Seattle

150 Years of Progress

James R. Warren

Published by

Heritage Media Corp.

Heritage Building

1954 Kellogg Avenue, Carlsbad, California 92008

www.heritagemedia.com

ISBN: 1-886483-52-3

Library of Congress Card Catalog Number: 2001090358

James R. Warren *Author*

Charles E. Parks *CEO/Publisher*

Lori M. Parks *Editor-in-Chief*

Stephen Hung *Executive Vice President*

Bart Barica *VP/Corporate Development*

Chuck Stubbs *Development*

Randall Peterson *CFO*

Administration	**Editorial**
Juan Diaz	Betsy Baxter Blondin *Managing Editor*
Debbie Hunter	Betsy Lelja *Softcover Managing Editor*
Azalea Maes	Sara Rufner *Project Editor*
Majka Penner	Mary Campbell
Scott Reid	John Woodward
Cory Sottek	

Design	**Production**
Gina Mancini *Art Director*	Deborah Sherwood *Production Manager*
Susie Passons *Assistant Art Director*	Jay Kennedy *Assistant Production Manager*
Marianne Mackey	Freddi Flores
Charlie Silvia	Dave Hermstead

Profile Writers

Anjali Banerjee

Tom Barr

Martha Burdick

Ranae Buscher

Jay Davis

Paul Freeman

Allen Gardiner

Mike Greenstein

Helen Taylor Hertz

Nora Horn

Vincent Kovar

Shannon Perry

Peter Stekel

Barbara Stewart

Gail Wood

Published in cooperation with the Greater Seattle Chamber of Commerce

www.seattlechamber.com

Printed by Heritage Media Corp. in the United States of America

First Edition

Dedication

I dedicate this book to my great-grandparents and their children who struggled across the plains in a wagon train the year following the Civil War and settled in the Pacific Northwest, a great place to live and to raise a family.

Table of Contents

6 Foreword

8 Acknowledgments

12 Prologue

18 Historical Photo Essay Seattle Yesterday: Looking Back

66 Chapter One The First Settlers Arrive on Elliott Bay 1851-1870

90 Chapter Two The Village Becomes a City 1870-1900

114 Chapter Three The Maturing Years 1900-1930

140 Chapter Four Depression and War 1930-1950

160 Chapter Five Postwar Seattle 1950-1980

186 Chapter Six Striding Into the Modern Age 1980-2000

200 Contemporary Photo Essay Seattle Today: Celebrating 150 Years

250 Partners Table of Contents

PARTNERS IN SEATTLE

252 Arts, Culture & Entertainment

272 Building a Greater Seattle

312 Business & Finance

334 International Trade

344 Manufacturing & Distribution

354 Marketplace

386 Networks

406 Nonprofit Organizations

424 Professional Services

436 Quality of Life

472 Sports & Recreation

482 Technology

498 Bibliography

500 Index

508 Partners & Web Site Index

4

Foreword

By Bob Watt,
President & CEO, Greater Seattle Chamber of Commerce

Welcome to *Seattle: 150 Years of Progress,* commemorating Seattle's 150th birthday. Noted historian and writer Jim Warren has written this beautiful publication about the greater Seattle area, which chronicles Seattle's growth and development, from our natural resources and neighborhoods to our politics, arts and technology. More than 200 vintage photographs, drawings and illustrations accompany the narrative to weave a fascinating story of the many people and events that have shaped this vibrant and diverse community since its founding 150 years ago.

In the pages of this book you will learn about Seattle's evolution from the pioneering days of Arthur Denny in the 1850s to the modern metropolis known for its coffee and culture, research and technology, manufacturing and international trade. Central to every community's development are the histories of the organizations and businesses that have provided its economic and cultural foundation. These corporate histories and profiles are too seldom recorded and yet have a prominent place in the shaping of our region. Here you will read about the companies and organizations that are continuing to make Seattle a place of immense opportunity.

We Seattlelites are proud of our well-educated, diversified and involved citizenry. We work hard and play hard, and recreation often involves the great outdoors in the local bounty of mountains, forests, lakes and ocean that surrounds us. We dedicate time to volunteer pursuits that enrich and improve our local community, from social services to the arts, and we are passionate about our local sports teams. Throughout this book you will become acquainted with the factors that make Seattle such a wonderful place to visit and conduct business for people from all over the world.

In learning about Seattle's early history and evolution to the thriving city it is today, you will see the threads of entrepreneurism that stretch from our original pioneers to our modern innovators in business, research and culture.

FOREWORD

Acknowledgments

By James R. Warren

Any writer of history is indebted to pioneers who wrote of their experiences and to those who acted as scribes for early settlers. We also owe a debt to early local newspapers and other publications and the persons who preserved them.

A special thanks to *The Seattle Post-Intelligencer* that has roots extending back to Seattle's first little weekly *Gazette,* first published in 1863, only a dozen years after Seattle was founded. The *Post-Intelligencer* also has donated its large and valuable collection of tens of thousands of news photograph negatives to Seattle's Museum of History and Industry, many included within these covers. PEMCO Insurance years ago donated the Webster-Stevens Collection of early historic photographs, some of which are used in this book. The MOHAI collections are gaining appreciation as the major source of images of Seattle's past.

Also thanks to Leonard Garfield, a longtime friend who now is the Executive Director of Seattle's Museum of History and Industry, and to museum staff members including librarian Carolyn Marr and photography experts Kathleen Knies and Howard Giske, who provided pleasant assistance. Thanks, too, to the library at the University of Washington and its easily accessible collection of the state's newspapers on microfilm. The Seattle Public Library's Northwest Collection also was utilized.

Thanks are due to Bob Watt, President and CEO of the Greater Seattle Chamber of Commerce, that sponsored this book and to his staff. Also thanks to the book's publisher, Heritage Media Corporation and its staff including Bart Barica, Cory Sottek, Betsy Blondin, Sara Rufner, Susie Passons and others for their friendly encouragement.

And last but far from least, thanks goes to Gwen Davis Warren, my wife of 52 years, for helping me understand new computer programs, for her accomplished editing, and for acting as a calming agent with an author who too frequently becomes impatient.

PROLOGUE

Seattle was founded later than Portland, San Francisco and several other Oregon and California towns because of what was called the Oregon Question. The 1815 Treaty of Ghent that ended the British-American War of 1812 restored all property taken by military force to the country that originally possessed it. For example, the treaty returned Fort Astoria on the south shore of the Columbia River to American control,

Unless otherwise noted, all photos in this prologue courtesy of the Museum of History and Industry

though a British fur company continued its operation. The agreement called for joint occupation of Oregon Territory by Britain and the United States.

The huge Oregon Territory of those years extended from the northern boundary of California to Alaska and from the Rocky Mountains to the Pacific Ocean. The only permanent white residents in the territory were employees of the British Hudson's Bay Company. However, U.S. trading ships had been sailing up and down the coast for 25 years bartering for furs with the American Indians. The captain of one of those ships, Robert Gray, on May 11, 1792, eased his ship across the treacherous bar that hid a mighty river from passing ships. As the discoverer of the river, he had the right to name it. He christened it the Columbia River after the vessel he commanded, the *Columbia Rediviva*. His discovery of the Columbia River gave the United States a historical claim to territory drained by that river. The Lewis and Clark Expedition to Oregon in 1804-06 increased the interest of Americans in the Northwest and provided further support for U.S. claims to the region.

Since no U.S. citizens lived in Oregon at the time, a joint occupation appeared satisfactory and the contenders agreed in 1818 to extend the joint occupation treaty for another decade and later extended it again. Negotiations continued sporadically and in 1823, the British suggested a solution. Earlier negotiations had established the U.S.-Canadian border along the 49th parallel from the Great Lakes to the Rocky Mountains. The British now proposed that the border be extended westward along the 49th parallel to the Columbia River and then down that river to the Pacific Ocean. This would have placed what is now Western Washington, including Puget Sound, under British jurisdiction. The United States refused that offer.

For the next 20 years the Oregon Question was debated in Congress and discussed in negotiations without finding agreement. During the 1830s a few Protestant missionaries traveled west to convert the American Indians. The British Hudson's Bay Company with its many French traders and trappers had attracted

several Catholic priests who baptized many Indians to that faith, including Seattle, a leader of the Indians living on Elliott Bay. The American missionaries, most of them from the New England states, wrote detailed letters home extolling the mild climate, great forests, fertile soils and natural bounty. When added to earlier descriptions provided by fur traders and explorers, Americans began to perceive of Oregon as a land of opportunity.

The Hudson's Bay Company, hoping Fort Vancouver and its other trading posts in what is now Western Washington would be located in Canadian territory, continued to promote the Columbia River as the demarcation line between Canada and the United States and advised all Americans to settle south of the river.

In 1844 James Knox Polk was elected president. He is remembered as a strong-willed man and is ranked as one of the country's better presidents. One of his major goals was to settle the question of who owned Oregon. Congress had been discussing the Oregon Question for more than 20 years and now that increasing numbers of American settlers were crossing the plains to Oregon he felt it was time to solve the problem. During his election campaign a memorable slogan was conceived: "54-40 or Fight!" meaning the United States claimed and would fight for Oregon to the southern tip of Alaska at 54 degrees, 40 minutes. Once elected, Polk decided to compromise and instructed his Secretary of State, James Buchanan, to suggest the border follow the 49th parallel all the way to the sea. When the British again insisted the border follow the Columbia River, Polk threatened to terminate the existing joint occupation agreement. The British then accepted the American proposal and the final papers were signed on June 15, 1846, establishing the U.S.-Canadian border at the 49th parallel from the summit of the Rocky Mountains to the sea with adjustments that allowed all of Vancouver Island to be Canadian territory. All doubts about the sovereignty of Western Washington were finally erased. Puget Sound belonged to the United States. Even before the boundary dispute was settled, a few Americans had located north of the river. Michael Simmons, for one, arrived in Oregon in 1845. In his party was a family headed by a popular mulatto named George Bush who was noted for developing fine farms. After hearing that the restrictive land laws of Oregon prevented "men of color" from residing in the Oregon Territory, the Simmons party ignored the advice of the Hudson's Bay Company and moved north to Puget Sound country. They believed British territory might extend that far south and they knew the British were less restrictive when it came to race. Months later, as the Bush family farm began to produce, a white family filed a claim on the property. This aggravated Bush's neighbors and they took the matter to the territorial representative who convinced Congress to pass a special bill assuring Bush the right to his claim.

Mike Simmons and others in his party started a village near the southern tip of Puget Sound and named it Newmarket. Today it is known as Tumwater. Immediately after the border question was settled, Edmund Sylvester moved north to found Olympia, and in 1851 Captain Lafayette Balch platted present Steilacoom. The first settlers at Port Townsend and Seattle arrived late in 1851.

In 1850, four years after the border was established, census takers counted only 1,049 Americans living north of the Columbia, most of them near that river. Elliott Bay lay quietly reflecting the huge firs and cedars on its banks, its surface occasionally ruffled by Indian paddlers. The natives often beached their canoes at a trailhead near where present Yesler Way meets First Avenue. For eons that trail had provided the natives a trade route to Snoqualmie Pass and the Kittitas Valley.

At the outset of the 1850s, no white families had claimed land on Elliott Bay. However, during 1850 a young man, 22-year-old John Holgate, arrived on Puget Sound seeking a site for a donation claim. He inspected the lay of the land on foot and by canoe, exploring from Olympia north to the Snohomish River. One day while ascending the Duwamish River he noted a prairie that he considered a perfect land claim. After returning to the Willamette Valley, he penned

John Holgate at age 22 explored the Puget Sound country in 1850. He wrote home extolling the area. As a result, several relatives in the Holgate and Hanford families migrated to Seattle in the mid-1850s.

a description in a letter to his family in Iowa. Holgate expected to return later and register his claim, but meantime Luther Collins appraised the same prairie and immediately filed a legal claim. When Holgate returned a few years later to find his chosen site occupied, he shrugged his shoulders and promptly filed a claim on Beacon Hill. After all, thousands of prime acres were available.

Word was filtering back to the Midwest from former neighbors and family members who had trekked to Oregon and were delighted with the mild climate, forests, fertile soil and natural bounty. Heeding such messages, the Denny Party of seven men, four women and four children left their homes in Cherry Grove, Illinois, and on April 10, 1851, began the grueling journey to the Willamette Valley in four covered wagons. The wagon train consisted of three generations of two families — the Dennys and the Borens. Arthur Denny served as leader of the group. He and his wife, Mary Boren Denny, and their two small daughters, Louisa Catherine and Margaret Lenora, occupied one wagon. Arthur's father, John Denny, for many years a widower with a large family, had recently married the widowed Sarah Latimer Boren. Sarah's son, Carson Boren, his wife, Mary, and daughter Gertrude, and Sarah's unmarried daughter, Louisa Boren, were part of the group. John Denny's four unmarried sons — James, Samuel, Wiley and David — were also members of the wagon train. To add to the confusion of names in these two families, David Denny and Louisa Boren were the first of the founders to be wed in the village named Seattle.

The Denny Party, as it traveled along the Snake River, experienced what Arthur Denny described as a couple of uneasy encounters with American Indians. A day or two later, they were surprised to overtake a wagon train of six men and two women camped near the Snake River. John H. Low, the leader, and Arthur Denny agreed the two groups should proceed together, for larger numbers provided greater safety.

When they arrived at their destination in the Willamette Valley on August 22, 1851, the Denny Party had survived 134 exhausting days of travel. A few days later, several of the party developed fever and chills, the common but dreaded ague, now believed to have been malaria. Mary Denny serves as an example of the hardiness of pioneer women. She was pregnant when their journey began, a condition considerably more evident by the time they arrived in the Willamette Valley four months later. Shortly after reaching their destination she suffered through the trauma of ague, then on September 2, 11 days after arriving, she gave birth to a son, Rolland H. Denny. On November 5, she boarded a small schooner with the others of the Denny party who had decided to continue on to Puget Sound.

The oldest male in the party, John Denny, and his wife and three of his four sons decided to stay in the Willamette Valley. The entire Denny Party probably would have settled there had they not met a man on the Oregon Trail who suggested a new destination. Arthur Denny's granddaughter, Roberta Frye Watt, authored *The Story of Seattle,* one of the few city histories based on diaries and memories of the founders. In it she quotes her grandfather:

> On leaving home for what we called the Pacific Coast, we had no other purpose than to settle in the Willamette Valley. But we met a man on Burnt River [that flows into the Snake near the present eastern border of Oregon] by the name of Brock who lived in Oregon City and had come out expecting to meet some friends, failing in which he turned and came back to The Dalles. He gave us information in regard to Puget Sound and called attention to the fact that it was about as near to the Sound from where we first struck the Columbia River, now known as Umatilla Landing, as it was to Portland, but as yet there was no road over the mountains by which it could be reached. My attention was thus turned to the Sound and I formed the purpose of looking in that direction.

While ill with ague in Portland, Arthur Denny was told that his younger brother, David, and John Low were about to drive Low's cattle north of the Columbia to winter pasture. He recalled Brock's suggestion and requested that David and Low travel on to Puget Sound to assess opportunities there. They agreed and hiked more than 200 miles following river valley Indian trails to Olympia, then a settlement of a dozen rough cabins at the southern

Fifteen years after arriving on Elliott Bay, Arthur Denny was prosperous enough to have this photo taken, one of few in existence of him as a younger man.

One day in the mid-1860s, Chief Seattle paused before the window of Seattle's first photography studio to study the pictures of white acquaintances. Photographer Sammis realized this was an opportunity. He invited the chief in to have his photo taken. This image is the only one existing of the chief. He closed his eyes against the bright light, but in some copies, his eyes were painted open.

tip of Puget Sound. Being the only settlement on the Sound, it also served as a rudimentary port of entry.

In Olympia, Denny and Low met Lee Terry, a native of New York, who also was inspecting the region, and Captain Robert C. Fay, who was preparing to sail north in his open boat to buy salmon from the Indians for the San Francisco market. He offered them a ride.

On September 25, 1851, Denny and Low stepped ashore on a peninsula jutting out from Elliott Bay. They were greeted in a sedate but friendly manner by a tall elderly Indian and several of his tribesmen. The old man spoke no English but they soon learned he was called Chief Seattle. The next morning Denny and Low hired two natives to paddle them in a tiny canoe up the Duwamish River to look for likely land claims.

Two evenings later while arranging their fir bough mattresses,

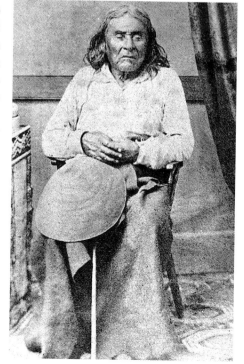

they heard distant voices speaking English. They hurried down to the water's edge and soon sighted a scow being poled around Duwamish Head. Luther Collins, his wife, and their daughter, Lucinda, stopped to visit. Collins explained they were headed with their household goods toward their new claim up the river. He mentioned three other men, two named Maple and one named Van Asselt, who had come north with him from the California Gold Rush and had selected claims adjacent to his. With darkness falling and still a couple of miles to go, the Collins family moved on.

The next morning Captain Fay stopped to tell Denny and Low that he was heading back to Olympia with his load of fish. John Low commissioned David Denny and Lee Terry to build his family a log cabin on the peninsula and sailed away with Captain Fay. Low then walked from Olympia to Portland. He carried with him a brief message from David Denny to his brother Arthur: "We have examined the valley of the Duwamish River and find it a fine country. There is plenty of room for one thousand settlers. Come at once."

Captain Robert Fay brought the first three men of the Denny party north to Alki in his small open sailboat. His wife was the Grandma Fay whose description of the Denny Party landing is quoted (right).

After the boat left, David Denny and Lee Terry began to work on Low's log cabin. Their only tools were an ax and a hammer, so felling the good-sized trees was a laborious process. The Indians helped them roll and lift the logs onto the walls of the cabin. As they began to frame the roof, Terry realized they needed a froe, a tool to split cedar shakes. The next day Collins poled by on his scow headed back to Olympia and Terry decided to travel with him as far as the Hudson's Bay post at Fort Nisqually, a few miles north of Olympia, to borrow the needed tool. This left 19-year-old David Denny alone in an unknown land with what he hoped were friendly natives as his only company.

It was a trying and lonely three weeks for young Denny. He continued working on Low's cabin until he cut his foot with the ax. Then a day later he came down with ague. On the morning of November 13, 1851, David awoke to the rattle of an anchor chain and crawled from under his shelter to see the small schooner *Exact*, skippered by Captain Isaac Folger, anchored offshore. Aboard were Seattle's founders, including the William Bell family that had joined the Dennys, Borens, Lows and Terrys as they left Portland. The often-quoted words of "Grandma Fay" describe their arrival:

I can't never forget when the folks landed at Alki Point. I was sorry for Mrs. Denny with her baby and the rest of the women. You see, it was this way. Mr. Alexander and me went on to Olympia, but the rest stopped there. I remember it rained awful hard that last day — the starch got took out of our bonnets and the wind blew, and when the women got into the rowboat to go ashore they were crying every one of 'em, and their sun bonnets with the starch took out of them went flip flap, flip flap, flip flap as they rowed off for shore, and the last glimpse I had of them was the women standing under the trees with their wet sun bonnets all lopping down over their faces and their aprons to their eyes.

Years later, Arthur Denny in an interview with historian Frederick Grant described the landing of Seattle's pilgrims with these words:

We were landed in the ship's boat when the tide was well out, and while the men of the party were all actively engaged in removing our goods to a point above high tide, the women and children had crawled into the brush, made a fire, and spread a cloth to shelter them from the rain. When the goods were secured I went to look after the women, and found on my approach, that their faces were concealed. On closer inspection I found that they were in tears, having already discovered the gravity of the situation. But I did not, for some time, discover that I had gone a step too far; in fact it was not until I became aware that my wife and helpless children were exposed to the murderous attacks of hostile savages that it dawned upon me that I had made a desperate venture. My motto in life was never to go backward and in fact if I had wished to retrace my steps it was about as nearly impossible as if I had taken up my bridge behind me. I had brought my family from a good home, surrounded by comforts and luxuries and landed them in a wilderness, and I did not think it at all strange that a woman who had, without complaining, endured all the dangers and hardships of a trip across the plains, should be found shedding tears when contemplating the hard prospects then so plainly in view.

And so it was that on November 13, 1851, the first of Seattle's founders arrived on Elliott Bay.

This sketch by Paul Gustin is taken from *Four Wagons West,* the book by Roberta Frye Watt.
It illustrates the landing at Alki on that chilly November 13, 1851.

Seattle Yesterday
Looking Back

All photos in this essay courtesy of the Museum of History and Industry

EARLY DAYS AT THE UNIVERSITY OF WASHINGTON

By 1890 the Seattle business district had expanded, preventing university campus expansion while the number of students was increasing. This forced the university to move to its present campus. This 1903 photo focuses on the first campus structure, Denny Hall, built in 1894 and named for Arthur A. Denny, a city founder instrumental in having the institution located in Seattle. To the left, Science Hall is under construction. It later was named for Professor Vernon L. Parrington who, in 1927, was awarded the Pulitzer Prize for his three-volume *Main Currents In American Thought.*

In 1899, to meet the increasing demand for on-campus living quarters, two dormitories were built — Lewis Hall, a men's dorm shown here, and the adjacent Clark Hall for women. These two structures plus the two mentioned on the previous page are still in use on the campus.

Husky football continued to gain fans. As a result, in 1920 the university began building a larger stadium on the lower campus. Since then, covered seating that soars high above the field has been added to provide good views for tens of thousands of Husky sports fans.

Rowing has been a major sport at the University of Washington for more than a century. The many silver cups that decorate numerous display cases indicate the success of Husky oarsmen. This 1921 crew posed in front of the Shell House that was built during World War I as a Navy military hangar.

Enoch Bagshaw, a famous Washington coach, chats with Husky halfback George
Wilson, winner of All-America honors in 1925. The University of Washington won the

During the first half of the 20th century, the press seldom mentioned women's sports. However, the university has long provided sports activities for women. These two coeds posed on a basketball practice court in the 1920s. Today, university women's sports teams are attracting increased attention from media and fans.

SEATTLE'S REGRADES

By 1907 the west half of Denny Hill was being sluiced into Elliott Bay, extending the city a couple of blocks into Puget Sound. Seattle residents began referring to the area as "The Regrade."

By the 1890s, steam-driven machinery eased the leveling efforts, and regrading speedily transformed the downtown area. This view is of Third Avenue being lowered at Columbia Street, reducing the steep slope rising from Second Avenue. A few of the more valuable structures were lowered to the new elevation.

Regradings have continued to alter Seattle's topography. Here the Interstate 5 freeway was being constructed through the heart of the city in 1963. (Columbia Street crosses Fifth Avenue in the extreme lower left corner of the photo.) Regrading continues to this day as huge new buildings are erected in the burgeoning Seattle metropolitan area.

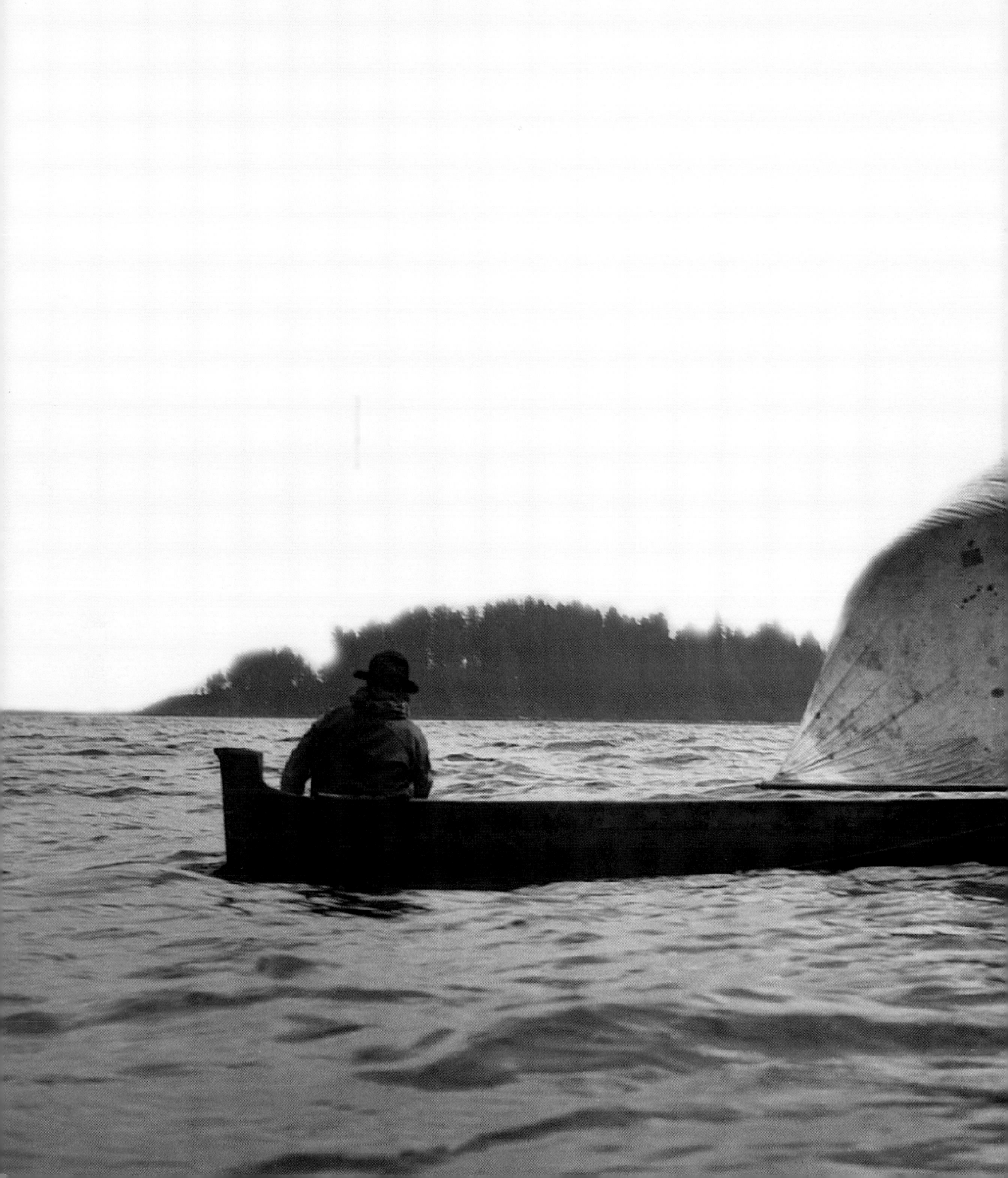

TRAVEL THROUGH THE YEARS

American Indians had developed a canoe transportation system on Puget Sound long before the arrival of white settlers. Early Seattle residents were often paddled around the Sound in these Indian dugout taxis, and several died when storm waves capsized the boats. After natives noted the sails on ships of the first European explorers, they adapted them to their canoes as shown in this 1890 photo.

By 1900, railroads were recognized as the major means of long-distance transportation. By then Seattle's Railroad Avenue was the site of a dozen tracks situated along the waterfront. As motor-driven cars and trucks were developed, the number of tracks gradually was reduced to the one or two that parallel the street renamed Alaskan Way.

Improved automobiles made longer trips into the mountains possible. Here a dealer demonstrates the ability of his 1923 roadster to handle higher elevations.

Seattle was hemmed in by lakes, rivers, canals and Puget Sound until ferry systems were developed and scores of bridges were built. Here the first floating bridge crosses Lake Washington to Mercer Island shortly after being dedicated in 1940. The bridge made it possible for eastside suburbs such as Bellevue, Kirkland and Redmond to develop more rapidly.

The latest transportation advances move travelers faster and at higher altitudes. Here is Seattle-Tacoma Airport on opening day in 1949. Now, more than half a century later, Sea-Tac has been greatly enlarged and hundreds of huge jet planes and smaller aircraft land and take off there every day.

SEATTLE'S BIG TIMBER

In 1907, the date of this photo, Douglas fir trees were felled by axe artists who carved smooth undercuts. Much of this work was accomplished as they balanced on springboards that raised them above the thick bottom bole of the tree.

Most mills were located on water where logs floated in millponds. During the 1920s several mil

Not all logs were sawed into lumber. Many tree trunks were used as telephone poles, wharf pilings and in other ways. As the photo shows, loading logs onto a ship on the Seattle waterfront in the 1920s was labor intensive.

The left quarter of this strange structure built in 1882 served as Seattle's first city hall. It was located on the east side of Second Avenue between Yesler Way and Washington Street. As demand for city services increased, sections were added without a master plan. Citizens dubbed the structure "The Katzenjammer Palace."

The Seattle Library occupied temporary quarters from 1868 to 1901. After Henry Yesler's death in 1892, the library was housed in his mansion that burned on January 1, 1901, destroying most of the books. Citizens decided then to ask Andrew Carnegie for $200,000 to build a permanent library. The structure, shown here, opened in 1906 and served for more than half a century before being replaced in 1960 by the present library.

Several historic structures are seen in this 1913 photo. Slightly left of center stands the clock tower of James Colman's ferry dock. To the right of the clock rises the Hoge Building that when completed in 1911 was the tallest structure in the city, but not for long. The steel skeleton of the L.C. Smith Tower rises nearby. After its 1914 completion, it dominated the Seattle skyline for nearly four decades.

Queen Anne High School, one of several surviving historic public school buildings, opened atop Queen Anne Hill in 1909. By the late 1920s, thousands of students had matriculated there. In 1981 the school district declared the building to be surplus. With the aid of Historic Seattle it was converted to living quarters called Queen Anne High School Apartments.

Two historic structures are shown in this early 1920s photo. The nearest is the long roofline of Pike Place (Farmers') Market, a public market that opened in 1907. For nearly a century, Seattle residents have flocked to the market to purchase fresh produce directly from farmers, ranchers, fishermen and dairymen. Beyond the market rises the silhouette of the old, gray stone Armory that was demolished in 1968.

WORLD WAR II IN SEATTLE

After the Japanese Navy attacked Pearl Harbor on December 7, 1941, West Coast cities feared they would suffer similar treatment. Seattle neighborhoods assigned air raid wardens and lookouts and trained residents how to react to incendiary and gas attacks. Here residents of Seattle's Madrona neighborhood train with smoke bombs.

Barrage balloons tethered with steel cables were raised above important defense sites to prevent attacks by dive
bombers, and smoke canisters were used in practices to conceal such sites.

On May 15, 1942, Congress authorized enlistment of women in the armed services. Two years later, this large contingent of the Women's Army Corps marched at Fort Lawton in Seattle. The fort property has since been converted into Discovery Park.

Seattle's center of patriotic activity during the war years was Victory Square, located on University Street between 4th and 5th avenues. There, in front of the Olympic Hotel, on a replica of Washington's Monument, the names of the local war dead were inscribed. The first Hero's Day ceremony of July 21, 1942, is shown in the photo.

52

In what is now considered an overreaction, Japanese-American families were moved to inland internment camps. Here, Seattle and suburban Japanese-American families were checked into the Puyallup Fairgrounds where they lived for several months while barracks were built for them in isolated inland locations. Most of the relocated were American citizens, and many young Nisei enlisted in U.S. military units to help win the war. Scores of them were killed on the warfronts.

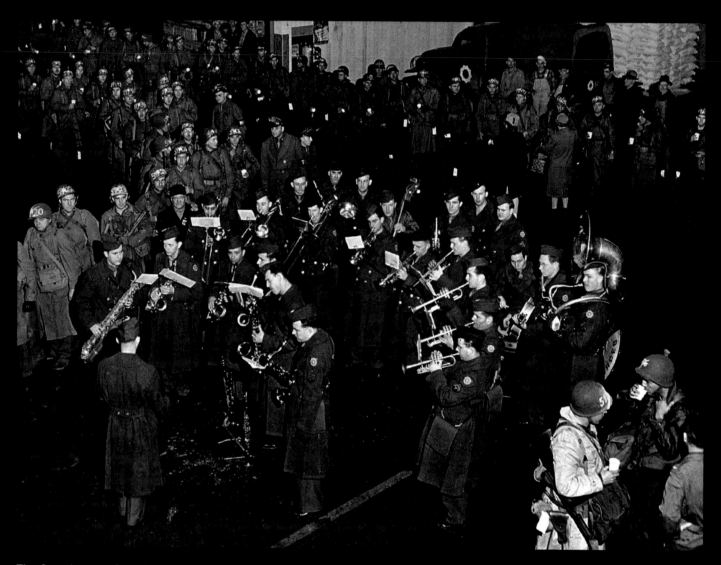

The Seattle waterfront became a major Port of Embarkation during the war. This early 1945 scene shows typical activities: an Army band plays, Red Cross ladies provide coffee and doughnuts as Army men line up in order of their numbered helmets to board a transport bound for a distant battle zone.

The city provided entertainment for the thousands of servicemen and women stationed in or traveling through the area.

The photo is of the 1942 U.S.O New Year's Eve dance at the Naval Reserve Station on Lake Union.

Several programs each month at Victory Square featured famous stars of radio, stage and screen who sold war bonds, reinforced patriotism and provided entertainment. Bob Hope, seen here, always attracted large crowds to laugh at his comedy and savor his patriotic statements. This photo is dated October 3, 1943.

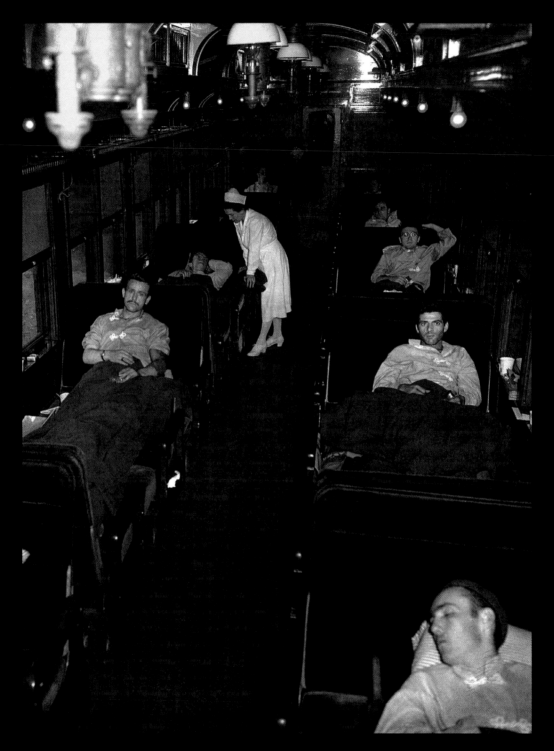

On May 11, 1943, the U.S. 7th Division invaded Attu, one of the Alaskan Aleutian Islands taken by the Japanese 11 months earlier. Before the island was retaken, more than 600 Americans were killed and 1,200 wounded, including these soldiers being transported by rail from a Puget Sound port to an Army hospital.

This Boeing Company photo depicts female employees helping to build a B-29, the large, long-range bomber that carried the two atomic bombs to Japan, ending World War II.

August 15, 1945, was a day never forgotten by Americans who experienced it. Known as V-J Day (Victory over Japan), it marked the end of World War II. Seattle newspaper extra editions headlined the historic event.

Within days of war's end, ships began transporting thousands of Americans home from distant warfronts. Here Red Cross nurses disembark on the Seattle waterfront.

On November 1, 1945, a ship arrived in Seattle carrying special heroes — survivors of the Bataan death march. The Japanese had invaded the Philippines on December 8, 1941. American and Filipino defenders were forced to retreat to the island of Bataan. That island fell on April 8, 1942, and the defenders were killed or captured. After more than three years, during which many prisoners died, the survivors were liberated when Allied forces took control of the islands. Survivors were treated for malnutrition and diseases, and four months later many of them arrived in Seattle.

For many years following World War II, bodies of Americans killed in battle were returned to the United States for burial in hometown and veterans' cemeteries. These 24 flag-draped coffins arrived in Seattle on November 16, 1947.

CHAPTER ONE

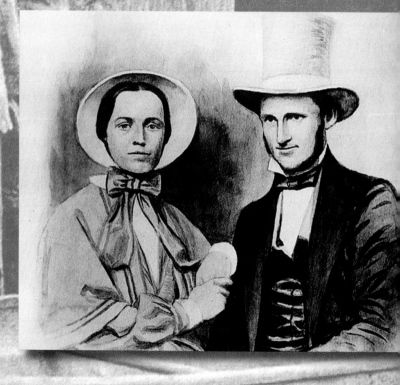

THE FIRST SETTLERS ARRIVE ON ELLIOTT BAY 1851-1870

On a wet and chilly November 13, 1851, the 12 adults and 12 children of the Denny Party landed on the beach at Alki Point and sought shelter from the elements, but there was none. The walls of a single cabin without a roof stood near the beach. As daylight faded, the women and children huddled around a campfire while the men hurriedly spread portions of a tent and Indian mats above the log walls as

These are the adult Seattle founders who arrived at Alki Point on November 13, 1851. These photos were taken decades after the event and do not include Mrs. William Bell, who died within a short time, nor Lee Terry, who returned to the East Coast after a few years.

temporary shelter from the rain. Exhausted, the parents and their children lay down close together in the crowded space, sharing body warmth as they slept.

Who were these 12 adults and 12 children who braved the elements, the deprivation, the isolation and the unknown American Indians to settle on an unexplored Puget Sound bay? The names of these founders of Seattle who arrived on the little sailing vessel *Exact* are inscribed on the historic monument on the beach where they landed. These were young folks: the oldest were John Low and William Bell in their mid-30s, the younger adults were Louisa Boren, 24, David Denny, 19, Charles Terry, 21, and Lee Terry, 19. The photo of the monument shows the names of the husbands are listed but their wives are indicated with two words: "and wife." The names of the single woman and three single males are on the monument and, on the far side, the names of the dozen children aged 9 down to the two babes in arms are spelled out clearly.

The next morning the men roofed the cabin with shakes and moved Mary Denny's small cook stove into the middle of the single room where it would supply warmth, dry the clothing and bedding, and provide heat for

(Far right) Children of Seattle's founding families who arrived at Alki Point on November 13, 1851 — in most cases these images were captured years later.

This historic monument lists the names of Seattle founders who arrived on the *Exact* in 1851. It is located on the site in West Seattle where they landed. The children's names are inscribed on the side away from the camera.

cooking. They then commenced construction of a second log cabin, this one for the Arthur Denny family. When it was completed, Arthur and Mary Denny and their three children, Arthur's brother, David, and Mary's sister, Louisa Boren, moved their belongings, leaving the first cabin less crowded.

Construction of the two cabins used all nearby trees small enough to produce logs that could be dragged and lifted without the aid of draft animals. With typical pioneer adaptability, the men built the next two cabins for the Bell and Boren families using cedar boards they wedged from nearby straight-grained cedar trees. Puget Sound Indians for eons had constructed large multifamily long houses of such boards and likely demonstrated the process for their new neighbors.

By the first week in December, flames crackled in the fireplaces of four cabins on the shore of Elliott Bay. The captain of the passing brig *Leonesa* sighted the little settlement, dropped anchor and rowed ashore to become acquainted. His name was Daniel S. Howard and he was looking for someone to supply pilings for wharves in San Francisco, a city crowded with Gold Rush hopefuls. The young settlers contracted to load the brig and began felling trees. John Low hurried down to his winter pasture to bring up his team of oxen and Lee Terry purchased a pair on the Puyallup River. In 16 working days the men loaded the *Leonesa* with 13,458 feet of piling. They had earned their first income from natural resources on Elliott Bay, had established trade with California, and sent Captain Howard on his way with a pocket full of orders for necessities.

They finished this task at noon on Christmas day, then cleaned up for the holiday meal. The women had patched up the clothing, the men had resoled the shoes, and everyone appeared bright and cheerful. Louisa Boren had thoughtfully carried in her trunk all the way across the plains a dozen little gifts, trinket boxes decorated with shells. These she gave as Christmas gifts to the children. The holiday dinner featured baked wild goose. During that first winter, the children missed having milk to drink, but clam broth served as a substitute. Though vegetables were in short supply, a barrel of dried apples had been brought up

The cabin built for the Arthur Denny family at Alki a couple of days after their November 1851 arrival was photographed shortly before the turn of the century. Note the wooden oxbow leaning against the right corner.

on the *Exact* and Arthur Denny managed to purchase 100 bushels of potatoes from the Hudson's Bay Company at Nisqually for $1 per bushel.

While John Low and Charles Terry decided to take land claims near where the party had landed and built the first cabins, Boren, Bell and the Dennys decided the site was unsatisfactory because of adjacent shallow water and the exposure to storms. In January 1852 these men began searching for a better location. Unlike many pioneer families seeking fertile farmland, these men were thinking of establishing a settlement of some kind. Arthur Denny, an experienced surveyor, led the search for an appropriate town site. They inspected the beach for several miles in both directions but found nothing to their liking. During February they realized that the bay where they had landed needed a closer inspection. They eyed the endless forests that would provide a major source of income and took a canoe to seek out waters deep enough to float lumber schooners and where forests fringed the tides so that trees could easily be felled and floated to ships and mills.

Needing a device to sound the water depth, they asked Mary Denny to loan them her only clothesline. After making them promise to return it, she untied it from the trees and handed it to her husband. The men promptly weighted it with horseshoes and hopped into a canoe to take soundings. They found deep water extended nearly to the bay's eastern shore where giant firs and cedars flourished on low bluffs above the tide line. On February 15, 1852, Arthur Denny unpacked his surveying

Dr. David S. Maynard arrived in March 1852 and selected a land claim south of Denny's and Boren's. He attracted commercial establishments by providing lots for free or at low cost. As a result, the early heart of Seattle developed on his property.

equipment and the men marked off the beach corners of their claims by driving a north stake at what is now the foot of Denny Way and a south stake at First Avenue South and King Street. Between these stakes William Bell selected the north section, Arthur Denny the middle section and Carson Boren the south section. David Denny, then only 20 years old, filed for 320 acres north of Bell's acreage in the name of his father, John, to hold it until he was 21, when he could claim it for himself. How deep into the woods each of these claims extended they did not know, nor was it a concern. Claims could not be filed until the Indian treaties were signed, giving the white settlers permission to take control of the land.

On March 31, as the Denny, Boren and Bell families prepared to move from Alki to their claims on the bay's east shore, Chief Seattle and his paddlers arrived with Dr. David S. Maynard in their canoe. Maynard would play a major role in the development of the village. He planned to hire local Indians to catch salmon for him, which he would salt in wooden barrels for shipment to San Francisco. Maynard, a medical doctor with few patients in the sparsely populated region, was proprietor of a small store in Olympia. He was considered too generous with credit and derelict when it came to collecting what was owed. His competitors were hoping he would leave town.

Maynard inspected the settlement at Alki where Charles Terry had opened a store in his tiny cabin stocked with flour, sugar, dried fruit and other staples, all highly prized by the Indians who traded with him by barter. Maynard concluded the Dennys, Borens and Bells were right, that Alki was not an outstanding location for a town. When shown the three claims on the east shore of the bay, he decided to join them. Denny and Boren moved their properties a few yards north to give the doctor access to the point of land then protruding into the mud flats south of present Yesler Way for his fish packing center.

On April 3, Bell, Boren and Maynard moved into cabins on their claims located in what is now the heart of downtown Seattle. Boren's cabin, the first to be completed, stood amid giant firs at what is now 2nd and Cherry where the Hogue Building, one of Seattle's first skyscrapers, stands today. Bell's cabin was constructed about a half mile to the north in what is still called Belltown. Maynard's first home was located near the present corner of First South and Main Street. Arthur Denny, again suffering with ague in his Alki cabin, was grateful to the healthier pioneers who built his family a cabin on the bluff near the foot of present Battery Street. He later moved to a clearing at what is now First and Marion.

Shortly after the pioneers had occupied their cabins, the brig *John Davis,* out of San Francisco, sailed into the bay looking for pilings. The founders' problem of depleted funds suddenly was solved and the shipmaster sailed away with his load of logs and also with orders from the settlers for food and other necessities that he would bring north from California on his next journey. With their few tools — augers, handsaws, and a broad axe or two — the pioneers were managing to make a living.

Before summer ended, a couple of additional settlers arrived on Elliott Bay, including a bright young lawyer named George V. McConaha and his wife, Ursula. A few days after they arrived, Ursula gave birth to a daughter, Eugenia, the first white child born in Seattle. A few weeks later Dr. Henry A. Smith, a 22-year-old medical doctor, paddled up from Olympia. He admitted to the settlers that he had had difficulty finding the settlement and in fact had rowed past it and turned around for a second try before noting the cabins in the woods. Smith took a land claim on the north side of Elliott Bay on an inlet known today as Smith Cove.

The settlement still lacked a name and a political election was in the offing. So it was that the small number of pioneers isolated on Elliott Bay found themselves in a voting precinct named Duwamps. An anonymous pioneer Olympia bureaucrat had so named the precinct because of the nearby Duwamish River and Indian tribe. Settlers soon agreed that a more euphonious appellation was needed and Dr. Maynard, an admirer of the affable elderly Indian leader, suggested the name "Seattle." The chief, however, reportedly was unhappy with the idea because tribal superstition warned that whenever a dead man's name was spoken, he would turn over in his grave. Arthur Denny, the first postmaster in the village, received the mail in his cabin after it was paddled up in a canoe from Olympia. He probably showed the chief how his name was the address on the envelopes. The old chief, it is said, eventually accepted the honor with dignified silence.

Creation of Washington Territory

Oregon was a large territory and the capital was nearly 200 miles from Seattle. As early as 1851 some residents of the Willamette Valley were agitating for creation of a separate territory in Northern Oregon. When the national Congress received a bill to split the territory, no opposition developed. As a result, on May 2, 1852, just six months after Seattle's founders arrived on Elliott Bay, Congress established Washington Territory and situated the capital in Olympia. President Franklin Pierce appointed Isaac I. Stevens, a graduate of West Point and an able engineer, as the first governor.

The settlers agreed that two of Steven's several announced objectives were of primary importance: locating a railroad route to Puget Sound and signing land treaties with the Indians. When the Indians understood they were being asked to give up the lands they revered, several tribes resisted. Most of the natives in the Seattle area remained friendly, thanks in large measure to Chief Seattle and to settlers who treated them fairly and paid them wages when they worked for them.

During the first five years of Seattle's existence, the population increased slowly. The isolation was a major detraction to would-be settlers. There was no quick or easy way to reach the settlement. The Indian trails that extended east across the Cascade Mountains and south to the Willamette Valley were passable for people and horses but not for wagons or other vehicles. Sailing vessels, the major transportation service for distances, took weeks to reach San Francisco and a week to sail to Portland.

Seattle's Earliest Businessmen

Earning a livelihood on the isolated Northwest frontier was a challenge, but Seattle's settlers found answers, sometimes by luck, but more often by diligent searches. These pioneers were unusual human beings in many ways. Members of the Denny party showed little interest in farming for a living. Most of them had experience on farms in the past and did raise produce, grains and meats for family consumption, but their major objective from the outset was to found a town and businesses. These dreamers struggled and several gave up and moved away, but as the population increased, those who stayed saw their real estate begin to appreciate in value. Here are a few examples of early business successes in Seattle.

Charles Terry was Seattle's first retailer. He brought with him from Portland on the *Exact* in November 1851, a stock of goods to sell including tinware, axes, tobacco, a keg of brandy, a keg of whiskey, a case of raisins, and a cage of laying hens. His cabin on Alki Point could be sighted from passing vessels and some stopped to trade. Whenever a ship left Elliott Bay for

San Francisco, Terry sent orders for items such as ammunition, flour, calico, molasses, sugar and other necessities. Some of his trade was with local natives who bartered fresh game, goose feathers, and hides for the sugar, molasses and tea they craved.

Terry also believed in advertising. The first issue of the first newspaper on the Sound, the *Columbian* of October 1852, carried this paid notice:

> Charles C. Terry, thankful for past favors, takes this opportunity to inform their numerous friends and customers that they still continue at their well-known stand in the Town of New York on Puget Sound where they keep constantly on hand and for sale at the lowest prices all kinds of merchandise usually required in a new country. N.B. Vessels furnished with cargoes of piles, square timber, shingles etc.

Dr. David Maynard's attempt to send salted salmon to San Francisco ended in disaster. The Indians had supplied sufficient salmon to fill nearly 1,000 barrels. The fish, well salted, was shipped toward the end of the summer. Perhaps because he was a novice at the process or because the barrels were hand made on site and much of the brine leaked from them, the entire shipment spoiled before it arrived. Undaunted, the doctor opened a general merchandise store he called the Seattle Exchange and that fall advertised in the Olympia weekly, *Columbian,* that he was "receiving direct from London and New York, via San Francisco, a general assortment of dry goods, groceries, hardware, crockery, etc., suitable for the wants of immigrants just arriving. First come, first served." Dr. Maynard, being a physician, tried to find a means of earning a living through his profession. He had received his training, much like other doctors of the time, by assisting older

As a reward for his support, President Franklin Pierce appointed Isaac I. Stevens, a West Point graduate, to serve as Washington Territory's first governor, as superintendent of Indian affairs and chief surveyor of a Northern Pacific Railroad route to the West Coast. Stevens was killed in the battle of Chantilly during the Civil War.

One of the first homes erected in what became Seattle, this cabin of Arthur and Mary Denny, was located at today's First and Marion streets. In 1853 it served as Seattle's first post office where Denny received the mail sack that was canoed up from Olympia once a week.

(Far right)
Dexter Horton arrived in 1852 and he and wife Hannah worked in Yesler's Mill, he as sawyer and she as cook for the mill hands. Horton later joined owners of a general store and in 1870 founded Seattle's first bank.

Henry Yesler brought the first industry to Seattle, a steam sawmill that produced the lumber to build much of early Seattle. He was said to be the town's first millionaire, but his riches derived more from real estate than the mill.

practitioners. He apparently had absorbed some of the rudimentary skills of his day and briefly had operated his own medical school in Chicago. After a short time in Seattle, he and his wife opened Seattle's first tiny hospital in their cabin, but the doctor was no businessman.

In October 1852, Seattle's first industrialist, Henry L. Yesler, arrived on a ship out of Portland and announced he was seeking a site for a steam sawmill. The settlers immediately perceived the importance this man's efforts could have for their settlement and began showing Yesler possible locations for the mill. He especially liked the "sag," where a small creek had eroded the bluff, leaving a flat area at the edge of the bay. A mill located there could utilize Elliott Bay as a millpond. The problem was that site was located on the dividing line between Boren and Maynard's claims. When told that all waterfront property in that vicinity had been claimed, Yesler considered locating his mill over at Alki and paced off a claim there before Seattle's founders decided they could not afford to let this opportunity escape them.

Arthur Denny remembered: "As there had not yet been any claims filed in the land office, which at this time was in Oregon City, Boren and Maynard each agreed to give Yesler a portion of their territory in order that he might obtain a claim also." They separated their properties by 420 feet, forming an access route from the sag up the hill to where Yesler could claim the remainder of his 320 forested acres. This narrow corridor developed as a corduroy road over which oxen skidded logs to Yesler's mill. As a result, residents began calling it the "Skid Road." Over time, several blocks of hotels and saloons were built along the road to serve loggers and other workers and the term "Skid Road" began to connote an unsavory part of town. The term was picked up in other cities, usually as

"Skid Row." And so it is that Seattle claims to have developed the first "Skid Row" in the country, even though city fathers quickly changed the name, first to Mill Street and then to Yesler Way.

The settlers welcomed Henry Yesler as well as his mill. He was older than they, a man of some means, a millwright who knew his business, and his would be the first steam sawmill on Puget Sound. They helped him build a structure to house his mill and a log cookhouse. As it was being completed, Yesler sailed for San Francisco to take delivery of the mill equipment he had ordered from the Midwest and that had been shipped down the Mississippi and around the Horn to California.

In his *History of Seattle,* Frederick James Grant describes Seattle in the summer of 1855 as having a total of about 40 homes, most of them clustered along three blocks of First Avenue South in the Pioneer Square area. He continued:

> The most important structure in the village was Yesler's sawmill. In more senses than one it was the life of the place. Here most of the men in town earned their money; here the ships came for cargoes and discharged their groceries. Its puffing, buzzing and blowing of steam made the music of the bay, and the hum of its saws was the undertone of every household. By its whistle all the clocks were regulated... It was not a large mill, having only some fifteen thousand capacity, but since the price of lumber was very high, the value of its output was not inconsiderable. The next house in interest was Yesler's log cook and mess-house. As the name implies this was the eating house of the mill hands. But in addition to that use it was town hall, courtroom, meeting house and hotel.

The forests surrounding the settlement soon attracted other mills. Tobin, Fanjoy, and Eaton operated a sizeable sawmill on the Black River near present Renton. A third mill began sawing lumber near the location of the Fremont Bridge on Lake Union. Others soon followed.

Most of Seattle's founders were nearly destitute when they reached Puget Sound. Arthur Denny, when asked by a visiting ship captain to take merchandise on commission to sell to the settlers and American Indians, agreed to try it and after a time found it a profitable business. After a few months he opened his own store at First Avenue South and Washington Street in a 20 by 30-foot structure built of lumber from Yesler's mill. In 1854 Denny stopped selling on commission and, with Dexter Horton and David Phillips to help finance and operate the enterprise, stocked groceries, hardware, dry goods and notions.

Dexter Horton and Thomas Mercer, after crossing the plains in the same wagon train in 1852, upon reaching Portland decided to visit the village on Elliott Bay. When Mercer returned to Portland to transport his three daughters to Seattle (his wife had died on the way to Oregon) he managed to drive his horses and wagon up the trails to Seattle. The effort was considerable for he was forced to widen the trail in many places. His two horses were the first drayage animals in Seattle and became favorite pets of the population. Mercer developed the first transport services in the settlement and selected a land claim at the southern base of Queen Anne Hill, along what is now called Mercer Street. While clearing that land, he paid Horton to help with his drayage business. Horton also worked from 1 p.m. to midnight at Yesler's mill and his wife, Hannah, cooked for the 14 Yesler employees.

A short time later Horton became a partner with Denny and Phillips in their general store. One day while minding the store, he was approached by a logger who had recently received his wages in coin and was fearful of losing them, especially if he stopped for a few drinks at the town saloon. Horton placed the cash in a sack with the man's name in it and hid it in the coffee barrel. Horton was a serious individual who quickly acquired a reputation for honesty, and soon others were asking him to keep their spare cash. He stashed funds in several hiding places around the store.

A decade later he concluded it was time to found a private bank in the growing settlement and sailed to San Francisco to learn what he could about lending, interest and other such activities. On his return in 1870, he and David Phillips founded Phillips and Horton Company to provide elementary banking services. The first bank was a tiny wooden shed. When Phillips died a few months later, the name of the bank was changed to Dexter Horton and Company. Later Arthur Denny, who purchased shares, became a vice president, and several other pioneers became involved. Through the years this tiny bank developed into

The original tiny wooden bank building at First and Washington streets was no predictor of the success that would follow. The Dexter Horton Bank, over time and with different owners and titles, developed into Seattle First National, the state's largest bank that recently was acquired by Bank of America.

Seattle's first hotel, the Felker House, was built by ship captain Leonard Felker. He hired a colorful woman named Mrs. Conklin to manage it. She was good at both cooking and swearing and the pioneers often referred to the hotel as "Mother Damnable's."

Seattle First National Bank, soon the largest in the state with many branches. In the late 1990s, Bank of America purchased this SeaFirst Bank that had been founded by Horton and Phillips more than 120 years earlier.

The first hotel in Seattle, the Felker House, was constructed near present Jackson Street and Western Avenue by Captain Leonard M. Felker, Master of the brig *Franklin Adams*. Local citizens usually referred to this hotel as "Mother Damnable's" or the Conklin House after the manager, Mrs. Conklin, also known as Mary Ann Boyer. She frequently was the subject of serious, but more often humorous comments, for she was an excellent cook but possessed a violent temper. When angry she turned to a profanity that caused even sailors to blanch. In fact, she could outswear her husband, an elderly sea captain, who had learned to remain in the background while she operated the hotel.

The farmers out in the Duwamish Valley, the Collins, Maples and Van Asselts, who had arrived a few weeks before the Denny Party, were doing well. Clarence Bagley wrote in his *History of Seattle*:

In 1853 the crop raised by L.M. Collins was valued at $5,000. The enormous size of the products of his farm excited surprise even here. He raised turnips weighting from 23 to 35 pounds each, potatoes weighting as much as four pounds each, and onions two pounds each. Already he was advertising 200,000 apple, peach, plum, cherry and other trees for sale at the low price of $12.50 per hundred.

Bishop Modeste Demers, a Catholic priest, preached Seattle's first sermon in Yesler's Cookhouse to a room full of Protestants.

Seattle's First Religious and Educational Services

Most of the city founders were churchgoing folks, when they had a church building in which to worship. The first religious service in Seattle was presented late in 1852, about a year after the arrival of the founders. Catholic Bishop Demers, who worked to save the souls of the Indians and the employees of the Hudson's Bay Company, one day visited the village and was requested by the settlers to preach a sermon. They gathered in Yesler's Cookhouse, every one of them Protestants, filling the benches to hear the Catholic priest present the word of God. A few weeks later Seattle's second sermon was delivered by Methodist Reverend Benjamin Close of Olympia, the first Protestant minister stationed in Washington Territory.

The Reverend David Blaine, a Methodist Episcopal pastor, and his wife, Catherine, arrived in Seattle late in 1853. He was the first resident minister and she was the first school teacher in the village.

Seattle's first resident minister, the Reverend David Blaine, along with his wife, Catherine, arrived in Seattle in late November 1853. They sailed to Olympia and visited a few days there with "Brother Benjamin Close." David and Catherine Blaine are well remembered in the city's history books. Their frequent letters from the Oregon country to relatives in New York were preserved and provide rare detailed accounts of the earliest days in Seattle. Reverend Blaine's first sermon in the settlement was delivered at Alki Point on Sunday, November 27, 1853, the day after they arrived. The minister, in a letter to his family, described their first experiences:

We were very kindly received and hospitably entertained at a Mr. [Samuel] Russell's, the only white family in the place [Alki] which contains eight or nine houses and a sawmill. The houses are used as stores and homes for bachelors. I preached in the afternoon and evening. In the evening after the sermon, a young man [it was Charles Terry] took his hat, of his own accord, and passed it around among the auditors, of whom I should think there were 30. He turned out the contents on the table and I scraped them off and put them in my pocket. When we counted the money it amounted to $12.50.

The Blaines then moved into the village proper, staying with Arthur and Mary Denny and their four children in the tiny two-room Denny home. Four adults and four children in two rooms! During their first week with the Dennys, Reverend Blaine preached two sermons at Bachelor's Hall, located near First and Cherry, and began organizing Seattle's first church to serve Methodist Episcopal parishioners and anyone else who cared to attend. His original congregation consisted of four adults including his wife, Catherine. Carson Boren donated lots for a church building and parsonage and Blaine began soliciting funds to pay for construction. Several of the settlers, having no cash, donated logs to be milled into lumber. The church slowly rose from the hillside, thanks to volunteer construction teams. It was finished in May 1855 and painted white. For a decade it was Seattle's only church. During the two years while it was being constructed, W.G. Latimer allowed the congregation to use his men's boarding house, Bachelor's Hall, for services. The second church in Seattle was Methodist Protestant and was painted brown. As a result, the pioneers usually indicated their church affiliation as white church or brown church. Several decades later, the two congregations combined as the United Methodist Church.

On January 1, 1854, Seattle's first elementary school classes were scheduled at Bachelor's Hall. These were subscription classes, meaning parents raised funds to pay Catherine Blaine $65 a month to teach at this private school. Mrs. Blaine was expecting a child so she scheduled the second semester of 14 young scholars in the tiny Blaine home. The students all had pioneer names such as Denny, Mercer, Bell, Phillips, Horton and McConaha.

The Indian Attack on Seattle

Progress was evident in the tiny village. Much of the forest had been cleared from the edge of the bay, exposing the pioneer cabins to sailing ships passing by. Several new families arrived, and Dr. Maynard attracted early businesses by practically giving them property from his land claim along the trail that was called Commercial Street and later First Avenue South. The local Indians under the influence of Chief Seattle remained peaceful and anxious to trade for the white settlers' foods and equipment. Henry Yesler employed a few of them at his mill and other settlers hired them for various chores.

Chief Seattle presided over the Suquamish and Duwamish tribes. As was the case with other tribes, diseases of the white men had rampaged through these people, drastically shrinking their numbers. Years earlier a Catholic priest had baptized the chief at the Hudson's Bay Company's Fort Nisqually and he was buried with both Catholic and tribal services in a little cemetery in the town of Suquamish, near the Indian reservation. After he died, his white friends erected a monument over his grave.

People would like to know more about Chief Seattle. It is said that he did not try to learn English because as a chief, he did not feel the need to do so. He was described as a wise old man, nearing 80 years of age, an orator with a voice his followers could hear a distance away. At least one of the chief's speeches was translated by Dr. Henry Smith, how accurately it is not known. The pioneers could not have learned the difficult Salish language quickly. However, several early pioneers and Indians conversed using the Chinook jargon, a trading lingo of a few French, English and native words. To translate the chief's speeches using that jargon would result in far from perfect results. Some of the younger Indians quickly learned English because early reservation schools prohibited use of the native language, but the old chief had passed on in 1866, before the schools were started. Probably what has been passed down about Chief Seattle is a mixture of history

Noted Seattle photographer Edward S. Curtis about 1915 posed American Indians as authentically as possible to record images of their society as it was before white settlers arrived. This picture shows a summer shelter of woven reeds, woven rain capes and hats, and a shovel-nosed canoe they used for transportation on local inland waters.

as remembered by the survivors of his people and folktales passed down by the early settlers.

The local American Indians had a developed society that revered nature and its largesse and intended to preserve it. They learned to appreciate everything that nature supplied. Tribes west of the Cascades did not live in teepees but in long houses made of boards wedged from the strait grained red cedar and in summer homes of woven mats and bark. They enjoyed berries, natural greens and vegetables, fish, venison and other meats. They learned to dry fruits and meats and stored the results in artistic baskets, some woven so tight they were waterproof. Their dugout canoes were works of art adapted to the area's rivers and bays. And with Chief Seattle as their leader, they remained peaceful with the white interlopers even when other tribes made war. They shared native knowledge with their white neighbors, helping the pioneers to survive their early years on Elliott Bay. Most of the Seattle founders gave the local American Indians credit for this assistance.

The natives of Puget Sound knew how to harvest nature's bounty. Here, while the tide is out, an Indian woman picks mussels from a rock. The Indians taught the settlers how to add variety to their diets by using local sources of natural foods.

An Indian attack near present Auburn in 1855 resulted in Mrs. Harvey Jones (below) and her husband being killed. Her three children (right) were saved when 7-year-old son, Johnny, led his small brother and sister through the woods to a friendly Indian family who rowed them to Seattle.

Indian tribes east of the Cascade Mountains, especially the Yakimas and Klickitats, were not so tranquil, nor were those across the border in British Columbia. In 1853 James M. McCormack, a white stranger in town, was killed and buried near Lake Union. Local Indians, reportedly animated by jealousy, told the settlers about the murder. Four natives were arrested, and after a brief trial two of them were hanged. During the trial, Sheriff Carson Boren locked one of the accused young men in his house to keep him from falling into the hands of vigilantes. When Boren was called away for a time, several settlers broke in, grabbed the youth, and dragged him to a stump to which they had nailed a noose. Boren, hearing of their activity, raced home in time to stop the vigilante action and later released the teen-age Indian.

During these years Governor Isaac Stevens was traveling around the territory trying to convince Indian leaders to sign treaties. The tide of white immigration was increasing. Several American males headed for a reported gold find near present Colville were killed while trespassing on Indian lands. With disagreements growing and new conflicts developing, the territorial Legislature called up the militia. In August and September of 1855, Indians from east of the mountains, incensed over prospects of losing much of their tribal land, reportedly were trying to convince Puget Sound Indians to join them in forcing the white settlers from the area. Some 200 soldiers from Steilacoom were sent to join volunteers already in the field watching for any marauding warriors. Territorial settlers meantime hurriedly built more than 60 blockhouses, including two in Seattle.

The bloodiest encounter of the local Indian battles occurred on October 28, 1855, on the White River north of present Auburn. The Indians massacred four men, three women and two children but several other children were rescued and carried to safety by local native acquaintances. These White River killings convinced even reluctant Army officers that a real Indian War was in progress. All Territorial Volunteers were called to duty. The Seattle Company recruited nearly every male in the village to serve. More than 430 Indians living in the

vicinity, including Chief Seattle, were moved across the Sound to their reservation near the present town of Suquamish.

The territorial Legislature earlier had memorialized Congress to station a man-of-war on Puget Sound to protect settlers from Indian marauders who traveled in giant war canoes from north of the border. The sloop of war *Decatur* on duty in Hawaii was ordered to Puget Sound and arrived in early October, much to the relief of residents.

On December 3, Army Lieutenant W.A. Slaughter and three of his men, members of a squad confronting natives from east of the mountains, were killed as they rested near the site of the White River massacre. With native unrest bristling near Seattle, many families took shelter in the blockhouse during nighttime hours and some families remained there day and night. Fearing that the Army and the warship in the bay might not provide sufficient protection, Seattle settlers experienced a worrisome Christmas in 1855. Edmund Meany in his *History of the State of Washington* wrote:

The year 1855, as it drew to a close, saw the Territory of Washington enshrouded in gloom. It was not known how many Indians had suffered. They always managed to conceal their dead and rescue their wounded. But it was known that a considerable number of white people had lost their lives, many others had lost their homes. The survivors collected into blockhouses for mutual protection. The Indians gave continuous evidence of their presence. Food was growing scarce — ordinary business was out of the question...

Early on January 26, 1856, the natives crept to the edge of the woods along present Third Avenue, intent on attacking the settlers in their homes. About 8 a.m. shots were heard, Indian yells followed, and the battle commenced. The warship *Decatur's* cannon began to fire into the trees, the volunteers loaded their rifles, and Indians' bullets smacked into blockhouse and cabin walls. Those settlers caught in their homes raced for safety in the blockhouse.

Emily Inez Denny in her book *Blazing the Way* described her personal experiences on that day:

Louisa Boren Denny, my mother, was alone with her child about two years old, in the little frame house, a short distance from the fort. She was engaged in baking biscuits when hearing the shots and yells of the Indians she looked out to see the marines from the Decatur swarming up out of their boats onto Yesler's wharf and concluded it was best to retire in good order. With provident foresight she snatched the pan from the oven and turned the biscuits into her apron, picked up the child, Emily Inez Denny, with her free hand and hurried out, leaving the premises to their fate. Fortunately her husband, David T. Denny, who had been standing guard, met her in the midst of the flying bullets and assisted her, speedily, into the friendly fort.

Emily Inez Denny wrote the book *Blazing the Way* and added illustrations such as this one. As the quote explains, during the Indian attack her father, David Denny, (lower right) rushed out to help her mother carry their daughter and an apron full of biscuits to the blockhouse.

The cannon of the *Decatur* blasted shot into the edge of the woods where the Indians' gunfire was originating. All morning, grapeshot and canister splintered the trees and plowed the earth but the Indians continued to fire back from behind stumps, logs and hummocks. At noon the Indians ceased firing long enough to dine on the pioneers' cattle that they killed and roasted over open fires. During that brief lull, many of the women and children were rowed to safety on the warship *Decatur* and the bark *Brontes* that were anchored off shore. A few men sneaked from the blockhouse to nearby deserted houses to recover guns and other valuables left by the residents in their hasty flight, realizing that under cover of darkness the Indians would likely steal them. Desultory firing continued until nightfall, then gradually ceased. When morning dawned, the hostile force had disappeared, taking with them everything they could loot from the houses and burning outlying homes as they retreated. The houses of David Denny and Thomas Mercer at the foot of Queen Anne Hill were not touched because local Indians explained to the warriors from east of the Cascades that these two men were tillicums (friends).

Later, local Indians told the settlers that the hostiles understood how grape and canister shells worked but the new delayed-action shells that "mox poohed" (exploded) a second time with destructive force were a mystery and a terror to them. The pioneers agreed that the warship cannon that fired those shells probably saved Seattle residents from being overwhelmed by the several hundred Indians in the attacking force.

Two white men were killed during the battle for Seattle. One was a young man new in the village whose name was Robert Wilson. He was crossing the porch of the Felker House when struck by an Indian bullet. The other was a teen-ager anxious to leave the blockhouse to join the men keeping the foe at bay outside. Though ordered to stay inside the fort with the women and children, he grabbed a musket, stepped outside the door and was immediately felled by enemy fire. Milton Holgate was 15 when he died and they hid his body under the

Adult pioneer Abbie Jane Holgate Hanford lived through the attack and later helped a relative re-create the scene artistically. The view looks west from about Third Avenue. The White Church is seen near right and Yesler's Mill is in the distance. The warship *Decatur* and the bark *Brontes* are shown in Elliott Bay.

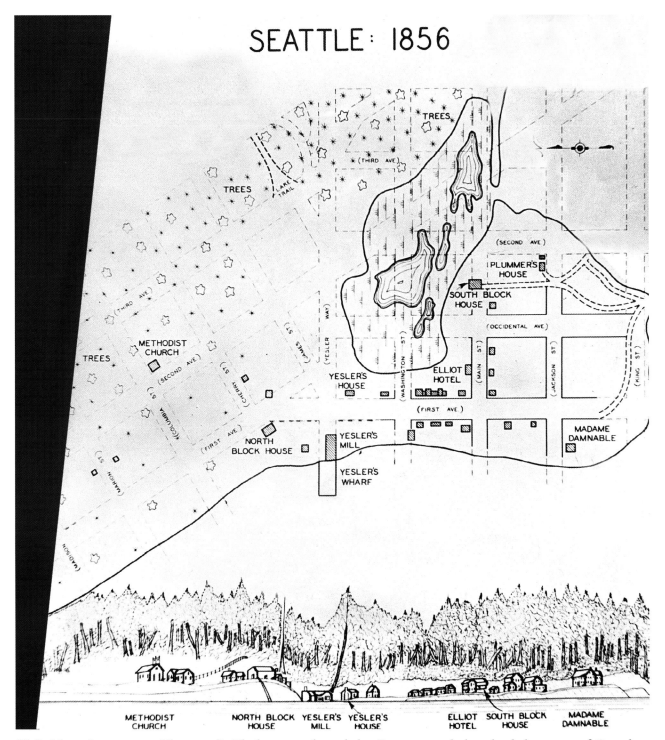

SEATTLE: 1856

U.S. Navy Lieutenant Thomas S. Phelps was aboard the *Decatur* and sketched this map of Seattle as it appeared during the attack. Note the two blockhouses. His placement of some homes was incorrect, but his effort added understanding to the situation. This map includes updates with new street names added.

blockhouse steps where his mother would not see it until after the battle. The number of Indians killed in the fracas was not known but William N. Bell reported "there were a number."

The pioneers gave several local natives credit for providing information that saved lives. Roberta Frye Watt wrote:

> In the week preceding the battle, rumors of an attack were brought by friendly Indians, one of whom was Curley. Curley's loyalty to the whites has been questioned by many, and undoubtedly the truth of the matter was that he was friendly to both sides. He would get a little ammunition and tobacco from Mr. Yesler, whom he knew very well since he had worked in the mill, and trade it for information which he would in turn bring back to Mr. Yesler. Indian Jim, whose sincerity was never questioned, also brought news to the whites; likewise the "klootchmen" [women] and other Indians who had worked in Yesler's mill and were his "tillicums."

Clarence Bagley also makes it clear in his *History of Seattle* that few local Indians were involved in the attack.

> During the entire period of the Indian war there were, within the immediate vicinity of Seattle, many Indians whose friendship for their white neighbors was sincere and loyal. Especially was this true of old Seattle and his tribe, and of Pat Kanim and his tribe of Snoqualmies... At one time, shortly after the White River massacre, Lieutenant Slaughter sent word to Governor Mason that Pat Kanim was following his party, evidently with hostile intentions.

Governor Mason forwarded this information to Captain Sterrett aboard the *Decatur*. The captain talked to Arthur Denny who insisted Pat Kanim was "well disposed toward the settlers." Denny insisted he had positive knowledge that Pat Kanim and his tribe were nowhere near where Lieutenant Slaughter was operating. Denny proposed that Captain Sterrett not disturb the Snoqualmies and let him assume responsibility for them. Captain Sterrett agreed that if Denny would contact Chief Kanim and ask him to come in for a meeting he would not pursue him. At the appointed time the chief arrived with his women and children loaded with a cargo of venison, horns and hides that he presented to Captain Sterrett. The captain expressed his great surprise and considered the meeting to be conclusive proof of the good faith and friendship of the Snoqualmies.

The Indian attacks put a halt to the settlers' plans and when they threatened to continue the siege at a later time, many early residents began leaving Seattle as soon as they could safely get away. The Indians burned William Bell's home in Belltown, which made life difficult for that family because Mrs. Bell was seriously ill. Shortly after the attack he moved his family to California, hoping the weather would improve Sarah's health. She died five months later, but Bell stayed in California 14 years before he became convinced it was safe for his family to return to Puget Sound, a move that would allow him to check the rumor that his land claim was becoming quite valuable. After the attack, several other settlers migrated to Oregon as quickly as passage on ships became available. The Reverend David Blaine accepted the call of a church in Portland, but he and Catherine delayed their departure until Charles Terry returned from a trip to the East Coast where he intended to visit the Blaines' relatives. With the minister gone, Seattle's only church was closed. Within a few months, the village population had shrunk from about 140 to 80 unmarried men and a dozen families. Pioneer historians called this Seattle's darkest hour.

Many of the families who stayed in Seattle lived in the dank and crowded blockhouse. The Indians had made off with the settlers' cattle, so the children had no milk. In March, Louisa Denny gave birth to a second daughter in the blockhouse. She and husband David named her Madge Decatur Denny, the middle name as a reminder that she had been born in the blockhouse called Fort Decatur after the warship protecting the settlers from Elliott Bay. A few historical remnants of Fort Decatur are preserved at the Museum of History and Industry, including the American flag hurriedly stitched together from scraps of cloth gathered by the women in the blockhouse.

This flag, preserved at the Museum of History and Industry, was stitched together from clothing scraps by the women in the blockhouse during the Indian attack. At the time new states were being added often, and they did not know how many stars to include nor how to arrange them.

Spring arrived and the farmers on the Duwamish River, protected by armed volunteers, ventured out to plant crops. This was a vital effort, for the Indian attack had stopped all trade and food was in short supply. By summer, the danger of further attacks appeared to be decreasing and in August the warship *Decatur* was ordered elsewhere. Still the village lay dormant. Years later Arthur Denny recalled the situation:

> Business was generally stagnant. Little in the way of building or improvement was attempted. Roads that had been opened before the war had mostly become well nigh impassable and some of them entirely so. Active efforts were not resumed to improve the roads and open communications until 1866, a period of ten years.

Clarence Bagley in his *History of Seattle* describes the depressing aftermath of the Indian attack with these words:

> There was little money afloat and little business. In this Maynard was no exception. He saw no promise of success in returning to a business life so he decided to become a farmer. He still had 260 acres unplatted of his donation claim and Charles Terry had about 320 acres at Alki. On the 11th of July, 1857, they exchanged properties. Terry moved over to Seattle and the Maynards moved to Alki.

That was a huge mistake on the part of Dr. Maynard, for within a few years his original claim was the most valuable in Seattle and his Alki property was practically worthless. The Indian attack slowly faded into history and eventually a few humorous memories became part of the story. Dexter Horton relished relating how the gunner of the *Decatur,* while aiming shot at the natives in the woods, aimed a little low and sent a cannon ball crashing through the lean-to in back of his store. The lead ball smashed through a dress belonging to Mrs. Horton and carried it flapping into the woods. Two months later the embarrassed Navy man insisted on presenting Mrs. Horton with a new gown.

David Denny enjoyed telling this story on himself. During the day of the Indian attack, shortly after he had helped his wife and family into the blockhouse, while rushing around to rejoin the battle against the attackers, his trousers got caught on something and in efforts to pull away, the seat split. Frantically he borrowed his wife's needle and thread, found a dark corner out of sight of the women, pulled off his britches, repaired the rip, quickly slipped back into them and rejoined the other men in efforts to keep the Indians at a distance. He always chuckled as he added, "You should have seen the size of the stitches I took that day!"

Normalcy slowly returned to the village. During those months several weddings were much enjoyed by the settlers, for friends of the couples invariably provided food and cake after the ceremony. One couple, Edmund Carr and Olivia Holgate, met while teaching Sunday school at the White Church. Cornelius Hanford, in his history, *Seattle and Environs,* tells how the community pulled together to celebrate such occasions.

> In the summer of 1856, a public wedding was made an occasion for festivities. When it was announced that Edmund Carr and Miss Olivia Holgate were to be married, the community took the matter in hand and projected a wedding feast for everybody. The market was nearly destitute of delicacies usually supplied for such an affair, but it is wonderful how pioneer women with scant provisions can delight appetites of the hungry when they try; they did try and made the feast a great success. One cow that was saved from slaughter by the Indians supplied milk, and there were chickens, eggs, venison, berries, different kinds of fish and oysters, the stores had on hand flour, sugar, butter and rice, and fresh vegetables were plentiful. Three large wedding cakes were made, One for the feast, one especially for Captain Swartout, commander of the warship Massachusetts, then in the harbor, and the third for other officers of that vessel. Those compliments were acknowledged by the booming of the ship's cannon in a salute to the bride and groom. There was no clergyman in Seattle, but the couple were married by E.A. Clark, justice of the peace.

After leading businessman Charles Terry married Mary Jane Russell at Port Madison, the groom purchased Bettman Brothers general store and became very active in the commercial life of Seattle. Mary Jane Mercer, Thomas Mercer's oldest daughter, who earlier had cared for her younger sisters after their mother died, was married at age 18 to Henry G. Parsons of Olympia. A few months later her sister Eliza became the wife of Walter Graham. Another bride was the popular Mrs. Ursula McConaha. This plucky widow lost her husband, George McConaha, Seattle's first lawyer and a member of the territorial

realizing these territorial services would bring employment and recognition to their community. During every legislative session, bills were passed to locate territorial institutions in specific towns, but usually without result because the legislature could find no funds for construction of facilities.

On January 29, 1855, four years after the Denny Party arrived, the Legislature voted to locate the University of Washington in Seattle, with a branch in Lewis County. Nothing happened and in 1858 the Legislature changed the site to Cowlitz Prairie in Lewis County, provided the county or an individual donated 160 acres for a campus. Again nothing happened. On January 10, 1861, Arthur A. Denny, a newly elected territorial representative, introduced a bill calling for designation of government lands dedicated to support of a university, selection of a campus site and election of university commissioners. The next day his bill was passed and for the second time the university was to be located in Seattle. Furthermore, Seattle residents Daniel Bagley, Edmund Carr and John Webster were appointed commissioners. The Reverend Bagley was named chairman to manage the effort. The act prohibited the commissioners from incurring indebtedness and said nothing about construction of college buildings. Denny and Bagley agreed they must act quickly or the next legislative session might again shift the university to another town.

Earlier Denny had offered to contribute 10 acres of his land claim for a campus. Now, he and Bagley hiked to the northern edge of his property where a tract of tangled brush and huge firs existed near present Western and Battery Streets. After a couple of sweaty hours of struggle trying to survey this jungle, Denny laid his instruments aside and called out, "Bagley, I'll give the knoll!" Denny earlier had considered donating the knoll located north of the village but realized it was one of the choice sites on his land claim. A later survey showed Denny had 8 1/2 acres at the top of the knoll, so Charles Terry with Judge Edward Lander donated the adjacent acre and a half. The site selection drew criticism from more than a few residents for being "out in the sticks." That campus was located at Fourth and University streets, where the Four Seasons Olympic Hotel stands today.

The next hurdle was to find funding to clear the campus of its huge trees. The Legislature had appropriated

Legislature, when a storm overturned his canoe as he was being paddled home from a session in Olympia. She took as her second husband the popular sheriff, Lewis Wyckoff. And out on the Duwamish, Henry Van Asselt married Jane Maple, the daughter of his neighbor.

However, for every man who found a bride, a half dozen sought in vain. As was frequently the case on the frontier, men outnumbered women by a marked degree. Women arriving single in the territory did not remain alone long, nor did the little pioneer girls when they reached their mid-teens. Louisa Catherine Denny, Arthur and Mary's daughter, turned 16 on October 20, 1859, and five days later married 25-year-old George Frye. That same year the Reverend Daniel Bagley arrived in Seattle to fill the role of Protestant minister and soon was noted for his ability to properly conduct weddings.

Establishing the University of Washington

Washington faced the usual problems of a new territory in developing needed public institutions. Many settlements dreamed of being chosen as the site for the capitol, the penitentiary, the insane asylum or the university,

Several weddings occurred after the Indian war. Charles Terry, one of the town's first successful businessmen, married Mary Jane Russell of Port Madison and they became a favorite Seattle couple. Terry later built one of the first nice residences in the city.

The Reverend Daniel Bagley was the founder of Seattle's second house of worship, the Methodist Protestant or Brown Church. He and Arthur Denny worked together to secure the placement of the University of Washington in Seattle.

The original University of Washington structure opened in 1861 when Seattle was home to about 200 residents. For 15 years the university did not graduate a college student, but the Seattle schools rented the structure for public school classes. Notice the school children playing in the yard. The Four Seasons Olympic Hotel now occupies this site.

no funds for the university and would not do so for 15 years. Clearing land on that 10 acres ended up costing from $275 to $325 per acre, a fortune in those days. At that time forested land was selling for only $1.25 an acre, and as a result Rev. Bagley quickly disposed of hundreds of acres of university lands near Seattle and sold large timbered tracts in Jefferson and Kitsap counties to mill companies.

Many men prominent in the town worked to raise funds to clear the campus of felled trees and construct the university buildings. Thomas Mercer (Mercer Street) and others hauled materials to the site. John Pike (Pike Street) served as architect and helped frame the buildings, and his son Harvey and others painted the structures. A.P. DeLin and O.C. Shorey carved the columns and put them in place. R.H. Beatty, O.J. Carr, Josiah Settle and Clarence Bagley installed flooring and attached shingles. Many other residents also were involved. The University Building, the president's house, a dormitory and two out-houses were completed. Interestingly, the plans did not call for any conveniences, not even a water pipe.

Seattle had its university but no territorial fund to operate the institution. Even so, the University of Washington opened on November 4, 1861, with Asa S. Mercer in charge. Young Asa had graduated from Franklin College in Ohio the year before and followed his older brother Thomas and two family friends, Dexter Horton and Daniel Bagley, to Seattle. Being the only secular college graduate in the town, he was selected as the first president of the University of Washington. On opening day 30 "scholars" of various ages were welcomed into the one classroom furnished for general education purposes.

Seattle had its university before a public school building existed in the town. The next spring Mrs. Ossian J. Carr taught private school classes in the university structure. By 1865, to meet the growing need for free public education, the town's citizens arranged for the school district to rent the University Building and reimburse the university for expenses. So it was that for several years the university served as Seattle's first public school. Not until 1876, 15 years after it opened its doors, did the university award its first degree, a bachelor of science diploma, to a young Seattle woman named Clara McCarty. Not until the late 1880s did students graduate every year.

All of this proves the city founders had remarkable foresight. When the university opened its doors, only a few hundred residents called the isolated town home. In addition, the Civil War was raging, slowing both population and business growth in the West. Furthermore, in those days only a tiny percentage of the population felt a need for education beyond the primary grades. Nevertheless, those founders realized a university would provide jobs, attract settlers and, most importantly, enhance Seattle's image as the leading settlement on Puget Sound. They persevered through difficult times and today the University of Washington is one of the largest and finest institutions of higher learning in the country and continues as a major influence in the development of the Seattle area and the state of Washington.

The Civil War Years

Within months of the Indian attack, Seattle residents faced the trauma of the Civil War being fought on distant battlefields. Because most had family and acquaintances in the Midwest, East and South, they impatiently awaited the news contained in letters and newspapers that took two months or more to arrive.

Back then a majority of the pioneers and territorial officials were Democrats and were opposed to interfering with slavery. After hearing of the Confederate attack on Fort Sumter, many of these pioneers began believing it was more important to preserve the Union. Rumors of a Confederate privateer off the coast and of efforts to enlist a Washington company of volunteers for the Confederate army caused concern, but the many common local problems kept partisanship from becoming very heated or long lasting. Edmund Meany described the situation in his history of the territory:

"While the majority of them adhered to the Democratic party, their democracy was fundamentally different from that in the East, and especially in the South. Every time the question of slavery arose the people of the Northwest spoke and acted in favor of free soil and against slavery. They would continue as Democrats but not pro-slavery Democrats."

In Seattle support was split almost evenly. Bagley, Horton, the Dennys and the Mercers were outspoken Unionists. Yesler, Maynard, Terry and Plummer were openly sympathetic to the South. Seattle women stitched

The only college graduate in Seattle available to serve as the first president of the university was young Asa Mercer who had followed his brother, Thomas Mercer, to the area.

In 1865 the Civil War was ending. Men of the village had felled a tree and installed it as the tallest flagpole in the territory. It rises at the end of the street on the right. Historian Clarence Bagley was 22 years old and lived in Seattle at the time. Sixty years later he identified the numbered structures: (1) S.B. Hine's general store, (2) Sires' Hotel and Saloon, (3) Yesler's Mill, (4) the Brown Church, (5) University of Washington on Denny's Knoll, (6) the White Church, (7) at top right, the Charles Terry home, (8) Occidental Hotel, (9) Kellogg Brothers Drugstore, (10) L.V. Wyckoff's Livery Stable, (11) Thomas Mercer's home, (12) Joe Williamson's store, (13) Welch and Greenfield's Dry Goods and (14) another saloon.

a 40-foot-long United States flag, while the men felled the tallest tree they could find to use as a flagpole to be erected near Yesler's Mill. That flagpole stands proudly in some of the earliest photographs of Seattle.

Several historically prominent Civil War officers served in Washington Territory prior to the conflict. Isaac I. Stevens and George Pickett were the two known best by local citizens. Stevens, a West Point graduate, served as the first governor of Washington Territory and later as a delegate to Congress. In 1860, as the war commenced, he volunteered for active duty and was appointed a brigadier general in September 1861. He distinguished himself during the battles of Manassas and Second Bull Run. Late on the afternoon of September 1, 1862, during a rebel attack at Chantilly, Virginia, when the regimental standard bearer was felled by Confederate shells, General Stevens rushed forward to raise the fallen banner for his men to rally around when he, too, was killed. To this day at Chantilly, a few miles out of Washington, D.C., on a stone memorial atop the hill where he died are etched Steven's name and date of death.

George Pickett was assigned to the territory during the U.S.-Canadian dispute over San Juan Island. This minor skirmish, known as "The Pig War," started when a British pig was shot while feasting in an American settler's garden. Pickett lived for a time in Bellingham with his wife, the daughter of an Indian chief, and their son. His wife died soon after their son was born and Pickett joined the Confederate army, leaving his son to be raised by friends in the Gray's Harbor vicinity. Pickett quickly advanced to the rank of general and was involved in many battles including the one at Gettysburg where he led the famous charge that bears his name. General Pickett married a second time in his home state of Virginia and apparently

never reclaimed his son, Jimmy, who, as an adult, earned a living as a Portland newspaper artist. When Jimmy died at a young age, apparently of tuberculosis, he was in possession of a trunk belonging to his father in which there was one of his Army swords.

Before the Civil War, Ulysses S. Grant as a young officer was stationed for a year at Fort Vancouver. General Phil Sheridan was also assigned there from 1855 to 1861. Other officers such as Colonel Silas Casey, longtime commander at Fort Steilacoom, and General George Wright and General E.O.C. Ord served in Washington Territory. Army fortifications later were named for all of them.

During the Civil War a telegraph line was extended through Seattle, allowing receipt of reports of the final battles to be received in Seattle almost as soon as in cities near the battlefields. This service appeared almost by accident. The first attempt to lay an undersea telegraph line across the Atlantic failed when the cable broke. Not sure they would ever succeed in that direction, a decision was made to route wires west across the country, then north to Alaska and across the Bering Sea to Russia and on to Europe. That telegraph wire, sometimes strung on trees, reached Seattle before the second attempt to lay cable across the Atlantic was successful. The first telegraph messages were received in Seattle on October 26, 1864, telling of Confederate army retreats and of the attempt by General Sherman to surround General Hood's army in a valley "and starve them to death." Seattle suddenly had almost instant communication with the rest of the country.

The Saga of the Mercer Girls

The shortage of single women created increasing concern among Seattle's pioneers. Lee Terry, for one, after a couple of years on Elliott Bay returned to his former home in New York where women were more plentiful. Thomas Mercer in the late 1850s suggested the territory make efforts to recruit young New England women to migrate west. That same year Charles Prosch, publisher of the *Puget Sound Herald* in Steilacoom, surmised, "There is no community in the Union with a like number of inhabitants in which so large a proportion are bachelors." The next year he editorialized: "Here is the market to bring your charms to, girls. Don't be backward but come right along, all who want good homes in the most beautiful country and the finest climate in the world."

Prosch's words convinced 96 young men to meet and discuss ways to convince young women to migrate to Puget Sound. A plan was developed whereby Asa Mercer, the first president of the new university and a man of ideas as well as ambition, would travel east to recruit the young ladies. Mercer visited several settlements on the Sound to raise funds to pay for his journey to Boston. Scores of young single males contributed what they could afford and in the fall of 1863, young Mercer boarded a ship headed for the East Coast. A couple of months later in Lowell, Massachusetts, he made several speeches before large audiences. His speaking ability, pleasant personality, and his descriptions of opportunities on Puget Sound convinced 11 educated young ladies to make the journey.

With Asa as chaperone, their itinerary took them to Panama and on horseback across the isthmus, then on to San Francisco, then north to Port Gamble on a lumber bark, and from there to Seattle in a small sloop. They arrived at 11 p.m. on May 16, 1864. That being shortly before telegraph service arrived, there was no way to communicate their time of arrival. They disembarked onto a dark and empty dock. The young women may have had second thoughts as they stumbled down the muddy street following Asa Mercer and a guide holding high a smoky lantern to lead them to the DeLin House at First South and Main Street where their rooms were waiting.

The next morning excited voices echoed down the streets of Seattle: "Asa and the girls are here!" A public reception was arranged at the University Building that afternoon and the residents turned out en masse to hear Dr. Maynard chair a meeting that offered prayers for the young women's happiness and prosperity. Asa Mercer was rewarded with a rousing cheer. All the while, the many young bachelors shyly studied the women, most of them aged between 16 and 20. Soon these women had been hired to teach school in Puget Sound towns such as Coupeville, Port Townsend, Port Ludlow, Olympia and Seattle, and most of them quickly wed local men. The oldest among them, Lizzie Ordway, was in her mid-30s and though she had suitors she did not marry, saying she preferred to reserve her affections for her young students. She taught in several districts and served as Kitsap County's superintendent of schools. In 1870 she opened Seattle's first public school, a two-story frame structure at Third and Marion. Classes started before the structure was completed. Clarence Bagley described the opening day scene in his Seattle history:

> So many scholars were present that the teacher was compelled to send home many of the smaller ones. [Miss Ordway said it this way: "I sent the younger ones home to ripen a little."] She announced that as soon as the school's lower story was finished there would be ample accommodations for all. Arrangements were made almost from the start to secure additional teachers as they should be needed. By May 1851, Miss Peebles had charge of the intermediate department of the public school and Mrs. C. M. Sanderson, of the primary department. In the intermediate department there was an average attendance of fifty pupils; in the primary department eighty-four names were on Mrs. Sanderson's roll with an average attendance of more than seventy.

To reward Asa for his success in bringing the young ladies west, he was nominated to be a candidate for the territorial Legislature representing King and Kitsap counties. He was elected by a huge majority and proudly claimed all those votes were generated without his "spending a nickel, making a speech, or buying a cigar or a drink of whiskey for anyone." But Asa, himself, was still without a wife, a situation that undoubtedly helped convince him to undertake a second expedition to the East Coast.

On this second journey he planned to enlist the aid of powerful politicians in the nation's capitol. Mercer's family had known the young Abraham Lincoln, and as a child Asa sat on his lap while Lincoln repeated some of his humorous stories. Now their former neighbor occupied the White House, and Asa planned to visit with him and ask for assistance in filling a ship with unmarried women to take to Puget Sound. It was apparent the Civil War was nearly over and dozens of government vessels were sitting idle. Within hours of his ship docking in New York, Mercer was on the way by rail to Washington, D.C. As he arrived at the nation's capitol, he noticed black crepe bows hanging on doors. He soon learned that President Lincoln had been assassinated the night before he arrived. Mercer was shocked, saddened and bewildered, but after a few days decided to seek assistance from others. He described his efforts with these words:

Lizzie Ordway, a teacher, came west with the first batch of Mercer Girls. Though she had suitors, she always said she preferred to reserve her affections for her students. She opened Seattle's first public school building and later served as superintendent of Kitsap County schools.

Asa Mercer's second trip east to find eligible women for Puget Sound's many bachelors was not as successful as hoped. But *Harper's Weekly* published a complimentary feature with sketches showing young ladies singing around a piano, dining, and sitting on deck. The saga of the Mercer Girls was the basis of a long-running 1970s television series called "Here Come the Brides."

Passing over the months of hard and continuous labor in the various departments of Washington, with the statement that I had seen everybody, from President Johnson down the line, all of whom approved of the enterprise but were afraid to aid, I finally called upon General Grant and stated my wants. Having been stationed for a number of years on Puget Sound, he knew the situation and promptly promised his aid. Calling at his office one morning he said: "Mercer, sit down and read the morning paper until my return. I am going over to the White House to meet the President and his Cabinet and will bring your matter to a head one way or the other." Half an hour later he returned, and as he entered the door his salutation was: "The Captain here will make out an order for a steamship, coaled and manned, with capacity to carry 500 women from New York to Seattle for A.S. Mercer, and I will sign the same." He explained that the President and all the members of the Cabinet approved the undertaking, but were afraid to assume the responsibility of making the order. They pledged themselves, however, to stand by Grant if he would assume the risk.

Mercer carried the order to release the ship to a General Meigs who promptly refused to honor it. After Mercer had tried other avenues, the reportedly unscrupulous Ben Holladay stepped up with an offer to help. Mercer mentioned he had been promised a ship at a reduced price but had insufficient funding even for the lower price. Holladay proposed that he would buy the ship and carry the passengers to Puget Sound for a nominal fee. Mercer, young and inexperienced with such business ventures, agreed and began issuing free tickets to the more than 200 young ladies who had expressed a willingness to sail to Puget Sound.

Then trouble struck. *The New York Herald* published a scurrilous article slandering Mercer and stating that all men on Puget Sound were rotten and profligate and would turn the girls over to houses of prostitution. That article was reprinted in newspapers across the country and even reached Seattle before Mercer returned home. Delays in fitting out the ship caused additional concerns and during the delay most of the young women, aware of the article, withdrew from the Mercer offer. Holladay raised the prices for the few still willing to continue the

journey. On January 16, 1866, Asa sailed for home with 36 unmarried young women, 10 Civil War widows, 13 men with their wives and children, and 14 single men. When they reached San Francisco, a group of local women who had read the *Herald* article met the ship to offer protection to the poor, misguided young ladies. Most of Mercer's girls, however, continued to trust Asa and promised him they would continue on to Seattle.

Now Asa faced another major problem. He explained it this way:

When I arrived in San Francisco I was broke — three lonesome dollars being my all. With hotel bills of the party to pay and transportation to Seattle to secure, the situation was somewhat embarrassing to say the least. Remembering the Governor's promise, I spent $2.50 sending him this telegram: "Arrived here broke. Send $2,000 quick to get party to Seattle." The next day I received a notice from the telegraph office to call, pay $7.50 and receive a dispatch awaiting me. Having but 50 cents, I could not buy the message. However, I called at the office and asked to see the superintendent. Explaining my impecunious state, I told him of the message to the governor, and suggested that he, the superintendent, open the dispatch and see if it contained an order for money. If so, I could pay, otherwise it was the company's loss. He opened the envelope and read, then burst into a hearty laugh, and passed the envelope to me. It was made up of over one hundred words of congratulation, but never a word about money.

While in New York Asa had purchased $2,000 worth of agricultural machinery, mostly wagons, to be shipped around the Horn to San Francisco and then on for use by residents of Seattle. He suddenly realized he might solve his problem if that equipment was still stored in San Francisco. He rushed to the office of the shipping company and luckily found the machinery was awaiting shipment in the warehouse. He managed to sell it for just enough to pay the fare of the women to Seattle. To save dollars and time he arranged for the young ladies to board several smaller ships that were scheduled to leave for Puget Sound. When all had arrived in Seattle, a welcoming event was scheduled in Yesler's Hall, with Reverend Daniel Bagley presiding. The Mercer Girls, as they soon became known, all appeared at the event to demonstrate their faith in the

This old Ramage Press printed papers in Philadelphia in the early 1800s before being sent to San Francisco in the 1850s. Then it was taken to Portland to print the *Oregonian*, then to Olympia to publish the *Columbian*. It printed papers in Stilacoom before being moved to Seattle to print the town's first paper, *The Gazette*, in 1869 and later *The Post-Intelligencer*. It could turn out only 50 to 75 four-page newspapers an hour and was called a "man killer." It is now retired at Seattle's Museum of History and Industry.

man who had sponsored their trip. These young women added sophistication and intelligence to Puget Sound, most of them marrying within a year or two. Several present residents of the Seattle area are descendents of those intelligent and adventurous young women.

An item in the local weekly of July 15, 1866, provides a conclusion to the Mercer Girl saga. It announced that Reverend Bagley presided at the wedding of Asa Shinn Mercer and Miss Annie E. Stephens of Baltimore. As the locals phrased it: "Asa finally convinced one of his girls to marry him."

Seattle's First Newspaper

In August 1863 James R. Watson began publishing a newspaper in Olympia, then the most important town in the territory, and in December moved his press to Seattle, where he published *The Gazette* each week, providing he could find sufficient news. He put the paper together in a room provided free by Henry Yesler. His press was an ancient Ramage model, the first printing equipment in California and Washington Territory, and the press that had produced the first newspapers in Portland, Olympia and Seattle. Today, that Ramage press is a treasured relic at Seattle's Museum of History and Industry.

During the latter years of the 1870s, progress was noted on several Seattle fronts. By legislative action Seattle was granted a city charter in January of 1869. The first ordinances of the new town passed by the trustees levied a tax to pay for wooden sidewalks on Front Street (now First Avenue), established laws against reckless driving of horse-drawn vehicles, and levied fines of $1 for each pig allowed to run loose in the city.

During Seattle's first two decades, the grim reaper claimed several of the original settlers: Luther Collins drowned in the Snake River while prospecting for gold; John Holgate, the first U.S. citizen to explore the Duwamish River, was shot in a dispute over a Nevada mining claim in 1868; Charles Plummer, one of Seattle's first prominent developers, died in 1866; and Charles Terry was only 37 when tuberculosis took his life in 1867.

Seattle residents proudly noted that the 1870 Federal Census counted 1,107 residents, proving their former village had really become a town. What's more, as Roberta Frye Watt explained: "This growth was more than an increase in population. The early townsmen were like a vanguard preparing for a multitude. There was an expectancy about the town as if the pioneers were standing on tiptoe peeking over the Cascades in expectation of the Railroad."

Historical Chaff from the Era

Why Our Streets Bend at Yesler Way

In 1853, as additional settlers arrived, a demand developed for residence and business town lots. Arthur Denny, Carson Boren and David Maynard decided to plat their properties fronting on Elliott Bay. On May 23, 1853, two plats were filed with the County Auditor. They were adjacent properties with streets alike in width and with lot and block sizes similar. However, they differed in street direction. Denny and Boren's streets ran parallel to the shoreline but Dr. Maynard insisted that his streets conform to directions of the magnetic compass. As a result, the streets bend where they meet at Yesler Way. Arthur Denny, the surveyor, wrote in his book *Pioneer Days on Puget Sound*:

All had gone smoothly until the time when we (Boren, Maynard and myself) were to record a joint plat of the town of Seattle, when it was found that the Doctor, who occasionally stimulated a little, had that day taken enough to cause him to feel that he was not only monarch of all he surveyed, but what Boren and I had surveyed as well.

Consequently Boren and I, on the 23rd day of May, 1853, filed the first plat of the town of Seattle. When, in the evening of the same day, his fever had subsided sufficiently, the Doctor filed his also.

Some have insisted Maynard's plan would have reduced the slope of the east-west streets, others insist the opposite is true. But it really is a century and a half late to be arguing about it.

Name Confusion

When the bill to separate northern Oregon as a new territory was discussed, residents suggested it be named Columbia Territory because of the magnificent river that marked part of its southern border. During debate on the bill, Representative Richard Stanton of Kentucky moved an amendment to change the name to honor the first president of our country. That, he thought, would prevent confusion between a Columbia Territory and the District of Columbia. On March 2, 1853, President Fillmore signed the legislation creating Washington Territory. Since that time, Washington, D.C. has become a more familiar name than the District of Columbia, a situation that causes confusion between Washington state and "that other Washington."

CHAPTER TWO

THE VILLAGE
BECOMES A CITY
1870-1900

After two decades of existence, Seattle still hardly showed as a dot on the map. Judge Cornelius Hanford in his history of *Seattle and Environs* described the 1870 village with these words:

"The town existed as a mere aggregation of houses, commingled with stumps, before the first survey was made for fixing the street grades. Until the city was incorporated [in 1869] there was no public fund available

Henry Yesler's little home at First and James was not pretentious. This photo from the 1860s shows Seattle's first water system, an open trough Yesler built from a spring on 4th Avenue to his steam sawmill. Notice the stumps and mud extending up to present-day Fourth Avenue.

Yesler's lumber mill was the major industry in Seattle through the 1870s and most pictures of the village include some part of it. Here Yesler's millpond in Elliott Bay is framed by the coal bunkers where ships pulled in close to load the black fuel from mines in Renton, Issaquah and Newcastle for transport to California.

By the mid-1870s, businesses were stretching along a recently graded but muddy Front Street, now First Avenue.

for improving the streets, and no authority existed for raising revenue for such purpose. The public road fund belonged to the county and was disbursed by the Board of County Commissioners. Most of what had been expended for the direct benefit of Seattle was practically wasted in the attempt to construct a wagon road along the beach southward toward Duwamish valley."

The road at the base of Beacon Hill, he explained, was built on blue clay and occasionally slipped onto the mud flats. The only permanent road was graded atop the hill, but the sharp ascents and descents at each

end caused problems. Eventually, the city built a boardwalk across the mud flats allowing easier access to the valley.

An event that captured the attention of Seattle residents in 1870 was the conquest of the mountain they looked for each morning. Mt. Rainier stood as an unconquered challenge, there being no record of a successful human ascent of the peak that rises more than 14,000 feet above sea level. That year Hazard Stevens, son of General Isaac Stevens, the first Territorial Governor, along with a friend, P.B. Van Trump, ascended over glaciers and rocky slopes to surmount the peak and, to the surprise of many, descended safely to tell and write of their adventure.

Several new businesses opened their doors along First Avenue South during the early 70s, most of them situated in inexpensive, one-story frame structures. In 1872 Schwabacher & Co. erected the first substantial two-story brick mercantile building and shortly thereafter, James M. Colman and Frauenthal Brothers built a similar structure on the waterfront. By then, two breweries, a couple of shoemakers, several blacksmiths, boilermakers, painters, carpenters, lawyers, doctors and dentists called Seattle home.

Regular steamship service between Puget Sound and San

(Far left)
The Intelligencer newspaper started as a weekly in 1867, became a daily in 1876 and combined with a failing publication called the *Post*. *The Seattle Post-Intelligencer* has been published ever since.

The side-wheeler *Eliza Anderson* was a common sight on Elliott Bay during the 1870s.

Francisco was inaugurated in 1874. The *Pacific* was the first vessel to sail on a regular schedule but unfortunately, after a few voyages she collided with a sailing ship and rapidly sank. Of the several passengers from Puget Sound aboard her, only two survived. During 1875 the Pacific Mail Steamship Company's *City of Panama* was scheduled for two trips a month from California to Puget Sound, a schedule later extended to Alaska. This move helped Seattle businessmen realize the considerable trading potential that existed with that northern territory. At the same time, small local steamers posted regular schedules for carrying passengers and freight between Seattle and outlying Puget Sound settlements. Locals soon were calling the little ships that buzzed around the Sound "the mosquito fleet." Those small steamers helped develop Seattle as the major business center on Puget Sound.

Seattle's first daily newspaper, *The Intelligencer,* began publishing in 1876 with David Higgins as editor. Two years later he sold it to Thaddeus Hanford who combined it with two other small papers. When a competing paper, the *Post,* began publishing in the small town, success for either was difficult. The two later were combined as the *Post-Intelligencer* that continues publishing to this day and is one of Seattle's oldest businesses. A few years back it gave its extensive news photo collection to the Museum of History and Industry and several are used in this book.

King County had severe financial problems during the 70s. Under the laws of Washington Territory, collecting taxes was an uncertain undertaking. When funds were not available, the County paid with warrants that when presented for payment were stamped "unpaid for lack of funds." The holder then became eligible for interest from that date until funds were available. In similar fashion, mill companies sometimes issued drafts payable through

a San Francisco office in 60 days. Those who supplied logs and performed other services for the mills usually needed the cash immediately. Captain D. B. Finch, owner and master of the steamer *Eliza Anderson,* scheduled a round trip each week between Olympia and Victoria, carrying supplies to all the towns between. He realized that if he acted as an informal banker and purchased delayed-payment drafts and warrants at 75 percent of par value, then cashed them in later at full value, considerable profit might accrue. He soon was recognized as one of the wealthier men in the maritime business.

The Fight for Railroad Service

As Seattle was being founded, steel rails were tying East Coast cities together. Among the first settlers on Elliott Bay were those who began dreaming of the day trains would carry much of the nation's freight to Seattle's waterfront where it would be transferred to ships for transport around the Pacific Rim. Nearly 30 years would pass before their dream became reality. Books have been written about Seattle's difficult battle to become a major rail center. What follows is a brief synopsis of that complex history.

At the dawn of the 1870s, the Northern Pacific Railroad was under construction from Duluth to an unselected terminus on Puget Sound. Seattle, the largest town on the Sound and located on a deep harbor, was a major contender. Nearly every issue of the *Intelligencer* newspaper featured articles about the importance of rail service to Seattle. Real estate values began to escalate. Hundreds of new residents appeared, including men like Orange Jacobs, John Leary, Thomas Burke and Robert Moran who became community leaders and promoters of rail services. Their hopeful anticipation received a jolt in July 1873

when the Northern Pacific sent Arthur Denny a terse telegram stating "We have located the terminus on Commencement Bay." Seattleites could hardly believe tiny Tacoma had been chosen.

Construction engineers of that time considered the Cascade Mountains to be almost insurmountable, so the first Northern Pacific tracks followed the valley of the Columbia River to Portland. The rails then were extended down the river to where a ferry was located that could float the railroad vehicles across to what is now the town of Kalama. From there the rails extended north to Tacoma. Seattle leaders, upset at their lack of success at attracting a railroad, realized most of Eastern Washington also remained without rail service and called several meetings from which an unrealistic plan emerged. It called for laying track from Seattle to Walla Walla where it would join the Northern Pacific cross-country tracks. Seattle volunteers began leveling a roadbed around Beacon Hill and the south shore of Lake Washington. Captain William Renton supplied funds to pay for laying track from coal mines in the town of Renton to a steamship landing on the Duwamish River. James M. Colman added financial support and supervised Chinese laborers as they extended the line to the Newcastle coal mines. By 1877 the black fossil

fuel was being delivered by rail to the King Street bunkers on Elliott Bay and was second in value to lumber among Seattle's exports.

A southerly rail extension was added from Renton through White River Valley towns to Tacoma, but the Northern Pacific used it only sporadically, leaving Seattle without regularly scheduled rail service. In response, Seattle residents managed to secure financing for a line to Sumas on the border with Canada where freight and passengers were transferred to the newly completed transcontinental Canadian Pacific. This Seattle short line was operated for two years before the Northern Pacific leased it. Seattle again found itself with intermittent rail service.

But a solution was on the way. During the late 1880s James J. Hill began building his Great Northern rail system westward from Minneapolis-St. Paul. Hill visited Seattle several times and selected this city as his Puget Sound terminus. In 1892 the Great Northern construction engineers tackled the Cascades by building switchbacks over 4,059-foot Stevens Pass. Eight years later a 2.5-mile tunnel was bored through the mountain reducing the highest track elevation to 3,382 feet. In the summer of 1893 the first Great Northern train traveled the distance over the completed system. So it was that 48 years after the founders arrived on Elliott Bay, Seattle became the western terminus of a major rail system.

Soon other lines also were serving Seattle. The Chicago, Milwaukee and St. Paul was the first to install track over Snoqualmie, the lowest Cascade Mountain

pass and one that leads directly to Seattle. A deciding factor in the Chicago, Milwaukee decision to build at that time was the proposed 1909 Alaska-Yukon-Pacific World's Fair, during which their rail cars transported thousands of visitors to Seattle to enjoy the exposition on the new University of Washington campus. Railroad service was instrumental in Seattle's progress, and over the next half-century, before auto and air travel became affordable and reliable, most long-distance travelers bought tickets on the railroads. Two extant historic Seattle depots attest to the importance of rail travel during the first half of the 20th century — the King Street Station built in 1906 and the Union Station built five years later. It took both to serve the many travelers.

The Active 1880s

The new decade began with a record snowfall. Just weeks prior to the appearance of the winter storm, Territorial Governor Elisha P. Ferry dispatched to the Department of the Interior in Washington, D.C. his annual report in which he described the mildness of the climate on Puget Sound and remarked that during some winters snow fell infrequently or not at all. Nature disputed this statement on January 8 with a storm of large flakes that continued falling for a week, burying the streets beneath five feet of snow. Collapsing barns killed several cattle in the Duwamish Valley and Seattle residents clambered up ladders to their rooftops to shovel off the crushing weight. A man from Ballard became the first resident to shuffle down a Seattle street on snowshoes, bypassing other pedestrians struggling through the snow. Later, six horses were hitched to a large snowplow and labored mightily to open the road to Lake Union. The weather forced schools to close for the week.

Founding of the Seattle Chamber of Commerce

The battle to secure railroad service helped convince Seattle businessmen that a Seattle Chamber of Commerce was needed. The original Chamber was founded in 1882 with objectives such as these: "to foster and develop resources and services of the Northwest, in spite of predatory aggression of railroad magnates, Eastern financiers, California corporations, and even a few local businessmen." In 1890, supported by more than 300

(Far right) This little log canal in 1884 was the first to tie Lakes Washington and Union together.

The log canal floated logs harvested from the hills around the lakes to this Lake Union sawmill. The Capitol Hill forest behind the mill recently had been clear cut. Since this 1886 photo was taken, the swampy south end of Lake Union has been filled for two blocks or more.

members, the Chamber incorporated and developed new plans. These included acquiring, preserving and disseminating valuable business statistics and information; and fostering, protecting, and advancing commercial, mercantile, manufacturing and other public interests of the city of Seattle. In addition the Chamber provided a meeting place for the members; maintained a restaurant and rooms devoted to social purposes; and planned to purchase, acquire, hold, lease, mortgage and sell real estate for the accommodation and purposes of the said corporation. In 1910 the Chamber excised some of these objectives and added the goal of furthering trade with Pacific Rim countries. Since then, the organization has shifted objectives several times in efforts to keep abreast of the advances of business, industry, and society. The Chamber of Commerce continues as an influential organization in the development of Seattle.

Excavating a Canal to Connect
Lakes Washington and Union to Puget Sound

Beginning in the 1860s several attempts were made to excavate across the narrow isthmus separating Lake Washington from Lake Union. Harvey Pike took a pick and shovel and began to dig but soon gave up. The city hired a contractor who demanded more funding, claiming he ran into hardpan but the city refused his demands and he quit. The Lake Washington Improvement Company in 1884 employed a Chinese labor contractor who with 25 workers completed the narrow canal shown in the photo. This allowed logs from the forested shores of Lake Washington to be floated to the mill at the southern end of Lake Union. The dream of large ships steaming to Lake Washington was realized 32 years later when the Lake Washington Ship Canal opened. The locks at Ballard

The trees Henry and Sarah Yesler planted in the 1870s beside their home at James Street and Yesler Way are famous in Seattle history as the hanging trees.

made it possible for large ships to steam from the saltwater of Salmon Bay to the fresh water of Lakes Union and Washington.

Two Memorable Unlawful Events

George Reynolds was a personable downtown merchant. On January 17, 1882, after supper at home, while walking back to his store, he was accosted by two armed men intent on robbing him. When he reached for his own revolver, they shot him in the chest and he died two hours later. The fire bell was rung summoning men to the fire hall where a vigilance committee quickly formed to search for the killers. Two members, as they passed a haystack on a wharf, noticed a shoe sticking out of the straw and on inspection found a foot in it. The two men they rousted from the hay were turned over to Sheriff L. V. Wyckoff and Police Chief J. H. McGraw, who promptly locked the suspects in the jail. When the vigilance committee heard about the arrest of the two suspects, they rushed to the

sheriff's office to demand the prisoners be turned over to them. Sheriff Wyckoff, his pistol in his hand, demanded they desist from violence and promised to produce the two suspects in court the next morning.

Justice S. F. Coombs opened court in Yesler's Hall at 9:30 a.m. and prisoners James Sullivan and William Howard were ushered in. After brief testimony, Justice Coombs said, "I am convinced that the evidence is sufficient to hold these men without bail to await action of the grand jury, and they are now turned over to the officers and remanded back to jail." A shout echoed in the courtroom, and the two prisoners were wrested from the officers and pushed through a door to the alley. From there they were forced out to James Street where scantlings were placed between limbs of small maple trees on James Street south of Yesler's residence (now the site of the Pioneer Building). Ropes were tossed over these beams and the suspects were dragged to where nooses could be placed over their heads. They were hanged by the neck until dead.

One of the vigilantes suddenly remembered that Charles Payne, the suspected murderer of a Seattle police officer, remained in a jail cell. A group of the men scurried back, chopped down an outside wooden door to the jail, battered down two iron doors, grabbed Payne and hanged him beside the other two. At the time many citizens and the local press defended the vigilante action, but other residents argued that rules of law should apply to citizens and suspected criminals alike. That was the last time that vigilantes in Seattle succeeded in taking the law into their own hands.

Six years later a lawless gang caused a different kind of trouble in Seattle. Over the previous decade, many Chinese men had been recruited to immigrate to the West Coast to help build the railroads. As the rails reached their destinations, these immigrants sought employment and migrated to the cities. The census of 1885 counted 3,276 persons of Chinese extraction in Washington Territory, and a sizable "Chinatown" had developed on Washington Street in Seattle. Contract labor for these men usually was arranged through Chinese merchants. Most of the Chinese worked as servants, miners, construction workers,

This contemporary sketch is of the three men being hanged by vigilantes in the trees adjacent to the Yesler home. The local artist included caricatures of several citizens of that time. Big Bill Gross, the black restaurateur, is shown in the lower right corner with two Chinese between him and Henry Yesler, who as usual was whittling on a stick.

laundry men or cooks. The Exclusion Act of 1880 was intended to restrict entry of more Chinese, but it was poorly enforced. When a financial recession struck the area, unemployed whites tended to blame the Asians for hiring on as "cheap labor." Radical leaders began ranting "The Chinese must go!" On September 25, 1885, an Anti-Chinese Congress assembled in Seattle, concluded that the Chinese were illegally living in Seattle, and issued an edict demanding that all Orientals leave Western Washington within a week.

On November 4 Governor Watson Squire proclaimed that all citizens must refrain from acting violently against the Chinese and that law and order must be maintained. On November 7 Sheriff John H. McGraw, realizing the tension was increasing, assembled several hundred citizens and swore them in as deputy sheriffs and also placed two local companies of the territorial militia on alert. President Grover Cleveland, when apprised of the situation, issued a proclamation stating that military force would be deployed if necessary and dispatched 10 companies of federal troops from Fort Vancouver to Seattle. Fifteen persons were indicted in Seattle for conspiracy to deprive the Chinese of equal protection of the law, but all were acquitted two months later. As the tension dissipated, the troops were withdrawn and a false calm settled over the city.

On February 6, 1886, a meeting was scheduled for those who wanted to force all Chinese out of the Territory. A committee of 15 was organized to visit Chinatown ostensibly "to inspect sanitary facilities for health violations." This was cover for a raid on the Asian population, the goal being to drive them away. The plan called for a member of the committee to knock on a door and ask permission to inspect the premises. He and several others then forced their way in and rummaged around to locate the resident's personal belongings, which were carried out to waiting wagons.

The Chinese and their baggage were then unceremoniously dumped on the dock beside the steamer *Queen of the Pacific* that was preparing to sail for San Francisco. Sheriff McGraw hurried to dockside and ordered the mob to disperse, but they ignored him. The fire bells clanged to rally militiamen and deputy sheriffs. Governor Squire, who happened to be in Seattle at the time, immediately ordered unlawful actions to cease and warned that any lawbreakers would be punished. He also called for the militia to assist in maintaining the law.

Meantime down on the dock, the Captain of the *Queen of the Pacific* refused to let the 350 Chinese aboard until their fares were paid. A collection was taken by the anti-Chinese hoard and enough was donated to buy tickets for about 100 of the Asians. At the same time Judge Roger S. Greene prepared a writ of habeas corpus charging that the Chinese were being illegally restrained. This writ,

served on the captain, enjoined the steamer from sailing. The captain was ordered to produce the Chinese in court the next day at 8 a.m.

At the appointed time Judge Greene informed the Chinese that if they wished to remain in Seattle they would be protected from those trying to force them to leave. Those expressing a desire to leave would have an armed escort to assure they safely reached the *Queen of the Pacific* when she was prepared to sail. All but a few of the Chinese opted to leave, but the ship had space to carry only 197, leaving about 100 to be escorted back to their domiciles to await the next vessel.

After the *Queen* had pulled up anchor, armed guards began escorting the Chinese remaining in the courtroom toward their homes, but they were met by an angry mob at First South and Main Streets intent on blocking the Chinese from returning to their living quarters. The home guard moved to the front of the Chinese to lead the way and to protect them from the mob. Sheriff McGraw commanded the crowd to disperse. A logger named Charles Stewart shouted for the mob to disarm the home guardsmen. As the soldiers' rifles were grabbed, shots were fired and four men fell. One of them was the troublesome Charles Stewart who died the next day. Sheriff McGraw was a near casualty when a bullet penetrated the tail of his coat.

At that critical moment a group of volunteers known as the Seattle Rifles raced up from the wharf to support the home guards. For almost an hour the mob milled about the military groups, shouting threats at the Chinese seated within the circle of armed protectors. After a time mob members began to disperse and the guards escorted the Chinese to their homes. Governor Squire declared martial law, ordered all saloons closed, and established a 7 p.m. curfew. The next day President Grover Cleveland proclaimed martial law and ordered U.S. troops to Seattle. When the governor called for the arrest of vagrants, many of the men involved in the mob action fled town. Later, Congress appropriated $276,000 to pay the Chinese for their losses.

News of the anti-Chinese riot was carried in newspapers across the nation. Most articles praised Seattle and Washington Territory for maintaining the peace and protecting the freedoms of residents during difficult times. Several families later said they moved to Seattle because of the way its people worked together to end the riot.

Seattle was progressive in another way during the decade, but the effect was short lived. In 1883, with local politicians leading the way, the territorial legislature passed a suffrage bill giving women the right to vote. Four

This sketch illustrates how troops protected the Chinese from the mob (upper left), the Chinese lining up at the dock to board the *Queen of the Pacific* (upper right), and the mob trying to prevent the Chinese from returning to their homes. Shots are being fired as the mob tries to wrest the guards' rifles away, resulting in four of the mob being wounded.

On November 18, 1889, several Seattle residents joined the crowd at the original state capitol building in Olympia to witness the inauguration of Washington's first governor, Elisha P. Ferry.

The several privately owned Seattle water systems used augured logs with wooden spigots to connect them. As they aged they often leaked, causing water pressure to drop.

The glue pot that boiled over starting the great Seattle fire was recovered in the ashes, blackened but whole. It is now an artifact at the Museum of History and Industry. Glue at that time came in hard balls that had to be softened by heating before use.

The Territorial National Guard was assigned to safeguard valuables and keep thievery to a minimum. Note the tents being erected in the background.

years later the Territorial Supreme Court ruled the act to be unconstitutional. Seven years later Washington women were given the right to vote in school elections; then in 1910, they were permanently awarded voting rights in all elections. That was 10 years before the U.S. Constitution was amended to allow all women who were U.S. citizens to cast a ballot.

The town's law officers and public officials played important roles in attempting to keep the peace during the late 1800s. They were unusual men. Orange Jacobs served as Associate Justice in the Territorial Supreme Court before being elected as the Territory's delegate to Congress. He then served as Seattle's mayor, helped write a new city charter and served many years as a University of Washington regent. In 1884 Watson Squire was appointed governor by President Arthur and after the granting of statehood he became Washington state's first U.S. senator. He lived in Seattle where he was president of Union Trust Bank. There were dozens of such men and women who struggled to help Seattle survive difficult times and helped reconstruct it as a stronger and wealthier city.

Washington Becomes a State

On February 22, 1889, Congress passed an enabling act authorizing Washington Territory to adopt a state constitution preparatory to admission into the union. A committee of 75 members was organized in Olympia on July 4, 1889, to draft a constitution that was signed by the governor and sent to President Benjamin Harrison for his signature. The schedule called for the first state legislature to convene on November 6 but the plan went awry. The President refused to sign the constitution because it had not been officially certified as required by law. That delayed the proclamation of statehood until November 11, 1889. Had the delay not occurred, Washington might have become the 39th state of the Union. Instead three other states — North and South Dakota and Montana — were admitted days ahead of Washington, making it the 42nd star on Old Glory. It then took a week to make the inaugural arrangements and on November 18, Elisha P.

Ferry became Washington state's first governor. His home was in Seattle but he was no stranger in Olympia, having served two earlier terms as an appointed Territorial governor. He gave his speech from the porch of the "temporary" statehouse that would serve as the capitol until 1903.

The Day Seattle Burned

The spring of 1889 was unusually dry. In the heart of the city one- and two-story frame structures fronted on wooden sidewalks and unpaved streets. Residences were spreading up First Hill and around the base of Denny Hill, below the slopes too steep to allow construction.

With railroads servicing the Northwest, hundreds of newcomers arrived in Seattle each year. Privately owned gravity-flow systems delivered water through augured fir logs connected with leaky wooden spigots.

Fire Chief Josiah Collins warned that water pressure was decreasing and that the volunteer fire department needed additional equipment. The scene was ripe for disaster.

Thursday, June 6, 1889, dawned sunny and warm. Fire Chief Collins had sailed for San Francisco to act as best man at a friend's wedding. Victor Clairmont's cabinet shop in the basement of a two-story wooden structure on the southwest corner of First and Madison was a busy place. A young Swedish immigrant was melting glue in a metal pot on a wood-burning stove. When his attention was distracted for a moment, the glue overheated and flashed into flame. A nearby worker grabbed a small board and placed it over the pot to smother the flame but the board also began to burn. The young

This view is south on Front Street (now First Avenue) from Madison Street. The fire had started about 10 minutes earlier.

The Great Seattle fire started in a building on the west side of First Avenue, a site now occupied by the old Federal Office Building built in the 1930s. By the time the photographer preserved this scene, the fire was so hot that buildings across First Avenue, including Frye's Opera House, had burst into flame.

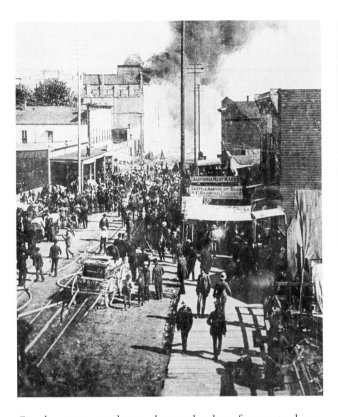

(Far left)
The fire jumped across Front Street and soon was devouring Frye's Opera House, the principal theater building in the town.

Rebuilding began immediately after ashes of the Great Fire had cooled.

Swede, a new employee, threw a bucket of water to douse the fire but that caused flaming glue to explode onto wood shavings on the floor. The entire building was soon wrapped in flames. A gusty wind from the northwest pushed the fire southward into adjacent structures. The

conflagration became so hot that the flames spread against the wind and crossed streets to set new blocks afire.

Firemen arrived and hooked up to the hydrants, but the intense heat kept them at a distance. They had no way of reaching the flames that were spreading in the flammable basements below street level. Burning brands, carried high by the rising heated air, dropped onto roofs blocks away. The waterfront wharves began to burn, destroying the railroad tracks and structures on them. As a lumber mill burned, the equipment crashed through the weakened floor into Elliott Bay. More firemen and hoses appeared and for a time the fire seemed under control. Fire equipment from Tacoma arrived on rail cars, but as additional

The devastation stretched for blocks along First Avenue.

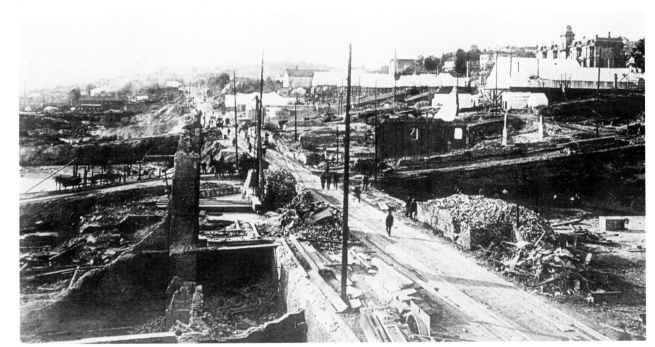

Looking south over the burned area the day after the fire

hoses were hooked to the water system, the pressure dropped. The water from the nozzles could no longer reach the heart of the flames. When it became obvious that many structures were doomed, efforts turned to removing valuables from the buildings.

By morning 116 acres of the business center of Seattle lay in smoldering ruin. Every downtown hotel was destroyed as were most rooming houses and restaurants.

Office buildings and downtown store structures were ashes and Dexter Horton's bank was a hollow shell, though his safe preserved the gold, silver and currency locked in it. All that remained of the brick Frye Opera House was a perilously leaning high brick wall. The large coal bunkers had burned, dumping tons of coal into the bay. Yesler's Mill and the historic buildings around it had disappeared. The residents of the city were appalled at the

The fire destroyed the wharves and the railroad tracks built atop them. In the background Duwamish Head can be seen shortly after it was cleared of its forest.

devastation but soon realized it could have been worse. The flames had been stopped from spreading into the residential areas to the east and north of downtown.

Reporters from several newspapers attempted to find the Swedish immigrant who reportedly had thrown water on the burning glue. Because his fellow employees had his name wrong (they called him "Berg"), he was not located for 16 days. A *Post-Intelligencer* employee found him and the next day the following interview was published:

> The chance incendiary who caused the recent disaster by fire was interviewed yesterday... He was down working on a new building at the corner of Third and Jackson streets. His name is John E. Back, and not "Berg" as heretofore given. He is a short, thick-set blonde of mediocre intelligence, aged 24 and a native of Sweden.
>
> How did you start the fire?" he was asked.
>
> He replied: "I can't tell. I put glue in and water on it, and I can't tell no more about it."
>
> Well, how did you go about it; what were you trying to do?
>
> "I cut some balls of glue and put them in the glue pot on the stove. I put in some shavings where there was little fire, and then went to work about 25 feet away, near the front door. After a while somebody said 'Look at the glue.' Another fellow, a Finlander from New York, then took a piece of board and laid it on to smother the glue, but the board caught fire. Then I run and took the pot of water to smother the fire and poured it over the pot of glue, which was blazing up high. When I throw the water on, the glue flew all over the shop into shavings and everything take fire."
>
> What did you do then?
>
> Then I tried to pull out my tool chest and burnt my hands. I lost the chest, and now somebody tell me to go to the relief committee for pay, and I go there pretty soon.
>
> Did you ever mix glue with cold water before?
>
> "No, I never did it before. I didn't know anything about it. I thought the fire go out with water."

John Back is not listed in the 1890 City Directory, so he likely left town after the interview.

Recovery activity began immediately after the fire when Mayor Robert Moran called town leaders together to develop plans to rebuild. Within two days gangs of laborers were cleaning up the ruins and stacking the

Dexter Horton's stone bank was gutted, but the iron safe in the back saved the valuables therein. Note the soldier guard.

reusable brick. After the ashes had cooled, merchants, with the help of the city, swept areas clean and erected tents as temporary stores and offices. Soon downtown streets were edged with white canvas and shoppers carefully trod on planks and new wooden sidewalks to do their shopping.

Amazingly, no lives were lost in the fire, although several stories were told of close calls. Several days after the flames had consumed the wooden interiors of the town's few brick buildings, a gust of wind shoved over a wall, killing one man and injuring another. The militia and city police were assigned the duty of guarding safes, safety

The standing walls of the few brick structures proved to be dangerous. The only two deaths attributed to the fire were caused when such walls collapsed.

Downtown Seattle became a tent city until permanent buildings were completed. Much of the city's commercial activity, including retail outlets, saloons, and professional services, including those of doctors and dentists, was continued beneath canvas.

deposit boxes, jewelry store sites and other possible locations of valuables in the ashes. For a time, parts of the burned area were declared unsafe and only workmen could enter to begin the cleanup. The fire made life miserable for many who had lived downtown, but on the other hand it cleared the business area of aging wooden structures. Within weeks, larger more modern buildings of noncombustible materials were rising. And the city adopted plans to combine the private water companies into a single municipal system.

Another positive result of the fire was the reaction across the country to what was called "the indomitable spirit" of Seattle residents. Banks wired information about their willingness to loan funds to rebuild the city, and mercantile companies inquired about developing Seattle outlets. In Boston the *Herald* published almost a full page of sketches and details of the Seattle fire. *Leslie's Weekly* carried graphic sketches of the fire damage. A *New York Tribune* poet, with tongue somewhat in cheek, attempted to commemorate the event in verse but was not sure how to pronounce the name of the town. "Which is correct?" he asked:

> "The town of Seattle was the scene of a battle
> In which the chief foeman was fire"
> Or:
> "The city of Seattle
> Was harmed but a leetle..."

A local pundit suggested that correct pronunciation does matter, but such awful poetry does not.

A month after the fire *The Seattle Press-Times* also waxed poetic. "Like the imaginary bird of ancient fable, Seattle has already begun to rise from the ashes of her former self and is putting on the raiments of magnificence and greatness."

Gay 90s City Activities

The amazing population increase during the 1880s resulted in a census count of 42,837 Seattle residents in 1890, 11 times the number of 10 years previous. Rapid population growth would continue through the new decade, forcing the city to undertake extensive improvements and to replat parts of the street grid. Fortunately, when statehood was granted in 1889, the Washington state constitution permitted cities of more than 20,000 inhabitants to write their own charters. Fifteen freeholders were elected in Seattle and during the next seven weeks they composed a charter that voters approved in

1890. For the first time Seattle residents controlled the destiny of their city.

To improve the street grid, First Avenue, then called Commercial Street, was straightened where it bent at Yesler Way. Yesler's Mill, built before the streets were platted, stuck out into the street, forcing First Avenue to jog up and around the mill. After the fire had burned the mill, the city paid $125,000 for a triangle of land that allowed First Avenue to extend north to Cherry Street where it was adjusted to run parallel to the shoreline and the other streets.

The 1893 Recession

Hard times swept west across the country after Baring Brothers, a major supplier of finances for the railroads, failed in 1890, and caused financial centers of the world to tighten their grip on capital. This caused some delay in rebuilding Seattle after the fire, but the enthusiasm and vigor of residents eased the trauma. Still, some of Seattle's founders lost their fortunes because of the recession.

Seattle had been one of the first U.S. cities to use electricity to power streetcars. City founder David T. Denny had invested heavily in real estate and trolley lines to serve the developing edges of the city. For several years he was considered one of Seattle's wealthiest citizens. Just prior to the recession, he and his wife, Louisa, moved into a fine new home on his original land claim at the foot of Queen Anne Hill. As Seattle banks felt the pinch of the recession, they began calling in their loans. Within months, David Denny found himself in dire straits. Unable to make all the payments due, Dexter Horton's bank foreclosed and laws of the day allowed them to take everything he owned, including that new home. David and Louisa moved to a small house at Licton Springs

One of Seattle's founders, David Denny, lost his wealth during the 1893 Depression and was forced to work into his 70s. In 1899 he was photographed in front of his cabin-office near Lake Keechelus, from which he supervised repair work on the Snoqualmie Pass wagon road.

The recession continued to smother growth plans until, in July 1897, a ship steamed into Elliott Bay carrying "a ton of gold."

The Alaska Gold Rush

The steamship *Portland* had departed Seattle for Alaska with a load of passengers and freight at just the right time and returned in 1897 with what the press headlined as a ton of gold from Klondike Creek. With the memory of the California gold rush of 40 years earlier enhancing their dreams, the present recession curtailing incomes, and new rail lines serving the area, Seattle soon was inundated with men intent on traveling north to file claims on the reportedly gold-laden streams. Seattle merchants began ordering supplies in great quantities and their insufficient storage capacity soon resulted in food, clothing and equipment being piled on sidewalks in front of the small stores.

On July 17, 1897, the steamer *Portland* arrived on Elliott Bay with "a ton of gold" from Alaska, starting the Klondike Gold Rush that quickly pulled Seattle from the recession.

north of Seattle and he, now elderly, took a job supervising construction of a wagon road over Snoqualmie Pass. Many town folks could not understand why the bank forced the likeable couple into poverty, considering that David's older brother, Arthur, was senior vice president of the bank.

Seattle banks banded together to survive the hard times and, though several faced bankruptcy, only one, Merchant's National Bank was forced to close its doors. By staying in business, these financial institutions rescued many merchants and industrialists from a similar fate.

Every ship that could float was placed in service to carry the Argonauts north to the gold fields. (The newspapers called them "Argonauts" as in the ancient legend of the ship Argo that carried Jason during his search for the golden fleece. The term had been used during the California gold rush.)

As a result of the gold find, Seattle, the seaport nearest Alaska, escaped from the recession earlier than most cities and in so doing gained recognition as "the gateway to Alaska." Only a small percentage of the miners returned

The government opened an assay office in Seattle in 1898, the same year the *Roanoke* arrived with $4 million in gold dust.

Seattle's little stores suddenly had big orders from men bound for Alaska's gold fields. As did many suppliers after filling their limited storage space, Cooper & Levy stacked merchandise on the sidewalk.

Army volunteers to serve for two years or less. Washington state was expected to raise one regiment of infantry, but so many young men rushed to enlist that Governor Rogers asked permission to raise a second regiment. His offer was refused because the same situation existed in other states. The First Washington Volunteer Regiment consisted of 12 companies, including two companies of Seattle men. All had trained with the state militia.

The First Washington Regiment was dispatched to the Philippines in November 1898 to help quell an insurrection led by

Several types of new businesses were founded to meet the needs of men headed for Alaska. The Yukon Mining School taught novices how to pan, sluice and rock the heavier gold from the lighter earth. They also taught miners how to train and utilize dogs to pull sleds and carry supplies.

with enough gold to make them wealthy, but the U.S. government established an assay office in Seattle in July 1898 that over the next decade purchased gold bullion from the Klondike and from Alaska valued at more than $174 million.

During the Spanish-American War, the U.S. Third Cavalry's temporary Camp Robinson at Woodland Park sheltered men and horses before they were dispatched to the Philippines. The men lived in tents and watered their horses in Green Lake. In 1901 Lake View Park on Capitol Hill was renamed Volunteer Park in honor of the Seattle soldiers who volunteered to serve in that war.

The Spanish-American War

The United States supported the attempts of Cuba to break free from Spanish control and eventually sent troops and ships to that island. When the battleship *Maine* was sunk, the cry "Remember the Maine" raised emotions across the country. The efforts to free the Spanish possessions gained immediate public support, and in April 1898 President McKinley issued a call for 125,000

Former mayor Robert Moran and his brothers operated a shipyard that in 1898 turned out 12 75-foot stern-wheeled steamers designed to navigate the shallow rivers leading to the gold fields.

Fort Lawton was first utilized during the Spanish-American conflict and was active through World War II and the Korean conflict. It was named in honor of Major General Henry Ware Lawton who was killed in action in the Philippines. The photo is of Fort Lawton during World War I days. After the Army deactivated the post, Fort Lawton was transformed into Seattle's popular Discovery Park.

In the early 1890s riders on the Yesler Cable Car received a thrill on the trestle that descended to Leschi Park on Lake Washington.

(Far right) For five years the good ship *Idaho* served as Wayside Hospital to care for derelicts and others on the waterfront. This damaged glass plate dated about 1904 shows the hospital a few months after it was abandoned.

The Madison Street Cable Company was incorporated in 1889 to build a line down Madison Street from Elliott Bay to Lake Washington where its pavilion offered entertainment and served as a dock for ferries serving Kirkland and other eastside settlements.

Aquinaldo, a Filipino leader who feared that American domination would differ little from that of the Spanish. Lieutenant John H. Wholly, a professor of military science and tactics at the University of Washington, ably commanded the regiment during 36 engagements with the enemy before Aquinaldo surrendered. Captain

Fortson of Seattle's Company B was one of 25 men killed in action. Another five officers and 98 men were wounded. When the regiment, now known as the "Fighting First," returned home on November 6, 1899, Governor Rogers declared a state legal holiday. Seattle was lavishly decorated and jammed with citizens to welcome the servicemen home. The new Army post atop Magnolia Bluff was named Fort Lawton in honor of U.S. Army Major General Henry Ware Lawton, who was killed during one of the Philippine battles.

The Cable Car Years

During the late 1880s increased electrical generation capability allowed streetcar services to be extended. Improved engineering resulted in cable cars with counterweights beneath the street that helped pull them up steep inclines. In 1888 the Lake Washington Cable Railway Company installed tracks out Yesler Way to Lake Washington with return tracks on Jackson Street. The Front Street Cable Company built a line that climbed the slope to the top of Queen Anne Hill. To this day the steep portion of Queen Anne Avenue is referred to as the counterbalance. Also in 1889 the Madison Street Cable Railway Company established service on Madison Street from the waterfront to 25th Avenue. Two years later this line was extended to Lake Washington. At the lake end of the line they and the other lines established pavilions, a zoo, boat rentals and other types of entertainment.

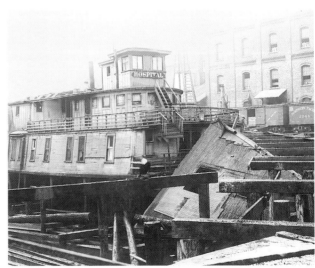

A Decade of Growth

In spite of the fire of 89, the recession of 93 and the war of 98, Seattle's population nearly doubled during this last decade of the 19th century, increasing from 42,837 to 80,761. Some of this growth was due to annexation of Magnolia, Lake Union, Green Lake and University neighborhoods, but most of it derived from families moving to the city from across the nation and from around the world. Seattle was developing as a truly cosmopolitan city.

As the population increased, many citizens worked to provide needed services:

• In the late 1890s Dr. Alexander de Soto appeared in the city. Of Spanish descent, he had received a good education as a surgeon. He joined a Baptist church and there met Captain Amos O. Benjamin, a former shipmaster, soldier and junk dealer. Benjamin had acquired the dismantled hull of the steamship *Idaho*. The two decided to turn the hull into a hospital to treat emergency cases from the waterfront and back alleys of Seattle. The Seattle Benevolent Society was organized in 1899 to operate this Wayside Mission Hospital on the remains of the *Idaho*. The city provided a site at the end of Jackson Street where for five years the old ship sheltered hundreds of destitute and derelict patients. The effort eventually led to the founding of the first City Hospital.

• Seattle residents have always liked to read. The pioneers tried valiantly to develop a public library beginning as far back as 1868 when $250 was raised to purchase books. Mrs. Henry (Sarah) Yesler was the first librarian but she could not convince all users to return the books and the number of volumes slowly decreased. In 1872 a library committee was elected to remedy the situation. Henry Yesler was named president and Mrs. Yesler treasurer. Dexter Horton agreed to contribute $500 to purchase books provided the committee raised $1,000 in matching funds. The Yeslers and others quickly matched his grant.

In 1873 the library was situated in a small building the Yeslers owned on First Avenue, then in 1877 it was moved to larger quarters in the YMCA. Again, over several years many of the books vanished. In 1888 the first Seattle Public Library board was elected and it persuaded Henry Yesler to give a triangle of property at Third and Yesler. The library moved several more times before in 1899 the books were carried to the late Henry Yesler's 40-room mansion at Third and James. It made a fine library, but two years later the mansion burned, destroying most of the 30,000 volumes. The remnants of the collection, most of which had been in circulation and avoided the

Henry Yesler's wife, Sarah, was instrumental in establishing a library in Seattle. She and Henry lost their only two children as infants and Sarah was active in several worthy causes.

fire, were housed in the former University of Washington building for a time while Seattle representatives convinced Andrew Carnegie to donate $200,000 to build the original downtown library at Fourth and Madison that opened in 1906. Carnegie later gave $105,000 more for equipment and branch libraries. That first Carnegie library was replaced in 1959, and now plans are being prepared for the third Seattle library to occupy that site.

This is the Seattle Carnegie Library fondly remembered by old-timers who frequently made use of its huge collection between 1906 and 1959 when it was demolished to make room for a new library. The 1920s photo shows the street-level restrooms and drinking fountain that were much appreciated by visitors of those days.
Seattle Post-Intelligencer Collection, Museum of History and Industry

When Hops Were King

For 30 years hop farms were one of the most successful agricultural businesses in the valleys around Seattle. Huge fields were developed around Issaquah and in the White and Snohomish River valleys. Ezra Meeker was given credit for introducing hop culture, but in one of the several books he wrote he corrects this information. His father, Jacob, who lived near Sumner introduced hop growing in 1865. Ezra took over from him, starting in 1867 with four acres that he expanded every year. For 22 years he made good profits on hops and convinced his neighbors to also develop hop farms. Meeker realized that England, considering all the ale they brewed, would be a good market and began exporting more than 10,000 bales worth more than half a million dollars each year. But in the mid-1890s this lucrative business ended. Meeker described the disaster with these words:

"One evening as I stepped out of my office and cast my eyes towards one of our hop houses, I thought I could see that the hop foliage did not look natural. Calling one of my clerks from the office he said the same thing — it did not look natural. I walked down to the yards and there for the first time saw the hop louse. The yard was literally alive with lice, and they were destroying the quality of the crop. It transpired that the attack of lice was simultaneous all along the coast from California to British Columbia... At that time I had more than $100,000 advanced to my neighbors and others upon their hop crops, all of which were lost. The people simply could not pay, and I forgave the debt... The result was that finally after a long struggle, nearly all of the hops were plowed up and the land used for dairy, fruit, and general crops, and is actually now of higher value than when bearing hops."

He concluded the story by saying a church group wrote to the *Seattle Post-Intelligencer* stating the crop failed because it was cursed by God. This upset Ezra and he wrote a lengthy letter to the newspaper in which he said: "This hop business they say was cursed by God. For myself I can inform them that as a citizen of Puyallup I contributed $400 to buy the ground upon which their church edifice is built, every cent of which came from the same hop business they say is cursed by God. I would thank God if they would return the money and thus ease their guilty consciences." Some of the parishioners responded with anger but did not return the $400. Meeker explained he didn't really want his donation back for he had written the letter while in a petty mood. He ended by conceding, "Our hops were finally destroyed — whether under the curse or not must be decided by the reader."

How Profanity Hill Earned Its Name.

Shortly after Washington was admitted to statehood, pressures for additional municipal services forced the county to spend $200,000 to build a larger courthouse and jail. After the structure opened in 1890, lawyer Cornelius H. Hanford and many others criticized the hilltop site. In his history *Seattle and Environs,* Hanford wrote:

"The ill-advised location of the courthouse was a cause of vexation to all the people who were obliged to transact business with the county officers. The courthouse site was on the brow of a hill 400 feet higher than the business district of the city, and the courthouse was built there because the county happened to own a block of ground on which the county commissioners chose to build the courthouse rather than to purchase a site that would have been accessible without inconvenience."

Late arriving citizens, usually lawyers, hurried up those steep stairs and strode into courtrooms short of breath and gasping out curses. As a result, the elevation became known as "Profanity Hill," a name retained until the new county-city building was completed in 1916 at the foot of the hill.

Hops were a major crop in the valleys of King and Snohomish counties for more than 20 years before the hop louse infested the fields and ruined the crops.

The Totem Pole Icon

In 1889 a group of Seattle's leading businessmen toured southern Alaska. While on the way home, they stopped at a Tongass village that displayed many Indian totem poles along the shore. Strolling through the village they found only children and elderly tribal members who did not speak English. They later were told the men were fishing and the women working in a nearby salmon cannery.

After admiring the many finely carved totem poles, they decided to take one home with them. Unaware of or disregarding the fact that the Indians revered the carved poles as memorials to ancestors, the men sawed one down and floated it to their ship. On October 18, 1899, it was erected in Pioneer Place in the heart of Seattle. The Indians rightly complained and the men involved were eventually fined for the depredation. That totem pole stood as a landmark for 40 years before being damaged by fire. Attempts at repair revealed it also was riddled with dry rot. Since the totem had become a true icon of the city, thoughts turned to finding a way to replace it. The City Park Department communicated with a Tlinget craftsman in Alaska who said he could duplicate the carvings. The remains of the first pole were shipped to him, and thanks to that craftsman the historic totem pole can still be admired.

This photo does double duty. It shows the Yesler Mansion that housed the Seattle Library until it burned. And high on the left is the new King County Courthouse atop Profanity Hill.

A crowd assembled on October 18, 1899, for the dedication of the original totem pole in Pioneer Place.

CHAPTER THREE

THE MATURING YEARS 1900-1930

City builders on Elliott Bay found the topography difficult to manage. The ice age of 10,000-20,000 years ago had gouged deep indentations and shoved up hills. As the ice melted, the lower elevations filled with water, leaving today's lakes, river valleys and Puget Sound. Seattle was founded on a site literally surrounded by water, mud flats and precarious hillsides. Several major facelifts were necessary before

Regrading Seattle's hills was a messy business. The lowering of Third Avenue, under way on the left, and excavation for the Central Building between Columbia and Marion streets tore up the landscape in 1904-05. The Central Building's location has attracted tenants for more than 90 years.

The southwest half of Denny Hill was nearly gone in this 1910 scene looking south from Sixth and Blanchard in Belltown.

Much fill dirt from Denny Hill was used to raise Seventh Avenue between Olive and Stewart streets. This 1909 photo illustrates how methods of earth hauling had advanced in just a few years from horse and wagon to rail.

the city could do much expanding. Fortunately technologies were being developed to make this possible and the right human engineer happened along when most needed.

The man was Reginald H. Thomson. The town had realized a trained and experienced city engineer was needed after workmen had dug a sewer trench along First Avenue that at one place ran uphill, causing sewage to boil over into the street. Thomson, a 25-year-old graduate of Hanover College in Illinois, moved to Seattle in 1881, was hired as a city surveyor and soon was drawing workable plans for

sewer lines and supervising construction of the Grant Street Bridge across the mudflats south of Yesler Way.

In 1892, as city growth accelerated, Thomson was promoted to city engineer with responsibility for paving streets, installing a city water system and building a municipal electric power plant. He began advocating bicycle trails in those pre-auto days and his department leveled a cinder trail along the west shore of Lake Washington that over ensuing years was widened, then paved as a thoroughfare for the first automobiles. Today it is known as scenic Lake Washington Boulevard.

Thomson next began the biggest job of his career — leveling Seattle's hills. In 1899 First Avenue was extended from Pine Street around the western flank of Denny Hill

Seattle residents were proud of their first streetcar that helped them avoid the muddy downtown streets. This 1884 photo preserves the scene on opening day.

north to Denny Way. Next he leveled Pike and Pine streets east through the southern edge of Denny Hill and eased their grades up Capitol Hill as far as Broadway. Most regrading was accomplished with shovels, the later ones mechanical, or by washing the hills away with water. The efforts continued over the three decades between 1900 and 1930 in all parts of the city. Nearly 50 million cubic yards of earth from the hills were used to fill ravines and tidelands. According to Clarence Bagley, that earth heaped into a pyramid half a mile long on each of its four sides would reach a peak 560 feet above the new street level.

Transportation Advances

The first streetcar rolled down Seattle streets in 1884. The Seattle Street Railway Company, owned by Frank Osgood, operated horse-drawn cars on 2nd Avenue tracks from James to Pike Street. One horse pulled the car on the fairly level streets but a second was needed to negotiate the hills. Documents in the Seattle Public Utility District archives relate that in 1886:

An old black horse stood at the foot of Pike Street waiting to assist the outbound car in negotiating the grade between First and Second Avenues; he needed no driver and was always on the job. As soon as the car approached, this old horse would walk out to the car and permit himself to be hitched with the other to the car and after performing his part of the work, walked slowly back and took up his position to await the coming of the next car.

Soon the tracks were extended north to Queen Anne Town and by 1886 out Westlake Avenue to Lake Union.

In 1889 the system was electrified and the motors were powered by overhead electric cable. Seattle's electric streetcar system was the first on the West Coast. Incidentally, the fare charged to board these cars was one nickel. By 1890 the tracks extended through Fremont and on to Green Lake.

Over several years, a dozen small, private streetcar companies were started up but most went bankrupt or were absorbed by larger companies. Stone and Webster, out of Boston, was called on to consolidate several of the smaller inefficient operations. Finally, in hopes of assuring reliable transit service, the voters in 1911 approved an $800,000 bond issue to allow the city to develop a municipal transportation system. The first city streetcar service ran from Third and Stewart to Ballard.

Easing Seattle street grades during the early 1900s disrupted all types of downtown transportation. At Third and Madison in 1907, passengers stepped aboard the trolley from small temporary platforms like the one visible at right center.

During rare winter snowstorms, streetcars often provided the only transportation to downtown Seattle. The big snow of February 1916 paralyzed much of the city. The Coliseum Theater at Fifth and Pike stands in the background.

Independent Asphalt Company was very busy in 1907 as Seattle began paving residential streets.

(Far right) Washington State issued the first metal license plates in 1915. This driver proudly displays his plates dated 1915 to 1923.

During the late 1920s, automobile travelers were insisting highways be improved. During the late 1920s, the road over Snoqualmie Pass was completely rebuilt.

In 1919 the city purchased the Stone and Webster holdings for $15 million, a figure most citizens considered too high. An unsympathetic state judiciary then ruled that the city system had to be self-supporting and could not use tax moneys in its operations. Even with those restrictions, the system managed to continue services during most of the Great Depression, but the struggle ended in 1938 when the city declared their transportation system to be bankrupt and Seattle representatives asked the state Legislature to act. That year a bill was passed allowing Seattle to apply for a U.S. Government Reconstruction Finance Corporation loan to replace worn equipment and deteriorated rails and to start the process of changing to rubber-tired buses.

Growth of Rail Systems

By 1916 more than 8,000 miles of rails served nearly all parts of the state. The Northern Pacific had installed 2,962 miles of railroad track; the Great Northern 1,570 miles; the Oregon-Washington Railroad and Navigation Co. 1,438; the Chicago, Milwaukee and St. Paul 1,039; and the Spokane, Portland and Seattle 427 miles. An additional 24 shorter lines also were operating in the state. The fastest way to travel east from Seattle was on the quick and comfortable special trains such as the *Oriental Limited* that stopped only at major cities.

During the 1920s, anyone traveling any distance used the railroads. Their service was the fastest and the most comfortable. This is the Great Northern's crack *Oriental Limited* arriving in 1927.

Increasing Numbers of Autos Appear on Seattle Streets

The first automobile wheeled down a Seattle street in 1900. It was little more than a horse-drawn buggy without the horse. Owned by Ralph Hopkins, shoe store proprietor and sometime realtor, the car was propelled by a rudimentary electric motor and its hard-tired wheels were too thin to move through mud, forcing the driver to sometimes drive on the wooden sidewalks. Each year improved automobiles became available and Seattle began surfacing its dirt, gravel and plank streets with brick and asphalt, and its wooden sidewalks with cement.

In 1906 more than 760 motor cars were counted in the state; 15 years later the new Department of Licenses counted 195,074. The count included 27,757 trucks, 929 buses (called stages back then) and 798 trailers.

Participants in the 1909 New York to Seattle auto race for the Alaska-Yukon-Pacific World's Fair passed over some difficult roads.

As more autos were driven on Seattle streets, accidents increased in frequency.

In 1909 the state began to license automobiles, but metal license plates were not introduced until 1915.

With popularity of autos increasing incrementally, the need for better cross-state highways became obvious. The first Seattle settlers found no roads, but slowly they carved paths through the forests, circumventing large trees and fording streams at shallow crossings surfaced with rocks or sand. The paucity of good roads resulted in the first farm products arriving at markets in canoes, scows or shallow draft steamers. But within a few decades rough roadways were being extended across the state. The Snoqualmie Pass Road, after years of labor, was opened in 1867 but every winter it was washed out at stream crossings and was crisscrossed by huge trees felled by winter winds. Cattle being herded from ranches in the Kittitas and Yakima valleys to Seattle packing plants accounted for most of the traffic over the pass.

In 1909 a New York to Seattle auto race was sponsored as part of the Alaska-Yukon-Pacific World's Fair. To give the participants a chance of successfully crossing over the Cascades, the Snoqualmie Pass Road was improved. To the surprise of the sponsors of the race, nearly 150 Northwest residents from east of the mountains also took the opportunity to drive over the pass to the exposition. The State Highway Department decided to make other improvements, and in 1915 the Seattle Automobile Club dedicated the new road with a picnic at the summit. By 1929 much of the roadway had been rebuilt, with curves

eased and grades reduced, and plans were under way to pave the road over the summit.

The Good Roads people publicized their dream of a concrete roadway from Seattle to Walla Walla, and from there north to Spokane, then west to Wenatchee, then down the Columbia River to Vantage and west to Ellensburg, where it would reconnect with the Snoqualmie Highway, at the time the only paved road over the Cascades.

Sam Hill, when he moved to Seattle before the turn of the century, brought with him a firm belief in the value of Good Roads. He energized the effort, publicized the possibilities, successfully lobbied for tax dollars, and during the first decades of the century convinced influential residents to join him in the Good Roads effort.

Early Air Transport

Charles Hamilton barnstormed into Seattle in March 1910 in his biplane that resembled a kite. Several hundred spectators bought tickets to see a man fly for the first time. The event was appropriately scheduled at the Meadows Racetrack that a few decades later became the site of the King County Airport and Boeing Field. Hamilton provided the crowd more of a show than they or he anticipated. After several minutes in the air, he flew low over the shallow lake in the middle of the race track, dragged a wheel and flipped the plane, bending parts of its pipe frame and spraining his leg. His bruises and those of his plane were successfully doctored and he flew away a day or two later to other adventures.

Five years later another barnstormer with a somewhat better plane caught the attention of young William E.

Seattle had one of the world's first service stations. John McLean, Standard Oil sales manager, realizing drivers had to buy gas in unhandy five-gallon cans, opened this gravity flow "filling station" at Holgate Street near Alaskan Way in 1907. He succeeded by feeding all 300 horseless carriages in the city.

growing number of scheduled flights out of Seattle developed during the 1920s. In 1926, regular flights to Los Angeles were inaugurated; in 1929 service from Seattle to Portland, Pasco and Bremerton commenced. During 1930, flights to Vancouver, Yakima, Spokane and San Diego became available and four years later the first transcontinental flights from Seattle to the East Coast began regular schedules.

Newspapers in the 1920s frequently carried aviation news on the front page. In 1924 the dirigible *Shenandoah* passed over the city before landing briefly at Camp Lewis, then floating on to San Diego. An interesting news report involved local pioneer Ezra Meeker, who in 1852 had traveled from Iowa to Oregon in a covered wagon. Now 94 years old, he boarded an airplane to fly back over this route and was amazed to cover the distance in three days instead of the four months it had taken him seven decades earlier.

The year 1927 brought a major flight accomplishment. In May of that year Colonel Charles Lindbergh became the first person to fly across the Atlantic Ocean. Thousands greeted him when he landed in Paris and this handsome, shy young man almost overnight became one of the best known human beings on the face of the globe.

Charles K. Hamilton barnstormed through Seattle in December 1910. He sold several hundred tickets to folks anxious to witness the first airplane to fly above their city.

Boeing. Boeing had arrived in Washington state in 1903 and made the acquaintance of Navy Lieutenant Commander Conrad Westervelt. They became good friends and on Independence Day 1915, both experienced their first airplane flight with a pilot looking for paying customers. Both men were thrilled at the experience and discussed it several times before deciding they could build a better plane. They promptly did put together a couple of the historic models known as the Boeing and Westervelt (B&W). The Navy soon transferred Westervelt to other parts of the globe, but William Boeing became serious about building airplanes in Seattle. Today his success and those of his employees are well recognized. Boeing directed the company for 19 years, developing it as The Boeing Airplane Company with subsidiaries that built aircraft engines and operated an airline that carried passengers, freight and mail.

Seattle businesses had tasted success with flight transportation and sensed the prospects for the future. A

(Far left) The Boeing Model 247 first flew in 1933 and soon chopped seven hours off the coast-to-coast record by covering the distance in just under 20 hours. United Airlines ordered 70 of these planes.

In 1852 Ezra Meeker crossed the plains in a covered wagon from Iowa to Oregon. In 1925 the 94-year-old Meeker boarded a plane to fly back over the route he had traversed 73 years earlier, but this time the journey took only three days instead of four months.

After his history-making flight across the Atlantic in 1927, Charles Lindbergh piloted his *Spirit of St. Louis* around the country promoting airfields. On October 10, 1927, he landed at Sand Point, toured the city and spoke of the need for a Seattle airport.

Once back in the United States, he flew his famous *Spirit of St. Louis* to nearly every state to promote construction of airfields. His efforts bore fruit in several localities including King County, where Boeing Field construction began the same year Lindbergh visited.

Modern Utilities Begin Serving Seattle

As the 1900s dawned, seemingly miraculous inventions began improving living standards. Actually, many of these new appliances had been invented before the turn of the century and since then had been improved and manufacturing costs reduced to where average families could afford them. Utility companies providing power for these appliances soon realized Seattle was a growing market.

Gas Lighting

Gas first was used to light Seattle streets in 1873 and by the mid-1880s was illuminating the homes of the wealthy. Two decades of competition ensued, during which several small gas companies attempted to gain control of the market. By the turn of the century, electric light bulbs were becoming more popular than gas lamps. In 1900 several pioneers including Dexter Horton, Arthur Denny and H.C. Henry incorporated Seattle Gas and Electric Company, hoping to supply both gas and electricity. The very next year the city council granted a 50-year franchise to Citizen's Light and Power Company that was financed by L.C. Smith and other Syracuse, New York, capitalists represented locally by James W. Clise. Samuel Hill meantime had gained control of most of the early gas market, and the competition remained heated until 1904 when Charles and Rufus Dawes, Chicago bankers who controlled gas plants in many cities, purchased majority stock and consolidated the competing companies as Seattle Lighting Company.

Electricity

Seattle Electric Light Company, one of the first suppliers specializing in production and delivery of electric energy, was founded in 1885 with George Hall as president and James M. Frink as vice president and superintendent. At this time, the potential profit of electricity generation was attracting investors similar to the ways computer-related and Internet companies have gained shareholders during recent decades. As do many new companies, Seattle Electric Light Company faced immediate difficulties. Shortly after being granted a city franchise, its dynamo was destroyed, delaying distribution of its first service until September 1886 when it sent electric current over wires to light a few downtown corners. The city paid a bill of $135.60 for that first month's service, a very high rate for the few existing street lamps. Meantime, the company

At the turn of the century these Seattle Electric employees installed and repaired electricity lines to homes and businesses.

In 1909 a Santo Electric Vacuum Cleaner was much appreciated by housewives.

was stringing lines to nearby businesses and homes, only to have its entire system destroyed by the Great Seattle Fire of 1889. The demands on the company became intense and it scrambled to build a plant to provide electricity for the most obvious needs. Within five weeks of the fire, downtown city streets again were being lighted by electricity.

As interest in the new lighting source continued to grow, competition developed. In 1890 Dr. E.C. Kilbourne, a dentist, founded a competing company and 60 days later began delivering current to subscribers. Additional private companies began competing, most of which failed or amalgamated with larger companies. In 1899 Stone and Webster, headquartered in Boston, began buying local companies. In 1903 it organized Puget Sound Power Company and built a large hydroelectric generating plant at Electron near Mount Rainier and a large steam power plant at Georgetown, a structure now considered a National Historic Landmark.

The most obvious electric generating plant in King County began producing power late in 1898 when Charles H. Baker designed and built a plant at Snoqualmie Falls. It had a capacity of 6,000 kilowatts and supplied power for lighting in Tacoma, Seattle and Everett, as well as smaller adjacent towns. In 1911 Puget Sound Traction, Light & Power Company purchased the Snoqualmie Falls plant as well as all properties under management of Stone and Webster. This company soon controlled all the light, power and railway properties in Bellingham, Everett, Seattle, Tacoma and most of the interurban rail lines from Bellingham south to Everett, Seattle, Tacoma and Puyallup.

The several small electric companies began consolidating. Puget Sound Power and Light was organized in 1899 to consolidate three small Seattle lighting and eight street rail companies. At that time, dynamos were belted to steam engines to generate electric current for lighting the city. During the 1920s, various kinds of electrical appliances begin to appear in the average home. The old ice box that required a fresh block of ice once or twice a week soon gave way to electric refrigerators, and electric heaters, vacuum cleaners and a myriad other electrically powered devices soon were available to ease a homemaker's labor.

As Seattle expanded rapidly, City Engineer R.H. Thomson began promoting the concept of municipal ownership of the lighting system. He was instrumental in securing state legislation and the necessary changes in the charter to allow the city to operate its own consumer-owned electrical system. Seattle voters in March 1902 approved a $590,000 bond issue to install generators on the Cedar River. The street lighting system of that time was purchased from Seattle Electric Company and connected to the city system.

As soon as street lighting systems were in place, the city added new generators so it could light commercial buildings. In April 1910, the lighting department was separated from the water department and the next year J.D. Ross was named superintendent and served many years.

By 1915, City Light receipts were more than $1 million annually. The system was furnishing power to 41,000 private customers and more than 15,500 street lamps, plus numerous port and government buildings. Clarence Bagley in his *History of Seattle*, published in 1916, concluded, "This makes the Seattle municipal light and power plant America's greatest publicly owned system and also makes Seattle America's best lighted city."

Seattle gained another distinction. For years it was the only major city in the U.S. served by both its own municipal power system and competing service from a private power company. In 1916, City Engineer Thomson proposed the city purchase the Puget Power system for $10 million but the City Council never voted on the suggestion. Four years later Superintendent J.D. Ross suggested the city acquire Puget Power properties inside the city limits, but again no action was taken. Discussion continued through the decades until in 1950 Seattle residents voted by a slight majority to pay $26.8 million for the private company facilities within the city. At the time it seemed a near death blow to Puget Sound Power and Light, but in the years following, the private company flourished by concentrating on the suburbs and cities that had no publicly owned power facilities.

Garbage Disposal

Garbage disposal is a problem faced by all municipalities. Back in 1910 Seattle awarded contracts to private companies to do the collecting but five years later transferred the responsibility to the City Health Department. Several improvements followed, including covering the garbage with earth. The Health Department had two scows built to haul garbage out to sea and fired up a huge incinerator to burn the rest of it. This procedure continued until 1939.

Over the years, parks, play fields, schools and industrial buildings have been built on former garbage dumps that were reclaimed. During World War II, avid recycling of paper, glass and metals reduced the amount

In 1915, employees and horses of the Seattle City Health and Sanitation Department were responsible for garbage pickup.

of garbage taken to the dump, but after the war the incentive for such efforts vanished. However, by the 1970s recycling was back in vogue. The more that is recycled, the less remains to be carted to the garbage dump and today that dump may be many miles from Seattle. At present, much of the city's garbage is hauled to a dry valley in Klickitat County.

Entertainment Becomes Big Business

The turn of the century found Seattle a growing metropolis with inadequate theater space. Several entrepreneurs soon noticed this shortage. In 1902 Alexander Pantages opened his Crystal Vaudeville Theater in Seattle. A decade later he controlled theaters in all parts of the West and contracted leading performers to entertain audiences in his theater chain. In 1907 Timothy Sullivan and John Considine opened Seattle's Coliseum Theater at Fifth and Pike, advertised as the largest theater west of the Mississippi.

A theater called La Petite heralded the future when it opened its doors in 1902. In its small auditorium Seattle audiences viewed many of the first commercial motion pictures, all silent, of course. Live theater also was attracting more customers. The Metropolitan Theater on University Street between

The Metropolitan Theater opened in 1911, almost alone on its block. Fifteen years later the Olympic Hotel was constructed around it.

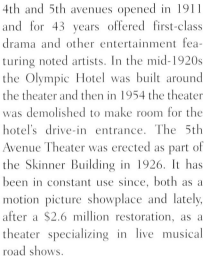

4th and 5th avenues opened in 1911 and for 43 years offered first-class drama and other entertainment featuring noted artists. In the mid-1920s the Olympic Hotel was built around the theater and then in 1954 the theater was demolished to make room for the hotel's drive-in entrance. The 5th Avenue Theater was erected as part of the Skinner Building in 1926. It has been in constant use since, both as a motion picture showplace and lately, after a $2.6 million restoration, as a theater specializing in live musical road shows.

The Fifth Avenue Theater as it appeared on opening night in 1926 — it still draws crowds.

The Palace Hippodrome was a favorite Seattle theater in the mid-1920s. The photo explains why this was so.

These folks are enjoying a day at the beach with an Edison phonograph and its tubular records. Notice that the young woman is properly chaperoned.

In 1914 Nellie Cornish opened the art school that has retained her name. The school trained stage performers as well as musicians. A couple of teachers at Cornish, Florence and Burton James, in 1928 established the Seattle Repertory Playhouse at 4045 University Way. This theater scheduled new plays, many by unknown playwrights, along with contemporary standards and classic dramas. It was popular through the Depression years but after World War II, the state Legislature's Anti-Communist Committee began a lengthy investigation of the staff. In 1951, after years of attack, the Repertory Playhouse closed.

The University of Washington Drama Department under Glenn Hughes was active during the postwar years. The Penthouse Theater, recently moved from its original site, was erected on the campus in 1938. About the same time the colorful Showboat Theater that sat on pilings above the waters of the ship canal attracted audiences. Several nationally known actors were trained at the university during those years. Seattle is home to a dozen other theaters of various kinds, some of them very successful.

The Alaska-Yukon-Pacific Exposition

Several positive occurrences spread sunshine on Seattle as the first decade of the 20th century was ending. The most newsworthy was the Alaska-Yukon-Pacific Exposition, the city's first world's fair. As it was being planned, the resulting nationwide publicity increased recognition of the city on Elliott Bay.

Before the fair, the Chicago, Milwaukee and Saint Paul Railroad decided to extend its line to Seattle, joining the Northern Pacific and Great Northern lines that had conquered the Cascades years before. The Chicago, Milwaukee, however, built over the lowest pass,

Snoqualmie, for some reason ignored by the earlier rail companies. The pass offered several challenges and forced the Chicago, Milwaukee to install temporary switchbacks over the summit. Later a tunnel was bored that reduced the grade to no more than 2 percent. The line began serving Seattle a few weeks before the fair opened.

Dozens of Seattle leaders worked to make the fair a success. Godfrey Chelander, secretary of the Arctic Brotherhood, had represented Alaska in its exhibits at the Lewis and Clark exposition in Portland in 1905. He suggested that Seattle develop a permanent Alaska exhibit. James A. Wood, city editor of *The Seattle Times*, suggested it be a grand show of products of Pacific Coast states, British Columbia, Yukon Territory, Alaska and all countries bordering the Pacific Ocean.

Soon a committee of leading Seattleites began organizing the events. The members of that committee, all well-known residents, included such names as John H. McGraw, Richard A. Ballinger, A.S. Kerry and H.C. Henry.

One of the controversial exhibits at the fair featured a Filipino Igorrote tribe living in a replica of their village on the fair grounds. Because their native costumes left them partially nude, ministers of a few churches were sent to view their dances. Most of them agreed it was educational but suggested young women have escorts when they viewed the exhibit.

(Far left) The cascades were at the center of the Alaska-Yukon-Pacific Exposition. Behind them is the U.S. Government Pavilion.

The most popular part of the fair was called the Pay Streak where some of the entertainment was reminiscent of that available in Alaska during the Gold Rush.

Visitors to the fair wanted to see Seattle while they were in town. Even after riding over rough brick-surfaced streets in a "Seeing Seattle" hard-tired vehicle, visitors exclaimed to reporters that they were enjoying their visit to the Northwest.

I.A. Nadeau was named director-general. An executive committee of 20 was chosen and 32 others served as a board of trustees.

The site chosen for the world's fair was the largely undeveloped University of Washington campus. At the time, the campus was forested except around the first few buildings. Professor Edmund Meany, a member of the faculty, saw ways the fair could benefit the university including the construction of badly needed buildings. The heart of the campus was cleared and converted to a park designed by Olmstead Brothers. The prominent campus view was to the southeast toward Lake Washington and beyond to the crests of the Cascade Mountains and Mt. Rainier. At the center of the fair site, terraced gardens were installed amid waterfalls and fountains.

Frequent streetcar schedules were arranged to carry passengers from downtown to the campus. Seattle was on its best behavior; the city was spruced up; and a special police force was trained. Promptly at noon on June 1, 1909, President Taft pressed a button in Washington,

D.C., sending a signal to unfurl a huge American flag atop a 187-foot flagpole milled from one piece of lumber. A national salute was fired and wheels began to turn in the machinery display. In the amphitheater that seated thousands, railroad magnate James J. Hill delivered the principal oration. Many other distinguished guests also appeared at the fair.

On Flag Day, June 14, a bronze statue of George Washington, a gift from the Daughters of the American Revolution, was unveiled. It still stands near the west entrance of the campus. On September 10 a bronze statue of William H. Seward, the Secretary of State who purchased Alaska from Russia, was unveiled in Volunteer Park. Seward's son and namesake, General William H. Seward, attended the dedication. Cornelius Hanford wrote:

> One thing about Seattle to live longest in pleasant memories of the present generation is the Alaska-Yukon-Pacific Exposition. It was an enterprise worth while, bravely undertaken, that united all the people in patriotic service, displayed genius, was carried through to complete success and had not a regrettable incident connected with it.

Attendance totaled 3,740,551; gate receipts totaled $1,096,476. After all bills were paid, $62,676 was declared surplus money and donated to the Anti-Tuberculosis League and the Seamen's Institute. Meany Hall and Auditorium, built as a permanent structure for the fair, was used by the university for more than five decades before it was replaced. Many of the "temporary" A.Y.P.E. buildings were utilized as classrooms, laboratories, a museum and libraries for half a century. All are now gone

Several years after the World's Fair had closed, most of the temporary buildings were gone. In the distance is Parrington Hall and in the foreground is the pool into which the cascades emptied during the exhibit. Today, nearly a century later, that pool is maintained as "Frosh Pond."

(Far left top) The Lake Washington Ship Canal under construction in May 1916 — on the left is newly paved Nickerson Street at the foot of Queen Anne Hill and on the right is Leary Way leading toward Ballard.

When the locks and canal were completed, the dike holding back the higher waters of Lake Washington was breached and several days later the two lake surfaces were the same height.

(Far left bottom) The Lake Washington Ship Canal crosses the upper part of this 1940 picture. The canal made it possible for the Seattle Yacht Club (mid-picture) to move to this protected inland site and still have yacht access to the Sound. On the far side of the canal is the University of Washington golf course, now the site of the Medical School.

except for a few nondescript smaller structures and the "frosh pond," now the site of the Drumheller Fountain.

As the first decade of the new century ended, the census counted 237,194 Seattle residents. When compared to the 80,761 counted in 1900, the increase was an almost unbelievable 194 percent.

Major Construction During the "Teen" Years

Between 1910 and 1920, several major construction projects were undertaken, one of the largest being the Lake Washington Ship Canal and locks.

Thomas Mercer in 1854, three years after the arrival of the city founders, had suggested that a canal might allow profitable access from Puget Sound to the fresh waters of Lake Union and Lake Washington. The possibility was discussed frequently over the next half century and in 1906 the Seattle Chamber of Commerce formed a Lake Washington Canal Committee that ably promoted the concept. The U.S. Navy agreed that a freshwater basin was desirable for anchoring its ships, and Seattle business interests spoke of extending port activities to the shorelines of the two freshwater lakes.

Of six potential routes, the 17 miles extending from Shilshole Bay to Salmon Bay to Lake Union and on to Lake Washington was chosen. There was one problem: Lake Washington was about nine feet higher than Puget Sound, so locks would be needed to raise and lower watercraft. Mills and shipyards in Ballard were concerned that when the locks were closed to raise the boats, their properties might be flooded. This and other problems were finally solved and in 1910 Congress appropriated $2,275,000 for construction of the locks, King County agreed to excavate the canal, and the city of Seattle accepted the responsibility for building the bridges across the waterway.

After several years the complex undertaking was completed and on July 4, 1917, dedication ceremonies attracted thousands. A flotilla led by the historic ship *Roosevelt,* which had carried Admiral Peary home after he reached the North Pole in 1909, led a parade of ships through the canal to Lake Washington with an "aeroplane" flying overhead. That evening fireworks illuminated the locks and bands played.

Hospitals

Several hospitals were constructed and enlarged during these years. In 1908 Dr. E.M. Rininger was building a 40-bed hospital at Summit and Olive streets when he became the city's first auto collision fatality. Dr. Nils Johanson and others of Scandinavian descent paid $91,000 for the nearly completed structure. Today it is known as Swedish Hospital, one of the largest and most noted in Seattle.

Mrs. Anna Clise is shown laying the cornerstone of the enlarged Children's Orthopedic Hospital on Queen Anne Hill in 1911. Also in the picture are Rabbi Koch and Dr. Gowen, and the tall gentleman on the right is Dr. Mark A. Matthews, pastor of the First Presbyterian Church.

When Anna Clise lost her 5-year-old son to inflammatory rheumatism, she began nine years of research seeking ways to provide better health care for youth of the city. At the time, children were treated in hospitals with adults. She enlisted women friends, her husband, James W. Clise, his business associates and several doctors in efforts to develop a facility for children. In 1908 they opened a cottage on Queen Anne Hill that became known as Children's Orthopedic Hospital. Three years later a new, larger facility was dedicated nearby. Then in April 1953, the hospital moved to its present site in the Laurelhurst neighborhood where it is near the University of Washington Medical School. Today the massive Seattle Children's Hospital has a worldwide reputation for its treatment of children.

Drs. Tate Mason and John Blackford established a group practice in 1917. They opened a hospital on Terry near Madison and named it Virginia Mason after Dr. Mason's daughter. It has developed into one of the city's major hospitals.

(Far right) The University of Washington Sports Stadium opened in 1920. Five years later, football games there attracted crowds like the one shown here. Tickets for the game cost $2.

The new Broadway High School opened in 1902. It was first called Seattle High School, then in 1906 became Washington High School. This caused confusion with the University of Washington, so in 1908 it was renamed Broadway after the street in front of it.

In 1947 a group of Seattleites formed Group Health Cooperative and opened a consumer-owned and operated hospital on Capitol Hill that provided comprehensive, pre-paid medical care. Today Group Health has several hospitals and clinics throughout the Puget Sound area.

Many other medical groups and facilities in the Seattle area help keep the city one of the healthiest in the nation.

Educational Facilities

Back in the early 1900s, increasing population figures combined with the broadening realization that higher education was important created a demand for additional school facilities. Broadway High School serves as a typical example of how the city tried to meet the need. Broadway was the first permanent building dedicated entirely to high school classes. The school district paid $13,000 for the lots at Broadway and Pine and plans were drawn for a $250,000 structure. Taxpayers criticized the cost and size of the structure, saying rooms would be empty for years to come. The building was completed in 1902 and two years later more than 1,700 students were enrolled and the structure was so crowded that an annex was added. During the 10 years after Broadway opened, three additional high schools — Lincoln (1907), Queen Anne (1909) and Franklin (1912) — were enrolling hundreds of high school students each.

The University of Washington also was adding buildings. Parrington Hall was completed in 1902, Meany Hall in 1909, and a dozen of the Alaska-Yukon-Pacific Exposition buildings were converted to accommodate engineering, music and physiology programs. During the second decade of the century, new buildings were erected to house home economics, fisheries, commerce, aerodynamics,

nursing and education programs. The most obvious new structure was the sports stadium that was completed in 1920. Then in 1926, the first part of the Suzzalo Library was dedicated. Two years later both the men's and women's physical education buildings were built. During the Depression years, with the help of WPA and other government programs, Bagley Hall, women's residents' halls and other structures began to fill the campus.

World War I

World War I began on June 28, 1914, the day Archduke Franz Ferdinand and his wife were assassinated by a Bosnian student. That same day Austrian troops invaded Serbia. Great Britain, France, Russia and Italy became allies. The enemy, known as "the Central Powers," were Germany, Austria-Hungary and Turkey. From the outset, Seattle residents avidly perused their newspapers, in those days the major communications medium from the war fronts.

Within a few months bloody battles were raging at the Marne, Ypres and on the seas. On May 7, 1915, a German submarine sank the passenger liner *Lusitania* with a loss of 1,198 lives, including 124 Americans. Still the United States retained its neutrality, though war clouds were being blown closer. Between July and November 1916 on the Somme battlefield, more than 1 million soldiers died, many of them during futile British-French attacks. On April 6, 1917, the United States declared war on Germany after German submarines sank several American ships. President Woodrow

Wilson announced "the world must be made safe for democracy." Seven months later, under the command of General John J. Pershing, Americans experienced their first battles. On August 8, the last German offensive failed and three months later, November 11, 1918, Germany signed the armistice and the war ended.

During the 19 months after America declared war, Seattle residents were involved in many ways. Young men of the city volunteered by the hundreds to fight for their country. Cebert Baillargeon, from a wealthy Seattle family, paid his way to England to find how he best could help the Allied cause. He was commissioned in the U.S. Navy and after the war served on the international board to arrange the terms of peace. William J. "Wee" Coyle, U.W. football star and later Lieutenant Governor of the state, was awarded a medal for his distinguished service as a soldier. Drs. James B. Eagleson and Harry E. Allen of Seattle organized Field Hospital No. 50 and cared for many wounded in France during the months of hard fighting by the American Expeditionary Force. There were scores of other

These World War I draftees paraded down Fourth Avenue on the way to the railroad depot to be transported to an Army post for basic training.

A large U.S. Navy Training Camp was established early in World War I at the University of Washington. Most of the sailors lived in tents on the north shore of the ship canal.

Seattle residents involved in the war efforts, one of whom was awarded the Medal of Honor.

Deming Bronson, born in Wisconsin in 1894, moved to Seattle with his family and played with the famous undefeated University of Washington football teams of 1912 to 1916. At the outset of World War I he joined the Army and was assigned as a first lieutenant in the 91st "Wild West" Division. The citation for his Medal of Honor tells how he was wounded several times but refused to leave his men during the battle near Eclisfontaine, France, on September 26-27. First he was "struck by an exploding enemy hand grenade, receiving deep cuts on his face and the back of his head." He refused aid and helped capture an enemy dugout that resulted in many German prisoners. On the afternoon of that same day he was wounded in the left arm by an enemy bullet, received first aid, then was directed toward the rear but disregarded instruction and, though suffering pain and shock, remained with his company during the night.

When morning came, the regiment resumed its attack but his company was shifted to reinforcement status, meaning they would be called only if needed. The lieutenant promptly joined E Company as it marched by after being ordered to capture the village. He strode to the front of the company and when enemy fire stopped the advance, he killed an enemy machine gunner that had stopped the company. When an enemy artillery barrage compelled Company E to fall back, Lieutenant Bronson, one of the last to retreat, was wounded in both arms by a high-explosive shell. Though bleeding profusely and feeling faint, he refused to let calls be made for a rescue party to

attempt to find him in the dangerous darkness. He remained with company survivors throughout the second night. The next day he was escorted from the front line to medical treatment and to a hospital to recover.

Eleven years passed before Bronson's bravery was recognized. On November 19, 1929, he and his wife, a former Walla Walla girl, were escorted to the White House where President Herbert Hoover pinned the Medal of Honor on Bronson's business suit. At the time he was Atlantic Coast Manager for General Paint Associates of San Francisco and later he became a lumberman in Roseburg, Oregon. He died May 25, 1957, and his cremated remains were interred in Arlington National Cemetery.

The war created an instant demand for more ships. Twenty large and small Seattle shipyards employed 40,000 men to produce the vessels. The largest, the Skinner and Eddy Shipyard, located near where today's downtown sports arenas stand, completed 75 ships during the war. As a result, the country learned that Seattle shipbuilders could turn out all sorts of vessels in record time, a fact remembered 20 years later during World War II.

Home front activities included "Minute Man" organizations that provided needed services, helped with patriotic

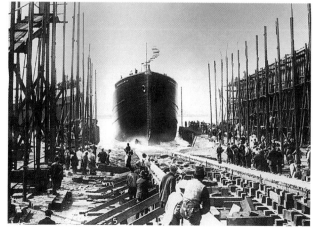

events and sold Liberty Bonds. Every Seattle man mobilized for active duty was sent off with a package of candy, cigarettes and reading material. A clubhouse for servicemen located in downtown Seattle provided low-priced meals. Relief funds were collected for needy families of servicemen. The Red Cross was active and Seattle young women sponsored a Victory Carnival that earned nearly $90,000 to donate to the Navy Relief Association and the industrial hospital. During "wheatless and meatless days" Seattle residents saved food for the hungry in war-torn Europe.

The war ended quite suddenly on November 11, 1918, leaving many partially completed vessels on shipyard ways, and a mothballed armada of 30 major unused vessels floated for several months on Lake Union. Other reminders of the war continued for several months after the armistice. Influenza took more American lives during and after the war than were killed on the battlefronts. Seattle hospitals were crowded for weeks with people ill with the virulent "Spanish flu." Theaters were closed at times and many persons donned cloth masks in public, hoping to prevent contagion.

The Veterans' Bonus Imbroglio

Most World War I service personnel resented the way their government treated them after the war. This bit of history is largely forgotten today, obliterated by the positive effects of the GI Bill of World War II.

World War I veterans' organizations such as the American Legion and Veterans of Foreign Wars asked for a bonus for servicemen who served during the war. They felt it was only fair to compensate them for the differences between their miniscule service pay and what they would have earned had they remained on the job at home. Congress in 1924 passed an Adjusted Compensation Act that would pay them $1.25 per day for overseas service

and $1 per day for service in the United States. However, the money was presented as a 20-year endowment policy for each veteran. They were allowed to borrow up to 25 percent of its value. Veterans grumbled but took no inclusive actions.

Five years later the Great Depression struck, causing widespread unemployment. Veterans, most of them with families, asked that they be allowed to take loans worth up to 50 percent of their endowments. Congress promptly passed the requested legislation but President Hoover vetoed it, saying he felt the action would damage the economy and would benefit all veterans whether or not they were in distress. The next year, after Democratic leaders proposed the entire bonus be immediately paid in cash, veterans organized a "Bonus Army" to demonstrate support. In June about 17,000 veterans rode boxcars, hitchhiked and walked to the nation's capitol where many camped in the open or in vacant government buildings.

On June 17 the House voted to provide $2.4 billion to pay off the total of the veterans' bonuses but the Senate defeated the measure. Instead they voted sufficient funds to pay for transporting veterans back to their homes. When an estimated 2,000 refused to leave Washington, D.C., the police were ordered to drive them out. In the following melee, two veterans and two policemen were killed. President Hoover then ordered Federal troops commanded by General Douglas MacArthur and Major Dwight Eisenhower to force the veterans to leave. Infantry and cavalry units and tank troops were called in to drive the veterans from the city. In general, citizens across the country reacted negatively to the methods used.

In May 1935, with the Depression at its worst, Congress passed a bill calling for $2.2 billion to immediately fund veterans' bonuses in full. Democratic President Franklin Roosevelt, fearing it would spur inflation and increase the Depression-wracked national debt, lobbied against the bill. The senate failed to override his veto.

In January 1936, a bill to pay the World War I bonus to veterans, most of them now in desperate financial straits, passed both houses but again was vetoed by the President. However, this time Congress overrode his veto. The act authorized issuance of nine-year interest-bearing bonds that veterans could cash in at any time. On June 15, more than 25 years after the war ended, $1.5 billion in bonus checks were mailed to the 3 million surviving World War I veterans. Most had previously borrowed the maximum allowed from their endowments so the usual payments were usually $300 or less.

Virulent "Spanish Flu" swept across the country at the end of World War I. Hundreds in Seattle were very ill with it and several died. The mayor closed theaters for a time and those who made contact with the public, such as this newsboy, were told to wear cloth masks to keep from being infected.

When it became obvious the general strike by Seattle workers could not be prevented, deputy sheriffs and Army reserves were called to active duty. Here they are being armed with guns they fortunately did not need to use.

The General Strike

Seattle made national headlines on February 6, 1919, when what was claimed to be the nation's first general strike closed down the city. The Bolshevik Revolution in Russia, disputes over war reparations in a divided Europe, racial lynchings in the South, the 1916 prohibition amendment outlawing the sale of liquor and beer, and heated confrontations between labor and employers created very unsettled times.

The Seattle chapter of the leftist organization Industrial Workers of the World (IWW) actively opposed the American Protective League, a conservative group that feared anarchy and sabotage was spreading across the country. In the last year of World War I, a female secretary of the Seattle IWW was sentenced to 10 years in prison for distributing antiwar leaflets, and two members of the Socialist Party received prison terms for agitating against conscripting youth into the armed services. Some corporate leaders declared labor union members were anarchists. The rational labor leaders and corporate officers attempted mediation, but the heat was too high, the misunderstandings too deep.

The general strike scheduled for 10 a.m. on February 6, 1919, silenced the city as about 60,000 workers left their jobs. Troops from Camp Lewis remained on alert but out of sight behind the walls of the new Seattle armory. An estimated 1,500 policemen, many of them temporary deputies, patrolled in nonbelligerent fashion. Labor leaders called for nonviolence from members. Union members continued delivery of milk to hospitals and the ill and delivered boxes of food to families with children. Light, power and gas services were not suspended except at some businesses. There were few radical orations, no massive marches and no picketing. The laboring men simply left work for home. By the third day of the strike, workers began to filter back to their jobs. Sensing support was dissipating, strike leaders called off the walkout on February 13. In the months following the general strike, labor organizations found they had lost both members and negotiating power that would take years to regain.

Troubles During the 20s

The third decade of the century also was troubled in several ways. President Warren G. Harding's appointees

During the 1919 general strike, labor members could pick up food to be delivered free to those in need, including their own families.

A flower-bedecked auto delivers President and Mrs. Harding (seen in the rear seat) to the Seattle Press Club on July 27, 1923. A few days later he died in San Francisco.

caused considerable scandal during the mid-1920s. Congressional committees began looking into rumors of unlawful activity that resulted in several different trials. The director of the Veterans Bureau was indicted for fraud and bribery, sentenced to two years in prison and fined $10,000. The biggest scandal involved the leasing of Navy oil reserves to private interests. A Senate investigating committee found that the President, acting with approval of the Secretary of the Navy, had transferred to Albert B. Fall, Secretary of the Interior, the duty of administering oil reserves at Teapot Dome, Wyoming, and at Elk Hills, California. Secretary Fall then secretly leased Teapot Dome reserves to oil operator Harry Sinclair and Elk Hills reserves to Edward L. Doheny. The scandal came to light when the Senate committee chaired by Thomas J. Walsh of Montana found that Doheny had lent Fall $100,000 without interest or collateral and Fall had received a loan of $25,000 from Sinclair. Congress charged this amounted to fraud and corruption. Fall was convicted of bribery and received a year in prison and a $100,000 fine. Sinclair was sentenced to nine months and fined $1,000 for contempt of court. The Supreme Court declared both leases of Navy oil reserve to be invalid.

In July 1923 President Harding, depressed by the scandals, decided to tour Alaska. On the way home, his ship stopped in Seattle where the President had lunch at the Press Club and spoke briefly, then he and his party reboarded their ship to continue on to San Francisco. On the way, Harding reportedly suffered an attack of ptomaine poisoning and then developed pneumonia. Reported to be recovering, he was taken to a San Francisco hotel where that night he died of apoplexy (today known as an embolism).

The Difficulties of Enforcing Prohibition

Washington state went dry in 1916 and four years later the National Prohibition Act outlawed consumption of intoxicating beverages nationwide. Many Seattle residents managed to acquire illegal liquor. The youngest of Seattle's police lieutenants, 34-year-old Roy Olmstead, an intelligent and respected member of the force, had noted the mistakes of several of the arrested rumrunners and the cash found in their possession. After a time he decided to join their game.

At 2 a.m. on March 22, 1920, he and his men were caught unloading liquor at Meadowdale Beach. He was dismissed from the police force, entered a plea of guilty, paid a $500 fine and was released on bail. Newspaper reports of the event resulted in him achieving local hero status. Now he seriously began his bootlegging career. His boats were loaded in Canada and usually unloaded at quiet Puget Sound bays, but sometimes at downtown Seattle docks. He never diluted his product, did not allow his men to bear arms, and his gross receipts sometimes exceeded $200,000 a month.

His success became common knowledge and federal agents could no longer ignore him. They chartered the fastest boats available, tapped his telephone line, and in November 1924 raided his home. He posted bail and continued rumrunning until a trial in 1926 ended with a four-year sentence at McNeil Island federal prison. He served 35 months and was released. He had found religion in prison and returned often to lecture inmates about his Christian Science faith. In 1935, after Prohibition ended, he received a pardon from President Roosevelt.

Olmstead and his wife, Elise, made history in another way. Radio broadcasting took root during the 1920s, resulting in a melange of signals, no station operating full time and their broadcasts often conflicting on the same wavelength. Olmstead and his wife, living in a large old

During Prohibition, any bootlegged liquor confiscated by law enforcement agencies was trucked to facilities where it was discarded. This 1923 photo was captioned "Load of Olmstead Booze."

house in the Mt. Baker district, turned a spare bedroom into a broadcasting studio. They soon broadcast the most powerful signal in the Northwest on their station KFQX. They developed several new types of programs, including a story hour for children during which Elise read to them, and they arranged for live broadcasts of dance orchestras from Seattle nightspots. When Olmstead went to prison, his station was acquired by other businessmen, but a couple of his employees at KFQX were hired by other stations and helped develop Seattle radio into an important source of news, information and entertainment.

The Great Depression Takes Hold

Stock market speculation sent prices unnaturally high, in part because stocks could be purchased with only 10 percent down. Many investors believed the stock market would continue its rapid rise. "Good times are here to stay!" was a slogan of the day. Then on October 23, 1929, the roof caved in as stock values dropped catastrophically. On one day, October 28, stock values fell $10 billion in 1920 dollars. Thousands of investors wrung their hands as their fortunes vanished. The Great Depression was beginning a decade of economic torture.

Historical Chaff from the Era

On May 22, 1927, the day following Charles Lindbergh's epic flight across the Atlantic, newspapers filled their front pages with stories about the "Flying Fool" and "Lucky Lindy." *The Seattle Post-Intelligencer* included an item from Paris describing how the exhausted aviator was invited to rest at the U.S. Embassy after his solo 3,600 mile flight that took more than 33 hours. Before retiring, in answer to a reporter's query, he explained, "The biggest trouble I had was in staying awake. I went to sleep several times, but was lucky enough to wake myself up right away. I was afraid of the sandman all the time."

The press estimated his successful flight would earn him a "pot of gold." He was awarded the Orteig prize of $25,000 for being the first to cross the Atlantic Ocean in an airplane. Reporters estimated he would receive at least $55,000 from other commercial ventures and perhaps $100,000 for theatrical and vaudeville appearances. The shy young man soon let it be known he was not interested in the latter type of work.

Employees of the Seattle Health and Sanitation Department were responsible for destroying the illegal alcoholic beverages. Officials watch as one man uncorks the bottles and the other pours the liquor down the drain. An interesting sign above the man with the hat warns that spitting on the floor, walls or equipment is prohibited by law.

CHAPTER FOUR

DEPRESSION AND WAR 1930-1950

President Herbert Hoover and many Americans during the 1920s promoted self-reliance as a virtue and believed the federal government should not become involved in the personal problems of citizens. The 1929 stock market failure was the harbinger of what would follow. As the Depression deepened, the President called upon the American people to be generous with those in need but again stipulated that

Local governments, including Seattle's, struggled mightily to aid destitute citizens. In the summer of 1931, a few of the city's progressive citizens formed the Unemployed Citizens' League that quickly recruited 50,000 members to organize self-help projects. They secured donated forest acres where loggers were put to work cutting wood for stoves and fireplaces. When they heard that fruit was wasting in Eastern Washington orchards for want of buyers, they sent families over the Cascades to harvest apples and other crops for distribution to the needy. Dozens of fishermen were hired to drop lines and nets in Puget Sound and commissaries were established to distribute the catch. As thousands of citizens were evicted from their homes and farms for lack of funds to pay mortgages and rents, a group of negotiators was appointed to find alternatives to evictions and to locate shelters for dispossessed families. A simple barter society was instituted where members could exchange services for goods.

direct aid to the individual citizen was not a duty of the federal government. As the situation continued to worsen, he altered his message. He said that if the time came when voluntary agencies, "...especially those in local and State government, were unable to find resources with which to prevent hunger and suffering in my country, I will ask the aid of every resource of Federal Government." As the situation became desperate for increasing numbers of families, he authorized $700 million to fund job-producing public works projects and established what he called the Reconstruction Finance Corporation to prop up industry and agriculture. Still more Americans felt the bite of the Depression.

Seattle Mayor Robert H. Harlin appointed a "Commission on Improved Employment" and proposed a million-dollar bond issue to finance the program. He assigned many of these relief efforts to the Unemployed Citizens' League, including distributing food to hungry families and finding temporary employment for as many of the 45,000 Seattle jobless as the budget permitted. But financing was inadequate and the city soon was forced to discontinue such efforts. The general election of 1932 resulted in a Democratic Party avalanche in Washington state. Every state representative elected was a Democrat allowing that party to control the Legislature for the first time since statehood.

Trying to Curb the Depression

As the Depression deepened, Seattle became a magnet attracting jobless men seeking work. Soup kitchens fed hundreds of hungry residents and at the city garbage dumps, families picked through the garbage

$212 million. Fearing a complete collapse of the state banking system, the state Legislature on March 1, 1933, passed a bank stabilization act. On March 2, Oregon and California went further by declaring bank holidays in their states, and the next day Washington followed suit. Two days later a national bank holiday closed every bank in the United States until each individually could demonstrate financial stability.

That same year the Legislature enacted a classified business tax but newly elected Governor Clarence Martin, a moderate Democrat, vetoed the parts that would tax agriculture and the professions. The remainder of the bill was referred to the state Supreme Court where the justices ruled it unlawful except for the $6 million they considered as emergency funding for public schools that were in desperate straits.

Again in 1935 state income tax legislation passed the Legislature, this bill establishing a 4 percent levy on incomes over $4,000 per year. The courts for the second time declared the action to be unconstitutional, leaving state leaders in a quandary as to how to fund vital services. During the 1936 session, as a last resort, both houses enacted a tax of two percent on retail sales, exempting gasoline, milk and bread. To collect taxes totaling less than a penny, an aluminum sales tax token worth one-third cent was produced. However, as World War II drew closer, aluminum was needed for the defense effort, so plastic and

As the Depression persisted, more and more indigents arrived in Seattle seeking work. They scrounged in alleys for discarded lumber and cardboard, on the beaches for driftwood to build shacks, and through the garbage dumps for anything of value. The new sports stadiums now occupy this site on First Avenue South.

for returnable bottles or other materials of value. Local relief coffers soon were emptied. The 1931 Legislature, increasingly aware of families suffering from hunger and cold, passed an individual and corporate income tax. This law was immediately vetoed by Governor Roland Hartley, a conservative mill owner from Everett. State income tax promoters countered by quickly securing sufficient numbers of signatures to place an initiative on the next ballot. This initiative was approved overwhelmingly 322,919 votes to 136,983, but the state Supreme Court promptly declared it null and void because the state constitution specifically decreed such an income tax to be unconstitutional.

In 1932 the newly elected Legislature in Olympia created the State Emergency Relief Organization and approved a $10 million bond issue to combat unemployment and provide necessities for families of the unemployed. By then more than a quarter of all state wage earners were without income, but the bond issue was immediately challenged as illegal. The state Supreme Court, after considerable debate, voted five to three to uphold the constitutionality of the effort, the majority arguing that "it is better to cure incipient insurrection by promoting prosperity than by use of bullets."

During 1933, depositors, fearing their banks were failing, rushed to withdraw savings. Many financial institutions, unable to meet the demand for instant cash, were forced to close their doors, an act that increased the pressure on the surviving institutions. Washington's bank deposits precipitously fell from $448 million to

The last half of Denny Hill was regraded in 1929, just before the Depression hit. With construction funds short and investors wary, the newly leveled blocks sat empty for most of the decade.

144

The objective of the Civilian Conservation Corps (CCC) was to put young men to work building park trails and other worthy efforts. They received board, room and clothing when needed and were expected to send most of their meager pay home. Here a crew at Longmire near Mt. Rainier is receiving lunch.

with no other source of income. Wages were dismally low, with salaries of $100 a month or less very common. Government programs such as the WPA and CCC paid about half that or less. The cost of necessities was reduced to amounts unbelievable today. Day-old bread was available for a nickel, wooden boxes holding 50 pounds of apples sold for a dollar, potatoes were advertised for two cents per pound, steak for 19 cents a pound, ice cream for a dime a pint. Gasoline was sometimes available for less than 20 cents a gallon, men's dress shirts were advertised at $1.29 each and a wool business suit for $19.95, and not many

paper tokens were substituted until the Legislature made it legal to collect the tax to the nearest penny.

During the Depression years, entire families became itinerants, the parents hopefully following job trails. Seattle was the destination of many such families who hoped big city factories and services would have more job openings than was the case in small towns and rural counties.

With so few employment possibilities, women were not considered for most positions other than teaching school and clerical work. Some school districts refused to hire married women, saving the jobs for single women

were sold at that price. Movie admissions often were a dime for children and 50 cents or less for adults. Several Seattle hotels advertised rooms for a dollar a night.

The arts, though suffering from lack of support, remained somewhat active during the Depression. The federal government funded a few work projects for writers, artists and musicians. Wealthy individuals such as Dr. Richard Fuller and his mother donated funds in 1932 to build the Seattle Art Museum in Volunteer Park. Fortunately, the year before the Depression struck, the Civic Auditorium was built and an ice arena and athletic

field were soon added. During those difficult years, symphony orchestras and opera and ballet companies sometimes performed in the Civic Auditorium, though the acoustics left much to be desired. And many games were played on the athletic field. The Army in 1939 built a large armory near the auditorium that in the 1960s was converted to the Center House and Food Circus. The Civic Auditorium was transformed into a new acoustically pleasing Seattle Opera House to be used during the 1962 World's Fair.

As the decade was ending, the grasp of the Depression began to weaken, first in the cities, then in rural areas. Jobs became more plentiful as the country began rearming against the aggressive dictators that threatened both Europe and Asia.

The Democratic Party landslides of the Depression years resulted in several longtime state political leaders, among them Warren Magnuson of Seattle and Henry Jackson of Everett, both first elected as congressmen, then as senators. Magnuson was serving as King County prosecuting attorney when Congressman Marion Zioncheck, who suffered periods of manic depression, killed himself by jumping from the sixth floor of the Arctic Building on Third Avenue. Magnuson was elected to his congressional seat and later to the Senate, serving a total of more than four decades in Congress. Senator Jackson developed the same sort of congressional tenure.

Air Transportation Comes to the Seattle Area

With attention concentrated on easing the pain of the Depression, two important stories that involved the Boeing Airplane Company did not receive much attention

from the public. The opening of Boeing Field (King County Airport) in 1931 resulted in the city having a creditable airfield that attracted some of the early airlines, one of which was United, a subsidiary of William E. Boeing's company.

The second Boeing story began unfolding that same year when the country's postmaster general changed the method of awarding airmail contracts. At the time, many of the country's 44 small airlines survived on earnings from U.S. mail contracts. The postmaster decided larger companies such as Boeing were more secure businesses with appropriate equipment to provide adequate airmail services. His decision forced several smaller companies out of existence.

In 1934 an investigative reporter published a syndicated story that charged mail contracts were not awarded to the lowest bidders, as decreed by law. Democratic legislators, now in control of Congress, complained to President Roosevelt, who, after several discussions, canceled existing airmail contracts and ordered the Army to assume responsibility for delivery of all airmail. This resulted in acrimonious hearings in the nation's capital during which arguments against the Army taking over mail routes were heard and fears were expressed that the large airlines were developing as monopolies. Attempting to reach middle ground, the President decided that contracts would be offered only to private airline companies that did not manufacture their own aircraft and engines. That excluded the Boeing Airplane Company because it produced both airplane engines and its own aircraft. Bill Boeing, who had been involved as a witness at one of the more acrimonious hearings, returned to Seattle in an angry frame of mind. Shortly thereafter he sold his Boeing Airplane Company stock, severed all relations with the company and retired. Twenty years later, in 1956, he succumbed to a heart attack at age 74 while cruising on his yacht. And so it was that the founder of the Boeing Company passed away as the company he had founded was leading the airline industry into the jet age.

Transportation stories made headlines all during the decade. In 1930 a Ford Tri-Motor passenger plane visited the city and a Ford dealer drove a new Model A convertible up beside it, posed some University of Washington alumni in appropriate places and took their picture. In September 1935, Seattle residents spent most of a day watching the Navy dirigible *Macon* soar over the city, after which it cruised on to moor at Fort Lewis. In 1939 the Seattle-Everett

University of Washington alumni members in 1930 posed with a couple of popular Ford products, a Tri-Motor airplane and a Model A convertible.

(Far right) Seattleites enjoyed dining in this whimsical "Twin T-Ps" restaurant on Aurora Avenue for nearly 70 years. *Seattle Post-Intelligencer Collection, MOHAI*

The Navy dirigible *Macon* had Seattle residents looking upward as it floated over Seattle in September 1935. *Seattle Post-Intelligencer Collection, MOHAI*

Interurban rail service that had been successful for more than two decades was forced by the Depression to suspend activity.

The very next year, with the streets becoming increasingly crowded with motor cars, accidents became a growing concern. A safety rally was scheduled at one of the busiest cross streets in downtown Seattle — where Highway 99 on Fifth Avenue passed Westlake and Pine Street. Farther out Highway 99, where it was called

Aurora Avenue, the Twin T-Ps became one of the city's first restaurants to successfully cater to motorists and would continue to do so for more than half a century.

Automobile ferries, an important form of transportation, gained prominence during the first half of the century. The streamlined *Kalakala* became a Seattle icon during the years of Depression and war when it transported thousands of war workers each day between Seattle and Bremerton, site of the huge Naval shipyard.

As the Depression was ending, traffic increased and with it a concern for safety. The thermometer indicates 60 traffic deaths in 1940, a cause for this safety rally at Fifth, Westlake and Pine streets. The "U.S. 99" sign indicates the main north-south highway in those days passed through this busy intersection. *Seattle Post-Intelligencer Collection, MOHAI*

The streamlined ferry *Kalakala* crosses Elliott Bay with one of her plainer sisters during the war years. *Puget Sound Maritime Historical Society Collection*

The *Kalakala* was usually crowded as it ferried workers from Seattle to and from the Bremerton Navy Yard during the war. Travelers appreciated the appearance of the vessel but not the vibrations and noise of the ride. *Seattle Post-Intelligencer Collection, MOHAI*

The World War II Years in Seattle

(Above)
The Boeing Airplane Company produced nearly 7,000 of these B-17s, and other companies built 5,750 of this Boeing bomber. B-17s dropped 55 percent of the explosives that fell on the Third Reich during World War II.
Seattle Post-Intelligencer Collection, MOHAI

As the Depression was fading, new products and services became available. In 1940 nylon stockings replaced those made of silk and cotton. That year the first floating bridge was completed across Lake Washington to Mercer Island. Citizens were purchasing better radios, some of them equipped with short wave receivers on which could be heard the news directly from the countries involved in the first battles of World War II.

Edward R. Murrow, raised in the area, was educated at Washington State College where he majored in radio speech and learned to broadcast news on KWSC, the college 5,000-watt radio station. By the time war broke out, he was an experienced radio newsman and was sent overseas to broadcast from the war fronts. His famous "This is London" series, carried on a national network of stations, was one of the most popular programs about the war. Millions of Americans heard him describe from the rooftops of London how the Nazi Luftwaffe was devastating the historic cities of England.

The speeches of Prime Minister Winston Churchill often were broadcast on American radio. Newspapers and magazines published stories describing how the indomitable British were fighting to prevent Hitler's Nazis from taking over their islands. Seattle residents flocked to motion picture theaters to view movies that dramatically portrayed the war effort in Europe. American opinion began to shift toward involvement as citizens realized the potential danger to North America if Europe fell to Hitler. In those pretelevision days, Seattle's new Telenews Theater, 1508 Third Avenue, attracted crowds to view newsreels from the war fronts and informative films about the war.

World War II began impacting Seattle businesses in the late 1930s. National defense efforts were generating jobs and the armed services increased their recruiting of young men. Several Seattle industries signed increasingly larger contracts for defense equipment and supplies, and the defense department was pleased with how quickly they began production, when compared to established large manufacturing companies where conversion to

wartime needs was often time-consuming and expensive. The war rapidly changed the Seattle production scene. Prior to the conflict, the city was not noted as one of the nation's large manufacturing centers, but by war's end it was praised for having supplied much equipment and materials vital to the final victory.

During the two years from 1940 and 1942, industries in the Puget Sound region received contracts worth $1.5 billion. Several of the first large orders went to the Boeing Airplane Company that in 1935 had tested its first B-17 "Flying Fortress" bomber. By 1940 the company had hired 4,000 employees and four years later that number had increased to more than 45,000. With two main plants located in Seattle and Renton and several small branch plants in nearby Washington towns, production of B-17s rapidly accelerated. New processes were developed that helped to speed the manufacture of the bombers. For example, instead of using a single long production line, engineers developed a multi-assembly system that increased output per man and utilized floor space more efficiently. Professor Stewart in his three-volume *Washington, Northwest Frontier* explained:

A modern airplane is an extremely complex bit of machine, and a great deal of the actual work of construction required engineering ability and training of a high degree. And men with the necessary qualifications were simply not available in sufficient numbers despite the fact that Boeing had been able in the early years to attract and to hold the services of a number of very gifted young engineers. This problem was solved by a very minute breakdown of the various jobs, which had to be accomplished, with simplification being the goal in every case.

By war's end, Boeing's Seattle plants had produced 6,981 of these complex B-17 Flying Fortresses. In addition, Lockheed turned out an additional 2,750 and Douglas 3,000, making a total of 12,731 B-17s. These Boeing bombers carried 55 percent of the explosives dropped on the Third Reich during World War II.

Early in the war, Boeing began developing a larger bomber with greatly increased cruising range. The first test model flew in September 1942. Called the Super Fortress or B-29, it could carry 20,000 pounds of bombs, had a 4,500-mile cruising range, and its ceiling was above

40,000 feet. But on February 28, 1943, tragedy struck when the engine of the test model caught fire. The pilot and crew attempted to circle back to Boeing Field but the flames spread across the wing and the plane kept losing altitude. With all control lost, the plane crashed into the Frye Packing Company just south of downtown, killing well-known test pilot Eddie Allen and the 10 crewmembers plus 30 employees in the packing plant. Because of the critical need for the plane, another test model was soon in the air and this time flew successfully. Within months, scores of the B-29s were rolling from assembly lines at the Boeing Renton plant.

A Foss tugboat towed this dry dock through the ship canal to a Lake Union shipyard in 1942. *Seattle Post-Intelligencer Collection, MOHAI*

Other Wartime Production

A total of 39 shipyards operated in the Seattle area during the war, many of them small but several large enough to construct or repair the largest warships. Todd Shipbuilding Corporation of Tacoma, as one example, during reorganization in 1939 acquired the former Sea-Tac Shipbuilding site on Harbor Island. Hundreds of ships, including destroyers, were constructed or repaired in its yards. Puget Sound Bridge and Dredge, also on Harbor Island, acquired the Lake Union Shipyard and the two facilities produced scores of vessels of various sizes for the United States and Allied navies.

Pacific Car and Foundry's large plant in Renton turned out Army tanks, tractors, cranes, trucks and logging equipment, all important in the war effort. They also developed

Pacific Car and Foundry produced trucks, cranes, tanks and other equipment at its large plant in Renton. *Seattle Post-Intelligencer Collection, MOHAI*

In 1943 workers and volunteers harvested a record 15,500 tons of cabbage in the White and Sammamish valleys and on the east shore of Lake Washington. These huge examples from Ivan Unbedacht's Kent farm were sold to a sauerkraut factory.

and were sole producers of a tank retrieval unit that towed hundreds of damaged tanks from battlefields to nearby repair facilities.

Traditional industries of the state were heavily involved in the war effort. Lumber companies produced building materials 24 hours a day and supplied needed products such as tannic acid from hemlock bark, cork from fir bark, and fire-resistant and waterproof plywood. Washington, a major agricultural state, helped feed the Allied armed forces as well as home front families. The state fishing industries provided fresh fish and other products of the sea, including millions of cans of salmon for the Army and other services.

The Relocation of American Japanese

On March 2, 1942, four months after the attack on Pearl Harbor, the Western Defense Command declared the three states fronting on the Pacific Ocean to be special military areas where residents of Japanese ancestry might be considered a danger. A plan developed to move them to inland relocation centers. During May of 1942, those living on Bainbridge Island were the first Japanese-Americans to be expelled and families in Seattle and Tacoma soon followed. It was a difficult time for these people but they handled the situation stoically even though they lost most of what they had labored for years to acquire.

At the time many Americans in the region argued that the Nisei were suffering racial discrimination. While it was true that Japanese military leaders had planned the attack on Pearl Harbor, those acquainted with local families of Japanese ancestry knew them to be patriotic Americans. Not one was ever convicted of espionage and most of the young men volunteered for military duty, many of them serving in the Nisei 442 Regimental Combat Team that earned more decorations for bravery than any other unit of similar size in the U.S. Army.

These families were moved to hurriedly erected barracks in uncomfortable desert or mountain settings. Some were there when they lost soldier sons in action in Italy and Germany or in the South Pacific where several worked as interpreters. The treatment of these families, many of them American-born citizens, left an indelible blot on the United States' World War II history page.

Army and Navy Bases in Seattle During the War

The entire Seattle waterfront was a hive of activity during the war. The Navy Port of Embarkation assumed control of most wharves, where all types of vessels ranging from troop ships to LSTs (Landing Ship, Tanks) were loaded with equipment, munitions, supplies and men bound for Pacific war fronts. The piers at Smith Cove became Navy property and were enlarged and barracks and office spaces added. The Alaska Communications system was headquartered in Seattle and local U.S. Coast Guard offices were busy helping direct the increased shipping on Puget Sound while alertly watching for hostile activity on the state's waterways. Sand Point Naval Air Station was one of the busier bases in the state and a large

On May 25, 1942, Americans of Japanese ancestry living on Bainbridge Island were the first in the area to be transported to inland relocation camps. The scene shows them walking to the ferry at Eagle Harbor. Many of these folks were American-born and all proved to be patriotic citizens. *Seattle Post-Intelligencer Collection, MOHAI*

(Far right) A typical wartime scene at the Seattle Port of Embarkation shows sailors, MPs and officers watching infantrymen with M-1 rifles and barracks bags board an LST for their journey to a Pacific war zone.

The Seattle Port of Embarkation was a beehive of activity all during the war. Even mud didn't deter service and port personnel from loading the LST in the background that soon would be transporting equipment and men to South Pacific battlefronts.

Navy structure with training rooms and offices was constructed at the south end of Lake Union. The Naval Reserve was headquartered there after the war.

Fort Lawton on Magnolia Bluff served as a staging area for troops embarking from Seattle for overseas assignment. Soldiers usually arrived in Seattle by rail from Fort Lewis or training facilities located in other states. Trucks transported them from the train stations to Fort Lawton where they were housed in large temporary barracks for a few days while being processed for overseas duty. They were given physical examinations, their inoculation records were checked, censorship regulations were explained, and clothing was issued that was appropriate for the climate at their destination. Thousands consumed three meals a day in Fort Lawton's large casual mess hall. Recreational facilities on the base included movie theaters, bowling alleys and service clubs. Post Exchanges sold tobacco, candy, ice cream and other food and drink at reduced prices, and church services were provided on the Sabbath. Shortly before shipping out, the men were placed on alert and strict censorship was imposed. Passes to town were no longer available, visitors were not allowed, and no

The quiet Fort Lawton of this 1937 aerial view became extremely active within a few years. Many temporary barracks and other structures filled empty spaces and the parade ground was the scene of soldiers being trained. For thousands of GIs this fort was their last home on U.S. soil before they left for overseas battle zones. Today the former fort serves as Seattle's Discovery Park.

communication was permitted with persons off the fort. This was an effort to prevent the enemy from learning shipping schedules and destinations. Seattle residents often gave friendly smiles and waved V-signs at trucks full of soldiers passing by on the way to the port. There the men were lined up with full backpacks and barracks bags and marched to the pier to board their ship as a band played lively tunes and Red Cross volunteers served coffee and doughnuts. The soldiers soon strode up the gangplank bound for an unidentified Pacific war front. Once at sea they would learn of their destination.

The headline says it all. Two smiling Seattle men realize half the enemy has been vanquished. *Seattle Post-Intelligencer Collection, MOHAI*

Life on the Home Front

Residents of Seattle during those war years remember vividly how food, tires and gasoline were rationed; how the air raid sirens were tested every noon; how the tethered barrage balloons rose overhead to protect against low-flying enemy planes. They recall crowded buses, streets full of men in uniform, and long lines of olive drab military vehicles loaded with service personnel passing by. They remember Victory Square on University Street in front of the Olympic Hotel, where on a replica of Washington's Monument the names of local war dead were added to a lengthening list. Dreading the possible information contained in telegrams, Seattleites opened them with trepidation for they frequently carried the message that a loved one, a relative or friend had been killed or wounded or was missing in battle. Of the more than one-quarter million of the state's young men and women serving in the armed forces, more than 6,000 were killed and nearly twice that many wounded. The names of the war dead are now permanently inscribed on the walls of the Memorial Garden at Benaroya Hall in downtown Seattle.

Every Seattle resident, old and young, male and female, was striving for victory, working long hours and often seven days a week during the war. Volunteers collected recyclable materials such as newspapers, metals and rubber, planted victory gardens, helped at the U.S.O and the Red Cross, volunteered at military hospitals, and in numerous other ways aided the war effort. And they constantly prayed for the safe return of husbands, brothers, sisters, cousins, uncles and friends. It has been said that Seattle residents per capita contributed as much or more toward the victory than did residents of any other American city.

The surrender of Germany on V-E Day, May 8, 1945, brought quiet rejoicing to Seattle but everyone realized the job was only half done. Now attention focused on the remaining tenacious foe. Seattle residents realized their city would grow even busier now that the full war effort was shifting to the Pacific Theater. Military planners and politicians warned residents that the invasion of Japan's home islands against a fanatic enemy might well result in the biggest blood bath of the war. Indeed, much blood was shed during the next four months as the Allies invaded and conquered island stepping stones leading toward

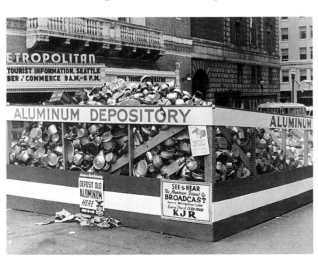

During the war years, Americans were asked to recycle metals, paper and rubber. Aluminum, especially, was in short supply. Seattle citizens deposited old pots and other aluminum scrap into this depository on University Street in front of the Olympic Hotel. Victory Square also was sited on this block.

Japan. As preparations began for the invasion of the final islands, dread increased, especially in families with sons in the Pacific. Service units that had been involved in defeating the enemy in Europe began boarding ships for transfer to the Pacific Theater. All Americans dreaded the coming invasions.

Allied service personnel in the Pacific could hardly believe the news. A new weapon of unprecedented destructive power had been dropped on Hiroshima on August 6, ravishing the city and killing tens of thousands. When the Japanese did not respond to a demand for unconditional surrender, a second bomb was dropped on Nagasaki. Boeing B-29s

carried the two secretly developed atom bombs to the enemy islands that forced the Japanese to surrender unconditionally. Japanese Admiral Takata, who was instrumental in convincing the emperor that Japan had to surrender, said, "American air power and the B-29 constituted the greatest single factor in Japan's defeat."

The official Japanese surrender occurred on August 15, 1945, known since as V-J Day. A huge celebration immediately swept the nation. Seattle citizens danced in the streets, service personnel hugged women and were hugged in return. Washington citizens were proud to learn

that plutonium for those two atomic bombs was purified at the secret Hanford plant in the central part of their state. A two-day holiday was proclaimed, but the joy of victory was moderated by thoughts of the more than a million young American service personnel who did not survive the war or who came home wounded. The long, costly, bloody world conflict had finally ended in victory for the Allied nations.

The Postwar Period

Over the next few months, thousands of veterans happily descended gangplanks at the Port of Seattle and soon were in railroad cars on the way to Army, Navy and Marine discharge centers all across America. These veterans carried cherished visions of home, family and friends and joyously anticipated resuming private lives that had been interrupted by nearly four years of war.

Nearly a quarter million Washington state men and women were eligible for the GI Bill, a term that originated with servicemen who had begun referring to themselves as "Government Issue," the same term used to describe their clothing and equipment. President Franklin Roosevelt signed the GI Bill on

June 22, 1944, providing several benefits for veterans as they returned to civilian life. The most popular of these benefits was a free college education. Universities and colleges in the Seattle area were inundated with students using the GI Bill. Campus living quarters and classrooms were crowded. Temporary portable structures were trucked in from former Army and Navy facilities and from housing projects near shipyards and wartime factories.

The GIs, most of them in their early 20s, had survived the Great Depression and nearly four years of war. They had lived in simple barracks, sleeping on Army cots or crammed into ships' holds. Many had experienced life in muddy, cold foxholes. They were glad to have survived those perilous years and now, older than most college freshmen, they earnestly pursued education and training and began seeking employment and wives.

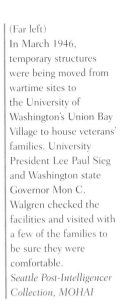

With the arrival of peace, several major building projects were quickly completed. Here is Seattle-Tacoma International Airport on opening day in 1948.

Seattle's Northgate was one of the nation's first shopping malls. This December 1949 view is looking east over the construction site.
Seattle Post-Intelligencer Collection, MOHAI

Peace brought many changes to Seattle. The first civilian autos that rolled off the production lines soon were resting in garages of proud owners. Home construction soared as returning service personnel began buying domiciles of their own, and older families with savings from the war years moved into larger, newer houses. Suburbs, where vacant land was less expensive, attracted contractors, some of whom built hundreds of tract homes to meet the surging demand.

Seattle experienced fewer postwar employment problems than anticipated. Veterans were assured the right to return to positions they held before entering the service, but many found their training and experience now made them eligible for jobs with higher pay. As postwar businesses developed, the city's appearance began to change. For the first time in 15 years or more, large commercial structures rose skyward, highways and bridges and airports were built, and passenger planes roared overhead. All sorts of new products appeared in the stores, many of them based on materials developed during the war.

In 1947 the state's first medical and dental schools were established at the University of Washington. During the 1948 Christmas season, thousands of residents stopped at Frederick and Nelson to view the miracle in the show window, a television set broadcasting programs from KRSC, later KING, the city's first television station. Within a few years several other Seattle television stations were broadcasting to the region.

Life in those immediate postwar years developed an unusual flavor. Thriving neighborhoods of young families developed where close friendships and block parties were common. Children walked together to school every morning and neighbors rallied to help community churches, educational institutions, and nonprofit organizations in need of assistance. This generation that had survived the Depression and a major war was thoroughly enjoying its good fortune. They had learned from experience that human beings succeed when they strive together to reach common goals.

Throughout its history, Seattle has suffered fewer prejudices than many cities. Within a decade of World War II, the city's neighborhoods and schools were desegregating. Most residents supported movements calling for equal opportunity regardless of race or religion. As a result Seattle gained a reputation as one of the country's more progressive metropolitan areas.

The decade of the 40s ended with one of the area's worst earthquakes on record. Measuring 7.1 on the Richter scale, it rocked the entire Puget Sound basin from the epicenter south of Olympia. Eight people were killed and many buildings were damaged, including several historic structures in Seattle's Pioneer Square area.

There is little doubt that the 1930s and 1940s in many ways were the most history-making and memorable years of the century in Seattle, a city populated with progressive and thoughtful citizens who were guiding their developing metropolis into what they hoped would be a brighter final half of the century.

Malmo Nursery Company, founded in Seattle in 1893, 50 years later was building these new facilities on 25th Avenue NE, now the site of University Village. *Seattle Post-Intelligencer Collection, MOHAI*

Historical Chaff from the Era

Prohibition lingered longer in Washington than in most other states. Residents had voted the state dry in 1916, four years before the 18th Amendment to the U.S. Constitution banned consumption of alcoholic beverages the country over. By the end of the 1920s, most Americans agreed that prohibition wasn't succeeding. As a result, the 21st Amendment to the Constitution was passed in 1933 repealing prohibition. Washington state liquor stores began selling liquor by the bottle, but a new state law banned the dispensing of hard liquor by the drink. Restaurants and cocktail bars worked for years to nullify the restriction, but not until 1949 was this law changed to allow diners to enjoy a mixed drink before dining out.

The State Department of Fisheries by 1948 was keeping an eye on the sustainability and health of native shellfish. They found healthy geoducks (gooeyducks), one of the largest if not the most beautiful of Puget Sound's edible mollusks, to be thriving.

Though Prohibition had ended nearly two decades earlier, Washington state laws prevented liquor being served by the drink until March 30, 1949. Customers of the Marine Room in the Olympic Hotel happily celebrated on that date.
Seattle Post-Intelligencer Collection, MOHAI

Department of Fisheries personnel in 1948 checked on the health and abundance of the large edible Puget Sound clams known as Geoducks.
Seattle Post-Intelligencer Collection, MOHAI

On April 19, 1949, the Puget Sound area was shaken by the worst earthquake on record. Eight people were killed and much property was damaged. At Yesler Way near First Avenue South, concrete cornices fell from several older Pioneer Square structures, damaging parked autos.
Seattle Post-Intelligencer Collection, MOHAI

CHAPTER FIVE

POSTWAR SEATTLE 1950-1980

The shift to a peacetime economy without slipping into a depression such as the one that followed World War I called for adroit and persistent planning. For the most part the effort was successful. The 1950 census counted 467,591 residents within the city limits, a confirmation that most of the families of the wartime population increase remained in the city.

By 1950, many veterans had completed their educations, married, and were producing families and purchasing homes. Here is a scene typical of the era, a street in Seattle's Wedgewood neighborhood.
Seattle Post-Intelligencer Collection, MOHAI

By the 1960s, Bellevue had its own major shopping square. 104th Avenue, now called Bellevue Way, is in the upper part of the photo. Across Bellevue Way at right center, under a long white roof, are Safeway and Bartell drug stores. They were still there in 2000.
Seattle Post-Intelligencer Collection, MOHAI

The veterans of World War II were older than typical students and many needed family housing as they completed college. The University of Washington brought in surplus wartime structures from shipyards to develop what was known as Union Bay Village. Through the 1950s hundreds of young families lived there as veterans earned degrees. The site now is occupied by the University's Center for Urban Horticulture program.
Seattle Post-Ingelligencer Collection, MOHAI

Seattle residents, deprived of both necessities and conveniences during 15 years of depression and war, began satisfying their immediate needs as factories switched to producing peacetime products. During the early 1950s, thousands of former servicemen and their wives were buying homes and producing families. They sometimes faced difficulties locating furnishings and appliances, but usually such shortages lasted only a few months. Lumber companies flourished as housing tracts spread across King County. Blossoming city neighborhoods and suburbs attracted retail centers, including new-style shopping malls that supplied young families with most every need. New schoolhouses were constructed to serve the increasing numbers of school-age children. Within two decades of the war, the Seattle School District was operating nearly 120 public schools.

Universities and colleges were aware that the GI Bill would help veterans afford college. They had expected a rapid growth in enrollment. Few, however, had foreseen the huge numbers of students that would continue matriculating as graduate students. All former armed service personnel, no matter their age or family financial situation, now could attend college. Included among them were thousands of slightly older men and women whose college plans had been delayed by lack of funds during the Depression decade.

World War II exerted democratizing pressures on an optimistic younger generation that expected, even demanded, the opportunity to earn advancement to a comfortable family life. Sons and daughters of poor families, members of minorities, persons from small towns and large merged on the nation's campuses and graduated as the best-educated generation to that time. Within a decade they began assuming leadership roles in their communities.

All was not serious with this generation. Like young folks that had matured before them, they frequently sought entertainment. Seattle's Seafair summer celebration began annual parades, hydroplane races and other events. Seattle's yacht clubs joined in celebrating the opening day of yachting season with yacht parades and boat races. When the circus came to town, young families filled the tents.

The annual summer Seafair celebration with its parades, pirates and hydroplane races attracted crowds. This 1951 Frederick and Nelson float was admired by the multitude as it passed the Fourth and Pine intersection.

All sorts of Seattle sailors have enjoyed the annual parade of yachts on opening day of boating season. H.W. McCurdy's yacht *Blue Peter* led the parade on April 29, 1950. The view looks west from the Montlake Bridge. *Williamson Collection, MOHAI*

Seattle Post-Intelligencer Collection, MOHAI

At mid-century, circuses visited Seattle each year. Ringling Brothers Circus elephants are shown being served lunch on August 29, 1955. A few hours later the tents behind them were filled with Seattle families enjoying the show.

The Korean Conflict

All was going well when, five short years after World War II ended, Cold War strains between the Communist world and the democracies heated up. Seattle's largest employer, The Boeing Company, had reduced its work force from about 40,000 to 11,000 as it completed its World War II contracts. A few months later the nation realized that the Cold War was turning hot and the company signed contracts for equipment to support United Nations armies in Korea. Boeing quickly rehired many of its former employees.

The Korean Conflict flared on June 25, 1950, when North Korean troops, led by columns of Soviet-built tanks, invaded South Korea. Seattle residents, aware they were living in the major U.S. port nearest Korea, soon noticed increasing activity on the waterfront. They began worrying about their sons, many of them veterans of World War II who had stayed in military reserve units now being called to active duty.

At the United Nations, which Russia was boycotting at the time, discussions centered on how to respond to the Communist attacks without fomenting a global atomic war. The decision was to send troops to help South Korea repel the invasion. During the time it took to transport men to the battlefronts, the South Koreans were forced into a corner of their country that became known as the Pusan Perimeter, where they managed to hold on until United Nations armies arrived. On September 15, 1950, Commanding General Douglas MacArthur's troops staged an amphibious landing at Inchon behind the enemy lines. The North Koreans, caught between two United Nations' armies, retreated. The U.N. forces pursued them north to the border with China.

Now the Chinese army entered the fray, ordering some 200,000 men and massive reserve forces to attack. The U.N. troops were forced into a hasty retreat and by January 4, 1951, Chinese forces had captured Seoul. In the hard-fought battles that followed, United Nations troops pushed the Chinese armies back to the 38th parallel that divided the two Koreas.

It was then that General MacArthur complained publicly that his efforts were being hampered by President Truman's refusal to allow him to order bombing of supply depots inside China. This led to heated debates in Congress, but President Truman, supported by the Joint Chiefs of Staff, did not budge. He ordered MacArthur not

Several shiploads of veterans of the Korean War arrived during 1954. The city arranged "Welcome Lane" greetings for the returning service personnel. The photo shows a truck caravan proceeding down Second Avenue on the way to Fort Lawton. *Seattle Post-Intelligencer Collection, MOHAI*

to discuss the disagreement publicly. The General promptly took the matter to the press after which President Truman removed him as commander of United Nations' forces and replaced him with General Matthew Ridgeway.

Korean Conflict peace talks commenced in July 1951 but remained deadlocked for two years during which both sides suffered heavy casualties as they battled for control of the Korean hills. Finally in July 1953, a cease-fire agreement was signed and the battlefield fell quiet.

Several Seattle factories produced materials for the allied cause in Korea, including The Boeing Company that turned out B-47 and B-52 bombers and jet-powered tanker transports that were vital to the allied cause.

More than 116,000 United Nations troops were killed in action in Korea, 54,000 of them Americans, 558 of them from Washington state and about half of those from the Seattle area. Early in the war, 18-year-old Joseph L. Hendricks had the misfortune of being the first Seattle youth reported killed on a Korean battlefield. After the cease-fire, thousands of veterans of the Korean conflict returned home through the Port of Seattle where they were warmly welcomed with bands, parades and entertainment.

Jet Passenger Service Begins

During all this, The Boeing Company also was busy developing the new jet-powered 707 airplane. William Allen, who assumed the presidency when Philip Johnson died in 1945, led the company as it gambled millions to develop this first jet passenger liner. The effort began in the early 1950s and a decade later the Boeing 707 was proudly jetting passengers to their destinations in record

times. The company's sales escalated in the years following, and derivative models of the 707 are being produced to this day. Boeing also successfully produced the BOMARC missile during those Cold War years.

The Era of Ill Will

The Cold War resulted in icy relationships between the United States and the populous Communist countries, principally China and Russia, and created trepidation across the land, including fear of a possible atomic war. Concerns of Communist influence in American politics resulted in exaggerated suspicions. Heated arguments developed between friends and neighbors. In 1947 the state Legislature, controlled by Republicans for the first time since the war, formed a Joint Fact Finding Committee on Un-American Activities with Albert Canwell of Spokane as chairman. Their objective was to scrutinize and question organizations suspected of Communist leanings. The committee eventually scheduled hearings in Seattle to query members of several organizations including the Building Service Employee Union, the Washington Pension Union, and several University of Washington professors about their political beliefs. When six of the university witnesses refused to answer questions, they were charged with contempt of the legislature. A committee of professors chosen by the faculty held long hearings and sent their recommendations to university President Raymond Allen who sent them on to the regents with his interpretation. The regents called for dismissal of three faculty members and probation for the three others.

Dozens of pickets marched during the hearings carrying signs demanding the Canwell Committee be demolished. Much heated rhetoric was heard both for and against the

effort. What was called the "era of ill will" persisted with parades against the Canwell Committee, heated orations and several trials. The U.S. Supreme Court eventually cooled the fracas by overturning all convictions that resulted from the hearings. Several of the more extreme legislators involved in the so-called "witch hunt," including Chairman Canwell, were not re-elected in 1948.

This type of activity bounced to the national scene in February 1950 when U.S. Senator Joseph McCarthy launched an "Anti Red Crusade" with a wild, unproven claim that he had in his possession a list of 205 members of the Communist Party working at the State Department. In succeeding months he accused countless others, including President Truman, of aiding the Communist Party. He finally went so far as to brand specific Army personnel as communists, to whom a lawyer for the Army Secretary retorted, "Have you no decency, Sir?" No one McCarthy accused was found to be a communist and in December 1954 the Senate voted to censor McCarthy for conduct unbecoming a senator.

The Beginnings of Metro

While ill will was evident on the national scene, more positive activity was permeating local politics. A Metropolitan Council was formed in Seattle to attack pollution, congestion, urban decay, and environmental destruction. In 1946 Mayor Gordon Clinton and the King County Commissioners appointed a Problems Advisory Committee with lawyer James R. Ellis as chairman. After considerable research, they proposed a 10-year

construction program to be funded with $125 million from federal grants and local taxes. The first project was to build more sewer lines and modern treatment plants in efforts to clean up algae-choked Lake Washington and other waters where "No swimming" signs decorated the beaches. As the sewage problem was corrected, the lake and Puget Sound began to clean themselves.

A committee of 48 citizens, again chaired by Jim Ellis, was responsible for drafting proposed legislation for development of a Metropolitan Municipal Corporation Act. When the proposal was in final form, it was lobbied through the 1957 legislature and a $145 million bond issue placed on the King County ballot. The act called for establishment of a Metro Council of eight members from Seattle and seven from suburban areas, to develop plans for regional sewer systems and rapid transit. Seattle residents voted in favor of the measure but a majority of suburban residents voted against it. The plan then was revised, reducing the bond issue to $80 million to improve the region's sewage system. Voters approved this measure.

In 1965 the "Forward Thrust" plan was laid on the table. It called for rapid transit, a domed stadium, new parks, a world trade center and major street improvements. A 200-member planning committee was appointed to cull through 2,000 project ideas and select the ones with highest priority. The committee recommended 13 different bond issues totaling $819 million plus two statewide bond issues worth $65 million. At the polls, citizens approved measures totaling nearly $334 million, the largest per capita public improvement plan ever passed by U.S. citizens to that time.

The final Forward Thrust report issued in 1980 listed the accomplishments of the effort, among them the construction of the Kingdome and the building of the Seattle Aquarium. Many neighborhood parks and playgrounds, sports fields, tennis courts and swimming pools were enlarged and improved. Also, the Forward Thrust funds paid for several new fire stations and additions to the Youth Service Center; and $12 million was expended on neighborhood landscaping, paving and street lighting. Seattle residents soon realized that the Forward Thrust program had indeed created a more livable city.

The 1962 World's Fair

The 1960 census counted 557,087 Seattle residents, an increase of 90,000 during the previous decade. However, growth was slowing and Seattle's leaders sensed something was needed to liven up the scene. In June 1955, four Seattle friends met in the bar of the Washington Athletic Club where their conversation turned to developing ideas for a second World's Fair. They discussed ways of celebrating the golden anniversary of the Alaska-Yukon-Pacific Exposition of 1909, an idea that was later discarded. The quartet of promoters — Don Follett and Denny Givens of the Seattle Chamber of Commerce, city councilman Al Rochester, and Ross Cunningham of *The Seattle Times* — soon were joined by other business leaders, among them Jerry Hoeck, an advertising agency executive.

In 1957 the Soviets blasted Sputnik into space, a feat that prompted Marlow Hartung, a colleague of Jerry Hoeck, to suggest that the fair feature the scientific progress expected to advance the world during the next century. The official title became The Century 21 Exhibition. An organization, a site and financing were needed, so the Seattle City Council memorialized the state Legislature to pass a bill calling for a World's Fair Commission. Governor Arthur Langlie signed the legislation and appointed Edward Carlson to chair the commission. The Civic Center was selected as the site because structures built there for the fair could be used for other events after the exhibition closed.

Many business and professional men and women were involved with the fair, among them William Street and Joseph P. Gandy. Several architects, including Paul Thiry, developed plans for the structures. Minoru Yamasaki, and Naramore, Bain, Brady and Johanson were employed to design the U.S. Science Pavilion (now the Pacific Science Center.) To pay for construction, the City Council placed a $7.5 million civic bond issue on the ballot that was overwhelmingly passed by Seattle residents. Newly elected Governor Albert Rosellini agreed that the state should match city expenditures. A budget of $4.5 million was established to build the Coliseum to house the Washington state exhibit. Thanks largely to Senator Warren G. Magnuson, the U.S. Government provided $12.5 million, most of it for the Science Pavilion. Ewen

Dingwall was named general manager of the event, and many nations and corporations signed on as participants.

Alweg of Sweden offered to build a monorail to carry visitors the 1.2 miles from the city center to the fairgrounds. In 1960 the Bureau of International Expositions sanctioned The Century 21 Exhibition as a World's Fair. Eddy Carlson, while visiting Stuttgart, Germany, was entranced by its tall tower with a restaurant at the top and came home with a suggestion of a similar landmark and observation tower on the fairgrounds. The Howard S. Wright Company built the tower that to this day serves as a trademark of the city, the 600-foot-high Space Needle. An exhaustive advertising campaign to attract visitors soon commenced.

On April 21, 1962, President John F. Kennedy sent the signal to open Seattle's second World's Fair by pressing the same gold key that had been used to start the Alaska-Yukon-Pacific Exposition in 1909. The fair garnered worldwide and national attention, and 10 million visitors congregated in Seattle during its six-month schedule. The exposition ended with a small profit, and more importantly it provided Seattle with the Opera House, the Pacific Science Center, the Coliseum, the monorail, the Space Needle, and several other buildings surrounded by attractive grounds.

(Far right) Late in 1961, construction at the World's Fair site was attracting attention. The view looks east from the U.S. Science Pavilion (now the Pacific Science Center) toward the Space Needle.

The Century 21 Exposition was shiny new when the photographer preserved this view of the completed grounds.

Publicity for The Century 21 World's Fair began well before the fair opened. The Coliseum was under construction in the background when these young ladies agreed to seat themselves on a temporary fence for a photo that surely would attract attention.

Alweg of Sweden built the monorail that transported fairgoers the 1.2 miles from downtown to the exposition at the Seattle Center. The monorail remains in service more than three decades later.

Many industrial exhibits attracted admiring crowds to view products and services of the future.

Modernizing Factors

Seattle was modernized in many ways during the 1950s and 60s. In 1953 the ribbon was cut to open the Alaskan Way Viaduct, which raised traffic above railroad tracks and streets leading to the waterfront. The new Interstate 5 replaced Highway 99 as the principal throughway, removing much of the traffic from downtown streets. New highway 520 branched east from Interstate 5 around the north side of Capitol Hill to cross over Lake Washington on the new floating bridge commonly called the Evergreen Point Bridge, though its official name honors Governor Albert Rosellini. As Eastside suburbs attracted population and businesses, including some of the first high tech firms, traffic increased and the freeway was extended to Redmond and beyond. However, not all the planned highway improvements were completed. The R.H. Thomson Expressway was to be routed through five Seattle neighborhoods and the Arboretum, but increasing opposition caused the plan to be abandoned, leaving a few completed but unconnected ramps near Highway 520.

The 1967 city elections energized the Seattle City Council by adding three younger members. The media

noted that this new generation assuming control of city government advocated neighborhood renewal programs, greater support of the arts, and citizen participation in developing answers to knotty problems. Rehabilitation of historic sections of the city became a priority and improvements began on several dilapidated Pioneer Square structures, resulting in art studios and offices for architects and small businesses. The Pike Place Market, where local farmers had sold produce directly to customers since 1907, was preserved, refurbished and enlarged.

A Decade of Protests

In the mid-1960s, the nation was in turmoil over activist efforts to develop greater opportunity and equal rights for minorities, especially the black population. At the time, most of Seattle's black families lived in the Central Area. Some of the "Great Society Projects" of that era were enacted to promote upward mobility, but these ran into occasional dissention across the nation. After Seattle voters defeated an open housing ordinance, efforts of local community leaders helped residents gain insight into neighborhood problems. Soon minority families were finding greater acceptance in most sections of the city.

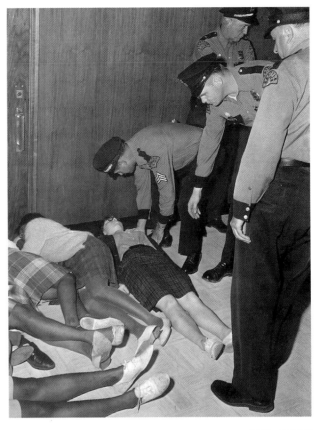

The struggle for equal rights for minorities increased in intensity during July 1963. The scene shows Seattle policemen attempting to gently remove participants from a sit-in at the Seattle Municipal Building. *Seattle Post-Intelligencer Collection, MOHAI*

Proponents of open housing gathered at Westlake Mall in March 1964, carrying signs reading "Stop Racial Discrimination Now!" and "Fair Housing for All." Several speakers explained why discrimination was harming the city. *Seattle Post-Intelligencer Collection, MOHAI*

At the end of an antisegregation march at City Hall, Mayor Gordon Clinton was with the Reverend Dr. Samuel B. McKinney as he spoke to the throng. The mayor seems to be enjoying one of McKenney's remarks. The date was June 18, 1963.

(Far left) University of Washington students against the Vietnam War showed their displeasure on campus by removing brick paving and posting a sign calling for the abolishment of Reserve Officer Training and military recruiting on campus. They also wanted classified war research moved off the campus. *Seattle Post-Intelligencer Collection, MOHAI*

presenting them with demands to open the campus to all. President Charles Odegaard met with the agitating students several times, calmed them and organized an Office of Student Affairs to hear their complaints.

During the Cold War in the mid-60s, open houses at Sand Point Naval Air Station invited Seattle residents to view a variety of Navy aircraft. *Seattle Post-Intelligencer Collection, MOHAI*

The Vietnam Conflict

In 1954 the French were forced from Vietnam and the country was split into a Communist north and non-Communist south. In 1960 the Communists began a

Students at the University of Washington strongly promoted equal opportunity for student-age minority youth. During the spring of 1967, the Black Student Union occupied part of the administration building and for a short time held members of the faculty senate hostage while

On May 5, 1970, students gathered in huge numbers to march against the Vietnam conflict. A Washington State Patrol riot squad talked with the leaders about their plans and made suggestions and explained why they should not stop traffic. *Seattle Post-Intelligencer Collection, MOHAI*

Seattle Post-Intelligencer Collection, MOHAI

On May 6, 1970, an antiwar demonstration attracted thousands, most of them students from the University of Washington and other campuses. They stopped traffic as they marched peacefully down the freeway and Pine Street to downtown Seattle.

terrorist campaign to topple the government in the South. The U.S. responded by sending military advisors and financial aid to South Vietnam. Suddenly defensive measures took on added importance.

In 1964, after a reported attack on U.S. ships in the Gulf of Tonkin, Congress voted to let the President take whatever action was necessary to prevent further Communist aggression. In February 1965, after seven Americans were killed in an enemy attack, President Lyndon Johnson ordered a continuous aerial bombing of North Vietnam and began a massive troop buildup that peaked in 1968 with 541,000 U.S. service personnel in Vietnam. The President reported the war was being won.

An extensive Communist attack in January 1968 forced major re-evaluation of the U.S. war effort and President Johnson decided not to run for re-election. Richard Nixon was elected the next president after pledging to end the war. A few months later he ordered air and ground forces to attack hidden enemy bases in Cambodia and Laos. This resulted in repercussions across the United States. In Seattle, on May 6, 30 state troopers stopped marching university students at the Roanoke Interchange with I-5 and the congenial students sat down, chanted, negotiated and left. The next day thousands of citizens, most of them students, marched down the I-5 freeway from the University District to downtown, stalling traffic for an hour.

On May 18, 1970, National Guardsmen, while attempting to quell Vietnam War protests, killed four students at Kent State University in Ohio. Worried parents

A jarring earthquake in 1965 dumped a brick wall on this car parked on South First Avenue. *Seattle Post-Intelligencer Collection, MOHAI*

suggested that Seattle police be allowed to help patrol the University of Washington campus. University President Charles Odegaard responded that the university would continue to police itself. The students continued to exert pressure on university administrators to take a moral stand against the killing at Kent State, but the president's bold leadership and meetings with students eventually diffused the tense situation in the University District.

In January 1973 the Nixon Administration signed an agreement to withdraw U.S. troops. The fighting in Vietnam came to an end, but not before some 57,000 American service personnel had lost their lives, nearly 1,100 of them from Washington state, including more than 400 from the Seattle area.

Other Events of the Rambunctious 60s

Seattle was shaken by a major earthquake in 1965 that registered 6.5 on the Richter Scale and killed five in the city. Many buildings were heavily damaged, especially those built on reclaimed fill.

Another type of earthquake resounded when Seattle rocker Jimi Hendrix debuted in his hometown and his recordings became bestsellers. Seattle resident Jim Whittaker made world headlines in 1963 when he became the first American to reach the summit of Mount Everest.

The 1965 earthquake knocked holes in this street beside the Union Railroad Station. The fact that this area was a tide flat that had been filled nearly a century earlier may have made it susceptible to such damage. *Seattle Post-Intelligencer Collection, MOHAI*

CHAPTER FIVE

The end of the 1960s was marked by what became known as the "Boeing Recession." Boeing, Seattle's largest employer, found it necessary to drastically reduce its work force after Congress shelved plans to develop a supersonic transport. Soon thereafter projected increases in air travel failed to materialize, slowing demand for the Boeing 747. Within a few years about 65,000 employees, two-thirds of its work force, had been released, causing the local economy to falter. That was when the memorable billboard appeared above a well-traveled street with the message, "Will the last person leaving Seattle please turn out the lights?"

But the lights never went out. Fewer than 15 percent of the jobless migrated elsewhere. Residents volunteered to work in food banks to keep hunger away from families of the unemployed, and federal, state and city projects were funded to provide employment for hundreds of the jobless. A group called "Seattle 2000" began developing plans for the future of its city that included preservation and enhancement of the natural environment, increased support for quality health care, and funding for a Community College system. The arts were promoted, methods to improve the administration of justice were considered, and a Seattle-King County Development Council was formed to explore ways to diversify the city's business and industrial base.

Democrat Dixie Lee Ray, the State's first female governor, followed Dan Evans in the governor's chair in Olympia. Here she confers with her assistant, Glen Rose. *Seattle Post-Intelligencer Collection, MOHAI*

Political Highlights of the Era

The state's two senators, Warren Magnuson and Henry Jackson, both adept politicians with 30 years' experience in Congress, had advanced through ability and seniority to powerful positions. In 1980 Slade Gorton defeated Magnuson and the former senator died a few years later. Henry Jackson, a serious presidential candidate in 1976, lost the nomination to Georgia Governor Jimmy Carter who was elected president. Senator Jackson died suddenly of a ruptured aorta in 1983, leaving the state for the first time in decades with little seniority in the United States Senate.

The first governor of the state of Washington to be elected to three successive terms was the moderate Republican Daniel J. Evans whose family roots were deeply embedded in Seattle history. He took office in 1964 and lived in the governor's mansion in Olympia until January 1977. He then served as president of The Evergreen State College in Olympia until appointed to fill Henry Jackson's seat in the United States Senate when that longtime senator died. The Washington state governor following Evans was Dr. Dixie Lee Ray, the first woman to be elected to that position. She had formerly served as a University of Washington professor, director of the Pacific

Seattle's first tall skyscraper, the SeaFirst Building, a 50-story monolith, changed the skyline when it was finished in 1969. From West Seattle it dominated the downtown profile. *Seattle Post-Intelligencer Collection, MOHAI*

Science Center and chairwoman of the United States Atomic Energy Commission. Ray served one term as governor that was stormy at times but memorable.

In 1972 the Watergate affair concerning the illegal entry into the Democratic Party offices in the Watergate Building in Washington, D.C. caused more discontent. Political and legal tussles extending over two years resulted in resignation of two of the President's aides, John Ehrlichman and H.R. Haldeman, who had been charged with covering up the details of the Watergate break-in. Ehrlichman was a well-known Seattle attorney before being called to Washington, D.C. Later, President Nixon, facing impeachment, also resigned.

Downtown Seattle Expands and Modernizes

Frenetic building activity in downtown Seattle during the 1970s astounded residents. Some among them considered it a renaissance in the heart of the city while others derided it as an attempt to ape Manhattan. As the structures stretched toward the sky, the Smith Tower suddenly assumed midget proportions.

The first real stunner was the $28 million, 50-story Seattle-First National Bank Building that was completed in 1969. Jokesters called it the black box in which the Space Needle arrived. It presaged a score of skyscrapers,

among them the 40-story Washington Plaza Hotel, now the Westin, also completed in 1969; the 27-story Hilton Hotel (1970); the 21-story Royal Manor Condominium on 8th Avenue (1971); the 21-story Park Place Office Building, 6th at University (1971); the 30-story Financial Center (1973); the Royal Crest Condominium at 3rd and Lenora (1973); the 40-story Bank of California Center (1974); the 40-story Rainier Tower (1975) and the 37-story Federal Office Building (1975). These were among the major new buildings erected in downtown before 1980. Since then other structures that scrape the sky have been added. They march along the downtown streets taller than the old-growth firs and cedars that covered those hills 150 years ago.

Seattle's folks have always been fond of their waterfront. The city founders astutely realized water transport would be the major connection with the world. It still is, though railroads, motorized vehicles, and aircraft long ago broke the monopoly once held by ships. During the 1960s and 70s, large steamers became scarce on the central waterfront and many wharves and piers were taken over by seafood restaurants, import and souvenir stores, an aquarium and firms providing sightseeing water tours. Larger vessels were directed to new facilities at the south end of the waterfront where cargo cranes as high

Seattle Post-Intelligencer Collection, MOHAI

Seattle's baseball aficionados, and there were many, followed the Seattle Rainiers at Sick's Stadium on Rainier Avenue. Seattle's first professional team, the Pilots, played here for a couple of years before moving to Milwaukee. Sick's Stadium was demolished in 1976 and baseball moved to the new Kingdome.

as skyscrapers and weighing hundreds of tons lift and stack heavy containerized cargoes into large vessels, filling their holds and decks in 24 hours or less. Much of the work of today's longshoremen has been mechanized, allowing them to work at computerized controls instead of manually loading and unloading cargoes.

The Arts Scene

In the mid-1970s the Seattle fine arts scene blossomed. Thanks to the World's Fair a decade earlier, the Seattle Symphony and Seattle Opera had an auditorium offering good acoustics and comfortable seats. For two decades,

the symphony had performed in the Civic Auditorium or the Orpheum Theater, the latter built to show motion pictures and vaudeville acts. During those decades, several active drama groups developed including the Seattle Repertory Theater and A Contemporary Theater (ACT). The Seattle Art Museum used two principal display locations — the museum in Volunteer Park and a branch in the Seattle Center Pavilion.

The Sports Scene

After World War II the biggest spectator sports attractions in Seattle were the Pacific Coast League Seattle

Rainier baseball team that played in Sick's Stadium on Rainier Avenue and the teams of the University of Washington and other colleges and local high schools. Various other sports groups scheduled amateur yacht races, tennis and golf matches and other events.

Television broadcasts of major league sports added to their popularity in the 1960s. The Seattle Supersonic basketball team was the first major league franchise in the city. They played their first games in the Seattle Center Coliseum (now Key Arena) in 1967. Major League baseball came to Seattle in 1969 when the Seattle Pilots played at Sick's Stadium, but the franchise soon shifted to Milwaukee. Actor-comedian Danny Kaye and local radio executive Les Smith obtained an American League baseball franchise in 1977 for the Seattle Mariners. The National Football League franchised a team in Seattle as the Kingdome was being completed. In this covered stadium, most of Seattle's professional football and baseball games were played over the next 22 years. As the millennium changed, the Kingdome was imploded and replaced by separate stadiums for baseball and football.

With new facilities attracting professional teams, local universities and colleges wondered if they might lose support for their teams. However, alumni and students remained faithful and attendance actually increased for several nonprofessional sports.

The Problems of Inflation

Inflation troubled most Seattle residents from the mid-1970s to the 90s. The *State of Washington Data Book* indicates that in 1980, for example, the cost of living in Seattle increased 16.7 percent. Home mortgage interest rates began a rapid ascent, causing a major reduction in the number of construction permits, forcing many young families to delay home ownership.

Demographic Changes

The suburbs, as they grew, continued to attract families and businesses, eventually causing the population to shrink in the Northwest's largest city. Seattle's 1960 population of 557,087 was reduced to 493,846 in 1980. However, indications were that the trend was being reversed. As the World War II generation aged and its longevity increased, many preferred to avoid yard work, home up-keep, and commuting to jobs, shopping and entertainment centers. Large condominium and apartment buildings rose along the shores of Elliott Bay and Lakes Washington and Union. Multifamily structures providing magnificent views sprouted atop Queen Anne and other Seattle hills.

Historical Chaff from the Era

During the 1960s one of Seattle's most popular residents was Bobo, a handsome male gorilla who had been rescued as an orphaned baby in Africa. Adopted and raised by the Bill Lowman family in Anacortes, he believed he was a human being. Eventually he grew so large and strong his family was forced to transfer him to the Woodland Park Zoo where he immediately became a star attraction. Families gathered to celebrate his birthdays and watch him eat cake. The publicity he received made politicians envious. Bobo would sit and study the humans who were studying him through the thick glass of his cage and occasionally he would entertain them with his antics, including imitating their actions. When he died in 1968, Bobo's obituary was published in the papers and his image appeared on television. Later a taxidermist mounted his remains and, to this day, they frequently are displayed for younger generations at the Museum of History and Industry.

The handsome gorilla BoBo was a favorite at the Woodland Park Zoo during the mid-1960s.
Seattle Post-Intelligencer Collection, MOHAI

During the 1950s, new model autos, including the stylish new 1955 Thunderbird, caught many an eye.

Seattle Post-Intelligencer Collection, MOHAI

Senator Warren Magnuson poses with a group of fellow Democrats at a 1956 party convention. Saluting the live party symbol are, from the left, Earl Coe, Senator Magnuson, Sheriff Tim McCulloch, and Mel Moe.

Seattle Post-Intelligencer Collection, MOHAI

In 1961 President John F. Kennedy visited Seattle. Riding with him are Senator Warren Magnuson and Governor Albert Rosellini.

CHAPTER
SIX

STRIDING INTO THE MODERN AGE
1980-2000

Explosions Open the Decade

On May 18, 1980, a huge explosion rattled dishware in Seattle and across the state. Mount St. Helens had erupted, shearing off about a quarter of its 9,677-foot peak with a blast that transformed earth and rock into dust, burning gases, hot lava, and boulders that were spread over the surrounding area. Some of the ash and smoke was blown high into the atmosphere and scattered around the world. Fifty-seven human beings in the vicinity of the mountain were killed by the eruption, hundreds of forested acres were blown flat, and countless animals, birds and fish died. Twenty years later nature had only begun to heal the scars.

On New Year's Day of 1983 a less damaging kind of eruption glued Seattle residents to their television screens as the University of Washington Huskies exploded against a tough Iowa team at the annual Rose Bowl game. The final score was Washington 28 and Iowa 8.

An aerial view of Mt. St. Helens two years after it erupted shows some of the devastation. Spirit Lake and Mt. Rainier are visible in the distance. ©1992 *photo by George White Location Photography*

Seattle's Businesses Prosper

During the 80s, The Boeing Company experienced more ups than downs, with its commercial airplane division accounting for about two-thirds of its income. In 1983 the company sold 149 commercial planes worth $6.3 billion and the military ordered planes worth $2.3 billion. By 1985 the economy was so bright that a headline in *The Seattle Times* read, "Led by Boeing, Seattle becomes World Powerhouse." The next year Boeing improved its record even more with the sale of 341 jets worth $19.25 billion. Eighty-three of these were jumbo 747s, while 213 were smaller 737s. The company also sold six 707 jets equipped with airborne warning and control systems (AWACS) to Great Britain. The year 1988 witnessed still another record at Boeing with the sale of 344 of their 737s, 161 of their 757s, 82 of their 767s, and 49 of the 747 models.

Microsoft Makes Headlines

Seattle became a center of computer-age activity during the 1980s. In 1982, Americans purchased nearly 3 million personal computers and the numbers were skyrocketing. Businesses and individuals in the Seattle metropolitan area were busily creating software to operate those computers and manufactured some of the computer equipment. By 1985, Microsoft's computer programs were in use around the globe and founder Bill Gates, not yet 30, was often in the news. That year the papers noted that the Microsoft campus, then located in Bellevue, was the largest of the area's several computer industry firms. By the end of the decade, Gates was recognized as the nation's youngest billionaire and his company was expanding a huge new campus in Redmond.

This 1990 view is of the Boeing Everett Plant with a 747 being completed in front of the huge factory. ©1990 *photo by George White Location Photography*

Seattle Center Activities

At the outset of the 1980s, the aging Seattle Center needed an overhaul. Ewen Dingwall, who earlier had managed the center, was hired out of retirement to solve several problems, the most pressing being a weak operating budget. Dingwall helped convince the City Council to double the city's annual funding to $1.9 million. Major attractions, including the 1983 Pacific Science Center's six-month exhibit of inventions and history direct from China, pulled in thousands of visitors. Business at the Center House and other facilities increased and city funding was generated to refurbish several buildings.

The growing Microsoft Campus in Redmond, the suburb east of Seattle ©1996 *photo by George White Location Photography*

©2000 photo by George White Location Photography

The Seattle Center is the site of three city icons: the Space Needle, the Monorail, seen in the foreground, and Experience Music Project.

This view of the Klahanie development on the Sammamish Plateau is toward the west and shows Lake Sammamish, Belleuve, Lake Washington, and Seattle.

A String of Murders

In 1982 the first bodies were discovered in what developed as a series of killings that continued through the 1980s. A total of 49 women, mostly prostitutes and young runaways, were believed murdered by an assailant the media dubbed the Green River Killer after several of the bodies were found near that river. Though officials worked diligently through the decade, the killer was never identified and the case remains open.

What was headlined as the worst mass killing in Seattle history occurred in 1983 when 13 people were shot during a holdup at the Wah Mee Social Club in Seattle's International District. The three men involved were later identified, tried and incarcerated.

Then in 1989, Ted Bundy, a handsome law student who had resided in Seattle, was electrocuted in Florida after being convicted of killing two college coeds there. During the trial he confessed to killing 11 women in Washington state, two in Oregon and two in Utah. And still another murder headline was published early in 1993 when Westley Allan Dodd, murderer of three young boys, was hanged at the penitentiary, the first person in 30 years to be executed in Washington state.

Unusual Weather

The 80s decade experienced its share of unusual weather. In 1985 a record low rainfall resulted in a very dry January. Ten months later 17 inches of snow fell and the lowest temperature on record was registered for that date: 10 degrees above zero. Two years later, the summer was hot and dry with only two inches of rain between June 1 and October 3. Surfaces of Seattle's lakes were measured at their lowest, watering of lawns was prohibited, and basic industries such as logging, fishing and agriculture were forced to curtail production.

The WPPSS Disaster

The Washington Public Power Supply System (WPPSS, pronounced WOOPS) delivered a financial shock in 1983 and generated headlines throughout the decade. Beginning in the 1930s, Washington state increasingly had relied on hydroelectric power, but in the 1980s demand was increasing rapidly. At the time, in parts of the world where waterpower was scarce, countries began constructing nuclear generating plants. WPPSS decided to build five such huge plants in the state. Several occurrences placed the effort in jeopardy. Similar plants on the East Coast and in the Soviet Union failed, endangering nearby populations. Then, WPPSS faced costs that

were soaring far over budget. Attempts to persuade utilities to pay for mothballing two of the plants were unsuccessful, forcing projects four and five to be abandoned. The matter went to court and the decision was that public utilities had signed construction contracts with WPPSS without proper authority to do so. After the state Supreme Court refused to alter the ruling, all nuclear plants but the one at Hanford were abandoned unfinished. Two decades later the Hanford plant also was shut down. The investors holding $2.25 billion in bonds sold to fund the nuclear plants found they held worthless paper.

Traffic Problems

When 1900 had arrived, Seattle residents were fascinated by the town's first automobile, a thin-tired electric that the owner sometimes drove on the sidewalk to avoid muddy streets. In 1914, for the first time in U.S. history, more autos than horse-drawn vehicles were sold. Three quarters of a century later, Seattle had the dubious distinction of being listed by the U.S. Department of Transportation as the city with the sixth-worst traffic congestion in the country. Part of the problem was the

The highways in the Seattle area have been vastly improved in the last two decades and still the traffic backs up at busy times. This 1992 scene shows the construction of the interchange of I-405 and Highway 520 in Bellevue. ©1992 photo by George White Location Photography

were criticized by some and lauded by others, while some argue up to 90 percent of the transportation budget should be used to construct more highways rather than to fund transportation alternatives. But as the area population continues to increase and the number of autos per family also increases, the problem worsens. Every working day, thousands of impatient motorists find themselves stalled in traffic jams.

Miscellany From the 80s

In 1983, homeowners were astounded to learn the average cost of a new 1,600-square-foot home in metropolitan Seattle had soared to a new high of $90,000. The next year, with sunlight seldom reaching some downtown Seattle streets, a city land use code was revised to limit the height and bulk of downtown commercial buildings, a move contested by many developers.

The Environmental Protection Agency in 1984 increased efforts to find the causes of pollution in the area. Governor John Spellman established a State-Federal Puget Sound pollution office. At the time a local man, William Ruckelshaus, was head of the Environmental Protection Agency and provided $1.6 million in federal moneys to pay for scientific efforts to find the causes of pollution and methods of overcoming it. A new environmental group called the Puget Sound Alliance came into existence. As the causes of the pollution were identified, among them untreated sewage, mill and manufacturing wastes, and garbage from ships and boats, attempts to clean Puget Sound waters began to succeed and the effort continues to this day.

During the mid-1980s, Seattle and Everett vied for the site of a new Naval base on Puget Sound. After several months of inspections, planning and estimating costs, Everett was selected to be homeport for the Navy fleet of 15 vessels. Two years later, construction began on the large facility, and several hundred Navy men and their families arrived to reside in Snohomish and King counties.

The advent of professional sports teams in the Seattle area did not reduce attendance at University of Washington football games as had been feared. In fact, Husky Stadium was often jammed full of fans, so in February 1987 a $12.7 million steel addition that would seat 20,000 was under construction on the north side of the field. The architects of the new seating matched it to the structure built years earlier on the south side. As the top section of the cantilevered addition was being completed, a few stabilizing guy wires were removed prematurely and the structure folded down like a bellows. Luckily, no employees

water and hills that surrounded the city, making highway construction difficult.

Another cause of traffic increase was urban sprawl that resulted in longer commutes to jobs and shopping centers. Klahanie development on the Sammamish Plateau east of Seattle is one of scores of such additions.

Until mid-century most jobs had been in the city, and traffic jams developed as more and more workers drove between their suburban homes and places of employment. Funding was poured into building highways to take care of the problem, but then in the 80s and 90s the suburbs began developing their own modern businesses that attracted employees from the city, causing even more severe rush hour congestion.

For years, engineers, committees and individuals have attempted to find solutions. Promoters of rapid transit, monorail service, improved metro bus routes, and additional Lake Washington bridges have been active. Residents voted to approve funding for several of these improvements only to have statewide initiatives approved that contradicted the plans. For example, car pool lanes

A lot of traffic crosses the enlarged Mercer Island bridge on Interstate 90 every weekday.

were killed or injured in the collapse. With the football season less than six months in the future, the contractors hurriedly removed the twisted steel and again commenced to put the heavy metal puzzle together. With considerable effort, they succeeded in having the new stadium completed for the first game in the early fall.

Seattle law enforcement agencies faced a new problem in 1986 — the sale of drugs by what was believed to be gang members who had moved north from Los Angeles. In 1987 and 1988 an increase in related violence, such as street shootings added concerns that a few Seattle youth were becoming involved with these gangs. The city police and citizens in affected neighborhoods mounted a successful effort to reduce gang activities.

King County citizens in 1988 voted more than two to one in favor of reinstituting the interurban rail system similar to the one that 50 years earlier had connected Seattle with Tacoma and Everett and all towns between. The plan was to have the service in operation no later than the year 2000, but at this writing the system is just beginning to serve as an alternative to personal automobiles.

During the 1980s decade, AIDS was recognized as a major health threat in Seattle. The state's first AIDS case was diagnosed in 1982 and over the next eight years more than 1,600 cases of AIDS had been reported. During that time the medical community increased efforts to educate citizens about the danger, explained how to avoid the disease, and predicted the epidemic would worsen in the future unless successful treatments were discovered.

Other medical notes: the University of Washington Medical Center performed 55 heart-transplant operations during the first five years of the program. Also, Seattle was recognized as a national model for employers wanting to ban smoking in the workplace.

1990s

As each new decade dawned, Mother Nature seemed intent on letting Seattle residents know who was in charge. In January 1990, she turned temperatures up and flooded the valleys of Puget Sound, then in February she buried Seattle beneath a heavy blanket of snow. At year's end she repeated her efforts with floods in November and a crippling snowstorm during the Christmas shopping season.

A wind and rainstorm on November 25, 1990, combined with human error, resulted in the sinking of some pontoons on the old portion of the Mercer Island Floating Bridge. Fortunately the bridge was being rebuilt and the new portion had been completed and could carry two-way traffic while the old half was rebuilt.

Then on May 2, 1996, a 5.3 magnitude earthquake, the most powerful in decades, shook the Seattle area. Fortunately, it lasted only 30 seconds and damage was minor, but it prompted a hurried evacuation of the Kingdome where a Mariners game was in progress. And for emphasis, on the day after Christmas, a paralyzing snowstorm bedeviled Seattle and environs.

Service personnel from Fort Lewis, McChord Air Force Base and the Whidbey Island Naval Air Base were dispatched to the Middle East after the Iraqi 1990 invasion of Kuwait. A total of 12,000 Washington servicemen and women were separated from their dependents during the war effort.

Nobel Prizes in Medicine Awarded to Seattle Doctors

Medical doctors in Seattle were awarded Nobel Prizes in medicine during the early 90s. Dr. E. Donall Thomas of the Fred Hutchison Cancer Research Center received the prize in 1990 and donated half of his $700,000 award to the research center in honor of his colleagues. Two years later two University of Washington professors, Edmond Fisher and Edwin Krebs, received the prize for their work on living cells, an effort that held the promise of finding ways to prevent diseases.

Sports in the 90s

The 1990 Goodwill Games in Seattle were declared a flop after sponsor Ted Turner faced multimillion-dollar losses. The expected sports fans did not appear, leaving not only the Kingdome but also local hotels and restaurants emptier than expected.

In 1994 tiles fell from the Kingdome ceiling, giving avid sports fans reason to clamor for a new stadium. As ceiling repairs were made both the Mariners and the Seahawks were displaced, delaying some games and forcing others to be played away from home. To add to the bad luck story, two workers using a high crane to work on the ceiling were killed when part of the equipment collapsed after brushing the ceiling.

The next year, as if to prove they deserved a new stadium, the Seattle Mariners captured the championship of American League West, and in the first round of the Championship Series defeated the New York Yankees, leaving a single team between them and the World Series. However, the Cleveland team refused to lose that series of games and advanced to the 1995 World Series.

Plans for a new Mariners stadium became more complicated in 1996 when the Metropolitan King County Council and team owners received bad news. A new roof design and other factors increased projected stadium costs by a stunning $45 million, inflating the total cost to $365 million.

The Supersonics won basketball's Western Conference Title in 1996 by defeating the Utah Jazz in seven games. But the Chicago Bulls bested the Seattle team for the NBA Championship even though Seattle did manage two home floor wins in the series.

Emerald Downs, the new racetrack near Auburn, opened its gates in 1996, four years after the closure of Longacres. Once again thoroughbred racing attracted Seattle area crowds.

The Local Economy
Seesaw Continues

By 1992, the U.S. economy was obviously making progress in overcoming years of recession caused in part by the earlier high interest rates and a depreciating dollar. Washington state's unemployment problem worsened in 1992-93 to where 7.2 percent of the work force was jobless, a 10th of a point higher than the national average. This influenced some Seattle voters during the presidential election, resulting in the majority supporting Bill Clinton rather than incumbent George Bush. President-elect Clinton promptly convened more than 300 business, labor and academic leaders to discuss U.S. economic problems and possible solutions. Seattle residents could follow the two-day program on CNN television.

The recession resulted in the demise of two local retail companies. Pay 'n Pak, the longtime building material specialists, and Frederick and Nelson, one of the city's most historic department stores, were forced to close down all their outlets. The state economy continued to sputter and unemployment climbed to more than 200,000.

The Boeing Company made headlines in 1990 with the introduction of its new 777 airliner. Two years later, after years of growth, the company suffered lagging sales as a result of the worldwide recession. The consensus of Wall Street brokers was that airlines would soon be buying many new planes in order to compete with the new and burgeoning low-cost carriers.

As the brokers predicted, by mid-decade Boeing was busy producing jets and had acquired orders for 625 of its various aircraft. In November 1996 it announced a $660 million contract for development of a new Joint Strike Fighter plane and two months later decided to merge with McDonnell Douglas, an acquisition that involved an exchange of millions in stock. Also during the year, Frank Schrontz retired as Boeing chairman and was replaced by Phil Condit.

In 1995 thousands of Boeing machinists in Washington, Oregon and Kansas went on strike. The walkout lasted 69 days before a contract agreement was finally signed in December.

The Federal Trade Commission approved the 1997 Boeing Company purchase of McDonell Douglas, making it the world's largest aerospace company. Two months later Boeing reported parts shortages and production problems that cost the company $1.6 billion, resulting in the company's first losing quarter in five years. By the year 2000, Boeing was again profitable and its shares were hitting new highs.

Technical improvements in health care resulted in ways to release hospital patients earlier and to improve care for various health problems. Health providers were urged to emphasize prevention and outpatient care to reduce medical costs. The results began to reduce incomes for health providers, resulting in consolidations and, in some cases, closing patient enrollments in health insurance plans.

High-Tech Gains Importance
in Washington State

The economic sluggishness of the previous few years was rectified in part by multimedia and high-tech developments of companies in Seattle and suburbs. Experimentation was under way in dozens of start-up companies to develop new uses for the data highway. Multimedia software was being produced that would combine words, pictures and sound. The market for such services, some experts promised, could provide almost unlimited employment opportunities.

Microsoft on August 24, 1995, released the new software program Windows 95 and it immediately became a bestseller the world around.

A newer Seattle-area billionaire, Craig McCaw, in 1994 sold his Kirkland-based McCaw Cellular Communications to AT & T Corporation for $11.48 billion. That same year he invested about $2.1 billion in Nextel Communications and in September of 2000, his Nextel stock was valued at more than $5 billion. Thus Craig McCaw joins Seattle billionaires such as Bill Gates and Paul Allen on the list of wealthiest Americans who reside in the Seattle area.

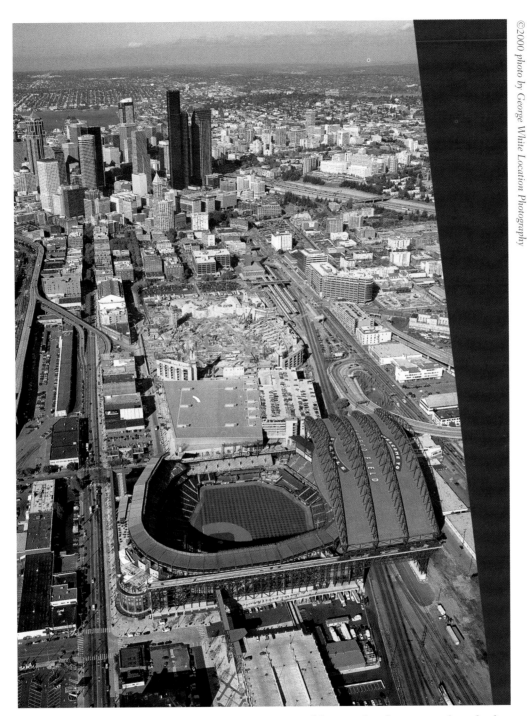

The new Seattle Mariners' SAFECO Field is in the foreground with the football-soccer stadium under construction to the north and beyond it the low-rise Pioneer Square area and the skyscrapers of downtown Seattle.

©2000 photo by George White Location Photography

Seattle at the turn of the millennium was judged one of the most livable cities in the country.

Politics Make Headlines

In 1994 the Republican Party surged to control of both houses of the U.S. Congress for the first time in four decades. Popular Tom Foley of Spokane, the speaker of the House of Representatives, was defeated in a bid for his 16th consecutive term by George Nethercutt, who promoted term limits and promised to serve no more than three terms. However, in 2000 he ran for a fourth term. In 1995 the state Republicans captured both the House and Senate in Olympia and proceeded to mimic the National Party by developing a "Contract for Washington State." They tossed out the recently passed landmark state health care law, cut taxes, and became critical of many state regulatory bodies.

In 1996, Seattle's Gary Locke was elected governor of Washington state, the nation's first governor of Chinese-American heritage.

In 1999 an Algerian named Ahmad Ressam traveled by ferry from Victoria to Port Angeles where customs agents discovered he appeared to be trying to smuggle bomb-making components into the United States. He also was found to possess a reservation card for a hotel near the Seattle Center. Since terrorist groups were active at various locations in the world, Mayor Paul Schell canceled the gala millennium New Year's Eve celebration scheduled at the Seattle Center. "It is safer to be prudent," he said.

Education

Two of Seattle's leading educators retired in 1995, William Kendrick as superintendent of Seattle Public Schools, and William Gerberding, president of the University of Washington. Kendrick founded his own consulting business to help school districts with strategic planning, restructuring and other issues he had dealt with while in Seattle. Gerberding was appointed to a group that oversaw the building of the new baseball stadium. He later helped raise funds for the Seattle Symphony and Opera, and taught University of Washington classes. In 1995, John Stanford, a former Army major general, was named Seattle's first black superintendent of schools. Charismatic and active, he proposed several changes to improve the system. He explained, "I'm not a politician and I'm not a survivalist. I don't care if I get fired or not. I'm here for the children." Progress was obvious in 1998 when he announced that doctors had found he was suffering from leukemia. In spite of receiving the latest methods of treatment, popular John Stanford died in November 1998 at age 60.

The Boom Continues as the Millennium Ends

Seattle business continued to boom and its population increased throughout the last years of the century. Heavy demand for homes and business space in Seattle constantly forced real estate prices upward. Homeowners opened their 1996 property tax billings to discover the value of their homes had increased in double figures again. The median price of homes in the area was approximately $175,000 and in some parts of the city averaged more than a quarter million dollars. King County's unemployment numbers in 1997 retreated to a 20-year low with fewer than four workers in 100 without jobs, a figure about 2 percent lower than the state average.

With good times rolling, arts and sports flourished. In 1996 the Leo Kreielsheimer Theater, named for the man whose estate was a major donor, opened at the Seattle Repertory. The next year the Frye Art Museum completed a $12 million remodel and King County voters at a special election approved taxes to help fund a new Seahawks football stadium. Multibillionaire Paul Allen, owner of the team, paid millions to advertise and pay for the election.

Seattle entered the new millennium as one of the world's most livable cities and with a population working to control growth in ways that will retain that accolade for future generations.

Historical Chaff from the Era

Seattle, the Most Livable of Cities

In 1990 the Population Crisis Committee proclaimed Seattle the most livable city in the world. Many citizens, including Mayor Norm Rice, declared themselves underwhelmed at the news, fearing such laudatory comments would attract more human beings to the area at a time when rapid population increases were eroding that lauded livability factor. During the mid-90s, several magazines ranked Seattle highly. *Newsweek* noted the city's young technology millionaires, the tasty coffee, and the easygoing lifestyle. *Money Magazine* complained that all the recent laudatory articles about Seattle were becoming tiresome and ranked the city in 9th place, whereas seven years earlier it had ranked it as the nation's No.1 metropolitan area. *Fortune* reported Seattle was the best city in which to balance work and family, and *Places Rating Almanac* concluded that the Seattle area ranked second in livability behind Southern California.

Seattle Today
Celebrating 150 Years

All photos in this essay by Gary Quinn*PhotoMagic unless otherwise noted

A part of the 1962 World's Fair, the Pacific Science Center has been refurbished and includes a new IMAX theater capable of 3-D projection.

PACIFIC SCIENCE CENTER

PUBLIC ENTRANCE

The Pacific Science Center is located at the southwest corner of the Seattle Center.

Seattle's skyscrapers watch over a modern seaport city.

Seattle Convention and Visitors' Bureau

The Cascade Mountains form the eastern backdrop for large automobile and passenger ferries.

Seattle Convention and Visitors' Bureau

The latest construction trend in Seattle is to give everyone a view of Puget Sound, and many condos have sprung up in Belltown.

The Seattle Symphony and Music Director and Conductor Gerard Schwartz are nationally recognized and have several outstanding classic recordings to their credit. Benaroya Hall's superb acoustics showcase the orchestra and guest artists.

Seattle Symphony, Photo by Fred Housel

The waterfront has many attractions, including fine eateries, boat tours, gift shops and this streetcar.

One of the newest additions to Seattle is SAFECO Field, home of the Mariners baseball team.

The King Street Station clock tower marks time for travelers on the rail.

The Hiram Chittenden Locks, one of the busiest in the world, raise and lower watercraft from the level of Lake Washington to Puget Sound.

Seattle Convention and Visitors' Bureau

The Port of Seattle is a major contributor to the economy of the region. It includes the Seattle-Tacoma Airport, a large containerized cargo-loading facility, marinas, and facilities for the North Pacific fishing fleet and passenger liners.

Port of Seattle, Photo by Don Wilson

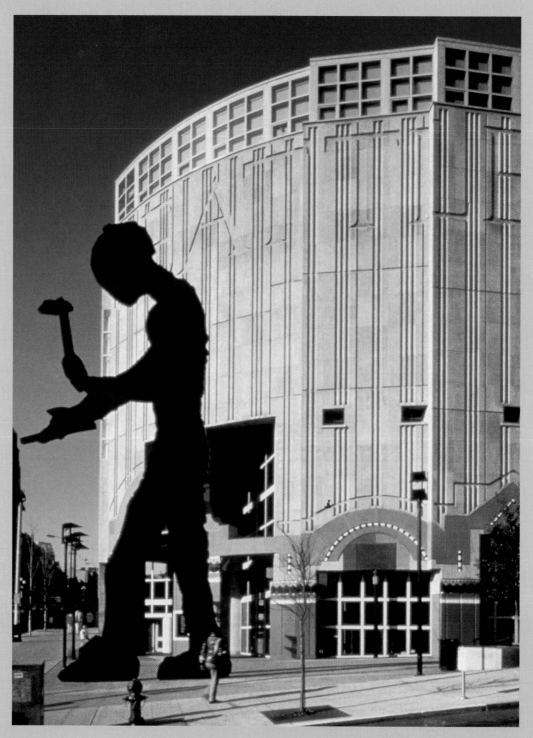

In 1991 the Seattle Art Museum, designed by architect Robert Venturi, opened to approving reviews. The large moving metal sculpture in the foreground is silhouetted against the museum building.

Seattle Art Museum, Photo by Susan Dirk

Seattle residents have retained some of the flavor of the past by preserving Pioneer Square where the city took root. Today, residents and visitors enjoy restaurants, galleries and lively clubs in the historic district.

Seattle Convention and Visitors' Bureau

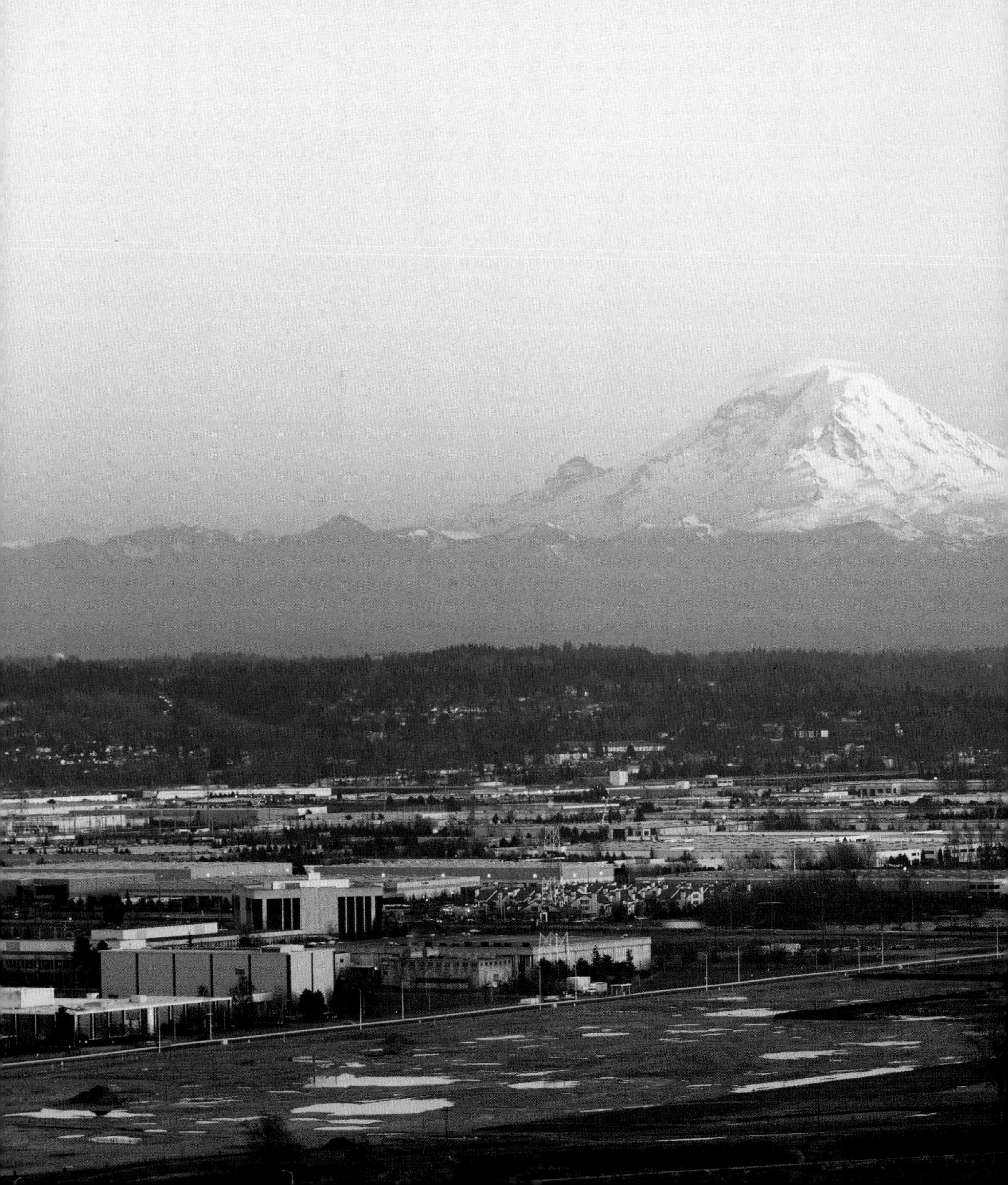

A winter sunset paints a heavily snowcapped Mount Rainier.

Court in the Square, across the street from the train station, provides a glimpse of how the structures in Pioneer Square looked when they were young.

The Smith Tower has been rejuvenated to its original polished marble and brass stature. The China Room deck still provides an inspiring view of Puget Sound.

Seattle offers yachting enthusiasts a multitude of opportunities to cruise on freshwater lakes, rivers, saltwater bays, and Puget Sound. Quiet coves abound where boaters can find solitude.

Seattle Convention and Visitors' Bureau

Seattle's dynamic waterfront provides interesting views and unique dining and shopping opportunities on the historic former ocean piers.

Seattle Convention and Visitors' Bureau

Another historic site is Pike Place Market where cobblestone streets lead to one of the country's last remaining working farmers' markets.

Seattle Convention and Visitors' Bureau

Pike Place Market offers fresh seafood and produce in addition to a grand array of arts and crafts.

Seattle Convention and Visitors' Bureau

Benaroya Hall, home of the Seattle Symphony, is a modern facility and a great place to hear the classics.

Lake Washington Ship Canal and Hiram M. Chittenden Locks connect saltwater Puget Sound to the freshwater bodies of Salmon Bay, Lake Union and Lake Washington.

The meticulously sculptured likeness of Noah Sealth, chief of the Duwamish and Suquamish people, with hand raised, welcomes visitors to Seattle, the city named after him.

Early springtime color is a welcome sight in the city.

Greenlake is one of the most popular spots for recreation, exercise and people-watching.

The Aurora Bridge, high above the west end of Lake Union, carries motorists to and from the city.

The University of Washington, one of the country's leading educational institutions, is known for its progressive medical school and a strong football program.

Springtime blossoms change the winter landscape.

Western passage to the sea from inland freshwater via the locks near Ballard

The Suzzalo Library on the University of Washington campus is characteristic of much of the architecture found there.

An aerial view of Seattle's waterfront situated on Elliot Bay

A spectacular view from the Bell Street Pier

New waterfront homeowners share the daily change of scenery in the Great Northwest.

The Smith Tower (in white) and what was originally the Columbia Tower (in black) share one commonality. They were both the tallest structures west of the Mississippi when they were built.

Partners Table of Contents
Partners in Seattle

Arts, Culture & Entertainment

Cruise West 254
Experience Music Project 258
Argosy Cruises 260
Cinerama Theatre 261
Corporate Council for the Arts/
   Arts Fund 262
On the Boards 263
Seattle Children's Theatre 263
Seattle Opera 263
Seattle Symphony 263
Museum of History & Industry 264
Nordic Heritage Museum 265
Pacific Northwest Ballet 266
Pacific Science Center 267
The Seattle Aquarium 268
Seattle Men's Chorus 269
Seattle Repertory Theatre 270
The 5th Avenue Theatre 271

Building a Greater Seattle

R.D. Merrill Company 274
Wright Runstad & Company 280
Conner Homes Co. 285
Clise Properties, Inc. 286
Turner Construction Company 290
Tarragon Development Company. . . 294

BRE Properties, Inc. 296
Kiewit Construction Company 298
Master Builders Association of
   King and Snohomish Counties . . . 300
Nitze-Stagen & Co., Inc. 302
Seattle-King County Association
   of REALTORS. 304
South of Downtown Development. . 306
Unico Properties, Inc. 308
Northwest Building LLC. 310

Business & Finance

Farmers New World Life
   Insurance Company. 314
SAFECO Corporation. 320
Guy Carpenter & Company. 324
HomeStreet Bank 326
Nowogroski Rupp
   Insurance Group. 328
Washington Mutual 330
Dain Rauscher 332

International Trade

Expeditors International of
   Washington, Inc. 336
Marine Resources Company
   International 340

Pacific Market International 342
Port of Seattle. 343

Manufacturing & Distribution

Isernio Sausage Company 346
Industrial Crating & Packing, Inc. . . 349
Division Five. 350
The Lucks Company. 352

Marketplace

Best Western Executive Inn 356
Budget Rent a Car 358
Elephant Car Wash. 360
Happy Guests International, Inc.. . . 362
Nordstrom, Inc. 364
Pike Place Market. 366
Pike Place Bar and Grill 366
Piroshky Piroshky 366
Studio Solstone Ltd. 367
Sur La Table. 367
Three Girls Bakery 367
Ballard Blossom 368
Bay Pavilion 369
Canlis Restaurant 370
Dunn Lumber Co. 371
Gary Quinn's PhotoMagic 372
Glant Pacific Companies. 373

Patron: Seed Intellectual Property Law Group PLLC

George White
Location Photography 374
Metropolis 375
Pike Place Fish 376
The Pink Door 377
Porcelain Gallery 378
Ray's Boathouse 379
Rock Bottom Brewery 380
Sorrento Hotel 381
Starbucks Coffee Company 382
Starwood Hotels 383
13 Coins 384
WorksiteMassage/
Optimal Performance, Inc. 385

Networks
Alaska Airlines 388
KING 5 390
KOMO 4 Television 392
Seattle City Light 394
Seattle Public Utilities 396
Sound Transit 398
The Seattle Times 400
United Airlines 402
710 KIRO 404
KCTS 405

Nonprofit Organizations
Children's Home Society
of Washington 408
Seattle's Union Gospel Mission 410
The Millionair Club Charity 412
The Seattle Foundation 414
World Vision 416
Center for Career Alternatives 418

Childhaven 419
Lifelong AIDS Alliance 420
March of Dimes 421
Senior Services of
Seattle-King County 422

Professional Services
Marsh & McLennan Companies . . . 426
McKinsey & Company 428
Bensussen Deutsch &
Associates, Inc. 430
Business Network International 431
MWW/Savitt 432
OfficeLease 433
Preston Gates & Ellis LLP 434
Shapiro and Associates, Inc. 435

Quality of Life
Children's Hospital &
Regional Medical Center 438
Economic Development Council . . . 440
Greater Seattle Chamber
of Commerce 442
Highline Community Hospital
Health Care Network 444
Planned Parenthood 446
Seattle Academy 448
Seattle Community
College District 450
Swedish Medical Center 452
Trendwest Resorts, Inc. 454
Bayview Manor 456
Corixa Corporation 457
Catholic Community Services and the
Archdiocesan Housing Authority . . 458

St. James Cathedral 459
Covenant Shores 460
Horton Lantz Marocco 461
Mount Zion Baptist Church 462
Northwest Center 463
Pilchuck Glass School 464
Plymouth Congregational
Church 465
Seattle University 466
The Art Institute of Seattle 467
University of Washington 468
University of Washington Academic
Medical Center 469
Washington Athletic Club 470

Sports & Recreation
Fox Sports Net 474
Full House Sports
& Entertainment 476
Seattle Seahawks 478
Seattle Mariners 480
Seattle Sounders 481

Technology
The Boeing Company 484
Fred Hutchinson Cancer
Research Center 486
Microsoft 488
UltraBac.com 490
InfoSpace, Inc. 492
LizardTech, Inc. 493
Nintendo of America Inc. 494
PWI Technologies 495
2WAY Corporation 496

Arts, Culture & Entertainment

Museums, cruise lines and the performing arts community provide
culture and entertainment for a vibrant Seattle.

CRUISE WEST

In 1951 a man came to Seattle with a story to share, a story of a land of wonders far to the north. The man was Chuck West and the land was Alaska. While Alaska and Seattle have had a long and historic link since the 1898 gold rush, Alaska remained remote, at least in perception, to most American travelers. Many misconceptions about the region persisted and most from the lower 48 states thought of Alaska only in terms of oil and ice. Chuck West knew different. This knowledge was to propel West through an adventure that would become much more than just a personal tale, to one of an industry unique as the land itself. Eventually, West's vision would found the first Alaskan hotel chain, the first motor-coach line as well as the first modern small-ship cruises, establishing him as the travel industry's "Mr. Alaska."

The story of Cruise West is itself infused with the frontier spirit. After returning from pilot duty in World War II, West became an Alaskan bush pilot, flying machinery, workers and supplies deep into the northern wilderness. There, he discovered a love for the land that shaped the course of his life. Alaska is well over twice the size of Texas, encapsulating varying climates from temperate rain forest to artic tundra. Its vast territory is host to a rich array of wildlife, majestic natural beauty and

a people who keep the pioneer spirit alive. Alaskans — like Seattleites — rarely called attention to their accomplishments during the early days. The early settlers of both regions were somewhat reclusive, inclined to wild territories and clear vistas. Even now Alaska is a land of wide-open spaces where it can be 250 miles to the nearest fast-food joint and just as far between porch lights. During the winter, the sky is woven with the graceful threads of the northern lights making a rich and rare tapestry of wonder. During the summer in Fairbanks, night comes only for a moment and people can be seen playing baseball at midnight while cabbages grow to science fiction proportions.

Despite all this, the idea of Alaskan tourism was initially met with skepticism as some of its towns are only accessible by sea or air. But the idea stuck with West and in 1946 he left his employer to launch the company that would become the progenitor of Alaskan tourism. The early days of the business (then called Arctic Alaska Tours) were a struggle but West was not to be deterred. Inspired but short on resources, some of his first ground tours were conducted in his personal car, a 1936 Plymouth sedan. His enthusiasm for the region was contagious and the business grew. However, a major obstacle to the company's

Chuck West first developed his enthusiasm for Alaska in 1945 as a bush pilot in the Arctic with Wien Air, a pioneer of Alaska aviation.

continued growth was communication. Overland mail was at the mercy of winter storms and long-distance telephone was both expensive and unreliable, so West looked southward to Seattle.

Near neighbors in the Northwest, the connection between Seattle and Alaska remained strong even after the gold rush days, as oil and industry stimulated trade between the ports. Seattle was also the embarkation point for ships and planes carrying the tourist trade north. In 1951 West opened his Seattle office on 2nd Avenue. Immediately it became apparent that the move was a good idea. Being 1,500 miles closer to the main U.S. tourist market streamlined communication with Seattle-based travel agents, ship companies and airlines. To establish himself, West also purchased two local travel agencies, Where-to-Go-Travel and University Travel Service, then moved his wife and family to the Magnolia Bluff in 1952. In Seattle, West found a people of a similar, if slightly more urban, frontier spirit.

The intervening years brought both great success and numerous name changes for West's initial company but the independent character behind it remained undimmed. After selling his then-named Westours to Holland America, West began to revive his original vision in a new company, Cruise West.

The family-owned business brought a new style of touring to the American market, that of small ships and up-close, casual, personal experiences. While Chuck West himself had been involved with maritime cruises for decades, Cruise West launched its first ship, the *Sheltered Seas*, in 1986. Still in service, the *Sheltered Seas* remains a popular venue, cruising the Inside Passage during the days and then disembarking its passengers in the evening to spend the nights in port. The fleet quickly expanded to include vessels with overnight accommodations while retaining its overall small ship character.

The first modern small-ship cruises to Alaska were developed by Chuck West in 1957 with two converted World War II-era British warships, the Castle-class corvettes *Glacier Queen* and *Yukon Star* (pictured).

On a Cruise West tour, the passengers are participants in the journey, not just spectators. This approach is in contrast to the 12-story ships used by the big-ship cruise lines. Such mammoth craft often dwarf the buildings of the ports they visit and contain visitors that may outnumber the town's population by as many as six to one. The largest Cruise West ship carries only 114 passengers, allowing the traveler to "get away" from the crowded hurly-burly of life rather than bringing it along. This community-conscious approach lets Cruise West passengers become easy friends on tour, while still allowing them to feel small when facing the grandeur of city-sized glacier flows.

The small size of the ships confers a further and perhaps even greater benefit. Most of Cruise West's smaller draft ships hug the coast, bringing passengers

The inauguration of the 90-foot motor yacht *Sheltered Seas* in 1986 was Cruise West's modern introduction to small-ship cruising.

Cruise West's style of up-close, casual, personal small-ship cruising allows a much more intimate involvement with icebergs, wildlife and waterfalls than is possible from a large cruise ship.

within mere yards of cathedral-like ice formations, grizzly bears foraging on the shoreline, and walls of blue-white ice calving off glaciers. The philosophy of travel on a Cruise West ship is to offer passengers meaningful encounters with their destinations, and the show is definitely outside. The vessels may not even adhere to a schedule determined in land-locked offices but may follow a serene pod of majestic humpback whales migrating from Mexico or stop

In 1991, Cruise West's *Spirit of Alaska* resumed offering the first Inside Passage cruises from Seattle since the Alaska Steamship Company ceased operation in the early 1950s.

to watch playful otters and tufted puffins. Visitors are often surprised at the abundance of wildlife. Moose, goats and wolves roam free over one of the nation's largest natural areas and overhead more bald eagles can be seen than anywhere else in the world. Small groups on small ships keep the pace leisurely and uncrowded. Passengers are not surrounded with Las Vegas-style shows or casino gambling. Instead, they socialize with the friendly crew, browse the ship's library and enrich their experience through on-board naturalist guides who offer background and anecdotes on the area's history, landscape and wildlife.

Cruise West vessels' size also gives them the maneuverability to gracefully access waterways that are too small for massive cruise ships. Passengers can cruise into the soaring fjords of Alaska to find glaciers that flow 5 miles wide and 40 miles long, famous fishing grounds, and quiet coves sheltered by towering cliffs. The agile craft also ply their way along some of the newer, southern routes offered on the Snake and Columbia rivers in Oregon and up San Francisco Bay to the verdant Napa wine country of California.

Though the ships may be small in comparison to the cruise-liners, they are hardly cramped. All cabins feature full facilities, most with view windows, and numerous lounges, walkways and deck space. In addition to the time spent on board, passengers may also enjoy frequent port excursions and a range of rail and motor-coach tours that extend the adventure ashore. In Metlakatla visitors can enjoy a native dance in a tribal longhouse, or in Sitka they may stop at St. Michael's Cathedral to view the dazzling collection of Russian Orthodox icons. Whether studying hand-carved tribal masks, exploring gold-rush towns or discussing history with a Ketchikan elder, each day deepens passengers' understanding and love of the land. Other tour options include inland adventures by helicopter, river raft or floatplane. Inland trips meander through places like the vast Denali National Park, home to the majestic Mt. McKinley and teeming with wildlife, or into the more cosmopolitan pleasures of the city of Anchorage.

These destination inroads are not limited to Alaska, however. A cruise into the Sonoma and Napa valleys of California ushers visitors into private winery tours and tastings while the Columbia and Snake River voyage features stops like

Lewis and Clark's Fort Clatsop and Multnomah Falls. The up-close adventures extend even farther with the popular Sea of Cortez sojourn in Baja, Mexico.

In 2001 Cruise West launched the flagship of its fleet, the *Spirit of Oceanus*. The oceangoing vessel's ice-strengthened hull and stabilizers allow it to cruise across new deep-water horizons and in even greater comfort. Its 12 top-deck suites each have a private teak balcony. All suites offer such amenities as in-room safes and satellite communications access. Though the vessel boasts conveniences like an elevator, hot tub and marble vanities, its intimate size of only 114 passengers makes this experience more reminiscent of cruising on an elegant private yacht than a package tour. The flagship's oceangoing capabilities have opened up many new vistas for Cruise West, as the company is now able to explore destinations in the Pacific Rim including Asia, Australia and the South Pacific. Passengers have responded enthusiastically and continue to swell the rosters of Seattle's tour industry, propelling Cruise West into the number one position for small-ship cruising.

The West family remains at the helm of Cruise West with founder Chuck West now chairman emeritus and son Dick West serving as both chairman and CEO. Under Dick's leadership, Cruise West's long-term plans will continue to steer the Seattle cruise industry forward into new markets.

In January of 2000, the Washington state House of Representatives honored Chuck West for his entrepreneurial nature and contributions to Washington state. Cruise West has grown to be an important Seattle employer and restored Seattle as a cruise gateway to Alaska for the first time since the 1950s. The House credits West and his company with bringing tens of thousands of guests to Seattle from all over the nation and the world. The line's cruises in the Puget Sound and San Juan Islands make Seattle itself a destination as well as an embarkation point.

Both the family and Cruise West also participate in the local community through sponsorship of local sports teams

During its first decade of small-ship cruise operation, Cruise West expanded from Alaska to British Columbia, the Columbia and Snake rivers, the California wine country and Baja Mexico's Sea of Cortez.

and academic scholarships. Cruise West also continues to help shape the face of Seattle business as its practices and ideals have garnered numerous awards from both local and national groups. These practices are based on West's adherence to what he calls "the Six Cs": concept, chance, competence, confidence, contacts and capital, though West is fond of adding a seventh "c" for courage.

Despite their accomplishments, Cruise West and its founder seem to measure success less in dollars than in service to their passengers and the continued growth of Seattle as an international tourist hub. Fifty years ago, Cruise West was just a dream and a story. Today, it is a million stories as each of its guests returns with a tale of their own.

In 2001, Cruise West will introduce its new flagship, the all-suite, 114-guest *Spirit of Oceanus*.

EXPERIENCE MUSIC PROJECT

Walking into Seattle's Experience Music Project (EMP) is a psychedelic journey through the history of rock 'n' roll. The museum, which opened June 23, 2000, is a tribute to American popular music, its origins, its most important figures, its changes and evolutions, its spirit and soul. EMP is like no museum seen before. Interactive, inventive, technologically state of the art, EMP is above all a comprehensive look at the phenomenon that is rock 'n' roll.

In 1991 Paul G. Allen, co-founder of Microsoft, now chairman of Vulcan Northwest, bought some Jimi Hendrix artifacts at an auction — a shard of mangled guitar, a felt hat. Allen felt that these pieces of history belonged in a museum. After some thought, he decided that he would build the museum. Hendrix was born and raised in Seattle; what better place to honor him and his contributions to rock 'n' roll? Allen's sister, Jody Patton, took over the project and is now its executive director. The museum soon expanded far beyond the initial idea. It would be difficult to talk about Hendrix, they felt, without talking about the wider implications of his work, those he influenced and

those who influenced him. Allen and Patton decided to build a museum that would trace the history of rock music from its earliest origins to the present and demonstrate the possibilities for its future. From this decision came EMP.

In 1995 Allen and Patton approached architect Frank O. Gehry. They wanted an architect whose building would capture the shapes, the colors and the attitude of rock music — its essential "swoopiness," as Allen termed it. Gehry was already well known for building the Guggenheim Museum in Spain and the University of Toledo Center for the Visual Arts, among others. Gehry's building incorporated the best of technology, popular culture, art and architecture. The multicolored, multi-shaped building is itself evocative of rock 'n' roll: the curves of a guitar, the rolling undulations of music. The colors were also rock-inspired. The blue is from a Fender Mustang guitar, the gold from a Les Paul guitar, the red is the red of a touring van, and the purple — of course — is tribute to Jimi Hendrix's "Purple Haze." The building required five separate layers: steel ribs covered by shotcrete under 2-inch insulation and 5-inch steel pipes. The entire

All "swoops" and curves, the Experience Music Project is reminiscent of a guitar and of the feel of music.

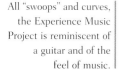

building was then covered by more than 4,000 pieces of metal "skin" which were chemically treated or painted to make the wild colors.

EMP is no less stimulating on the inside. Visitors enter the museum and walk directly into the Sky Church, a huge room full of music. A visual display on a massive screen reinterprets the music into light and shapes. Visitors are fitted with a MEG (Museum Exhibit Guide), a portable audio, video and image presentation system. MEG was designed completely in-house and is unique to EMP. By pointing the MEG at displays, visitors can listen to different narrations on their headphones. Visitors thus conduct "private" tours, setting their own pace and listening to those presentations that most interest them. There are four galleries in which visitors can use MEG: Northwest Passage, the Guitar Gallery, the Hendrix Gallery and Milestones.

With more than 4,000 pieces of colored "skin," the Experience Music Project is like no other building in the world.

The Northwest Passage Gallery traces the roots of rock music in the Pacific Northwest. Because of its location between mountains and ocean, Seattle was isolated from the rest of the country, and thus the music of Seattle is unique. With little information or influence from outside, Pacific Northwest musicians made their own sounds. From the rhythm and blues scene of the 50s, through Paul Revere and the Raiders and The Wailers in the 1960s, through garage rock and punk and heavy metal to the grunge phenomenon of the 1990s, Northwest Passage follows it all. On their MEGs visitors listen to snippets of songs such as The Ventures' "Walk — Don't Run" which became the theme for the television show "Hawaii Five-O." Visitors also hear interviews with band members while they look at displays of albums, costumes, instruments, even lyrics scribbled on envelopes.

The Hendrix Gallery follows the course of Jimi Hendrix's career from his early days as an R & B guitarist on the "chitlin' circuit," through his meteoric career in England and at home, to his death in 1970. Arguably the most important music figure to emerge from Seattle, Hendrix is a cultural icon for all lovers of rock 'n' roll. The gallery contains some of Hendrix's costumes, his prized white Fender Stratocaster guitar, handwritten lyrics, videos of concerts, and interviews with friends and colleagues.

The Milestones Gallery looks at some of rock's most popular figures and movements. Exhibits feature Elvis, Chuck Berry, Eric Clapton, Janis Joplin and Bob Dylan, among others; some of the movements included are R & B, punk, hip-hop and skate rock. Exhibits explain where artists came from and how movements got started: all designed to show the history of rock music and demonstrate the creative process, how music genres changed and expanded and how music has affected the rest of the world.

EMP is a totally unique experience. Interactive to a degree that no other museum can claim, its visitors can immerse themselves in a rock 'n' roll world. Lectures and concerts are conducted in the JBL Theater. The Guitar Gallery is a trip through the evolution of the guitar. On stage in the "You're a Star!" exhibit, people get a taste of what it is like to be a rock musician in concert. At the Sound Lab, visitors play instruments, while the Artist's Journey is a funky, fun-fair ride into some aspects of rock 'n' roll history and the influence of particular genres such as funk.

Equal parts education and entertainment, EMP was established not only to teach visitors the history of rock music, but also to inspire the next Jimi Hendrix or Janis Joplin. It is a commentary on the impact and importance of music and popular culture in society. And, like rock itself, the museum will continue to change and evolve as new artists and new aspects of the genre appear on the scene.

ARGOSY CRUISES

Embraced by the Puget Sound, Seattle has long viewed the water as both a source of great beauty and a means of transportation. From the shining waters of the lakes and sound to the proud mountains ringing the area, Argosy Cruises showcases a region that is rich in natural splendor. In 1949 Capt. Lynn Campbell founded the Spring Street Water Taxi Company to provide ferry service to the Kitsap Peninsula. Within a short time, the fleet grew and began to include tours of the historic Seattle waterfront. Following this, the business was renamed Seattle Harbor Tours.

The small fleet grew with the city and soon provided a variety of vessels as diverse as their destinations. To reflect its continued growth from a single ferryboat to a fleet of ships, the company was renamed Argosy Cruises in 1994. The new title was inspired by the Greek legend of the adventurer Jason and his mighty ship, the *Argo,* to reflect the variety of cruises and vessels it offers.

The Spirit of Seattle is used throughout the year for public cruises, weddings and corporate events and is the official Christmas Ship™ in December.

The Royal Argosy, launched in May 2000, is a fine-dining lunch and dinner ship unlike any other in the United States.

Argosy has 13 vessels located on the Seattle waterfront, Lake Union and Lake Washington.

Nothing illustrates Seattle's historic partnership with the water like touring it from out on the waves. Since the fleet's founding, Argosy's narrated cruises have carried over 2 million visitors from Seattle's waterfront to experience unparalleled views of the historic houseboat district, Mount Rainier, the Space Needle and the luxurious homes lining Lake Washington. A special favorite is the cruise through the Hiram Chittenden Locks. This trip takes visitors between the majestic salt waters of the Puget Sound and the freshwater sights of Lake Washington. The journey is not only scenic but also educational, as Argosy guides explain the workings of the famous locks that are the key to the city's waterways. Argosy also extends its on-the-water learning environment to local students through an educational outreach program.

In 2000 Argosy launched what has become perhaps the pearl of its fleet: *The Royal Argosy.* In partnership with the owners of such nationally recognized restaurants as the Metropolitan Grill and Elliot's Oyster House, Argosy has added *The Royal Argosy* to the list of the city's best eateries. The ship boasts three professional galleys, four distinctively elegant dining areas and business facilities alongside a carefully crafted regional menu. The freshly prepared entrees feature the highlights of Northwest cuisine like char grilled chinook salmon and Portobello napoleon. This dedication to hospitality makes the Argosy fleet a popular attraction for the area's visitors but also a tradition among residents, too.

Every Christmas, Argosy also produces the much anticipated Christmas Ship™ Festival. The ship-to-shore festival visits numerous locations throughout the area for evenings of bonfires, live music and caroling. The Argosy vessels are joined by other ships from around the area, forming the world's largest holiday flotilla. Proceeds from the festival are donated to the Seattle Times Fund for the Needy, helping to brighten the holidays for hundreds of thousands of Puget Sound families.

Over the past half-century, Argosy Cruises has grown into a lasting Seattle tradition marking the region's intimate bond with the water. Argosy proves that the best way to truly experience Seattle is from the water.

CINERAMA THEATRE

When inventor Fred Waller showed the first Cinerama film at the 1939 World's Fair, his experimental motion picture fascinated crowds. Waller used 11 separate projectors and a dome-shaped screen to surround the audience, creating a 3-D effect. After the war, Waller simplified the process to use only three cameras, and included a spectacular stereophonic sound system. Audiences were immersed in a total theatrical experience and they loved it. Unfortunately, Cinerama films were expensive to produce, and by the 1970s most movie houses capable of showing Cinerama films were closing or converting to less costly 35mm films. In the entire world, only one Cinerama theatre remains.

In 1997 Paul G. Allen, co-founder of Microsoft and chairman of Vulcan Northwest, was visiting his local video store when he noticed a petition taped to the counter. Seattle's Martin Cinerama was due to be torn down and a grassroots campaign had been started to save this piece of local and cinematic history. Opened in 1963 with the regional premiere of *The Wonderful World of the Brothers Grimm*, the theatre had had only a brief time of glory. The last Cinerama-style film was shown in 1969; by the 1980s, multiplex theatres were pulling movie fans out of the city and away from Martin Cinerama. The theatre was reduced to showing second-run films just to survive, but that didn't last long. Soon the theatre was falling into disrepair. Allen, who had visited the theatre as a child, stepped in and bought the Cinerama in 1998, saving the only remaining movie house capable of showing the special three-strip films. A multimillion-dollar restoration brought the Cinerama back to its former glory, and the theatre reopened in April 1999.

The Cinerama has been decorated to evoke a 1960s feel. Bold colors, scattered glass tiles on the walls, wallpaper inspired by a 1963 wallpaper sample book, wild carpeting and red mohair seats all recall the heyday of the Cinerama. Even the popcorn and drink containers are designed in the retro-futuristic style. A step into the Cinerama is a step back in time.

Today the Cinerama primarily plays first-run, 35- and 70-mm films on a standard screen set in front of the special Cinerama screen. Cinerama movies are shown only on special occasions such as the Seattle International Film Festival. But any trip to the Cinerama is a treat. Though the theatre may have been designed to recall an earlier age, many of the facilities are state of the art. The sound system consists of 56,000 watts of power delivered to 65 speakers. The theatre was designed by an acoustical engineer to have the same sound quality as a symphony hall. Although the theatre only has one screen, more than 800 people can watch a film at one time. Rear-window captioning, listening devices for the hearing impaired, narration for the blind, and buildingwide wheelchair accessibility mean that everyone can enjoy films at the Cinerama. Thanks to Paul Allen and his team, the unique experience of Cinerama films was saved — along with the last movie house of its kind.

Funky 1960s décor gives the Cinerama a "retro-futuristic" feel.

CORPORATE COUNCIL FOR THE ARTS/ARTSFUND

Seattle's transformation from a sleepy port town to one of the most desirable addresses in the country is inextricably linked to the development of its cultural life.

By the 1930s, Seattle could boast a symphony and an art museum. But it was not until Seattle's 1962 World's Fair that the arts began a breathtaking growth. The fair lifted a window shade to the world and sparked a passion leading to investments of $1 billion in cultural facilities by the close of the century in a growth that paralleled and supported the region's development as an international crossroads.

(Top left)
Pacific Northwest Ballet:
Olivier Wevers,
Christophe Maraval,
Timothy Lynch and Ross
Yearsley in *Ginastera*
Pacific Northwest Ballet
Photo by Angela Sterling

(Top right)
Seattle International
Children's Festival,
Tammako-za Taiko
Drummer
SICF

(Bottom left)
Seattle Art Museum:
"Puget Sound on the
Pacific Coast"
Albert Bierstadt,
oil on canvas,
Seattle Art Museum
Photo by Paul Macapiaz

(Bottom right)
Seattle Repertory
Theatre: Maggie Lacey
and Dan Donohue in
Game of Love and Chance
Seattle Repertory Theatre
Photo by Chris Bennion

Responding to the proliferation of arts groups following the fair, business and civic leaders in 1969 created a much-needed umbrella fund to allow corporations and individuals to channel cultural donations. This organization became Corporate Council for the Arts/ArtsFund, which has raised more than $50 million for operating fund grants to scores of nonprofit arts organizations in King and Pierce counties.

Strong leadership has driven CCA/ArtsFund's success. Companies like Boeing, SAFECO, Weyerhaeuser and Microsoft have provided the cornerstone of funding and effective leadership on CCA/ArtsFund's 60-member board of trustees. Peter Donnelly, who for two decades headed the Seattle Repertory Theatre, in 1989 returned from a three-year stint in Dallas to become CCA/ArtsFund president. Since then, annual fund-raising has more than doubled and the agency has launched several significant initiatives.

Perhaps most important among them is CCA/ArtsFund's highly regarded annual allocations process. In it, corporate grant makers and private philanthropists commit many days to reviewing applications and interviewing leadership from some 75 arts groups. The process is regarded as thorough and fair by both funders and beneficiaries and encourages management excellence of arts organizations.

CCA/ArtsFund is actively expanding its base of support beyond the core of corporate contributions. More than 1,000 individuals contribute directly or through ArtsFund workplace giving programs offered by dozens of companies and public sector agencies.

The strength and flexibility of the allocations system has attracted endowments and innovative entrepreneurial assets. CCA's ArtsFund Foundation now houses seven endowments with targeted uses. In recent years, the agency received as a gift from the pioneer Bullitt family one-third ownership of Classical KING-FM 98.1 (Seattle Opera and Seattle Symphony each received one-third). As a gift from the Kreielsheimer Foundation, CCA/ArtsFund also received ownership of the four-story Century Building. Each of these assets provides significant grant revenues.

CCA/ArtsFund's central position with business and arts has made it an effective advocate on important arts issues. In 1991, with support from The Boeing Company, the agency founded Building for the Arts, which provides a formal system through which arts capital projects from throughout Washington secure up to 20 percent of project costs from the state. Now written into statute, the program has provided more than $32 million to some 70 projects from Neah Bay to Spokane.

A strong and accessible cultural life with a wealth of performances, exhibits and arts education programs makes the Puget Sound region attractive for businesses, their employees and their families while making a strong positive impact on the region's economy. With its growing base of support and entrepreneurial spirit, CCA/ArtsFund will help Seattle's cultural life to keep pace with the growth and stature of the region.

ON THE BOARDS, SEATTLE CHILDREN'S THEATRE, SEATTLE OPERA & SEATTLE SYMPHONY

On the Boards/Behnke Center for Contemporary Performance

"...pushing the definition of performance theater and dance to its furthest boundaries."

— *The Seattle Times*

Located in Seattle's historic Queen Anne Hall, On the Boards was founded in 1978 by performing artists who wished to establish a home in which to create and present new works in dance, theater, music and multimedia.

OtB is unique in its dual mission of introducing Northwest audiences to the best in international contemporary performance and fostering Northwest artists in their journey towards international distinction. Today both international artists and arts organizations recognize On the Boards as the major contemporary performance center in the Northwest.

Seattle Children's Theatre

Imaginative, inspiring and educational, Seattle Children's Theatre productions and programs empower

young people to make discoveries about themselves and the world around them while building a lifelong interest in the arts. With an emphasis on developing new scripts, SCT produces professional theatre for the young, with appeal to people of all ages, and provides theatre arts education taught by professional artists. SCT is the second-largest resident theatre for families in the nation, performing in the Charlotte Martin and Eve Alvord Theatres at Seattle Center. It has served 3 million patrons since it opened in 1975 and provided over $7 million in free and subsidized tickets.

Seattle Opera

Founded in 1963, Seattle Opera is a top-flight opera company. Under General Director Speight Jenkins, Seattle Opera has fueled its reputation for producing theatrically compelling opera. Landmark achievements include productions of Floyd's *Of Mice and Men*, in its world premiere; Prokofiev's *War and Peace*; Debussy's *Pélleas et Mélisande* (designed by glass artist Dale Chihuly); and Wagner's *Tristan und Isolde*.

Seattle Opera is best known for its presentations of Wagner's *Ring*, which began in 1975 under founding General Director Glynn Ross and have continued since 1983 under Jenkins. Seattle Opera's *Ring* draws an international audience and has been acclaimed as the Northwest's premier cultural event.

Seattle Symphony

The Seattle Symphony is the oldest and largest cultural institution in the Pacific Northwest. With over 200 performances a season, more than 75 CD recordings and 18 seasons under Music Director Gerard Schwarz, the orchestra is noted for its advocacy of contemporary American music. Seattle Symphony presents programming for all ages and interests in Benaroya Hall, which opened downtown in 1998 and received the prestigious

American Institute of Architects 2001 Honor Award for outstanding architecture. A leader in symphonic music education, the symphony launched *Soundbridge* Seattle Symphony Music Discovery Center in Benaroya Hall to act as a hub for its many education and community programs.

(Far left)
On the Boards' Behnke Center for Contemporary Performance

(Below)
Seattle Opera's 1998 production of Richard Wagner's *Tristan und Isolde*
Photo by Gary Smith

(Far left)
Seattle Children's Theatre's production of *Cyrano*
Photo by Chris Bennion

(Below)
Maestro Schwarz conducts the Seattle Symphony in Benaroya Hall.
Photo by Dan Lamont

MUSEUM OF HISTORY & INDUSTRY

Since 1952, the Museum of History & Industry — known to generations of Puget Sound residents as MOHAI — has been the region's premier history center, bringing metropolitan Seattle's remarkable story to life for thousands of visitors and school children each year. With a priceless collection of rare objects and vintage photographs, MOHAI invites the community to discover, explore and celebrate its rich heritage through challenging exhibits, engaging programs and extensive educational activities.

A visit to MOHAI holds something special for children, parents and grandparents. Changing exhibits let visitors step back to the era of early America settlement and the days of Skid Road. It transports visitors through the devastation of the Great Seattle Fire and the excitement of the Gold Rush. MOHAI tells the story of Seattle's maritime heritage, the coming of the railroad and the rise of aviation. It charts the growth of major industries and tells stories of the men and women whose lives helped shape the Pacific Northwest. And during the Sesquicentennial era, MOHAI presents *Metropolis 150,* a retrospective look at the people, events and ideas that shaped the community since the first permanent American settlers arrived in 1851.

To make history come alive, MOHAI boasts the largest collection of historical materials in the Northwest — 100,000 machines, garments, toys, paintings, furniture, maritime artifacts, neon signs, household objects and many other tangible connections with Seattle's past, ranging from hatpins to hydroplanes. The museum's holdings also include a remarkable collection of more than 1 million photographs and a library with over 200,000 archival records including personal diaries, corporate papers, correspondence, maps, posters and more.

Throughout the year, MOHAI is transformed into a living classroom where students come face to face with the past and glimpse their own role in creating the future. MOHAI also offers the Seattle area's only teacher training in history. MOHAI moves beyond the museum's walls with off-site programs like the award-winning *Nearby History*, bringing the tools of history to libraries, community centers and senior housing.

MOHAI maintains strong partnerships with other historical organizations, serving as a home for the collections of the Puget Sound Maritime Historical Society and the Black Heritage Society of Washington State, a founding partner of the online History Link Web site, and an active collaborator with both the King County and Seattle library systems. Each year, MOHAI offers special forums for historical discussion, and it annually hosts the meetings of the Pacific Northwest Historians Guild and the Association of King County Historical Organizations.

As the community grows and changes, MOHAI, too, is expanding with a new regional history center at the crossroads of the Central Puget Sound, adjacent to the Washington State Convention and Trade Center in downtown Seattle — a unique place for students, residents and visitors to explore the diverse heritage of the region and its impact on the future. The past will have a bright future indeed at the new MOHAI in downtown Seattle.

"Fort Decatur, January 26, 1856" — This oil painting from MOHAI's collection, painted by pioneer Emily Inez Denny, depicts early Seattle settlers rushing to the block house during the Battle of Seattle. The U.S. sloop-of-war *Decatur* is anchored in Elliot Bay.

NORDIC HERITAGE MUSEUM

Almost 3 million Nordic immigrants came to America between 1840 and 1920. Land and resources in their countries had become scarce and crops were failing. The immigrants had hope for better opportunities in the New World and, indeed, became active in every aspect of American life. Their skills in fishing, farming and logging proved especially useful in the developing Pacific Northwest. And their contribution has not been lost. Seattle's Nordic Heritage Museum is filled with exhibits that pay tribute to these early immigrants from Denmark, Finland, Iceland, Norway and Sweden.

The Scandinavian immigrants' dramatic journey to the Pacific Northwest comes alive in the Nordic Heritage Museum's comprehensive Dream of America exhibit. Gallery after gallery of life-sized scenes, artifacts, photographs and personal stories illustrate the awesome trek from Ellis Island and Eastern cities to homesteads in the Midwest and then on to the forests and fishing boats of Washington state. The museum's Heritage Rooms display a myriad of colorful folk costumes and typical household items the immigrants brought with them to enrich their life in the new land.

The Nordics' often remarkable achievements as brave fishermen and active loggers, carpenters, farmers and miners are chronicled in the museum's Promise of the Northwest exhibits. A gallery devoted entirely to fishing and another to logging illustrate how skillful Scandinavians found work in those industries.

The achievements and lifestyles of the early Nordic immigrants as they adapted to their new environment are celebrated in five country-specific galleries. They include typical scenes of home, church, work and cultural activities and also show many traditions the immigrants became famous for in America — Icelandic literary talents, Finnish sauna and carpentry, Norwegian maritime skills, Danish businesses and Swedish entrepreneurial expertise, to name just a few. Renowned Scandinavian business people also are highlighted, such as John Nordstrom (fashion), Ole Bardahl (motor oil) and Karsten Solheim (Ping golf club).

While the museum enriches more than 65,000 visitors a year with these exhibits and others that rotate through its changing galleries of contemporary Scandinavian art and handicrafts, it also is a tremendous resource for the community. Among its offerings are music and reference libraries, a Scandinavian language institute, a lecture series on contemporary issues, a variety of educational programs, the "Mostly Nordic" concert series, and a wealth of children's activities and family-oriented festivals and events.

Emphasizing the migration of early settlers to the Pacific Northwest but also focusing on the present, the museum fulfills its mission of collecting, safeguarding and presenting the Nordic-American heritage. Located right in a neighborhood where many of those settlers first lived, it is the only museum in the United States to honor their legacy.

To keep that legacy going, the museum's Oral History Project is collecting memories of first- and second-generation immigrants who lived or worked in the area before 1960. While contributing to the area's growth, many of them also achieved great success in business, the arts or government — including two U.S. senators from Washington state, Warren G. Magnuson and Henry (Scoop) Jackson. But more importantly, as they built a better life for themselves and their children, the immigrants and their descendants wove their Nordic heritage into the tapestry of American life and culture.

This part of the Dream of America exhibit shows how the immigrants voyaged by ship to the New World and saw the Statue of Liberty as they neared Ellis Island.

PACIFIC NORTHWEST BALLET

In 1977 Kent Stowell and Francia Russell arrived in Seattle, family in tow, to become the new artistic directors of the city's struggling ballet company. At the time, Pacific Northwest Dance (PND), then under the umbrella of the Seattle Opera, had little money and even less direction. Stowell and Russell were, essentially, beginning with a clean slate. Accomplished dancers themselves, they were used to the intense physical and emotional demands imposed by their profession. Dance is work, but building a reputable dance company from scratch is a rare achievement indeed. Fortunately for Seattle, a determined Stowell and Russell did not see the difference.

One obstacle after another — openly hostile media, few professional dancers, a school that lacked coherent structure and curriculum — quickly taught the pair how to deal with adversity as part of their daily routine. Their struggles made them all the more determined to prove their competence to the PND Board, the local critics and, most of all, the public.

A year later, the Opera Board decided the ballet was more of a liability than an asset, and suggested it be cut loose. Stowell believed this was exactly what the ballet needed. He told his board that if the ballet could not stand on its own, it should not be in Seattle. Shortly after that, Pacific Northwest Ballet (PNB) was born.

A newly independent PNB continued to limp along through organizational and leadership changes, not to mention dwindling finances. However, passionate about establishing themselves as a viable company, everyone involved with PNB believed that sooner or later things were bound to change.

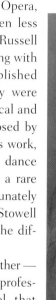
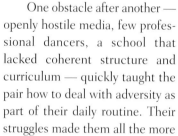

Kent Stowell and Francia Russell, artistic directors of PNB since 1977

PNB Company dancers in *Ballet Imperial* Photo by Angela Sterling

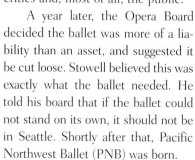

Then a remarkable thing happened — actually, two. PNB's production of *Swan Lake* in 1981 and *The Nutcracker* in 1983, both risky and expensive undertakings, gave the company its long-awaited success. Ironically, both were Tchaikovsky ballets — his first and his last. *Swan Lake* proved to critics and audiences alike that Seattle could not only pull off a major ballet, but also do so with artistic agility and style. PNB's brave new production of *The Nutcracker*, with choreography by Stowell and costumes and sets designed by children's author and illustrator Maurice Sendak, received national accolades. *Newsweek* told readers that *The Nutcracker* alone was worth a trip to Seattle. *The Nutcracker* continues to be an annual winner for PNB, attracting new audiences and increased revenue every year. In fact, many Seattleites consider it a "can't miss" holiday event.

Today, Seattle is fortunate to be among a handful of U.S. cities with major ballet companies, including San Francisco, New York, Houston and Boston. PNB has emerged as a reckoning force in professional ballet with a world-class facility and school, and unstoppable talent — 48 dancers and counting. The school, which has been an integral part from the beginning, is critical to the company's vitality. "The school is not only key to developing the 'PNB Style' of our dancers," says Stowell, "along with our Outreach Program, it provides a strong link with all segments of our community."

That support system continues to give PNB its creative freedom to reach for higher levels of excellence and to express to the world its own fresh and vibrant style.

PACIFIC SCIENCE CENTER

Imagine a face-to-face encounter with a giant robotic dinosaur or the thrill of climbing to the top of Mount Everest. How about a visit to a place where tropical butterflies flutter overhead? These are just a few of the adventures a person can experience at Pacific Science Center.

Second only to the Space Needle in popularity at the 1962 World's Fair, Pacific Science Center was born at an exciting time — when space exploration was in its infancy. Significant events like the launch of Sputnik 1, the first artificial satellite, and Russian cosmonaut Yuri Gagarin becoming the first human in space helped to generate a renewed interest in science.

Several decades later and counting, Pacific Science Center continues its mission to increase the public's understanding and appreciation of science, mathematics and technology through interactive exhibits and programs — and, of course, to make it fun for all.

George Moynihan is largely responsible for guiding the facility's success. Now in his 21st year as executive director, Moynihan remains passionate about science education. "We have entered the 21st century with the mission we began with — bringing science and kids together."

Under Moynihan's tenure, outreach programs and traveling science exhibits were conceived and have since become a major component of Pacific Science Center's objectives. People are often surprised to learn that the center serves more school children through its outreach efforts than it does through regular admission. The Science on Wheels program, for example, serves all 39 counties in the state of Washington. Colorful vans touting names like "Blood and Guts," "Physics on Wheels," "Rock and Roll," "Space Odyssey" and "TECH," among others, travel the state bringing hands-on workshops to elementary and middle-school children. For many, this will be their only exposure to an interactive science "experience" all year long.

But it's not just vans that are bringing science to the people. Pacific Science Center has dozens of outreach programs ranging from popular camp-ins, where children come to learn about science and spend the night next to lifelike exhibits, to Salmon Steward workshops at local streams and community leadership programs for teachers.

Adding to its appeal, Pacific Science Center is the only facility in the United States with two IMAX® theaters — guiding visitors daily on adventures from the ocean floor to the top of Mount Everest and out into space for flights on board the space shuttle. For astronomy buffs, there is a 27-foot, domed planetarium where visitors can participate in interactive shows and ask questions. In short, Pacific Science Center offers some science and some fun for everyone.

Over the last six years, major renovations have brought even more exciting changes. Visitors can now enjoy the new Seattle Rotary Discovery Lab, the Ackerley Family Exhibit Gallery and the popular Boeing IMAX Theater that boasts the latest in 3D technology.

With over 1 million visitors a year, Pacific Science Center continues to educate and entertain, making the wonders of science a pleasure for all who come to experience it firsthand — the kind of experience that evokes the question, "How about a little science with your fun?"

Pacific Science Center, a Seattle landmark since 1962, delights visitors of all ages.
Photo by Michael Walmsley

THE SEATTLE AQUARIUM

To visit The Seattle Aquarium is to take a trip beneath the surface of Puget Sound. This nationally recognized aquatic center on Seattle's waterfront exhibits approximately 30,000 specimens representing nearly 400 species of fish, invertebrates, marine mammals and birds from the waters of Puget Sound and beyond. The Aquarium also offers classes and outreach programs, special events, and outdoor environmental adventures designed to excite the senses while raising awareness and appreciation of the aquatic world. With deforestation, pollution and overpopulation destroying many of the richest habitats on earth, The Aquarium aims to educate the public to make informed decisions that will ultimately protect and preserve the vulnerable Puget Sound wilderness.

The Seattle Aquarium opened in 1977 as a division of Seattle's Department of Parks and Recreation. This window to Puget Sound presents Pacific Northwest fish in their natural habitats. The world's first aquarium-based salmon ladder and fish hatchery display the entire life cycle of Pacific salmon. Invertebrates include the giant Pacific (world's largest) octopus. Entertaining marine mammals — sea otters and seals — preen or sun at the water's surface or swim and dive underwater. Diving birds plunge for potential meals while shore birds dig long beaks into the sand.

Visitors can touch sea creatures and ask questions at the Discovery Lab. Waves crash through tide pools containing anemones, hermit crabs and barnacles. A watershed display shows all the vital habitats water passes through from the mountains to the ocean. Beneath its waterfalls, lively river otters offer a comparison with the laid-back but much-loved sea otters next door. The Seattle Aquarium is one of very few housing both types of otters, and in 1979 it achieved international acclaim for becoming the first facility in the world to breed sea otters successfully from conception to adulthood.

The Aquarium's most spectacular exhibit is the 400,000-gallon Underwater Dome. A myriad of magnificent fish — silvery salmon, huge lingcod and sharks, brightly colored rockfish and enormous sturgeon — swim around or lurk near the bottom of a spherical room encircling visitors. So popular is the dome that it is often rented in the evening for weddings and other events. During daytime hours, a particular highlight is a public feeding of the dome's fish by scuba divers. Many animals, including fur seals, sea otters and diving birds, also take their meals at regularly scheduled public feedings where naturalists answer visitors' questions.

While its emphasis is on Puget Sound, The Seattle Aquarium also is home to unusual aquatic life from other geographic locations including enchanting leafy sea dragons native to Australia. Open every day of the year, the aquarium serves more than half a million visitors annually. through award-winning exhibits, programs and special events, The Seattle Aquarium seeks to excite, involve and inform people of all ages. To make sure these efforts continue long into the future, supporters are already planning a new expanded aquarium on Seattle's waterfront to serve as a hub for environmental education for the city as well as the entire Pacific Northwest.

(Far right)
Visitors love to touch the sea creatures in the Discovery Lab's tank.

Spectacular fish surround viewers in the 400,000-gallon Underwater Dome.

SEATTLE MEN'S CHORUS

Who would have thought that a 22-man group of enthusiastic singers in Seattle would evolve into Washington state's largest choral organization and the largest gay men's chorus in the world? Seattle Men's Chorus, founded in 1979, did just that. With well over 200 singers now, it is the third-largest musical arts organization in the state (after Seattle Opera and Seattle Symphony) and has the widest audience and budget of any community chorus in the United States.

Seattle Men's Chorus held its first concerts in 1980 with about 40 singers. After that, the group began to grow quickly and vary its presentation style dramatically by incorporating creative and colorful costumes and scenery with its constantly improving musical sound. It also started attracting new audiences by performing with well-known guest artists and commissioning some of the world's leading composers.

Now each year Seattle Men's Chorus puts on more than 20 major concerts that maximize the possibilities of choral performance and have enormous popular appeal. More than 40,000 people attend the subscription series at Seattle's new Benaroya Hall and historic Paramount Theatre, and many more see the chorus (or its two smaller ensembles) in other local presentations. National and international audiences appreciate the singers on tour at some of the country's most prestigious halls, on televised concerts and on live Internet broadcasts. They also can be heard on 10 CDs the chorus has released since 1990.

Although the chorus members are of diverse backgrounds, professions and interests, they are in many ways like a family, united in the pride they take in their singing and in being gay men. They strive to make their music superb, but to them it is more important that the music builds community — both among themselves and with their audiences. "Music is the means, not the reason we exist," said Artistic Director Dennis Coleman. "We want our music to bring people together and help break down the barriers that sexual identity issues can still create."

In connection with that goal, Seattle Men's Chorus members enjoy serving as positive role models for other gay men and conveying the message that gay and straight people are more alike than unalike. For instance, their Youth Ticket Program provides more than 1,200 free tickets a year to gay, lesbian, bisexual and questioning youth through many social service agencies and schools. In the Seattle Men's Chorus environment, the youth feel like they belong — sometimes for the first time — and a number of them eventually become members.

Chorus outreach also includes helping AIDS organizations and other causes by participating in countless benefit performances each year, presenting special concerts to raise money for school music programs that have been severely cut back or eliminated, and setting aside concert tickets for interested groups who can't afford them. Whenever they sing, members of Seattle Men's Chorus hope their audience will appreciate their glorious harmony and share in the unity and joy expressed through the common language of music.

Governor and Mrs. Gary Locke with members of Seattle Men's Chorus who performed at the 2001 inaugural festivities

Seattle Men's Chorus members don their reindeer garb for a performance in their annual holiday concert.

SEATTLE REPERTORY THEATRE

One of the truest indicators of a community's cultural health is the vibrancy of its artistic community. That community is thriving in Seattle, due in no small part to Seattle Repertory Theatre (The Rep). One of America's largest and most respected professional, resident theatres, The Rep is internationally known for its artistic and technical achievements. Not surprisingly, it enjoys the patronage of nearly 20,000 season ticket holders and draws more than 200,000 people each year.

After opening in 1963, The Rep performed its first 20 seasons at the Seattle Center Playhouse. In 1983 it moved to the new Bagley Wright Theatre and PONCHO Forum. The Leo Kreielsheimer Theatre was added in 1996, giving Seattle Repertory Theatre more than 1,300 seats in three of the finest producing facilities in the country.

For more than 40 years, The Rep has challenged and entertained its audiences with an eclectic range of exceptional classic and contemporary productions. The works of playwrights as revered and diverse as William Shakespeare, Arthur Miller, Tennessee Williams and Wendy Wasserstein have graced its stages. Plays by legendary writers George Bernard Shaw, Eugene O'Neill, Anton Chekhov, Edward Albee and Neil Simon have also been performed, as well as special presentations and dramatic readings. In 1990 The Rep received a Tony Award for Outstanding Regional Theatre, in part for its history of nurturing a body of exceptional work by the most respected playwrights, directors and actors.

One of the reasons for The Rep's respected position in American theater — and one of the reasons for its vitality — is a genuine commitment to discovering and developing works by talented new playwrights. Many plays that went on to receive national acclaim had their beginnings at The Rep, including Herb Gardner's *I'm Not Rappaport* and *Conversations with My Father*, and Wendy Wasserstein's Pulitzer Prize-winning work, *The Heidi Chronicles*. The organization also actively seeks out new works, soliciting submissions each year for its New Plays Workshop Series; the best entries are then read or staged in the PONCHO Forum.

Recognizing that the continued robust health of theater in the Pacific Northwest is dependent not only on the development of new writers but on nurturing new audiences as well, The Rep also sponsors a variety of highly successful and innovative community outreach programs to introduce area students to the exciting experience of live theater. Each season it offers in-school residences and matinees for almost 10,000 high school students, classes taught by artist residents, "Careers in the Arts" seminars, workshops for teachers and student scholarship tickets.

In order to enjoy a balanced quality of life, a city — especially one with Seattle's national reputation for the arts — relies on the contributions of a flourishing theatrical community. Theater not only entertains but also reflects and explores the complexity of life. It presents new ideas and offers inspiration and hope. Seattle Repertory Theatre has enthusiastically taken up that gauntlet for almost half a century, creating a legacy that is undoubtedly its greatest production.

The Matsumoto sisters Rose (Michi Barall), Grace (Kim Miyori), and Chiz (Lisa Li) say farewell to their family farm in Seattle Repertory Theatre's world premiere production of Philip Kan Gotanda's Sisters Matsumoto. Photo by Chris Bennion.

The shepherd Silvius (David Gehrman) pleads for Phebe's love (Akemi Royer) in William Shakespeare's comedy As You Like It. Photo by Tim Fuller.

THE 5TH AVENUE THEATRE

The 5th Avenue Theatre opened in 1926 as a vaudeville house, heralded as one of the first theatres in the nation to be designed in an Asian motif. Under the precise supervision of architect Robert C. Reamer, the interior was modeled after three of ancient Imperial China's most stunning architectural achievements: the Forbidden City, the Temple of Heavenly Peace and the Summer Palace. Reamer possessed such a genuine concern for authenticity in design that he employed Gustav F. Liljestrom, chief designer for the S. & G. Gump Company of San Francisco, a firm famous for its hotel and theatre interiors. Together, they created The 5th Avenue — a theatre whose decor is nearly as breathtaking as the quality of entertainment presented within.

> ## "THE 5TH AVENUE THEATRE IS A NATIONAL TREASURE."
> ### — HELEN HAYES, JUNE 16, 1980

When vaudeville gave way to moving pictures, The 5th Avenue led the way in providing top-flight entertainment, thanks mainly to the showmanship of James Q. Clemmer, one of the first great film exhibitors in the Northwest. Clemmer had a knack for show business. Adding to the dramatic impact of the current feature, a Wurlitzer Pipe organ would rise from the center of the orchestra pit at the precise, suspenseful moment; ushers wore costumes in keeping with the theme of the current film — from swashbuckling pirates to swaggering cowboys — and the great booming voice of "Little Jimmy," a huge overstuffed bear in the lobby, called out to children during the Saturday matinees.

In 1978 The 5th Avenue closed its doors and seemed destined for the same fate as the Metropolitan and the Orpheum, two of Seattle's once splendid, now demolished theatres.

Happily, in 1979, 43 companies and business leaders set the stage for the rebirth of The 5th Avenue. Their mission was to save and restore one of the most ornate and unique theatres of our time and to provide firm financial footing so that the historic theatre could thrive and enhance Seattle's rich cultural community. The group formed The 5th Avenue Theatre Association, a nonprofit organization, and underwrote a $2.6 million loan for the renovation. The entire renovation was completed without local, state or federal funds, setting a precedent for theatres across the country.

After the renovation, The 5th Avenue emerged as Seattle's premier home for national touring shows. During the next decade, the theatre played host to such legends as Katharine Hepburn, Carol Channing, Richard Harris, Mickey Rooney, and Lauren Bacall — to name just a few.

In 1989 The 5th Avenue Musical Theatre Company was established as a resident nonprofit theatre company. Offering a mix of locally produced musicals and the best of touring Broadway, the company enjoys the support of more than 25,000 subscribers, making it one of the largest subscription-based theatres in the nation. Instrumental in both the development of new musicals and the production of revivals and forgotten gems from the musical theatre canon, The 5th Avenue is nationally recognized as one of the shining stars of the musical theatre stage.

In addition to musicals, The 5th Avenue Theatre hosts concerts, lectures, films and special events. In total, the theatre is in use 75 to 85 percent of the year, serving more than 300,000 patrons annually.

Generations of Seattleites grew up going to the movies at The 5th Avenue Theatre.
5th Avenue Archives

The interior of The 5th Avenue Theatre is modeled after the Throne Room of the Forbidden City in Beijing. Built in 1926, the theatre was originally a vaudeville house and reigned as one of Seattle's premier movie palaces for more than 50 years.
Photo by Dick Busher

Building a Greater Seattle

Seattle's development, lumber, construction and real estate
industries as well as property management and investment
companies shape tomorrow's skyline.

R.D. MERRILL COMPANY

Thomas Merrill, father of R.D. Merrill

Richard Dwight (R.D.) Merrill, a timber pioneer and family man who loved the outdoors, had a vision to replant the forest in the Pacific Northwest and build a business that would last for generations. In the 1890s he established the timberland enterprises that would later become the cornerstones for the R.D. Merrill Company, a private holding company, and as he envisioned, Merrill family descendents still own and direct the company today. Charles B. Wright III, a fourth-generation Merrill, is the current chairman.

R.D. enjoyed showing his children the adage that a bundle of matchsticks could not be broken, while a single one could easily fracture. The same was true for the Merrill family: the history of their joint business ventures is one of a collective pioneering spirit dating back to the 1850s. In that decade R.D.'s father followed the timber industry from Maine, where he had worked as a farmer and timber operator, to Michigan where he discovered great stands of spruce and hemlock. Along with his sons R.D. and Tom, and a son-in-law Clark Ring, the senior Merrill launched several new enterprises, but he mainly focused on his timber business. Together the family cut and harvested logs in upper Michigan and on the Michigan peninsula.

In the 1880s R.D.'s brother, Tom, traveled to the Pacific Northwest and found a 35,000-acre tract of timber in the Pysht River tributary, 40 miles west of Port Angeles on the Olympic Peninsula, at the foot of the rugged Olympic Mountains. Sitka spruce, western hemlock and Douglas fir dominated the forests. Today Douglas fir remains the primary commercial timber source in western Washington.

In 1888 Tom Merrill and Clark Ring established Merrill & Ring Timber Inc. with the purchase of the Pysht Tree Farm, which is now the oldest tree farm in Washington state still operated by its original owners. Tom Merrill also acquired scattered holdings in Canada, along the coast of British Columbia and to the northern tip of Vancouver Island, at a time when transportation was generally limited to canoes and other small boats. The Merrill family also acquired holdings as far south as the redwood forests in northern California.

In the 1890s, after he finished his degree in mathematics at the University of Michigan, the young R.D. Merrill brought his new bride to the Pacific Northwest. Washington state was an exciting frontier: it had finally achieved statehood in 1889, and the new transcontinental railroad brought an influx of settlers. With the economy in full swing, Washington led the states in lumber production. R.D. became the Merrill family's "operator in the field," managing the company's Pacific Northwest business.

A Man Before His Time

While Tom Merrill and Clark Ring eventually chose to return to Minnesota and Michigan to manage their properties, R.D. remained in the Pacific Northwest and formed partnerships with other timber enterprises in Washington and British Columbia. An aggressive and opportunistic businessman, R.D. was equally compassionate and forward thinking. Known for providing loggers with improved living

Bottom row: Brothers T.D. Merrill (right) and R.D. Merrill (center), and Clark Ring (left), brother-in-law of T.D. and R.D; top row: Managers and timber cruisers for Merrill & Ring Lumber Company and Timber Company

Merrill & Ring Logging Company headquarters camp at Pysht, Washington

conditions, he was the first to supply mattresses instead of hay in the bunkhouses, and he even brought in occasional movies. He was also known for serving the best food in the Northwest logging camps.

When most timber companies had not yet adopted sustained yield practices, R.D. foresaw the benefits of replanting trees to ensure second and third crops. Other businesses failed partly because they practiced a "cut and get out" exploitative logging philosophy, quickly exhausting supplies. R.D. Merrill practiced silviculture, which involves studying the relationship between the forest and its environment as well as the development, care and reproduction of timber stands. Merrill replanted seedlings and cut no more than he grew.

Recognizing responsible management of Merrill & Ring's Pysht properties, the American Forestry Association certified the operation as one of the first official tree farms. The first tree farm was Weyerhaeuser Company's nearby Clemons Tree Farm. Timber from the Merrill & Ring Pysht Tree Farm produced the finest lumber from Sitka spruce, which was used to build strong yet lightweight airplanes in World War I. During World War II, Sitka spruce was used for the manufacture of British medium lightweight Mosquito fighter-bombers.

In the early 1900s R.D. Merrill and his relatives continued to focus on developing their timber holdings. In 1926 the R.D. Merrill Company became officially incorporated. R.D. Merrill and his wife, Eula, invested their capital into the company in the form of a variety of shares, mainly in the Polson Logging Company and the Merrill & Ring Lumber Company, which later became the Merrill & Ring Joint Venture (the Pysht Tree Farm). However, R.D. Merrill Company remained a separate company with its own shareholders, including R.D. and Eula Merrill and their daughters, Virginia Merrill Bloedel and Eulalie Merrill Wagner, with one additional qualifying share each given to Timothy Jerome and Maurice McMicken, company employees.

Early directors meetings focused on recapitalization matters, declaration of dividends and routine elections of

A logging scene in the early 1920s of the Merrill & Ring Timber Company at Pysht, Washington

officers and directors. The company began with a total value of $4 million in contributed capital and invested in the stock market and later in private business ventures. By 1969, R.D. Merrill Company's investment portfolio had grown to approximately $9 million. The company formed an investment committee chaired by Bagley Wright, father of Charlie Wright. Several local investment managers as well as full-time tax specialists and accountants were hired.

Leading the Industry

R.D. Merrill Company grew to become a successful business as strong as its magnificent fir forests. Lumber ranked first among Washington's forest products until paper and pulp production became the dominant industries in the 1950s. By this time R.D. was in his 90s and had long since formally retired. His daughter Virginia Merrill Bloedel succeeded him as chairman until 1965 and was followed by R.D.'s only grandson, Corydon Wagner III. Unofficially, R.D. never retired. He remained a visionary with an entrepreneurial spirit who encouraged his son-in-law, Corydon Wagner Jr., and grandson, Corydon III, to search out new timber enterprises. R.D. saw a promising future for the wood products industry in the British Columbia interior.

The ever-united Merrill family heeded R.D.'s advice, and after much investigation, his son-in-law and grandson

Richard Dwight Merrill at his roll-top desk in the old White-Henry-Stuart Building office in Seattle, where the Rainier Tower now stands

Wagner's imports into the United States on a 5 percent wholesale commission, along with other outside lumber sales transactions. At its peak, Merrill and Wagner Ltd. employed 500 workers and realized good profits. A variety of problems, including railroad strikes and the need for capital plant improvements, eventually led to the sale of the company to Weldwood of Canada in 1976. R.D. Merrill Company retained 80 shoreline acres containing a lodge and campsite on the north arm of Quesnel Lake. Cariboo Pacific Corp was also liquidated in 1983.

Expanding and Forming New Partnerships

A number of acquisitions followed over the years, such as the purchase of Western Lumber Company of Aberdeen, Washington, which was sold in 1974. R.D. Merrill Company also invested in the Union Bond and Mortgage Company, which owned four small banks near Port Townsend and Port Angeles, Washington. In 1981, faced with increasing competition from large national banks, R.D. Merrill Company sold the small banks to Seafirst Bank.

In 1978, proceeds from the 1976 sale of Merrill and Wagner Ltd., along with a bank loan, were used to purchase Pacific Marine Schwabacher Company, a Seattle Pioneer Square city block including several buildings, a prized Northwest franchise that marketed Mercury marine outboard engines, and a well-known wholesale hardware business. The hardware business consisted of warehouses in which an inventory of over 40,000 items were bought, packaged and sold wholesale to customers such as Ernst Hardware and Pay N Save companies. The items were processed through an elaborate series of computerized conveyors, and sorting and packaging systems.

focused on the Williams Lake area of British Columbia in 1961. The R.D. Merrill Company acquired four different lumber companies, which were combined to become Merrill and Wagner Ltd., the forerunner of a new series of operating businesses controlled by the R.D. Merrill Company. Some of the Merrill family members and Peter Garrett, Clark Ring's grandson, were stockholders. Garrett managed the Merrill & Ring properties when R.D. Merrill retired. Today Peter Garrett's son-in-law manages the Merrill & Ring properties.

Merrill and Wagner Ltd. was formed with the acquisition of British Columbia Provincial cutting rights with an annual quota of 80 million board feet as well as a number of bush mills, which R.D. Merrill Company replaced with a modern sawmill and veneer plant. The same shareholders also owned Cariboo Pacific Corp of Tacoma, a sales company that marketed Merrill and

Merrill Place Building, formerly The Pacific Marine Schwabacher Building in Pioneer Square, March 2001

The business remained successful until Ernst Hardware, a customer that accounted for 70 percent of the hardware company business, went into the wholesale business as well. Left with few options, the R.D. Merrill Company converted the buildings into retail space and offices that became known as Merrill Place. Among Merrill Place's distinguished tenants were the Seattle Mariners baseball team, Adobe Software and the now defunct Empty Space Theater. R.D. Merrill Company sold Merrill Place in 1996.

Merrill & Ring Inc. established a sawmill operation in Port Angeles in 1959 and shared management with

Western Lumber Company until the mid-1960s. Although profits fluctuated, the bottom line steadily increased when the company entered the log exporting business. The Port Angeles sawmill was eventually sold to Oji Paper of Japan, which had acquired Merrill & Ring's neighbor, Crown Zellerbach, and sought to increase its acreage for the pulp mill expansion.

Today Merrill & Ring Timber Inc. holds 60,000 acres of productive timberland in Canada, New Zealand and western Washington state. Canadian holdings include 12,000 choice acres of British Columbia coastal and island timberlands to the northern tip of Vancouver Island. A number of fourth-generation family partnerships have benefited from the British Columbia holdings, receiving timber and lands spun off from Merrill & Ring ownership.

The Pysht Tree Farm, a Merrill & Ring Joint Venture, continues to operate in accordance with sustained yield considerations. A model of what R.D. Merrill envisioned — replanting trees for generations to come — the tree farm has a sustained yield cut of 25 to 30 million feet of timber per year, primarily western hemlock and Douglas fir. The Pysht Tree Farm is also an important place for students and adults to see how responsible timber operators work to safeguard the environment. To shield salmon runs, the company provides shade over the Pysht River. Stands of timber are extensively thinned to protect the property from disease and fire and are replanted for the future production of wood for shelter. Tours are conducted to show the public that the company practices responsible logging to conserve watersheds and wildlife habitats.

Merrill Gardens: Retirement Living for the 21st Century

In 1993 William D. Pettit joined the R.D. Merrill Company as president and chief operating officer. In 1994 Charlie Wright III came aboard as chairman. Wright took over for Corydon Wagner III, chairman emeritus. With the Merrill family's characteristic entrepreneurial, forward-thinking spirit, Pettit and Wright pursued business opportunities to diversify the company and keep up with a rapidly changing economy. The company invested in areas such as technology companies, resorts and real estate, and in the process acquired its first

The Manor at Canyon Lakes, a Merrill Gardens community in Kennewick, Washington

Merrill Gardens at Puyallup

Seated: Charles B. Wright III, chairman of the board and chief executive officer; standing: William B. Pettit, president and chief operating officer for the R.D. Merrill Company

independent and assisted-living community in Seattle. The new Merrill family venture, Merrill Gardens, was formed as an alternative to traditional retirement housing.

The Seattle purchase gave R.D. Merrill Company valuable insight into the way that the assisted-living industry operates. The company also learned design and construction techniques as it built another retirement community from the ground up in Monroe, Washington. After a year or two, Merrill Gardens took off and continued to expand along with the nation's need for more retirement housing.

In 1999 the company received a $15 million round of equity funding and acquired another owner and operator of senior housing communities, Torch Health Care Inc. of Irving, Texas. Eight of Torch's 18 communities were in Texas, with the rest in the South and Southwest. Through continued construction and acquisition of existing communities, Merrill

Gardens now operates over 60 rental retirement communities with more than 5,000 units in 14 states. It has become the largest operator of rental retirement communities in Washington state and one of the top 20 operators in the country. Recent revenues have been in the $80-90 million range.

In the tradition of R.D. Merrill, Merrill Gardens is dedicated to quality and built on a strong foundation of family, community, long-term commitment and entrepreneurial spirit. Merrill Gardens communities provide the best in retirement living by supporting the independence, individuality, privacy and decision-making abilities of each resident.

Merrill Gardens buildings are all different in physical structure and appearance, reflecting the characteristics of the surrounding area and the needs of residents. For independent living, Merrill Gardens offers private

apartments with a variety of floor plans. Assisted-living services provide more care, with individually tailored service plans for seniors who need help with specific daily activities such as bathing and dressing.

Merrill Gardens also offers carefully planned, home-like communities for people with Alzheimer's disease and dementia. Residents live in a comfortable atmosphere that offers a dignified, secure and supportive lifestyle. A highly qualified staff develops and implements individual plans of care specific to each resident's needs, and receives continual training in the care of those with dementia.

Recreational and therapeutic activity programs help to create a supportive environment. Activities are designed to stimulate memory through conversations and reminiscences, while scenic drives encourage positive social interaction. Family members can discuss concerns or ask questions in ongoing support groups conducted by staff, either one-on-one or in a group setting. Merrill Gardens also offers temporary, 24-hour respite care to give caregivers and loved ones a much-needed break from routine.

R.D. Merrill Company invested significant resources in its independent and assisted-living communities at a time when the industry was just beginning to flourish. Some industry estimates indicate that demand for assisted-living facilities will increase 150 percent by 2005. Bill Pettit and Charlie Wright foresaw the success of Merrill Gardens as R.D. Merrill had predicted the benefits of sustained yield forestry practices a century before.

Giving Back to the Community

The Merrill family's keen vision extends well beyond its business ventures. Known for their community spirit and philanthropy, R.D. Merrill's descendants remain active in a variety of charitable, cultural and human services organizations in the Seattle area. Virginia Merrill Bloedel donated the Bloedel Reserve, including the Bloedel family's former home on Bainbridge Island, for the public's benefit and enjoyment.

The Bloedel Reserve comprises approximately 150 acres, including 84 acres of second-growth forest. The remaining acres contain beautiful landscapes of gardens, ponds and meadows. The primary purpose of the Reserve is to provide the public with an opportunity to enjoy nature through quiet walks in the gardens and woodlands. The Bloedel Reserve includes many native species of plants and animals as well as a bird refuge where ducks, geese and swans live among the native sedge and ferns. Great blue herons and kingfishers feed on trout specially stocked in the pond. The Japanese garden features a rock and sand Zen garden created by Dr. Koichi Kawana, a professor of landscape architecture at the University of California.

Eulalie Wagner, Corydon Wagner III's mother, also donated her private estate, Lakewold, to a new public, nonprofit organization called Friends of Lakewold, which is dedicated to serving the educational, recreational, cultural and environmental interests of the community. Lakewold, a Middle English term meaning "lake woods," nestles between Puget Sound and Mount Rainier in the Lakes District 10 miles south of Tacoma. The property encompasses 10 acres on the west side of Gravelly Lake. A series of individual gardens features a variety of plants including roses, rhododendrons, ferns and alpine trees.

Corydon and Eulalie Wagner bought Lakewold from the Griggs family in 1940, and the Wagner children spent a happy childhood there. Over the years Eulalie became an accomplished landscape designer who enjoyed working in the garden. She continued to live at Lakewold after her husband passed away in 1979. In 1987 she donated the estate to Friends of Lakewold with the stipulation that an endowment fund be raised to ensure that the gardens would always be tended. She clearly stated her motivation: "As we become more and more city creatures, living in manmade surroundings, perhaps gardens will become even more precious to us, letting us remember that we began in the garden." In accordance with Eulalie's wishes, Friends of Lakewold has a mission to preserve and maintain Lakewold Gardens and the Wagner House for the benefit of the general public and for community events. Lakewold Gardens officially opened to the public in 1989. Although Eulalie Wagner died in 1991, her spirit remains at Lakewold Gardens.

A Rich Legacy

Richard Dwight Merrill's dream remains in the hearts and minds of his descendants, who remember his favorite parable that a united family, like a bundle of sticks, is infinitely stronger than any single person acting alone. From the company's pioneering beginnings in the timber industry to the remarkable success of Merrill Gardens, R.D. Merrill Company remains a strong, family-owned business a cut above the rest.

Heading into the 21st century, the R.D. Merrill Company is governed by a directors' board of 10, half of whom are members of the Bloedel branch of the family, the other five from the Wagner branch. Four members are third-generation descendants of R.D. Merrill; six represent the fourth generation.

In addition to Merrill Gardens, R.D. Merrill Company's dominant enterprises are still timberlands and other financial assets, including a general portfolio of stocks and bonds, as well as ownership interests in venture capital funds and publicly traded security funds. Although the company continues to grow and explore new business opportunities, R.D.'s original vision has never been lost. As descendants continue to replant the forest, the R.D. Merrill Company will prosper for generations to come.

Peter Garrett, current patriarch of the Ring family and grandson of Elizabeth Palmer Merrill and Clark Lombard Ring, March 2001

Eulalie Merrill Wagner and her husband, Corydon Wagner Jr.

WRIGHT RUNSTAD & COMPANY

When one glimpses Seattle's remarkable skyline, it's hard to believe that just 50 years ago its tallest building stood just 15 stories. Today the Emerald City is dotted with a variety of uniquely designed skyscrapers and superbly designed office buildings built in just the last few decades. From glass domes and cascading rooftop terraces to materials that reflect the natural beauty of the area, Seattle is an architectural delight to behold. Much of the thanks for these magnificent improvements goes to Wright Runstad & Company.

Wright Runstad & Company is the Northwest's leading developer of premier commercial office space. While the company's award-winning office buildings can be found up and down the West Coast from Los Angeles to Anchorage, Seattle is its home and its best showcase. Wright Runstad & Company was founded in 1972 by H. Jon Runstad and the late Howard S. Wright, and today is owned by its four active principals: Runstad, Douglas E. Norberg, Jon F. Nordby and Walter R. Ingram. Based upon a culture of integrity, quality and service, the extraordinary people of Wright Runstad & Company have built more than 14 million square feet of office space — 517 stories in Seattle, Bellevue, Portland, Boise, Los Angles and Anchorage. In 1999 and 2000 alone, the company built 2.2 million square feet.

Wright Runstad & Company's first foray into the world of commercial office development took place six miles north of Seattle's central business district. Built in 1974, the 210,789-square-foot Northgate Executive Center is a business and professional center consisting of three buildings that house several insurance companies and a branch of the University of Washington.

The next year, the developers turned their focus to Boise, Idaho, and built One Capital Center, a 14-story building. The project was the first building to be constructed in Boise's downtown redevelopment area.

After One Capital Center, Wright Runstad & Company ventured to Alaska to work on the Calais Office Center. Located in one of Anchorage's most valued business locations, the center consists of an eight- and a five-story building each with bronze insulating glass curtain walls. Later, Wright Runstad & Company would return to Anchorage to build a 313,000-square-foot building as headquarters for the Sohio Alaska Petroleum Company.

In 1978 Wright Runstad & Company started work on the prominent Cedars-Sinai Medical Office Towers located in Los Angeles. Both buildings are framed in concrete, sheathed in glass and connected via a skybridge to the Cedars-Sinai Medical Center.

The company returned to the Northwest in 1980 to build its tallest building up to that point, the 34-story 1111 Third Avenue. With 557,715 square feet overlooking Elliott Bay and the Olympic Mountains, the building exterior is built of precast concrete with dual-glazed, solar bronze glass. A beautiful, landscaped pedestrian plaza at the base is a favorite feature of the downtown Seattle business crowd. The building houses law firms, government offices, banks and several other prestigious companies.

During that same year, Wright Runstad & Company built 1001 Fifth Avenue in Portland. Located in the transit mall in the downtown area, the six-sided building rises 23 stories and is encased in partially reflective charcoal-gray glass with a rose-colored granite base. With more than 370,000 square feet, 1001 Fifth is nothing but modern. It presently houses a bank, government offices and financial services companies.

Back in Seattle in 1983, Wright Runstad & Company opened its largest building yet. Now known as the Wells Fargo Center, the Third Avenue building was built as the First Interstate Center. It contains more than 944,000 square feet of prime office space. The 47-story tower has six sides and is situated diagonally on a full block of Seattle's downtown area.

The building's double-glazed gray glass windows beautifully offset the Spring Rose polished granite exterior. The building is regarded as one of the downtown area's finest people places thanks to its three-level outdoor plaza filled with restaurants, shops and service businesses. During the summer, a variety of concerts are offered free of charge, encouraging both downtown visitors and employees to enjoy the weather and the music in the shadow of one of Seattle's tallest skyscrapers.

Just a few blocks away sits the Washington Mutual Tower, one of the most prominent buildings developed by Wright Runstad & Company. The *New York Times* named the tower one of the nation's three best new office buildings in 1988. Boasting truly unique public places that people enjoy year-round, the 55-story classically designed tower houses Washington Mutual Bank and the region's largest law firm, Perkins Coie, along with many of the city's most prestigious tenants. It offers outstanding views of Elliott Bay, Lake Union and the Cascade and Olympic mountain ranges. The 1.1 million-square-foot building is constructed of granite and emerald-green glass and features a pedestrian plaza as well as three levels of shops, services and rooftop gardens. A public atrium overlooks the plaza and the Metro transit tunnel is accessed through the tower's lobby.

In 1994 the Washington Mutual Tower earned the Urban Land Institute's (ULI) Award for Excellence. The ULI is an international non-profit education and research institute that studies land use and real estate development policy and practice. Established in 1979, the ULI Awards have the highly regarded reputation of reflecting the ULI's mission to provide responsible leadership in the use of land in order to enhance the environment.

Just across the street, Wright Runstad & Company developed another unique project known as the Second and Seneca Building. This stunning 22-story office building includes a lighted, green dome that serves as a

Washington Mutual Tower was named one of the nation's best new skyscrapers by the *New York Times* when it was completed in 1988. In 1994 the 55-story landmark tower earned the Urban Land Institute's Award for Excellence.
Photo by James F. Housel

(Below, left)
Sitting along the Seattle Waterfront, the World Trade Center's three buildings were completed in 2000. The complex serves as home to the Port of Seattle and Internet platform developer RealNetworks.
Photo by James F. Housel

Wright Runstad & Company used the traditional brick façade of Seattle's Pioneer Square for its King Street Center. Completed in 1999, the building houses King County's Departments of Natural Resources and Transportation.
Photo by Harrier Burger

The Second & Seneca Building's green dome serves as a beacon to the ships and ferries traveling across Puget Sound.
Photo by James F. Housel

beacon to the ships and ferries making their way across Puget Sound. Seven rooftop terraces cascade to the west, offering fantastic views of the Olympic Mountains and Elliott Bay. Images of Seattle's skyline, as well as the Northwest's incredible sunsets, are reflected in the eight-foot-high windows found on each floor. The building is now home to a number of well-known financial institutions, law and architecture firms and the biotechnology company Immunex.

Further north, the World Trade Center presides over Seattle's waterfront. Consisting of three structures all developed by Wright Runstad & Company since 1998, each offers spectacular views of Elliott Bay and the Olympic Mountains. World Trade Center West, owned by the Port of Seattle, has four office floors and underground parking. It houses several organizations engaged in international trade activities as part of a network of 306 World Trade Centers in 92 countries. World Trade Center East has six office floors, a five-floor garage and a skybridge that connects it to the Bell Street Pier complex. Microsoft currently leases the east building. World Trade Center North, the most recent addition to the complex, houses a five-story office tower and a large parking garage. It is leased to Internet audio and video infrastructure provider RealNetworks.

Just a bit north of Seattle's central business district is the 1800 Ninth Avenue building. This 16-story office building, completed in 1990, is composed of alternating panels of precast concrete. Bands of reflective glass form the exterior of this steel-framed rectangular building while granite-clad columns frame the handsome two-story entrance. Built for Regence BlueShield, the building is located near the freeway and is just two blocks from the Metro transit tunnel.

Wright Runstad & Company has also developed buildings for one of the region's most sophisticated medical facilities. The Elmer J. Nordstrom Medical Tower, completed in 1986, and the 1101 Madison Medical Tower, completed in 1994, are both adjacent to Swedish Medical Center. The buildings were designed to provide technology and flexibility along with plenty of space for the hospital's physicians. The 1101 Madison building was constructed above a seven-level garage originally developed by Wright Runstad & Company in 1992 and features a skybridge connecting it to the adjacent Arnold Medical Pavilion.

Another building Wright Runstad & Company recently completed is King Street Center, an eight-story office building located in Seattle's historic Pioneer Square. Adjacent to the landmark King Street Station, the

315,000-square-foot building conforms to the period architecture and unique building ornamentation of past years, yet is modern in every sense of the word. The building incorporates a variety of artwork provided by several contemporary artists. King Street Center houses King County's Departments of Transportation and Natural Resources.

Wright Runstad & Company's most recent development is a project built across Lake Washington, about 10 minutes east of Seattle. Located in Bellevue's downtown area, Key Center is a 22-story office building containing nearly half a million square feet of prime office space. Sheathed in a combination of light materials, soft reflective glass and light aluminum trim, the building was designed to maximize the remarkable 360-degree views of Lake Washington, the Seattle skyline and the Olympic and Cascade mountains. Another attraction of Key Center is its spacious pedestrian plaza, which connects with the public spaces of neighboring Rainier Plaza to create a one-acre public park in the heart of downtown Bellevue. The building is adjacent to Bellevue's Metro transit center and convention center.

Wright Runstad & Company began paving the way for Key Center and a new wave of high-rise office development in Bellevue years ago. The company built One Bellevue Center, Bellevue's first skyscraper, in 1983. The unique-looking structure is a 12-faceted, 22-story office building with a flush façade of light blue-gray, partially reflective glass. The ground level enters onto a 30,000-square-foot landscaped plaza near NE 4th Street and 108 Avenue NE. Wright Runstad & Company followed up three years later with Rainier Plaza, a 25-story building with more than 430,000 square feet.

Also in Bellevue, although further removed from the downtown area, is the 83-acre Sunset Corporate Campus. While the first Sunset building was developed in 1992, Sunset North was completed in 2000. It includes three five-story buildings comprising almost one-half million square feet of office space located along the I-90 corridor in Bellevue, one of the region's fastest-growing business centers. The campus includes a fitness center, a deli and a neighborhood park. The natural beauty and central location of the campus have attracted an impressive cross-section of tenants from the high-tech industry.

The largest single project developed by Wright Runstad & Company, and perhaps the least recognized, is Microsoft's corporate headquarters. The company was responsible for overseeing the first 2.1 million square feet of Microsoft's original clustered campus in Redmond. The

The 22-story Key Center is the latest building developed by Wright Runstad & Company. Its public spaces connect neighboring buildings, creating a beautiful one-acre park in the heart of downtown Bellevue.
Photo by James F. Housel

first phase of the project included building four two-story buildings each containing 60,000 square feet of space. During the second phase, a star-shaped building design was continued for the 5th and 6th buildings. Structures built as part of Phase III are twice the size of the first six buildings but have similar designs and exterior finishes. Buildings developed in Phase IV feature a linear design and open spaces through the use of extensive plazas.

Wright Runstad & Company also developed Microsoft's manufacturing and distribution center in Bothell. Even though the building is more functional in appearance than most of Wright Runstad & Company's other showcase office buildings, this building's glass curtain wall, rising two stories, gives the building a unique feeling of spaciousness and unique design.

Developing high-quality office space for technology companies is a skill for which Wright Runstad & Company has enjoyed great success and recognition. In 2000 it was honored once again by receiving a second Urban Land Institute Award for Excellence (only three Seattle-area buildings have been so recognized and Wright Runstad & Company developed two of them), this time for the redevelopment of the former Marine Hospital — the PacMed Building. The 12-story art deco tower rises 472 feet above sea level and is one of Seattle's most

Mt. Rainier looms behind the Amazon.com Building. In 1999 Wright Runstad & Company completed the renovation of the historic U.S. Marine Hospital and created a unique space for the Internet retail giant's world headquarters.
Photo by James F. Housel

prominent landmarks. Listed on the National Register of Historic Landmarks, it had been virtually vacant for more than 10 years before renovation and now serves as the world headquarters for Internet retail giant Amazon.com.

The beautiful lush campus is located on 10 acres situated in the midst of Seattle's Beacon Hill district. It has sweeping views of downtown Seattle, Elliott Bay, the Olympic and Cascade mountains, and a stunning view of Mt. Rainier to the south. The renovated tower was completed in 1999 and is now a highly flexible and visually dynamic office facility for Amazon.com. Construction of an additional 220,000-square-foot expansion building began in 2001. The new complex is situated in front of the original tower and terraces down the steep hill below the building to keep the view of the historic tower intact.

After opening seven new buildings in a 15-month period in 1999 and 2000, many companies would take a well-deserved break. But Wright Runstad & Company is not about to rest on its laurels and is already working on the next pages of its development portfolio.

Over the next two years, Wright Runstad & Company is creating a new gateway to downtown Seattle located near Interstates 5 and 90. The 500,000-square-foot office complex along Dearborn Street, known as Dearborn@5/90,

will be situated between the Jose Rizal Bridge and Rainier Avenue South. In a unique exchange for land, the company is giving Seattle Goodwill's program facilities, administrative offices and retail store a much needed $8 million facelift. Not only will Goodwill's 60-year-old facility gain the benefits of the renovation, the land gained by Wright Runstad & Company is also allowing the development of a high-tech urban campus at the intersection of the area's most important freeways, I-5 and I-90.

Wright Runstad & Company is also developing a 750,000-square-foot, campus-style office complex on 6.8 acres on the southernmost shores of Lake Washington. Southport is adjacent to the 2.5 square mile Gene Coulon Park and will be ideally suited for high-tech companies. Built next to luxury apartments, streetscapes lined with shops, restaurants and a lakefront promenade, all under development by another company, Southport will be the next destination community on Lake Washington. The site has incredible views of Lake Washington, the Seattle skyline, the Olympic Mountains and Mt. Rainier.

It's easy to see how Wright Runstad & Company has grown from a small office inside the Howard S. Wright Construction Company, to one of the most respected office developers in the Pacific Northwest. The company's corporate offices, located in Seattle, contain administrative offices, marketing and financial management resources, and project development teams. In addition, the company has on-site property management teams located in Portland, Boise and Anchorage.

Considering the seamless coordination required in operating and managing large, complex office properties, Wright Runstad & Company has established an impeccable reputation with tenants, lenders, investors, suppliers and the community. The company actively supports a long list of nonprofit groups such as United Way and Seattle Works, a group that encourages people who are just starting their careers to give back to the community. Wright Runstad & Company is also known for supporting education, human services and the arts. In fact, the University of Washington recently created the Runstad Center for Real Estate Studies.

Shaping skylines with office buildings of exceptional design and quality, providing outstanding service to tenants and generously giving back to the community are the trademarks of Wright Runstad & Company. The company and its employees have left an indelible mark on the Pacific Northwest and will continue building for the future, helping Seattle evolve as one of the world's greatest cities.

CONNER HOMES CO.

Conner Homes Co. has beaten the odds. Many family businesses flounder in their efforts to transition leadership from one generation to the next, but Conner Homes has recently managed a graceful shift in power from father to son. Years of planning eased the succession, but also helpful was the fact that Charlie Conner and his father, Bill, share a common philosophy and a commitment to value and service. The younger Conner may bring a more modern management style to the job but, like his father before him, he continues to build on a strong foundation that took shape more than 30 years ago.

Bill Conner began his career as a civil engineer. In 1958 he went to work with his brother building houses and apartments in the Seattle area, and in 1964 he incorporated Conner Development Co. on his own.

Charlie Conner began working for his dad in sixth grade. He toiled at the construction sites every summer, learning the trades and developing a work ethic he would carry forward into adulthood. After graduating from the University of Washington with a degree in finance, Conner briefly considered starting his own development company. But in 1978 he took his dad's offer to join the family firm as a superintendent. For the next decade, his responsibilities increased and the company continued to grow, reaching nearly $30 million in revenues by 1988.

About that time, Bill Conner began to plan his retirement. Conner Development Co. was gradually phased out, and in 1999, the senior Conner built his last house, the company name was changed to Conner Homes Co., and Charlie was named president.

Conner also became president of the Conner Group, the company's real estate division. Not many homebuilders have in-house realtors, but the Conners believe no one can represent their product better than their own staff.

At Conner Homes customer service is paramount. Homebuyers consult with staff on the home's specifications and interior design, and each buyer receives an orientation on the home's systems and warranty. In addition, Conner Homes surveys its customers after the sale, after move in and again a year later. Conner says these surveys are invaluable. He reads every one and uses owner comments to improve service and quality.

In 40 years the Conners have built more than 3,600 homes, developed more than 1,800 lots, won countless awards for design, service and marketing, and served their community and industry.

Bill Conner was president of the Seattle Master Builders Association and the Washington State Home Builders Association and a leader in many civic and professional organizations. Charlie Conner was president of the Master Builders Association of King and Snohomish Counties in 2000 and gives his time to several professional and educational groups.

His motto is "value to the homebuyer." His mission is to provide that value through quality building, excellent service and mindfulness of the environment. And whether Conner Homes Co. passes to Charlie's two daughters, employees or into other hands, Charlie hopes the company will sustain these principles far into the future.

Charlie Conner, president of Conner Homes, oversees the thriving home-building company and tends a family legacy that is more than 40 years old.

> IN 40 YEARS THE CONNERS HAVE BUILT MORE THAN 3,600 HOMES, DEVELOPED MORE THAN 1,800 LOTS, WON COUNTLESS AWARDS FOR DESIGN, SERVICE AND MARKETING, AND SERVED THEIR COMMUNITY AND INDUSTRY.

CLISE PROPERTIES, INC.

From its earliest days in Seattle, Clise Properties has earned widespread respect and admiration for its farsighted business philosophy — a philosophy founded on an unwavering and inspired vision of what the company and Seattle could ultimately be. Numerous commercial real estate development companies have come and gone, but Clise has endured and prospered for more than 100 years. Through its civic contributions — the founding of Children's Orthopedic Hospital, developing Seattle's downtown corridor and linking the city to the rest of the world — Clise has created crucial opportunities for generations of Northwesterners and helped Seattle grow and prosper as well.

A closely held, privately owned company with significant longtime holdings in the downtown corridor, Clise Properties has played a pivotal leadership role in the development of many of Seattle's best-known landmarks. It built and manages the Pacific, United Airlines and Denny buildings. The company is also responsible for two longtime downtown fixtures, the Westin and Securities buildings. From its earliest days, Clise has willingly accepted the responsibility and opportunity of aiding and shaping the future of Seattle. In keeping with a family tradition of civic involvement that has been handed down through four successive generations of Clises, the company develops and manages its properties not merely for profit but with an eye toward improving the quality of life of the city it has called home since 1889.

J.W. Clise

Clise Properties' founder, J.W. Clise, was born in Wisconsin in 1855. Raised as the son of a dairy farmer, J.W. set his sights on a more adventurous life and set out for California at the age of 18. He settled instead in Denver, where his burgeoning entrepreneurial skills led him into successful cattle ranching and lumber ventures. In Colorado J.W. also met the young woman who became his wife, Anna Herr.

In 1889 J.W. and Anna migrated to the Northwest at the urging of Clise's sister, who had invited him to visit Seattle and see firsthand the city's great beauty and untapped potential. Ironically, J.W. arrived in Seattle while the embers of the Great Fire were still smoldering — too late to see the city of which his sister had written so glowingly, but fortuitously in time to join in the rebuilding. Having brought with him an appetite for new ideas and an intuitive appreciation for new opportunities, J.W. immediately fell in love with Seattle and wasted no time in founding a real estate company that eventually grew into mortgage banking, shipping and real estate enterprises.

J.W. possessed an uncanny knack for persuading investors to participate in development projects. He also had the self-confidence to conceive and pursue a bold future for his company and its struggling city. As a result, J.W. became one of the best known real estate developers in the region and played an integral part in the rebuilding of Seattle. He would remain at the helm of Clise Properties for the next 50 years, making his mark on Seattle by bringing typewriter magnate L.C. Smith to town and arranging the financing for the Smith Tower, which, for many years after its construction in 1914, was the tallest building west of the Mississippi River.

Charles F. Clise

Born the year after his parents arrived in Seattle, J.W. and Anna's son, Charles F. Clise, is known in the company annals as a master of acquisition. He helped his father steer the company through the challenges of the Great Depression, and succeeded J.W. as head of the company in 1939. By

(Left to right) J.W. Clise and Charles F. Clise

that time Charles had already built the Securities Building, a downtown landmark that has served as the Clise Properties corporate headquarters since 1919. His most important and lasting contribution, however, was his belief in the potential for the area then known as the Denny Regrade. Charles' vision for the Regrade would prove to be pivotal in shaping the company's fortunes into the next century.

In one of Seattle's most ambitious civic projects, Denny Hill had been graded and dumped into Elliott Bay in the 1920s to make the terrain more suitable for anticipated residential and commercial growth. Soon after, the Great Depression occurred and the same developers who had eagerly acquired land in the Denny Regrade began selling off their properties at deflated prices or completely abandoning them as worthless. Having learned from his father's example,

Charles astutely recognized the developing real estate panic as a long-term opportunity. Having also inherited his father's optimism and faith in Seattle, Charles held fast to the belief that the city's projected growth in the area would resume once the Depression was over, and he immediately began acquiring a unique assemblage of properties in the Regrade. Even though it would be several decades before his vision was realized, the Denny Regrade — now known as the Denny Triangle — formed the principal properties that the company would begin developing in the 1990s.

A.H. Clise

Upon Charles' death in 1961, his son, 41-year-old A.H. Clise, became president of Clise Properties. By this time the company was nearing its 75th anniversary and had achieved the stature of one of Seattle's most successful commercial real estate developers. Because of its long history as one of the city's guiding forces and most generous benefactors, it had also become one of Seattle's most prominent and respected companies.

The business and civic climate had changed from J.W.'s and Charles' eras, creating different challenges that called for a leader who could preserve the company's past achievements and acquisitions in preparation for the future. A Marine lieutenant colonel who was decorated for his service in World War II, A.H. met that challenge during his tenure as president, shepherding the company and its hard-won properties through the decades leading up to Seattle's population boom in the 1990s. Even though the Puget Sound economy was somewhat stagnant during his presidency, A.H. not only maintained the company's solid fiscal and social position but also managed

The Securities Building, the corporate headquarters of Clise Properties since 1919

(Left to right) A.H. Clise and A.M. Clise

After a brief internship with another company, A.M. joined the family business in 1980. He was named president six years later, and succeeded his father as CEO in 1993. The company has blossomed under A.M.'s leadership, and — after decades of patiently waiting for the appropriate time — is finally making Charles' dream for the Denny Triangle a successful reality. As part of an ambitious and comprehensive 10-year plan, Clise Properties began development in 2000 of a major new addition to the Seattle skyline — the 1700 Seventh Avenue Tower. A visually striking, 23-story, 500,000-square-foot structure, the tower will serve as the national headquarters for another longtime fixture of the Pacific Northwest, the Nordstrom retail chain. Several other major projects will follow in the wake of the 1700 Seventh Avenue Tower, eventually transforming the Denny Triangle into one of the company's — and Seattle's — crowning achievements.

In the present commercial real estate environment, the risk and costs are so high that most development in urban areas is being done by conglomerates. "It is very unusual to find a smaller, family-owned company that is playing at their level," A.M. Clise observes. Yet Clise Properties continues to thrive in a world of mega-corporations, and stands as their equals. Having been established as an integral part of Seattle for more than a century plays a part in the company's stature, as does the far-sighted acquisitions policy followed by J.W. and Charles. But the key to the company's longevity and continued growth is a carefully planned and executed conservative business philosophy of thoughtful development that allows Clise to stay relatively debt-free and avoid the common pitfall of over-leveraging assets. The company is also not typical of commercial real estate developers in that it not only develops properties but continues to own and manage them for the long term. As a result, Clise has

to slowly and steadily increase its business. When he died in 1993, A.H. left as his legacy a prosperous, debt-free company with a potentially brilliant future.

A.M. Clise

A.M. Clise is the fourth generation of his illustrious family to head Clise Properties. Born in Seattle in 1949, he is the third native son to lead the company — a feat seldom matched by any other company in the country. A.M. graduated from the University of Nevada, Las Vegas (UNLV), where he demonstrated his leadership skills at a young age by serving as the captain of UNLV's basketball team, the Running Rebels.

positioned itself to weather the type of periodic regional economic fluctuations that have so often caused the demise of Puget Sound developers.

The second major component of the company's successful philosophy is its longstanding dedication to making Seattle an extraordinary place to live. Clise Properties has never viewed itself as a commercial island in a civic sea, but rather as an institution with a social responsibility and moral connection to the rest of the community. Continuing to build on more than a century of commitment to commerce and service, the company is actively involved in a wide range of associations dedicated to enhancing the Puget Sound, including the Downtown Seattle Association and Building Owners and Managers Association of Seattle and King County. The president and CEO, A.M. Clise, also serves on the board of trustees for the Pacific Northwest Ballet.

Of Clise's many contributions to the city of Seattle, perhaps none is as important, enduring and dear to the hearts of the Clise family as its involvement in the founding of Children's Hospital. After losing a son due to a lack of available medical services, J.W.'s wife, Anna Herr Clise, vowed that no Seattle mother or father would ever suffer a similar tragedy. Sharing her husband's ability to rally supporters around a worthy cause, Anna spearheaded a drive to build a children's hospital that would offer the medical care needed by Seattle's families. The facility opened in 1907 under the name of Children's Orthopedic Hospital, and was dedicated from the outset to providing care for all children, regardless of their families' ability to pay. Today, Children's Hospital annually provides $30 million in uncompensated medical care. It has become a renowned treatment and research facility that provides difficult-to-find, specialized care for children from all parts of the country. Having been steadfast in its support of the hospital since its inception, the Clise family is still actively involved, with A.M. serving on the board of trustees.

Since its earliest days in fire-ravaged Seattle, Clise Properties has always been guided by an unshakable sense of responsibility — to the family, to its illustrious legacy, and most of all, to the city of Seattle. Whether it is helping Children's Hospital, supporting the arts, or developing the Denny Triangle, the company always has its eye on the long-term future of the city as a whole. Adhering to its own principles of "thoughtful development," the company is guided by genuine concerns for the city's welfare, environment and aesthetic sensibilities. It takes seriously its role as a steward with opportunities and civic responsibilities. "We will treat our opportunity to help shape this city with respect," A.M. Clise explains. "We are proud of our 100-plus-year history, and look to the future with an equal amount of pride and sense of responsibility."

| The Westin Building

TURNER CONSTRUCTION COMPANY

When Turner Construction Company opened its Turner Northwest office in 1976, the company already had nearly 75 years of building experience behind it. Since its start, Turner Northwest has been crafting some of the most beautiful, innovative and functional buildings around Puget Sound and beyond, continuing a tradition of excellence that began in 1902 in New York. Today, Turner Construction is a worldwide industry leader and the largest general builder in the United States, taking on more than 1,000 projects a year. More than 60 percent of Turner's business comes from repeat customers, proving that its reputation is its best advertisement.

The World Trade Center on Seattle's waterfront

(Far right) The Two Union Square building in downtown Seattle

Henry C. Turner and DeForrest H. Dixon began their business after receiving the licenses for a new steel-reinforced concrete that would soon change the way buildings were constructed. For some time the company was known for being the "concrete specialists" and built primarily industrial buildings and warehouses. When the patents were thrown out in 1907, Turner adapted by expanding its scope. By 1929 the company was known as a great builder of "finely-finished" buildings. Turner was no longer occupied with just warehouses but now also built elegant retail establishments such as the original Macy's and Bloomingdale's. Hotels, offices, shops, research laboratories, medical facilities and sports arenas — Turner Construction has built it all.

Turner Northwest established itself with Seattle's Two Union Square building, completed in 1989. A complex project, Two Union Square was built with high-strength

concrete in a composite structural system. In keeping with Turner Construction's origins, the concrete used in the Two Union Square building is extraordinary: tested at more than 20,000 psi, the material is as strong as steel and four times stronger than conventional concrete. The 56-story office tower has 10 corner offices on each floor rather than the usual four, thanks to the building's innovative and stunning configuration. Those who work in the building probably rarely think about the concrete that went into its making; they'd rather enjoy the glorious views from Two Union Square — Mount Rainier to the south, Lake Union to the north, Lake Washington and the Cascade Mountains to the east, and Elliott Bay and the Olympic Mountains to the west. Such challenging, sophisticated constructions are Turner's specialty.

The Fred Hutchinson Cancer Research Center does life-saving work in the Puget Sound area and around the world. When the building of its Phase II biomedical research laboratory project hit several major snags, the "Hutch" turned to Turner Northwest for help. An exceptionally complex mechanical project, the laboratory needed special ductwork and systems that would provide labs with gasses and de-ionized water. By the time Turner came on board, the project was $4 million over budget. Turner was hired to perform pre-construction services only. If the company did well, it would be hired on for the duration. Turner took the challenge very seriously. A team of experts was assembled that included a special mechanical estimator and an expert on research lab construction. The team found places to save money and opened up the bids to other subcontractors. On the strength of its performance in pre-construction, Turner Northwest was awarded the general contractor/ construction management contract for the lab. The Phase II lab was completed on time, and the work was so exceptional that Turner was hired to perform the next three projects on the Hutch campus.

Educational and health care facilities are major areas of focus for Turner Northwest. Turner enjoys a healthy, long-standing relationship with the University of Washington and has been involved in the construction of the Biomedical Sciences Research Building, the addition at the University Health Sciences Complex and the Research and Training Facility at Harborview Medical Center. Medical research buildings have special needs such as large laboratories and controlled environments. By working closely with the university and the project architect, Turner was able to construct buildings that met those needs. Success on these projects led to awards of other University of Washington contracts, including the construction of the Fisheries building and the Chemical Oceanography building and the renovation of the Suzzallo Library.

Sports facilities have long been a significant portion of Turner's business. In 1909 Turner Construction built a colonnade on Harvard's football stadium, and in 1916 it built Franklin Field in Philadelphia, Pennsylvania. In the Pacific Northwest, Turner's most famous sports project is undoubtedly the Seattle Seahawks' $360 million, 72,000-seat football stadium and exhibition hall. Turner Northwest has worked with Seahawks owner Paul Allen before; Allen is also owner of the Portland Trailblazers,

The University of Washington Fisheries building

Fred Hutchinson Cancer Research Center, Phase II

and in 1995 Turner completed construction of the Rose Garden Arena in time for the start of the Portland Trailblazers' basketball season. Heralded as one of the most innovative sports venues in the country, the Rose Garden was an overwhelming success. Allen's team hoped to duplicate that success in Seattle.

The project was not without difficulties. First, the existing stadium, the Kingdome, had to be demolished to make room for the new, open-air football/soccer stadium. The implosion of the Kingdome was undertaken by Turner, and it was one of the most anticipated demolitions in Seattle history. On March 26, 2000, people lined the streets to catch a view of the 17-second-long implosion. It went off without a hitch, and the next day workers began to clear the rubble to make way for a new, state-of-the-art football stadium. Because the neighborhood where the stadium would be built had seen so much construction,

Allen and Turner Construction were concerned with the tolerance of the locals for more noise, dirt and disruption. Fortunately, Turner is experienced at carrying out construction without negatively impacting the neighborhood in which it is working. Even though construction of the Rose Garden Arena in Portland was carried out right next door to the operational Memorial Coliseum, not a single show was missed and traffic wasn't affected. In Seattle, Turner consultants studied the potential problems of traffic, dust, parking and noise and put controls in place to minimize these irritations. Turner Northwest believes that it isn't just putting up buildings, it's helping create and shape local communities. This attitude makes Turner sensitive to community issues and successful in raising and maintaining community support while it builds.

One way of generating community support in environmentally conscious Seattle is through construction that preserves the environment. So-called "green" building is a major Turner Construction initiative, and the company is a leader in the drive to make construction more environmentally sensitive. Before the Kingdome was demolished, interior furnishings were either donated to local charities or auctioned off, with the proceeds going to the King County Parks and Recreation Department. After the Kingdome was demolished, 97 percent of the debris was recycled. Any material that would contaminate the recycling process was removed in advance of the demolition. Dumpsters marked "wood," "steel," "concrete," etc., were set up around the site, and sorters made sure that the debris was separated into the proper containers. Concrete from the Kingdome was used to raise the site the two feet necessary for the construction of the new arena, reducing waste and eliminating the need for as many as 4,500 trucks and trailers to take away the waste concrete and bring in new concrete. As of November 30, 2000, of the approximately 128,250 tons of waste generated by the Kingdome implosion, only 3,420 tons were sent to landfills. This massive recycling effort saved the project more than $3 million and untold additional stress on the local environment. Turner hopes to inspire other construction companies to follow its example and employ more responsible building practices.

Innovation is a Turner Con-struction hallmark, and Turner's Special Projects Division (SPD) is particularly creative in its work. Formed in 1988, the SPD is largely involved in renovations, tenant services and small freestanding buildings. With a client base that includes such corporate giants as amazon.com, Immunex, the Bon Marche and Puget Sound Energy, Turner's SPD is the largest in the Northwest. The SPD emerged from the Two Union Square building for which it did all the interiors work — more than 1.1 million square feet of office and retail space. The key, according to Turner SPD staff, is attention to the client's needs and wants and the ability to fulfill them. Because Turner is such a large company, it has resources that other construction companies just can't match. Thanks to this broad range of expertise, the SPD has been able to take on such diverse projects as construction of Infospace; Casey Family Program, Seattle Division; Courtside Club/Premier Club, and Immunex Corporation.

Turner SPD has worked on several projects at Amazon.com. Not only is the client unique, but the building it occupies is also one-of-a-kind.

The implosion of the Kingdome, March 26, 2000

Architect's rendition of the Seattle Seahawks' stadium

Amazon.com headquarters are located in the former Pacific Medical Center complex. Turner SPD worked closely with the architect to make the building ready for occupancy by a high-tech company, and the work was completed on time and on budget. Additionally, Amazon.com needed a renovation and structural upgrade done on an office building in downtown Seattle, and it had no time to spare. Electrical needs required a transformer vault, offices and open workspaces had to be built, and reinforcements of the existing structure were needed to bring the building into compliance with seismic codes. The project was fast-tracked, and intensive work allowed the building to be substantially complete in just five months.

Turner Construction's ability to handle difficult situations and solve thorny problems is a key element to the company's continued domination of the industry in the United States. To solve difficulties, Turner relies on its network of highly experienced professionals. On every project, Turner encourages close, continuous communication between the Turner team, the architect and the owner. To ensure success on every project, Turner assembles a team of experts whose combined knowledge and experience covers every aspect of a job. Matching staff and resources to the client's needs streamlines the process from contract to completion. Frequently Turner is involved with a project in the planning stages, sometimes as long as three years before the first shovel of dirt is turned over.

Every job is different. When Turner Northwest was approached to participate in the construction of Boeing's sheet metal facility, the project presented some unusual challenges. Construction of the building required excavating underwater, and the site was underlain by the Oskilow Mud Flow, a build-up of trees, boulders and mud which had slid off the north face of Mount Rainier several thousand years ago. On site, 90 wells pumped 4 million gallons of water a day. Utility tunnels had to be dug underground, and foundations were laid for more than 150 separate pieces of equipment. More than 640 workers were required, some working swing shifts to keep productivity at a maximum. Painters did their work at night to minimize fumes and disruption that would interfere with other crews that worked during the day. In the end, the 900,000-square-foot facility won Turner the 1990 "Grand Award for Excellence in Construction" from the Associated General Contractors of Washington. It was the first such grand award the local Associated General Contractors had ever given.

Although Turner Northwest draws on experts and resources nationwide, the company prides itself on being a Seattle local. The Turner Northwest offices focus strictly on the Northwest, namely Washington, Oregon, Idaho, Montana and Alaska. Staff members live in the cities in which they work, connecting Turner Northwest to the communities in which it builds. When Turner Northwest opened its offices, its intention was to build a local reputation for excellence equal to Turner Construction Company's national and global reputation. Turner Northwest has forged and maintained strong ties with local subcontractors, designers, developers and crafts people. By consistently taking on challenging, cutting-edge jobs requiring sophisticated technology and know-how, Turner Northwest has proven that it can build anything and build it with the highest level of quality.

The reception area of Great Northern Annuities Insurance and Securities

The Courtside Club

TARRAGON DEVELOPMENT COMPANY

Pacific Northwest natives Joe Blattner and Michael Corliss know that a solid business, like a solid building, needs a good foundation. In January 1995 they combined their skills in finance and construction and opened Tarragon Development Company. With expertise in land acquisition, market analysis, land entitlements, design, construction and property management, Tarragon has become a leader in commercial development in the Puget Sound region and is expanding into other Western states.

For those seeking state-of-the-art retail, office, industrial or living space, the partnership of Blattner and Corliss is a match made in heaven. Their extensive backgrounds in real estate development and their complementary attitudes

toward business make Tarragon a dynamic and competitive company. Corliss, who studied business finance, was already at work on his first construction project — a 36-unit apartment building — just six months after graduation. Blattner, a Washington State University graduate, worked as operations manager and senior project manager for a large construction company. With their combined skills, Tarragon Development has been able to take on unusual projects and turn out success stories.

Tarragon Development Company is first and foremost a development company with quick access to resources and tactical expertise. The company looks for projects that take advantage of the varied strengths and expertise of its staff and that allow the company to add value to under-used property. Unique opportunities are what attract Tarragon's interest, and the company specializes in finding raw land and taking it through the often complex entitlement process. The ability to take on many kinds of projects and work in all segments of design and construction gives Tarragon Development a broad and diverse portfolio.

Tarragon Development Company has an established track record of collaborative and profitable relationships. A straightforward communication style, streamlined decision making, and intuition are trademarks of Tarragon's approach to real estate development. This gives Tarragon a real edge: when opportunities arise, Tarragon can move quickly to take advantage, winning out over larger, less nimble companies. Tarragon is always interested in unique projects. Tarragon built Valley South Corporate Park, and the 190-acre industrial project has been winning awards ever since. All the buildings are designed and constructed as high-quality and state-of-the-art industrial facilities.

Another Tarragon Development Company enterprise is the AIA Seattle award-winning Saffron urban village project, located in Sammamish, Washington. The property has approximately 50,000 square feet of upscale retail shop space, along with professional service space and 99 apartments, all above a 200-stall underground parking garage. Saffron is designed to be pedestrian-friendly: wide sidewalks and common gathering areas encourage

Tarragon's award-winning Valley South Corporate Park
Photo by Matt Todd Photography

A rendering of Tarragon's Lakeland Town Center by Fuller Sears Architects
© *Fuller Sears Architects*

people to walk and leave the car behind. Saffron is designed to give residents all the conveniences and activities of "downtown" life without the hassle of traffic and parking.

Saffron is just one example of how Tarragon is constructing today's residential and business spaces with an eye on tomorrow. Designing, building, leasing and managing, Tarragon Development Company is involved in every part of a project, and this long-term focus is an important part of the company's success. Tarragon primarily builds to own, and therefore structures are designed and constructed to be at the leading edge of the market — now, and 20 years from now. And with the rapid changes in the way building space is utilized, that's even more difficult than it sounds. More business is being done in less space than ever before, and Tarragon designs its buildings to make maximum use of the available area — a real benefit in Seattle, where real estate is at a premium.

In Seattle and around Puget Sound, Tarragon Development is involved in various types of projects, an example of Tarragon's flexibility in design and construction. Tarragon is personally committed to delivering on unique opportunities, continually expanding the types of projects it designs and builds. Another Tarragon project is a grocery-store-anchored shopping center located within a 690-acre community in Auburn called Lakeland Town Center. The planned community, Lakeland, includes over 3,400 homes, a 15-acre park, a neighborhood shopping area and two elementary schools.

In addition to its building projects, Tarragon Development is very involved with the Seattle and Puget Sound communities. Tarragon actively supports and is a member of NAIOP (National Association of Industrial and Office Properties), CREW Northwest (Commercial Real Estate Women's Association), Seattle Downtown Association, Seattle Chamber of Commerce, the International Council of Shopping Centers and the YWCA, particularly the Angeline Center for homeless women. Additionally, through professional affiliations and YWCA, Tarragon is involved in various community outreach programs designed to help women and families re-establish or learn economic self-sufficiency and

Washington Professional Center © Patrick Barta, Patrick Barta Photography Inc.

independence. Tarragon Development believes in being a part of the communities where it builds, and the company demonstrates this philosophy in grass-roots involvement.

Tarragon Development believes in taking care of its customers. With its focus on long-term relationships, it plans to keep those customers for many years into the future. Tarragon is always willing to listen to tenants, designing buildings to suit particular needs or making renovations to keep up with changes in the marketplace. It plans to further expand geographically, entering into even more areas around Puget Sound, as it also expands the kinds of structures it designs and builds. This, in addition to Tarragon's emphasis on innovation and customer service, will ensure that Tarragon Development continues to build the spaces in which Puget Sound lives, shops, eats and does business well into the future.

Saffron — the mixed-use, AIA award-winning "urban village" development is designed to be pedestrian friendly. © 2000 Patrick Barta, Patrick Barta Photography Inc.

BRE Properties, Inc.

Many companies claim to be changing the way people live, but BRE Properties, Inc. (BRE) is one of the few who are genuinely keeping that promise. A real estate investment trust focused on the development, acquisition and management of apartment communities, BRE is anything but a typical developer. The company's understanding of the connection between customer satisfaction and loyalty is the foundation of an ongoing mission to provide high-quality multifamily homes with architecturally advanced designs, the most desirable amenities in the industry and professional service from well-trained associates. More than just providing housing, BRE creates valuable and innovative Lifestyle Solutions™ for busy professionals who want comfort and convenience.

Founded in 1970, the San Francisco-based company is led by Chairman John McMahan and President and CEO Frank C. McDowell. The highly respected McDowell was brought into the company by McMahan in 1995 and soon broadened BRE's focus. Concerned primarily with ownership until that point, the company expanded to include property management and multifamily developments by acquiring REIT of California in 1996 and the assets of Trammell Crow Residential-West in 1997. The following year, after having owned developments in the Northwest for many years, BRE opened its Seattle office to manage those properties and develop its new Pinnacle line of luxury multifamily communities.

Under McMahan and McDowell, BRE has grown into a $2 billion company. With a portfolio focused on the Western United States, BRE owns and operates approximately 82 apartment communities totaling more than 22,000 units in California, Arizona, Washington, Oregon, Utah and Colorado. True to the company's innovative style, BRE's developments are anything but homogenous, ranging from suburban garden-style apartments and townhomes with attached garages to urban infill and mid-rise flats over street-level retail. In addition to new developments, the company also rejuvenates older apartment communities with extensive exterior and interior rehabilitation. In the Puget Sound area, BRE operates three new upscale multifamily communities designed for singles, couples and families who are renters by choice: the Pinnacle Sonata in Bothel, featuring 268 luxury townhomes; Pinnacle Bluffs on Lake Washington, 180 apartments located in a picturesque setting on the lake's southern edge in Renton; and Pinnacle BellCentre in downtown Bellevue, featuring 248 apartments and 9,200 square feet of retail and restaurant space.

Unlike most apartment communities, where the resident turnover rate is high, BRE's properties attract and keep residents who stay significantly longer than the industry average. The company's innovative approach to multifamily development is what sets it apart. BRE uses sophisticated market research and customized surveys to understand its residents' values, priorities and needs, then goes the extra mile to meet those criteria. Its communities attract residents by offering strategic locations at competitive prices and keep them by providing unparalleled amenities and customer service.

BRE knows that because time is precious for busy professionals and their families, location becomes a primary concern. One of the hallmarks of BRE communities is their placement in highly desirable locations that are close to major employment and transportation centers. By offering conveniently located homes, BRE makes it possible for residents to spend less time commuting to and from work, supermarkets, day care or school, and more time enjoying family and leisure activities.

Setting the pace for the industry, BRE communities offer amenities that create a residential experience second to none in

Pinnacle Sonata |

quality, aesthetic appeal and convenience. Each development is beautifully landscaped, built in a contemporary design with quality interior finishes, and offers maintenance-free living. Amenities can include gourmet kitchens, full-size washers and dryers, master suite fireplaces, reading libraries, state-of-the-art fitness facilities and private movie theaters with surround sound.

For residents whose workplace is in the home, BRE communities offer a total telecommute solution in the form of full-service business and Internet centers, and executive conference centers. The Pinnacle communities also feature always-on, high-speed Internet access, e-mail portability, Web site hosting and local area networks through VelocityHSI™. These lifestyle solutions through technology also make it possible for residents to place and track maintenance requests, conduct virtual online garage sales, send messages to their neighbors, transfer utilities, and pay their rent without having to mail a check or go to the rental office. Because VelocityHSI™ works with televisions and Web appliances, it is also available to residents who do not own a computer. By making the apartment of the future the apartment of today, BRE has carved out a market position that is light years ahead of the competition. In honor of the company's innovative amenities, *Multifamily Executive* magazine awarded it the Best Use of Technology award in 1999.

BRE realizes that amenities alone cannot always ensure long-term relationships. The company believes residents must also feel connected and valued, comfortable not only with their physical surroundings but also with the way they are treated within their community. As a result, BRE is as innovative in its approach to customer service as it is in its amenities. Whether sponsoring communitywide social events, facilitating the sharing of commuting options, or linking residents electronically, the company strives to create and nurture a sense of community among the people who call its developments home. Its intention is nothing less than

| Pinnacle BellCentre

to revolutionize the way customer service is provided in multifamily communities.

As demographic shifts in the United States continue to create an expanding population of renters-by-choice — from busy new professionals in the expanding technology sector to the first wave of Baby Boomer retirees who have tired of maintaining a home of their own — it becomes increasingly important for upscale multifamily housing to offer convenience and technological functionality with a touch of elegance and an atmosphere of home. After 30 years of creating such model communities, BRE Properties understands the needs of this emerging market and is committed to not only maintaining but also enhancing its high-touch, high-tech Lifestyle Solutions™.

| Pinnacle on Lake Washington

KIEWIT CONSTRUCTION COMPANY

No matter where people go in Puget Sound, chances are they'll find a Kiewit Construction Company building, or they'll drive on Kiewit-built roads to get there. Kiewit Construction Company's Pacific Building District is responsible for airports, hotels, sports stadiums, schools, theaters, offices and roads all over Seattle and Greater Puget Sound. And Kiewit's reputation for quality work done on time and within budget is as rock-solid as the structures Kiewit builds.

Andrew and Peter Kiewit founded their company in 1884 in Omaha, Nebraska. Sons of a bricklayer themselves, they knew the value of quality construction work. From constructing buildings, the company quickly expanded and began building roadways, bridges and tunnels. The company expanded geographically as well, and Peter Kiewit broke into the Pacific Northwest market rather dramatically in 1939.

In the winter of 1939, the United States was preparing for involvement in World War II. Young men were being drafted, and Fort Lewis needed barracks to house its inductees. Peter Kiewit Sons' Co., as the company was then called, was awarded a contract to build 760 barracks, each designed to hold 64 men. Fort Lewis also needed roads, utilities and support facilities.

The 27-story, "four star" Starwood W Hotel includes 417 guest rooms, a fine dining restaurant, meeting and ballrooms, and four levels of below-grade parking. It was completed in September 1999.

The new 244,000-square-foot Ballard High School, completed in August 1999, replaced the original building built in 1914. The new school has state-of-the-art features such as an in-house television studio, fiber-optic cabling, and closed circuit television.

Kiewit agreed to build all of these — in 90 days. The project was made even more challenging when the United States Army doubled the order to 1,540 buildings but didn't increase the time frame or price per unit. Immediately, 10,000 managers, engineers, carpenters and other skilled workers began pouring in from Omaha and across the nation. Road equipment, idle for the winter in Nebraska, was transported by train or truck to Fort Lewis. Despite cold, wet, foggy weather, workers managed to turn out one completed barracks building every seven minutes. The $7.5 million project was completed on time and within budget. The Fort Lewis construction didn't generate a lot of profit for Kiewit, but it helped establish Kiewit as a presence in the Northwest.

From the Fort Lewis barracks, Kiewit Construction Company went on to build many structures that are well-known to Seattle residents. Among them are the Sears, Roebuck & Company building, finished in 1945 (now Starbucks' headquarters); the original Sea-Tac Airport parking garage; the Department of Veterans' Affairs hospital; several buildings for the 1962 World's Fair; and many buildings at the University of Washington. Kiewit is also responsible for major sections of Interstates 5 and 90. Large, high-profile projects are a Kiewit specialty. The company's ability to operate under considerable pressure and within time and budget restraints guarantees that Kiewit will always have plenty of work in Puget Sound.

One notable example of Kiewit Construction's gift for shining under pressure is the Seattle Kingdome. When the original contractor walked off the project, Kiewit was called in to complete the half-finished building. Engineering mistakes complicated the job: the forms for the concrete roof ribs had become wedged in place. Kiewit workers engineered a way to release the forms and move them into position for the remaining pours of concrete. All the unfinished construction work was completed in time for the opening game of the Seattle Seahawks' 1976 inaugural season.

When it came time for a new stadium to be built for the Seattle Mariners, Kiewit, in partnership with The Hunt Group of Indiana, won the contract. The Hunt/Kiewit team completed SAFECO Field in only 27 months. The stadium's most notable feature, the unique retractable roof, weighs in at 12,000 tons and has become such a Seattle landmark that local residents joke that Seattle has only two kinds of weather: "roof open" and "roof closed."

Seattle's Pacific Science Center also bears the Kiewit stamp. The original buildings were constructed by Kiewit for the 1962 World's Fair, and since 1995, Kiewit has completed six more projects for the Science Center. In 1995 Building 3, along with exterior fountains and ticket kiosks, were renovated, and a generous donation from the Kiewit Foundation led to the naming of Building 3, "Kiewit Pavilion." Additionally, Kiewit built the Boeing 3-D IMAX Theater, the Ackerly Exhibit Gallery, the Butterfly Pavilion and the James A. Claypool Memorial Parking Garage.

In August 1999 Kiewit completed construction on the new state-of-the-art Ballard High School. From the outside, Ballard High School, with its brick facade and arched entryways, greatly resembles the 1914 structure it replaced. On the inside, the school boasts such modern features as an in-house television studio and fiber-optic cabling. In downtown Seattle, Kiewit completed the 27-story Starwood W Hotel with minimal disruption to the heavy pedestrian and vehicular traffic of the area. Challenging and unique building projects such as these have always attracted Kiewit's interest and given the company the opportunity to shine.

Kiewit's unique decentralized management structure also broadens Kiewit's scope: while decisions about Puget Sound area projects are made in the Pacific Building District office in Renton, resources can be drawn from its national parent company, Peter Kiewit Sons' Inc. in Omaha, Nebraska. The 19 decentralized district offices frequently work together, enabling Kiewit to cover every aspect of a project: materials, equipment and expertise. Ownership of the company by its employees means that there are always owners on site.

SAFECO Field, completed in July 1999, includes 47,600 seats, suites, Mariner's administrative offices, the Stadium Club, restaurants, state-of-the-art clubhouses, and retail and concession operations. The most notable feature is the unique 12,000-ton retractable roof.

Kiewit Construction Company has had a significant impact on Seattle and Greater Puget Sound, even beyond the buildings and roads: it donates time and resources to the Boy Scouts, the Girl Scouts, the YMCA, and Boys and Girls Club of King County, among others. Kiewit has an annual fund-raiser for the United Way, with the corporate office matching employee contributions. Donations from the Kiewit Foundation promote local educational activities for youth, especially programs that involve engineering and construction projects.

In 1939 Kiewit Construction Company built barracks — lots and lots of barracks. Since then it has built nearly every kind of building imaginable. Any Puget Sound area resident or visitor has enjoyed the fruits of Kiewit's labor. With its hard-earned reputation for quality construction, Kiewit Construction Company will continue to play a major role in the building of the Northwest for a long time to come.

The Pacific Science Center IMAX Theater is equipped with the latest 3D technology, a digital sound system and over 400 seats. It was completed in October 1998.

MASTER BUILDERS ASSOCIATION OF KING AND SNOHOMISH COUNTIES

A handful of Seattle builders met in 1909 to promote the American dream of home ownership. In the first decade of the 21st century, Master Builders Association of King and Snohomish Counties will celebrate its 100th year representing all facets of the residential construction industry in the greater Seattle area. United by a common goal, MBA members include single and multifamily builders, remodelers, developers, architects, designers, contractors, suppliers, manufacturers, bankers, landscapers and others associated with the home building industry.

The group's vitality is evident in its incredible growth. The MBA today has 2,800 member companies employing more than 80,000 workers, making it the second-largest home building association among the 800 in the country. The association is chartered by the National Association of Home Builders and, along with the other 16 local state associations, forms the Building Industry Association of

Master Builders Association began in downtown Seattle more than 90 years ago.

Community service has always been at the heart of many of the association's activities.

Washington. Together, MBA members build and remodel more than 85 percent of the homes in King and Snohomish counties.

Although the concerns and issues affecting the building industry have changed over the years, the focus of this nonprofit trade association has always remained constant and is the cornerstone of the association's mission: to ensure the economic viability of the industry and the livability of the region.

"We are the voice of the housing industry, working diligently to build communities that meet all the housing demands of the consumer in all market segments," says Sam Anderson, executive officer of the MBA.

From the economic booms in the first and last decades of the 20th century to the intermittent downturns, the builders and contractors of the greater Seattle area have continued over the years to search for better ways to represent and promote the building industry and serve the housing needs of the region's residents.

The association's roots go back to the time of building the grand, stately homes on Queen Anne Hill, Capitol Hill and the ridges above Lake Washington. As the decades marched on, the association guided the Puget Sound through its growing pains, helping to settle labor disputes, establishing stricter cost controls, and finding more efficient ways to build and meet the area's varied housing demands.

To raise professionalism, industry expertise and consumer knowledge, MBA educated its members, provided for the needs of home buyers and informed the government and the public about housing issues.

In 1939 the MBA reached out to the public and sponsored the first Seattle Home Show, a tradition that continues each February and October in the Stadium Exhibition Center. Fifty years ago, MBA began the country's first Remodelors™ Council to bring a higher degree of professionalism to that industry. Always on the lookout for ways to protect consumers, the association offered a Home Owners Warranty in the 70s to assist consumers making a new home purchase. With the new millennium, the MBA launched a Dispute Resolution Process that offers a method for consumers buying or remodeling a home to solve problems, should they arise. The association continues to educate and inform through its Home Show booths and seminars, a new remodeling magazine, an industry Web site and public events such as new and remodeled home tours.

Along the way, builders, remodelers and associates have found many ways to extend a helping hand to the less fortunate in their communities. Through a variety of service projects, MBA members build and remodel homes for children and the temporarily homeless, build wheelchair access ramps, donate materials to various projects and raise money for a variety of local charities. That commitment to the community and to the industry remains a hallmark of the organization today.

Through the Master Builder Education Foundation, college students in construction-related trades are awarded thousands of dollars in scholarships each year. The Association's 501(c)(3) not-for-profit corporation, Master Builders Care Foundation, gives back to the community through Dream Playhouses, Rampathon and its Master Builders' HomeAid Chapter, which works with nonprofit community care providers to build or renovate facilities housing the temporarily homeless.

For the past 20 years, the most critical issue in the industry remains how to provide affordable housing for the majority of the region's residents. To address this concern, MBA has stepped up its government affairs involvement, working with local governments on sensible growth management and increasing its political efforts to elect housing-friendly candidates.

The Growth Management Act of 1990 (GMA), which has among its goals to contain urban sprawl, provide adequate transportation infrastructure and increase economic development, has created new challenges and opportunities for the champions of affordable housing. While increased environmental regulations and longer permitting times raise the cost of building homes, the land supply through GMA has been severely diminished, driving up lot prices. MBA constantly reminds state and local officials of their responsibilities to make housing more attainable to all citizens.

The association works with elected officials, local government and community groups to allow builders to meet the housing needs of area residents while protecting the environment. Partnerships with such groups as local economic development councils, chambers of commerce, the Housing Partnership and 1000 Friends of Washington find areas of common ground which help realize the goal of affordable housing and manage growth in a way that makes more sense for all.

New homes built with environmentally friendly materials and methods are certified as Built Green™.

To meet the needs of those who want more environmentally friendly and sustainable homes, MBA launched its Built Green™ program in partnership with King County, Snohomish County and various community groups. The comprehensive program identifies homes that are built with environmentally friendly and energy-efficient materials and methods and educates builders and consumers about the many ways available to help preserve the area's ecosystem and protect the salmon habitat.

After almost 100 years of serving its members and the residents of the Puget Sound community, the association continues to provide quality, assurance, expertise and leadership. MBA members receive services, programs, legislative representation and membership opportunities unparalleled by any other trade association. For homeowners, the MBA is the ultimate resource, providing reliable information and the names of quality professionals who can help in any area of building or remodeling a home.

MBA remodelers answer the public's questions at the Seattle Home Show.

NITZE-STAGEN & CO., INC.

A private real estate investment and develop-ment company that has one eye on the community's future while simultaneously keeping an eye on preserving its past is a rare gem indeed. Yet, Nitze-Stagen & Co., Inc. of Seattle has shown a remarkable prowess for doing just that.

The vision of Peter Nitze and Frank Stagen was realized in 1970 when the two men formed an investment company that today continues to offer expertise in the areas of commercial office, industrial and retail properties. Nitze-Stagen's staff of more than 22 people, most of whom have been with the company for at least a decade or more, have helped the company make immeasurable contributions to the Seattle area, including its renovations of Union Station, the Frye Museum, the SODO Center and Merrill Place.

Part of Nitze-Stagen's continued success is a com-mitment to its involvement in the downtown Seattle area. Its vision of a thriving hub of industrial, manufacturing and shipping industries has led to its daring renovations and purchases of properties long abandoned by conven-tional investment wisdom. As President Kevin Daniels explains, "We want to leave a stamp on what happens in Seattle." Nitze-Stagen has accomplished that and much more by engaging its resources in the preservation and renovation of long-forgotten landmarks.

Perhaps one of the company's more notable ventures is the SODO Center, now known as Starbucks Center. In 1990 Nitze-Stagen acquired and funded the renovation of the former Sears Building on First Avenue South.

The Starbucks Center has become an economic powerhouse in Seattle.
Photo by Wayne Bartz Photography

Containing 1.9 million square feet, the SODO Center was once considered a waste of space. Daniels succinctly summed it up when he recalled, "It was noon on December 7, 1990, during the Christmas retail season, and there were three cars in the parking lot."

SODO is now considered an "economic powerhouse," according to a former Seattle mayor. Today, humming with activity, the center houses a vast array of clients and three national retail chains as well as the Starbucks Coffee Company's corporate headquarters. Olympic West Sportswear, one of the nation's largest manufacturers of outerwear garments for companies including Lands End and L.L. Bean, is just one of the many building tenants bringing economic growth to the area. Storage tenants include the University of Washington, Pacific Science Center, City of Seattle and The Intiman Theatre.

Nitze-Stagen also renovated Merrill Place, a land-mark office block containing some 200,000 square feet on First Avenue South in Pioneer Square. The project is now home to a supercomputer manufacturer and Internet-related companies. Merrill Place has become the center of development and employment opportunity for the surrounding community. Concurrent with the total office renovation of these historic buildings, 16 rental apartments sitting astride the office block were totally renovated into 12 luxury condos.

Of all Nitze-Stagen's undertakings, Union Station is probably the best known. This seven-phase project included the restoration of Union Station as corporate headquarters for Sound Transit and the construction of a new 1,150-stall garage that will offer daily parking for the project as well as sports and special-event parking conve-niently situated within walking distance to SAFECO Field, the Stadium Exhibition Center and the new Seattle Seahawks Stadium. The garage also is easily accessible for downtown special events parking because the Metro Bus Tunnel's southern entrance is located next to it.

Inside the Great Hall at Union Station, the 55-foot-high, cream-colored, barrel-vaulted ceiling, with its skylight, inlaid square plaster blocks and gold insignia of the original Oregon-Washington Railroad and Navigation Co., has been restored to its original splendor. The brick exterior, marveled for its neoclassical lines, has been cleaned to return it to its original look. On the lower level, origi-nally known as the baggage room, the waiting area for immigrants and a small emergency hospital, the concrete floor has been raised to accommodate miles of advanced cabling for the myriad of equipment needed to operate a rapid transit system.

An employee garden was created in a ground-level courtyard. Upstairs, on a floor that flanks the arched waiting-room ceiling, Sound Transit executives and staff occupy offices finished with Douglas fir woodwork. Former ticket offices, cafeteria space and the Ladies Waiting Room are now a Transit boardroom and workspace.

The balance of the Union Station development was completed by the spring of 2001, seven years ahead of schedule. Occupants include Amazon.com, Vulcan NW, Accenture Consulting and Watchguard Technologies, to name a few. The result is a high-technology park that services the needs of tenants in the newly completed office campus of 1.1 million square feet in Seattle's oldest neighborhood, while simultaneously embracing the renovated Union Station.

In recognition of this outstanding achievement, the Puget Sound Regional Council, the designated transportation planning organization, presented the VISION 2020 Award to Nitze-Stagen. The VISION 2020 Awards annually honor innovative projects that help achieve the region's adopted growth management, economic and transportation strategy. The company also received the Historic Seattle 25th Anniversary Special Recognition

Award for its blending of old and new into a commercial success without sacrificing quality or historic relevance. In addition, the project was named the winner of the 2000 National Preservation Award by the National Trust for Historic Preservation.

The Frye Museum, named after Charles and Emma Frye, is another elegant renovation that has become a splendid example of incorporating the past with the future. Visitors to this extraordinary museum, originally provided for by Charles Frye upon his death in 1940 and completed in 1952, houses German, French and American art collected during the Fryes' excursions to Europe in the 1920s. Upon entering the foyer, visitors are enveloped in an elegant lobby. Surrounded by an outdoor reflecting pool, waterfall and courtyard garden, the café, museum store and education wing round out the expansion. State-of-the-art lighting and climate control enhance the visitor's experience of the collection. Nitze-Stagen coordinated the design and construction of the renovated museum, which was completed in 1998.

Nitze-Stagen's deep sense of commitment and investment in the Seattle community have given it an excellent reputation that is locally and internationally recognized. With an unwavering focus on reinventing the past and renovating for the future, Nitze-Stagen & Co., Inc. continues to inspire a passion for history, economy and culture throughout Seattle and the Northwest.

Merrill Place is an employment mecca for the surrounding community.

(Far left) The entrance to the Frye Art Museum offers a first glance of the renovated museum.

Union Station, completed by spring 2001, serves as corporate headquarters for Sound Transit. *Photo by Lara Swimmer Photography*

SEATTLE-KING COUNTY ASSOCIATION OF REALTORS

Handing the keys to a first-time homebuyer is an exhilarating experience. It doesn't matter if the home is a fixer-upper, a brand new structure or something in between. It doesn't matter if the buyer is young or old or if the buyer is single or married. Anyone who witnesses the new owner's excitement, joy and sense of accomplishment understands the essence of the American dream.

Homeownership matters. In the words of Henry Cisneros and Jack Kemp (former U.S. secretaries of Housing and Urban Development), "In addition to stabilizing neighborhoods, homeownership strengthens the family structure, helping children stay in school and out of trouble." They observed that homeowners are more likely to vote in local elections, and they volunteer time and talents to charities, recreational leagues and religious organizations.

Recognizing that homeownership isn't just about shelter, since its formation in 1908 as the Seattle Real Estate Association, the organization now known as the Seattle-King County Association of REALTORS® (SKCAR) has worked on behalf of property owners to promote the rights and responsibilities of homeownership. Members of SKCAR also belong to the Washington Association of REALTORS® (WAR) and the National Association of REALTORS® (NAR). The term REALTOR®, first adopted in 1916, is a licensed collective trademark that may be used only by members of the National Association of REALTORS® and its local associations. As part of NAR, also established in 1908, its founders envisioned four purposes that remain central to NAR's purpose today:

- access to all available real estate experience, skills and information;
- expansion of existing knowledge through education and research;
- strength to establish ethical standards, and
- advocacy for sound public policy on the many issues affecting real estate.

SKCAR also believes that safe, decent and affordable housing forms the foundation of strong communities. Homeownership contributes to a region's well-being. It enhances civic, economic, business and employment stability. It also adds value in ways that are sometimes difficult to quantify. It brings families together in a shared desire to make their neighborhoods safe. It brings neighbors together as advocates for good schools. It fosters new friendships.

Promoting homeownership is central to the REALTOR® mission, but it represents only part of the association's scope of services and commitment at local, state and national levels. The Seattle-King County Association of REALTORS® comprises approximately 4,900 real estate licensees and affiliated interests. Membership in this nonprofit trade organization is voluntary.

Collectively, there are around 760,000 members who voluntarily accept and abide by a Code of Ethics that distinguish REALTORS® from other real estate licensees. Since 1913, this code, which is predicated on the Golden Rule, has come to stand for competency, fairness and integrity. Considered a living document, it undergoes regular review and revision to amplify its ethical principles and to accommodate current legal, cultural and national perspectives. In many instances, the code is stricter than state law.

REALTORS® also act as advocates of vital quality-of-life issues. The legislative and political priorities include such far-ranging concerns as protecting private property rights and the mortgage deduction to promoting stewardship of the environment and smart growth.

Other services encompass education programs for REALTORS® and consumers and professional development and designations for members. Risk management, legal assistance, insurance and other services are also offered. Member benefits also include publications, database programs and discounts on an array of products and services.

1909 Board of Directors for the National Assn. Of REALTORS®

The association also promotes volunteerism and community service. Each year, SKCAR, in partnership with other organizations, presents the Seattle-King County First Citizen Award. This award recognizes a King County resident, family or organization that exemplifies outstanding public service and leadership.

Hugh Russell conceived the award during his tenure as president of SKCAR in 1939. It symbolizes appreciation on behalf of Puget Sound area residents to those who, through voluntary actions, devote themselves to the well-being and prosperity of their community.

First Citizens are recognized for their unselfish commitment to civic causes, whether by supporting humanitarian organizations, charitable and educational institutions, arts groups, the environment or other concerns. Visionary leadership and philanthropy to meet ever-changing community needs are also considered. Individually and as a group, award recipients are recognized as inspirational role models for compassionate citizenship.

In 1999 the *Puget Sound Business Journal* joined SKCAR as a partner and co-presenter of the First Citizen Award and civic banquet that celebrates community involvement. Past recipients include a cross section of prominent leaders alongside the unsung heroes whose good deeds have enriched people's lives and made neighborhoods and workplaces desirable places for families and businesses.

Past recipients of the Seattle-King County First Citizen Award include:

Herb M. Bridge, 2001; The Bullitt Family, 2000; Paul Brainerd, 1999; Jack A. Benaroya, 1998; Walter B. Williams, 1997; Stanley O. McNaughton, 1996; Mary Gates & Family, 1995; Phil M. Smart, Sr., 1994; Constance W. Rice, Ph.D., 1993; Lester R. Sauvage, M.D., 1992; Buster and Nancy Alvord, 1991; The Rev. Wm. J. Sullivan, S.J., 1990; R.C. "Torchy" Torrance, 1989; Samuel Stroum, 1988; John W. Ellis, 1987; Robert W. Graham, 1986; Fredric A. Danz, 1985; Victor Rosellini, 1984; T.A. Wilson, 1983; Dr. Dale E. Turner, 1982; C.M. "Mike" Berry, 1981; James M. Ryan, 1980; Gordon H. Sweaney, 1979; John M. Fluke, 1978; W.J. "Jerry" Pennington, 1977; Rabbi Raphael Levine, 1976; Dr. Wm. B. Hutchinson, 1975; Ned and Kayla Skinner, 1974; Dr. Dixy Lee Ray, 1973; John D. Ehrlichman, 1972; Glynn Ross, 1971; Norton Clapp, 1970; William B. Woods, 1969; James R. Ellis, 1968; Mrs. Henry B. Owen, 1967; Milton Katims, 1966; Edward E. Carlson, 1965; H.W. McCurdy, 1964; George F. Kachlein, Jr., 1963; seph E. Gandy, 1962; Ben E. Ehrlichman, 1961; Michael Dederer, 1960; Mrs. A. Scott Bullitt, 1959; Nat S. Rogers, 1958; Gordon N. Scott, 1957; Rev. A.A. Lemieux, 1956; Deitrich Schmitz, 1955; William M. Allen, 1954; Frank E. Holman, 1953; Henry Broderick, 1952; George Gunn, Jr., 1951; Thomas M. Pelly, 1950; Dr. Raymond Allen, 1949; Ernest Skeel, 1948; John H. Reid, 1947; Royal Brougham, 1946; W. Walter Williams, 1945; Children's Orthopedic Hospital, 1944; Phil Johnson, 1943; Kenneth Colman, 1942; William O. McKay, 1941; Dr. Wendell Fifield, 1940; Richard Eugene Fuller, 1939.

SOUTH OF DOWNTOWN DEVELOPMENT

Vulcan Northwest believes in partnering with the community to create relevant, lasting projects that are supported by and benefit the larger community. Neighborhoods should be healthy and comfortable places to live, work, play and learn, and Vulcan Northwest wants to help communities recognize their possibilities and realize their goals. One area of particular interest to Vulcan is Seattle's historic south downtown (SODO), an area primarily concerned with industry and transit which plays a critical role in Seattle's continuing growth and prosperity. Vulcan Northwest wants to be a partner in preserving SODO's history and shaping its future.

preserve its individual cultures and histories. With this directive firmly in mind, Vulcan Northwest has carried out several major projects in the area including the Washington State Football/Soccer Stadium, the Washington State Stadium Exhibition Center, the 505 Union Station building, the preservation of historic Union Station and the redevelopment of Palmer Court.

The publicly owned Washington State Football/Soccer Stadium was first envisioned when Ken Bering, then-owner of the Seattle Seahawks football team, decided to move his team to California. One of the sticking points for Bering was the aged and out-of-date Kingdome, which did not generate enough revenue to support the costs of running a world-class team. The Seahawks needed a new stadium, and the ancillary revenue which would come with it, in order to field a competitive team. Then Paul Allen stepped in. He agreed to buy the team with the condition that the people of Washington state be his partner in building a new stadium. The issue was put to a public vote, and the people agreed. The Kingdome was imploded in 2000 and construction of the new stadium began.

In 1997 Paul Allen created a new company called First & Goal to manage the development, construction and operation of the stadium and exhibition center. Ellerbe Becket, in association with LMN Architects,

A graphic representation of the completed football/soccer stadium
© Ellerbe Beckett

Seattle's south downtown area encompasses three unique and distinct districts: Pioneer Square, the International District and Duwamish. Situated close to the old docks, Pioneer Square is one of the most historic areas of Seattle. Once Seattle's financial district, now the area's beautiful, old brick buildings house much of Seattle's creative community, among them galleries, bookstores, gift shops, advertising firms and software developers. The International District is home to many of Seattle's Asian businesses and families. And Duwamish, in the heart of Seattle's industrial area and working docks, is the lifeblood of the city. Vulcan believes that all three districts are important and that any development should respect and

oversaw the stadium's design; Turner Construction built the structures. The open-air facility seats 68,000; 70 percent of seats are protected from Seattle's predictably unpredictable weather. A showcase for the Americans with Disabilities Act, the stadium was meticulously designed to provide state-of-the-art facilities for fans with disabilities. And the stadium's look is in keeping with its surroundings, reflecting the architectural styles of neighboring buildings and showcasing the natural beauty of the Pacific Northwest.

The Stadium Exhibition Center, nestled between Safeco Field and the football stadium, is a flexible, multipurpose public facility. Washington residents voted in favor of building the Exhibition Center when they passed Referendum 48 in June 1997. Development managers First & Goal were able to bring the project to completion before the demolition of the Kingdome, allowing exhibitions to continue uninterrupted. Owned by the public, the Exhibition Center consists of 325,000 square feet of exhibit space and a 2,000-car parking garage. The center hosts a variety of events such as the Home, Boat, Auto and RV shows, the International Sportsmen's Exposition, and the Christmas in Seattle show. The Exhibition Center opened on October 30, 1999. Thanks to the large size of the center, Seattle can now host popular events that may have formerly been out of Washington's reach.

The Union Station project was an important victory for the preservation of historic Seattle. As an anchor for the redevelopment of the south downtown area, the old train station is at the heart of SODO's evolution. Vulcan Northwest, in partnership with Seattle development company Nitze-Stagen, bought the Union Station train station and the vacant land immediately to the south of it, and began a 7.5-acre, $250 million makeover. Seattle's bus, train and light rail services come together at Union Station, making it the city's transportation hub. The area links together the International District and Pioneer Square while respecting and preserving the histories and characters of both districts throughout the development. The renovated train station is now the home to Sound Transit and provides beautiful and much-needed public gathering space.

One example of the area's refurbishment is the 505 Union Station building. An 11-story office block offering 290,000 square feet of office space, "505" was the first office building to be constructed in Seattle's Union Station. Each side of the building takes into account the neighborhood it faces, creating a unique architectural gem. The north side faces Union Station and is a series of glazed-glass windows reminiscent of a waterfall. This side leans back, forming a shining backdrop for its historic neighbor. The west side, with its glass curtain wall and metal detailing, is a nod to the artistic atmosphere of Pioneer Square. The east and south faces are

Part of Vulcan Northwest's partnership with Seattle communities, the 505 Union Station building was constructed to fit in with neighboring buildings and the local environment.

more traditional, in deference to the International District and future developments. Landscaping was also designed to reflect the building's Asian neighbors. Asian botanical varieties grace a public garden between 505 Union Station and the former railroad building. Combining modern and historical urban designs, 505 Union Station, like all of Vulcan Northwest's south downtown projects, is designed to fit harmoniously with its surroundings.

Vulcan Northwest's projects in Seattle's south downtown area have started what many call a renaissance for the SODO district. The football/soccer stadium, the exhibition center and the Union Station refurbishment have all pumped new enthusiasm and new blood into a historically important town. Residents and visitors alike are finding reasons to come back, and south downtown is thriving once again.

With more than 300,000 square feet of exhibition space, the Stadium Exhibition Center can host even the largest events.

UNICO PROPERTIES, INC.

The history of Unico Properties, Inc. is inextricably linked with the history of downtown Seattle — specifically with a piece of land once known as Denny's Knoll, now the heart of downtown Seattle. By skillful development and management of this tract since the 1950s, Unico single-handedly moved Seattle's financial district from Pioneer Square to the downtown area where it still resides. Today, Unico manages some of the most familiar buildings in the Seattle skyline — including One and Two Union Square, the Financial Center and Rainier Tower — while the company expands its presence into other major Western U.S. markets.

Denny's Knoll was a heavily forested hill of 8.3 acres when pioneer Arthur Denny endowed it to the Territory of Washington in 1861 for the purpose of building a university. The Knoll, extended to 10 acres by additional gifts from Denny's neighbors, housed the University of Washington — the first university in Washington state. The university quickly outgrew Denny's Knoll, however, and in 1895 it moved to its current site on Lake Washington. In December 1907 the Metropolitan Building Company took over the leasehold for the property.

Metropolitan retained the lease for nearly 50 years. The area became known as the Metropolitan Tract, as Metropolitan's buildings began to dominate the city's skyline. The White Henry Stuart Building (now the site of Rainier Tower) and the Cobb Building were the first to open their doors in 1909. Several more buildings would be constructed by Metropolitan, culminating with the Skinner Building, completed in 1926. But it wasn't until Unico won the bid for the new lease in 1953 that Seattle's downtown really began to take shape.

Roger Stevens, a man associated more with the theater than with real estate deals, recognized the Tract's possibilities and became the visionary behind Unico. A true developer, Stevens dove wholeheartedly into any project interesting enough to keep him engaged. And the Metropolitan Tract, with its geographic advantages, definitely caught Stevens' attention. Situated on the side of the hill that dominates Seattle's downtown, the area is relatively flat, forming a plateau. The city's financial district was, at that time, located at the bottom of the hill, in Pioneer Square. Stevens realized that the Knoll could be far more attractive to potential investors than Pioneer Square:

people doing business on the Tract would not have to hike up and down the steep hill, and they would be away from the dirt and noise of the docks. Furthermore, the campus that once sat on Denny's Knoll was one of the few places in downtown Seattle to survive the great fire of 1889.

Armed with these convincing arguments, Stevens easily persuaded four other business professionals to join him in forming a company to bid for the leasehold on the 10-acre tract. University Properties, as Unico was then known, was awarded the contract from the University of Washington regents and it immediately

(Far right) One Union Square (left) and the award-winning Two Union Square (right)

(Right) Rainier Tower at night

started improving and modernizing the buildings that stood on the Metropolitan Tract.

The first step to exploiting the area's potential was to encourage retail businesses within the Tract to expand. Fashionable specialty stores opened on Fifth Avenue, making it the "smart" place to shop. New buildings further extended the Tract's office space: the Puget Sound Plaza was completed in 1960, the IBM Building in 1964, the Financial Center in 1972, and Rainier Square and Rainier Tower in 1977. The development of businesses within the Tract attracted the attention of Seattle's banks and lending institutions, and between 1959 and 1976 the balance of Seattle's financial power shifted from Pioneer Square to the Metropolitan Tract. Continued renovations of existing buildings guaranteed that the Tract would remain the heart of downtown Seattle in the years to come.

Building on the success of the Metropolitan Tract, Unico completed One Union Square in 1981 and Two Union Square in 1989. These two properties stand adjacent to the Tract, linking the Washington State Convention and Trade Center with the financial and retail heart of the city, further strengthening the downtown core.

Unico's careful focus on long-term planning and construction of long-term relationships has brought stability and prosperity to the downtown Metropolitan Tract, with a reputation built on customer service. An interdisciplinary approach to leasing and management means that Unico is involved with its properties throughout their life cycles. Buildings are assessed to determine their value in the market, and plans are drawn up to maximize each building's potential. Unico selects tenants carefully and works with them to address physical space concerns and to plan any necessary alterations or improvements. Innovations in technology have created new challenges and changed the look of the traditional office. To keep up with these changes, Unico helps its clients create effective, productive and livable work spaces.

However, Unico's involvement with the greater Seattle community extends far beyond the lease agreement with the university and the rental of property to businesses. Unico and its employees are very active locally, working with the Seattle Chamber of Commerce, United Way, the Boy Scouts, Seattle Aquarium, and Woodland Park Zoo, among others. Seattle's 5th Avenue Theater owes its continued existence in part to Unico, which for a time donated the revenues from its rental back to the nonprofit organization established to restore the theater to its original splendor.

The addition of an investment advisory team in 1996 added another dimension of service to Unico's existing management, leasing and construction capabilities. With its 1997 purchase of the Wells Fargo Plaza in Tacoma, Unico made good on its commitment to begin moving outward from Seattle. Subsequent purchases in Bellevue and Renton solidified Unico's position as a major force in Washington. The company has since expanded into Boise, Idaho; Portland, Oregon; and San Francisco, California, with its sights set on other Western markets. Investing and competing in new urban office markets not only expands and diversifies Unico's portfolio, but also provides the company with new opportunities and growth that attracts the best professionals in the industry.

Unico Properties, Inc. has shaped Seattle's skyline and has helped keep Seattle's downtown vibrant and productive in an era when many city centers are in decline. Denny's Knoll, which once housed and educated 16 students, now boasts nearly 2 million square feet of office and retail space and has helped make Seattle the dominant commercial center in the Pacific Northwest.

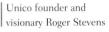

Looking north along the Metropolitan Tract — Fourth Avenue in the early 20th century

Unico founder and visionary Roger Stevens

NORTHWEST BUILDING LLC

Northwest Building LLC is among the top commercial-real estate investment, development and management firms in the region. The company has developed some of the largest industrial parks in the Puget Sound, including Lakewood Industrial Park, Port Commerce Center and The Park in Puyallup. Northwest Building also manages all of its assets, which today total over 2.7 million square feet of space.

Company founder Norton Clapp introduced Northwest Building in 1979. The company was an amalgamation of various family-owned real estate assets and companies. The company's flagship, the Norton Building, was built in 1958 at a time when construction of a new office building in Seattle represented challenge and forward thinking. The Norton Building, named for Clapp's grandfather, Matthew G. Norton, was the first major downtown office building built since before the Depression.

The 21-story, $12 million structure was also Seattle's first thoroughly modern skyscraper, complete with air conditioning, three floors of underground parking, sweeping views and a top-floor dining club. At its dedication Clapp stated, "The Norton Building is designed and built for the future... If, someday, succeeding generations reading these words look back, they will, perhaps, learn and understand that this building was built for them."

Today most of the family enterprises are housed there. So is one of the world's top accounting firms, Arthur Andersen LLP, and the award-winning architectural firm LMN Architects.

Clapp's belief in his community was not limited to one area or municipality. In an address to the Seattle Chamber of Commerce in 1966, he envisioned a great Puget Sound community working together to improve shared interests. Northwest Building actively supports development and community enhancement throughout the region including Seattle, Auburn, Puyallup, Fife, Tacoma and Lakewood.

By the late 80s Northwest Building turned its focus to industrial development and real estate equity investment. Current industrial projects owned and managed by the company include:

Lakewood Industrial Park, one of the largest industrial parks in the region totaling over 2 million square feet of distribution, warehouse and manufacturing space. It is located in the heart of Lakewood adjacent to I-5 and SR-512. The park is a carefully master-planned setting with boulevards in place, utilities underground and extensive landscaping throughout.

The Park In Puyallup, over 1.5 million square feet offering distribution and manufacturing space, business park facilities and build-to-suit sites from one to 20 acres in size. It is sited at the intersection of three major highways, SR-167, SR-512 and SR-161. Conveniently located within the Puyallup city limits, The Park uses municipal utilities and services already in place.

Port Commerce Center, a joint venture development with the Port of Tacoma located near I-5 and conveniently served by rail service. Access to the entire port area is easy from this location.

The Norton Building |

Northwest Building LLC is a wholly owned subsidiary of Matthew G. Norton Co. The company was named in honor of Clapp's entrepreneurial grandfather who was instrumental in founding and building Weyerhaeuser Co. Like the company's namesake, Matthew G. Norton Co. is today active in funding and adding value to great companies through its venture capital activities.

Norton Clapp passed away in 1995, but his legacy endures through Matthew G. Norton Co., Northwest Building and countless other achievements that helped shape Seattle and the Puget Sound.

Business & Finance

Insurance providers, banks and investment companies offer support
for a host of Seattle organizations.

FARMERS NEW WORLD LIFE INSURANCE COMPANY

Life insurance isn't what it used to be. For many decades tradition held that the family breadwinner bought an insurance policy to protect his loved ones in the event of his early death. Simpler times called for simpler policies. However, over the years life has become more complicated, and like every other aspect of American society, the business of life insurance has evolved with the changing culture.

Today people require different benefits from their insurance at different stages in their lives, and they need insurance that is tailored to fit their unique situations. The needs of a retired couple vary from those of business owners, newlyweds, young families, middle-aged parents of college students, single parents and individuals. Family models vary widely, people are living far longer than they used to, and new times call for new ways of doing business. People have no patience with traditional business practices, but they still want to have complete faith in the strength of their insurance provider. Thus no established insurance company can afford to sit back and rest on its reputation, regardless of its merit.

The Seattle-based Farmers New World Life Insurance Company (FNWL) is a company with a sterling pedigree and a long history, but relying on the tried-and-true plays

no part in the way it does business. FNWL stays ahead of the changing times, constantly challenging itself to create innovative approaches to the life insurance business. It is a point of pride for FNWL that the company anticipates its customers' needs long before most customers are even aware of them, and it has pledged to be what its mission statement calls "compellingly convenient" to all its customers. With more than 90 years in the business, FNWL is a forward-thinking company in the competitive insurance industry.

Life insurance is designed to protect families in the event of a tragedy and to provide for the secure financial future of those who are left behind. Farmers agents understand that life insurance is an integral part of long-term financial planning, including planning for the unexpected. Because it is difficult for most people to anticipate the consequences of accident and death, a trusted insurance agent can give guidance and advice. Keeping a home, sending children to college and maintaining an established lifestyle are the all-important benefits that provide a family with a security blanket should the unforeseen occur.

The situation of one young family illustrates how essential a good policy is in a crisis. Their Farmers agent was a friend through their church, and the couple had asked him to take a look at their existing policy. He found that the coverage provided by the husband's employer would be insufficient should anything happen to him, and he drew up an FNWL plan for the couple. Sadly the husband, a firefighter, died on duty shortly afterward, devastating his young widow and their children. After her husband's death, one of the first calls she made was to their Farmers agent, who was able to assure her that her family's future was financially secure.

The majority of potential life insurance customers have little idea of their true needs, and it takes a trusted expert to guide them through the intricacies of the various policies and products that are available. That's why the Farmers network of agents is so important to the success of the company. Farmers agents are community-based people. They live where their customers live and they care deeply about the families they serve. Many of their relationships begin as friendships, and likewise, over time many of their customers become personal friends.

Planning a life insurance program begins with understanding what policies are available, what risks a family

Current Home Office of Farmers New World Life, located on Mercer Island

may face, an analysis of every customer's needs and a clear understanding of the unique goals of every individual. Dreams play a part, too, because some of life's greatest joys occur when people's dreams come true. Prudent planning allows families the freedom to hope for the best, which is why the partnership between FNWL and its customers is a very personal one.

A Strong, Secure Company

While the personal touch is what appeals to customers, the big picture is equally important. FNWL is a wholly owned subsidiary of Farmers Group, Inc., the country's third-largest provider of auto and home insurance. As of year-end 1999, FNWL was ranked 35th out of more than 2,000 life insurance companies when measured by volume of policy coverage in force. FNWL is also the sixth-largest writer of universal life insurance in the United States. The company consistently receives the highest ratings from industry analysts. More than 1 million people hold policies through FNWL, and the company has more than $4.7 billion in assets.

Those 1 million policyholders know that they are entrusting their money to a company with a strong reputation for financial stability. Safety and success are the watchwords of FNWL, which pursues high-quality, low-risk investments. FNWL is a leader in the industry for allocating its investments in a diverse and safe portfolio. When the company's financial strength is measured by its capital ratio (the ratio of capital, surplus and investment reserves to assets), the FNWL average is nearly double the industry average. This figure is a solid indication of its exceptionally strong financial position.

Since the A.M. Best Company introduced a system of insurance ratings in 1976, FNWL has consistently earned an A.M. Best rating of A+, indicating superior. The ratings are assigned after a series of tests that measures company performance and competency in the various fields of insurance, among them underwriting, control of expenses, adequacy of reserves, capital and investments. Other industry analysts have awarded the company similarly high ratings.

A Farmers representative at home in the community
©*bohemian nomad picturemakers/ Kevin Morris*

The safety of FNWL is guaranteed by several factors that govern the life insurance industry. Life insurers are legally required to maintain specified surplus levels to protect them, and they must maintain a reserve liability account whose requirements are set by state law. All insurers are required to submit annual statements of their financial conditions to the government of every state in which they do business. Additionally, from time to time a state's insurance department will examine life insurance companies and intervene if any weakness becomes apparent.

A Life Insurance Plan for Every Situation

When customers choose FNWL as their life insurance carrier, they will select from several plans that have been

C. Paul Patsis with the executive staff of Farmers New World Life
©*bohemian nomad picturemakers/ Kevin Morris*

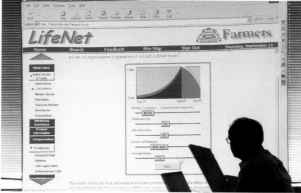

blending its years of experience with its dedication to innovation. Company President C. Paul Patsis sums up the company's guiding philosophy: "Our role in the marketplace is to bridge the gap between people's fears and worries and their dreams. We help them achieve this by offering a full range of insurance and investment products, which protect them and help them accumulate assets."

New Technologies, Innovative Thinking

FNWL is always looking to the future. Ever conscious of changing market trends, the company has enthusiastically embraced new technologies as the means to better serve the needs of its customers. Today these new technologies include the Internet and the future of E-commerce. President Patsis, an ardent advocate of innovation, asserts: "Our guiding statement around here is to innovate every single day. The Internet offers the perfect tool to do just that."

FNWL pioneered the first Internet-based technology for Farmers Group Inc., which was called LifeNet. LifeNet is a virtual assistant for agents to help them be more efficient and deliver "just in time" solutions to their customers. Farmers agents have access to "just in time" product knowledge, online brochures and numerous calculators to use with their clients. As an FNWL Web site currently available to agents only, LifeNet contains a wealth of information to help them provide better service to their customers. LifeNet, an electronic wholesaler, is available 24/7 to provide assistance to Farmers agents. FNWL was the first business unit within Farmers to offer this innovative tool. The site contains such vital information as new company products and tips on how to offer a higher level of service. Agents can easily keep track of their customers' policies and remind them about expiration dates. Access to instant rate quotes speeds the time in which an agent can present a complete policy plan to a prospective customer, and customers appreciate the shorter wait time.

On the public site, which is available to consumers, each type of life insurance plan is outlined, including the subcategories of term life, whole life and universal life. Customers who want to understand the variations among policies can use "real time" calculators and tools to figure out their financial goals, predict the amount of retirement income they will need and determine the amount of income that is right for them. Once people have read through the various insurance plans, they are in a better position to discuss their needs with their Farmers agent.

carefully designed to meet almost every foreseeable need and situation. FNWL primarily offers variable life and annuity products, universal life, term life and cash value insurance, as well as flexible premium, single premium and equity-indexed annuities. FNWL has also recently entered the long-term care insurance market. A Farmers agent is the expert who interprets the details of each plan and recommends the appropriate coverage.

FNWL has designed its life insurance plans to suit the diverse needs of its many policyholders. It has done the meticulous planning so that its customers can select the policies that best suit their needs, their incomes, their families and their futures. Determined to reinvent the way an insurance company does business, FNWL concentrates on observing current trends, anticipating future needs and

Nearly a Century of Service

Service has been a company watchword since 1910, when FNWL started in Spokane as the Roman Catholic Life Insurance Company of America. Even back then, the company's goal was to grow and expand its services, and within seven months it changed its name to New World Life Insurance Company and offered insurance services to the general public. It sold its first life insurance policy in 1911. Ten years later the company was selling policies to customers throughout Washington, Oregon, California, Idaho, Montana, North Dakota, Minnesota and Wisconsin.

In 1930 the growing company moved to Seattle and settled in a remodeled second-floor loft over Friedlander Jewelers at 5th and Pike streets. Along with the rest of the country, the company endured the long years of the Great Depression before business picked up during World War II. In 1942 the company purchased Seattle's first skyscraper, the 15-story Alaska Building at 2nd and Cherry streets, but it didn't move in until 1946 because the Coast Guard was headquartered there during the war.

By 1953 Underwriting Associations of Farmers purchased a controlling interest in the successful life insurance company, whose name was changed to Farmers New World Life Insurance Company. Business continued to increase so that the company outgrew its office space and moved again in 1958. This time FNWL settled in its current community on Mercer Island. By then FNWL was doing business in 25 states.

In 1965 FNWL purchased a 93 percent share of Ohio State Life Insurance, a move that helped accelerate its already rapid growth. By 1966 so many new employees were working at the Mercer Island headquarters that the site was expanded to 37,000 square feet. In 1982 the company had again outgrown its office space and sold its building to the city of Mercer Island. FNWL built its current home nearby, a five-story office complex with 150,000 square feet.

A savvy investor who purchased shares in FNWL back in 1953 and then held on to them for decades would have seen the stock soar, matching the phenomenal growth of the company. One hundred shares of stock purchased that year for $34 a share were worth $8,500 two years later. By 1960 the value of the stock rose to $11,025. Seventeen years later those same 100 shares had escalated in value to $189,244. In 1988 the original investment of $3,400 was now worth more than $1 million.

For FNWL, investing in the future has meant constant innovation and the incorporation of every new technology that will help it become more efficient. As early as 1960 the company compiled one of the first "plain language" policies. For the first time, ordinary people could read their insurance policies without the help of a legal expert, and the language also incorporated the friendlier use of "you" and "we" to refer to the customer and the company. Two years later a revolutionary rate book was introduced. It included visual selling tools to assist the agents in selling policies and reduced premiums for women. In 1965 FNWL became the second company in the industry to introduce a nonsmoker policy.

Employing technology to help people ©bohemian nomad picturemakers/Kevin Morris

Former Farmers New World Life Home Office on Mercer Island

In 1966 FNWL installed its first computer, an IBM 360, the world's first computer system. It enabled FNWL to accelerate its processing procedures. One year later, with 150,000 policyholders, the company converted to the Consolidated Functions Ordinary policy administration computer system, increasing its efficiency even more. The first computerized proposal service, which helped the company's agents calculate premiums faster than ever before, was introduced in 1969 when the company's total insurance reached the $2 billion mark. In 1983 the IBM 3033 computer was installed and began processing 5 million instructions per second. Two years later a system that worked at three times the speed was in place. FNWL continues to invest in new technology to help it keep pace with its ever-expanding business.

A Good Place to Work

With its business focused on helping people protect themselves and their families, it's natural that FNWL has an active community outreach program. Through the Farmers Group, the company is a member of the steering committee of Connect America, a nonprofit coalition of business, community and religious sponsors whose goal is to engage more people in community service as a means to help solve serious social problems. The national organization, based in Washington, D.C., focuses on volunteer service as the most powerful way to bring people together and numbers among its sponsors some of the most prominent businesses in the country. Farmers Group has also sponsored a National Geographic Special, "Inside the White House," in cooperation with its in-house Partners in Pride committee, as well as a PBS video called "Through the American Promise."

Locally FNWL supports public service organizations by direct corporate donations to such groups as the March of Dimes, the Special Olympics, Corporate Council for the Arts, the Mercer Island Half Marathon, Public Television station KCTS-Channel 9, the YMCA of Greater Seattle, Big Brothers and Big Sisters of King County and Lifelong AIDS Alliance. The company encourages its employees to contribute to the United Way and supports their donations by matching them 100 percent.

FNWL has also created a Partners in Pride team, a group of employees responsible for coordinating the company's involvement in local nonprofit events. Thanks to the diligent efforts of the committee, more than half of FNWL's employees involve themselves directly in one or more community activities. Partners in Pride provides the

FNWL employees with information on the various volunteer opportunities available throughout the Seattle area.

Partners in Pride sponsors activities such as a United Way Day of Caring and a handball competition and barbecue for the participants of the local Special Olympics. The committee also organizes clothing drives for a number of organizations and an annual toy drive every holiday season. Employees are encouraged to tutor at local schools as a way to involve themselves directly with the young people of their community, and every year FNWL sponsors a concert for the local Mercer Island senior center. FNWL employees also participate in the Adopt-a-Highway program, organize school supply drives and assist the public television station with its fund-raising. In addition, the partnership supports local organizations by offering parking and event facilities when they are needed.

Such community support is possible because of the loyalty and dedication of the FNWL employees. Six hundred people work at the Mercer Island Home Office, with 160 joining the company there in the year 2000. The Mercer Island Home Office serves FNWL customers in the Western region of the United States. An additional 150 employees work in Columbus, Ohio, to serve policyholders in the Eastern part of the country. Employee loyalty is very strong. Among those employed for more than two years, the average length of service is 10 years.

The friendly staff of Farmers New World Life ©bohemian nomad picturemakers/ Kevin Morris

People enjoy their jobs with FNWL and encourage their family members to join the team; currently more than 25 families have multiple members employed at the Mercer Island Home Office.

The strength of the FNWL commitment to its customers and its community has been at the heart of its success. This commitment has led to astonishing growth for nearly a century, growth that will continue steadily as the company consistently focuses on innovation and service. With the customer always coming first, FNWL prides itself on being number one in quality among life insurers, in Seattle and across the nation.

The beautiful Seattle skyline ©bohemian nomad picturemakers/ Kevin Morris

SAFECO Corporation

The bat cracks and the baseball arcs high into left-field seats. Thousands of cheering fans rise to their feet and the announcer screams, "Good... bye... baseball!"

It's a summer evening at SAFECO Field, one of the jewels of Major League stadiums. The Seattle Mariners are slugging it out with the New York Yankees. Coast-to-coast in major television markets, millions follow each pitch "live from SAFECO Field." Still more around the world track the SAFECO action in real time over the Internet.

The global village of the new millennium is a world apart from the rough-and-tumble Seattle of the early 1900s. That was before computers and the Internet — before electric typewriters or television. It was 1923 when an enterprising insurance salesman, Hawthorne K. Dent, launched General Insurance Company of America, later to gain national prominence as SAFECO Corporation.

Fountain pens, felt hats, metal cabinets and steel desks were familiar symbols of that original SAFECO company. Eight decades later hardly anything is the same. The steel desks are gone and in their place sit computer terminals linking company agents, employees and customers coast-to-coast for policy service, new business and electronic commerce.

The regional upstart now belongs to the major leagues as one of the nation's largest insurers of homes and automobiles. It is a leader in small business coverage as well as complex commercial policies. It sells life and health insurance to individuals and businesses, plus retirement plans and annuities. It's one of the largest writers of surety bonds for Fortune 500 corporations, and provides loans and leases through its commercial credit subsidiary to businesses for equipment acquisition. It manages a respected and growing family of mutual funds, as well as outside investment portfolios. It is the pre-eminent company distributing most of these products and services through independent insurance and financial partners.

SAFECO's brand is carried into every living room in America through such high-profile marketing initiatives as the naming rights to SAFECO Field, the Seattle Mariners' baseball stadium, a creative national television and radio advertising campaign and extensive direct-response marketing programs.

Business in the 21st century turns on customer service, speed and convenience. SAFECO stakes its success today on a blend of the old and new, on time-honored values and leading-edge technology. Its diverse and talented work force of some 12,000 employees serves customers and distribution partners from more than 100 offices coast to coast, with the biggest concentrations based in the company's University District corporate headquarters in Seattle and its wooded, suburban office campus in Redmond, Washington.

SAFECO's Redmond campus is headquarters for SAFECO Life & Investments, the Seattle region, the national supply facility and soon the company's huge data center. Recently opened in nearby Bothell is a state-of-the-art national contact center where employees communicate with customers around the clock by mail, telephone and e-mail.

But one point that hasn't changed since the beginning is the way SAFECO distributes its products. They are sold not by employees but by independent

Hawthorne K. Dent, SAFECO founder

The staff of General Insurance Company of America — SAFECO's predecessor — in 1923

insurance and financial partners. It's a point of pride — SAFECO believes the majority of customers, including those who buy over the Internet, value the service and support of a local advocate and adviser in their own community who can help them with complex purchases as well as support after a loss.

The challenges of today's fast-changing business world are great, but so were those facing SAFECO's founders. In the early 1900s insurance was a sometimes dangerous business. Marketing territories were large and closely guarded by the companies that claimed them. Dent's own father, also an insurance salesman, once was severely beaten for encroaching on a competitor's "turf." It didn't dissuade him, nor did it stop Dent from eventually changing the industry forever with his unique ideas of selectivity and selective pricing.

When Dent was a child in Portland, Oregon, in the 1880s and 90s, most houses were heated by wood fires. Delivering wood to people's basements was a way for young boys to earn some money — usually about 75 cents per cord. Dent realized he could unload wood faster into those houses with convenient basement windows, so he charged these customers only 60 cents. This philosophy of better prices for better customers would remain with him his entire life and become the basis of the new company eventually known as SAFECO.

Dent tried many jobs as he grew up but couldn't find one that fully challenged him. Not until he was hired by Northwestern Mutual Fire Association did he find his niche. He established himself as a creative and fearless salesman.

Northwestern was a mutual insurance company. In profitable years mutual policyholders receive dividends that effectively lower their premiums. Dent felt this system was unnecessarily risky, with too much money being distributed as dividends. More of the company's profits, he felt, should be placed in a surplus to offset times of extraordinary losses.

In 1921, after working his way up to executive vice president, Dent left his 20-year career with Northwestern to set up his own business.

His idea was to start a stock insurance company that would also combine the best qualities of the mutual companies. Because mutual companies issued dividends and therefore had less surplus money to cover losses, they accepted only business that was determined to be a better-than-average or good risk. Stock companies, on the other hand, did not pay dividends and therefore had money available in case of catastrophic losses.

The original General Insurance Co. sign at the corner of N.E. 45th Street and Brooklyn Avenue

Dent's idea was to create a hybrid company that would integrate the concept of superior risk selection with the financial strength of stockholder investments. Policyholders would not be subject to assessment liability in times of loss but would still enjoy dividends in times of gain. Agents would have to be persuaded to write only preferred-risk policies and not spread bad-risk policies among several insurance companies, counter to the standard operating procedure of the time. Dent needed willing agents, savvy investors and, he reckoned, about $2 million to set his plan into motion.

To earn the company a good reputation and attract investors, Dent enlisted some of the biggest names in Pacific Northwest finance and industry. He convinced these leaders to invest and also take positions on the

company's first board of directors. They included such men as O.D. Fisher, president of Fisher Flouring Mills, James T. McVay, president of the Metropolitan Bank of Seattle, and Frank D. Martin of Weyerhaeuser. These names lent prestige and gave potential investors a sense of security. In 1923 General Insurance Company — SAFECO's predecessor — was born.

Dent predicted other companies eventually would follow General's lead to remain competitive. In time he was proven correct, but at first he had to convince his own board to remain on the path he had set. He continued to push his policy of low-risk business and by the 1950s General's success was the envy of the industry.

In the 1950s the insurance industry underwent a dramatic change. Widespread ownership of automobiles, and laws requiring drivers to have accident insurance, introduced a whole new field of competition and forced insurance companies to re-evaluate how they did business. Instead of digging in its heels and refusing to change as many companies did, General proved itself one of the most adaptive and innovative companies in the country.

Until this time General, like most insurance companies, had distributed its products through independent agents. The usual commission these agents received was 25 percent of the premium. Direct-writing companies, on the other hand, distributed through "captive" or "exclusive" agents who received about half the standard commission. This saved their companies substantial money and allowed for lower-priced premiums.

Direct writers were able to offer insurance at discounts ranging from 10 to 40 percent below General's prices. The competition was no longer between stock and mutual companies. Direct writers, prosperous from capturing so many auto insurance policies, had begun looking at more traditional insurance markets. In response to this threat from direct writers, General conceived its most daring and original plan — creation of Selective Auto and Fire Insurance Company of America (SAFECO).

SAFECO was largely the brainchild of General's Harold Pigott. Pigott was among the first to recognize the problem of direct writers. The solution, Pigott said, was to lower the company's production costs, including agents' commissions. A new auto insurance company, streamlined and efficient thanks to advances in computer automation, could best meet the challenge of the direct writers. Pigott's proposal was received with enthusiasm and in September 1953 SAFECO became the fourth company in the General's group.

Selective Auto and Fire Insurance Company of America (SAFECO) was an instant success. So popular was the company's acronym that barely two months after it started doing business its name was formally changed to SAFECO. The company used an eight-point program to make its business more efficient and profitable:

- Applications had to be signed by both the customer and agent.
- Cash payment was required with the application.
- Policies would be active until canceled by either the customer or company.
- Billing would be automated.
- Bills would be sent directly from SAFECO rather than collected by the agent.
- Merchandising and advertising would promote SAFECO to potential clients.
- New sales techniques would be developed and taught at workshops and seminars.
- Agents would be supported by SAFECO administrative personnel.

Radical as they were at the time, these eight points were SAFECO's closely guarded secrets to success. The program worked so well that in 1968 the board of directors voted to change the parent corporation's name from General Insurance to SAFECO.

SAFECO has remained one of the nation's most successful insurance and financial corporations by recognizing and exploiting new opportunities. In 1957 it entered the life insurance business and in the 1960s it introduced mutual funds and a commercial credit company. Popular advertising campaigns, especially those featuring the Pink Panther cartoon character, increased SAFECO's visibility. In the 1990s SAFECO further diversified through the acquisition of American States Financial Corporation and WM Life Insurance Company. These additions increased SAFECO's distribution channels and national presence. With the purchase of the London-based R.F. Bailey (Underwriting Agencies) Ltd., SAFECO took a step into the international marketplace.

SAFECO ensures continuing success by investing in its employees. They are encouraged to grow personally and professionally through in-house educational seminars and courses, and receive tuition reimbursement for education pursued at regional colleges and universities. SAFECO fosters an atmosphere of diversity, cooperation and respect.

This respect extends outside the office. SAFECO believes it has a social responsibility to share with the community it has served for so long, and assists many charities and community events. It sponsors an annual United Way fund drive, offers financial education to help people better understand financial issues, and works with the "Strengthening America's Neighborhoods" program to help Seattle solve problems of economy and safety. It also supports local arts programs. SAFECO strongly promotes programs aimed at finding solutions to domestic violence. By providing grants to improve local communities and by encouraging employee volunteerism, SAFECO makes Seattle and the Pacific Northwest a healthier place to live.

SAFECO is, as always, looking to the future. Continued diversification, e-commerce and a strong presence on the Internet, greater visibility and name recognition all are part of SAFECO's plan. Hawthorne Dent died in 1958 but his company continues to grow and thrive, thanks largely to the traditions of service and innovation he instilled in its employees.

From the beginning, Dent exhorted his workers to provide the best service they could, to minimize costs so that savings could be extended to customers,

The SAFECO Tower building in Seattle's University District

to look for new ways to do business, to improve existing service and to continue to grow. Dent's vision and drive and the dedication of SAFECO employees have taken SAFECO from a little upstart to the national leader that sets the industry standard.

SAFECO employees volunteer time and energy for a "Strengthening America's Neighborhoods" project. *Photo by John Freeland*

GUY CARPENTER & COMPANY

When catastrophe strikes, consumers, businesses and institutions turn to their insurance companies to help them recover or start over again. Earthquakes, hurricanes, wildfires, freezing temperatures that damage citrus crops, and any number of natural or man-made disasters can severely challenge even the largest insurance companies. To ensure their ability to pay all claims in the event such a disaster occurs, insurers rely on the safety net of reinsurance. Through reinsurance, insurers partner with other companies — reinsurers — who, as an investment, will assume a portion of policy risk in exchange for a portion of policy premiums. The global network of Guy Carpenter & Company is the most respected intermediary and provider of reinsurance services worldwide. An industry leader, Guy Carpenter has played a crucial role in redefining and revolutionizing reinsurance since its earliest days.

The company was founded in 1922 by Guy Carpenter, a young man who had worked in the insurance business since the age of 15. Carpenter had served as the manager of the Cotton Insurance Association, a pool of insurance companies formed to spread the risk associated with harvesting, warehousing

Guy Carpenter, founder of Guy Carpenter & Company

and transporting cotton. Acquiring reinsurance for cotton was a complicated, time-consuming and inexact process at the time because rates were based almost exclusively on the previous year's record and had to be renegotiated at the start of each season. Since conditions could fluctuate dramatically from one year to the next, it was virtually impossible for companies to anticipate long-term rates and plan for the future. Dissatisfied with the inefficient system, Carpenter devised a revolutionary approach that based premiums on an average of the previous several years. By making it easier for clients to anticipate and manage costs, the Carpenter Plan went on to modernize the entire reinsurance industry.

The new system worked so well in the cotton industry that Carpenter started his own company to apply risk averaging to other types of reinsurance. After some initial industry resistance to changing the way risk was calculated, Carpenter overcame the opposition once and for all by bringing his new company under the umbrella of the respected insurance giant Marsh & McLennan Companies in 1923. Soon after, Guy Carpenter set the industry standard for contract language and earned a lasting reputation as the country's premier reinsurance intermediary.

The depth and breadth of its expertise and service is what places Guy Carpenter at the pinnacle of the reinsurance industry. The company employs a high-quality, motivated and professional staff that combines exceptional service with insight, information and integrity. With years of experience dealing with local markets on a worldwide basis, the insurance giant reorganized into eight regions and specialties in 2000. This ongoing globalization initiative links all of Guy Carpenter's offices in 20 countries into a new global network with unrivaled resources, making it possible for brokers to access the company's unique capabilities and expertise in every office around the world. By making all products and services consistently available, the company can

When disaster strikes, Guy Carpenter is often involved behind the scenes in designing financial programs for insurance companies.

WATER OVER ROADWAY

offer a complete range of services to each client, regardless of the client's location.

Under the leadership of President and CEO Sal Zaffino, Guy Carpenter now employs 2,000 professionals in more than 30 offices around the world and has played a key role in some of the largest and most innovative risk transfer arrangements in the industry. Because insurance companies offer coverage in virtually every area and specialty — each with its own unique risk and coverage requirements — the reinsurance market is also multifaceted. Guy Carpenter is known for its expertise across the entire spectrum of reinsurance and for its ability to deliver an ever-widening range of products and services including

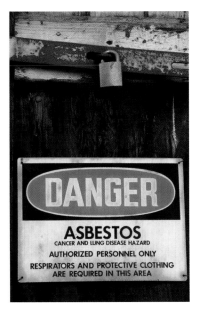

natural hazard modeling, traditional property catastrophe insurance, and reinsurance for niche and emerging areas such as agriculture and health care. The company is also the industry leader in securing reinsurance in such fields as life, accident and health; casualty; fidelity and surety; finite risk; professional liability and individual risk.

Using the superior market intelligence of its Market Information Group, Guy Carpenter can work with clients on a multiline approach or concentrate on specific areas, helping companies plan business strategies for fluctuating conditions and find the type of reinsurance that offers them the best investment. Once that has been determined, Guy Carpenter provides dynamic financial analysis and aggressive market negotiation to obtain the best possible terms for the client. The process continues with superior post-placement and support services.

The company is particularly known for its superior ability to provide clients with an objective picture of catastrophic risk. Guy Carpenter Instrat provides world-class actuarial services and offers the most advanced quantitative risk assessment tools to minimize the level of uncertainty in catastrophic reinsurance. Instrat's multidisciplinary group of professionals is highly experienced in the intricacies of different models and dedicated to analyzing reinsurance

options from all quantitative viewpoints: financial, statistical and scientific. Using analytic tools that not only meet but define the current state of the art, Instrat first provides the best available modeling and analysis, then structures the reinsurance agreement and places the client's treaty. Many of the largest and most complex insurance companies in the world have relied on Guy Carpenter to optimize their property exposure profile.

The field of reinsurance has changed dramatically since Guy Carpenter revolutionized risk analysis in the 1920s. As the range of risk has grown in scope and complexity with each passing decade, insurance coverage has also expanded and become more complex, increasing the importance of reliable modeling, thoughtful analysis, and expert investment and placement advice. The company's professionally diverse staff, its highly accessible global network and a longstanding commitment to innovative solutions have deservedly made Guy Carpenter & Company a giant in reinsurance. Yet with so many changes within and without, the company has remained faithful to its founder's vision, adapting and growing for one primary purpose: to be its clients' finest advocate and most trusted adviser.

Guy Carpenter is an innovator in spreading the financial burden of unforeseen events.

Guy Carpenter develops reinsurance programs to protect insurance companies from catastrophic occurrences such as hurricanes.

HOMESTREET™ BANK

If a company could clearly depict its philosophy in its name alone, a prime example would be HomeStreet Bank. Its name reflects the company's history of providing funding for homes, apartments and commercial buildings, and financial services to individuals and businesses. A family- and employee-owned Northwest institution for 80 years, HomeStreet Bank has been and remains dedicated to helping people achieve their dream of acquiring a home and realizing financial security.

HomeStreet Bank was started in the early 1920s, at a time when Seattle was experiencing a post-war slump following the tremendous economic growth that had occurred during World War I. With a vision not common in those days, a group of local business people in Seattle's University District were convinced that the economic conditions offered a prime opportunity to help people find the capital to build new houses, apartments and commercial buildings.

After a rocky start, W. Walter Williams, the company's first employee and longtime president, was able to develop HomeStreet Bank, then known as Continental Mortgage and Loan Company, into a strong community financial institution. This was due in part to his conservative business sense as well as his foresight and willingness to take advantage of new tools offered by the federal government for home ownership, such as the FHA program and later, the VA program.

By 1940, HomeStreet was helping to meet the area's rapidly rising demand for housing and wartime factories brought about by World War II. The company developed more than 200 new homes for the ever-increasing numbers of "war workers." By the end of 1944, it was the third-most active mortgage lender in King County.

When the war ended in 1945, the company suffered a serious economic slowdown, as did Seattle and the rest of the country. But change was in the air. The post-war demand for consumer products such as new homes and cars led to the birth of the American suburb. HomeStreet was one of the first in the region to recognize and act upon the changes this would bring.

To meet the growing demands of residents who were building homes outside of Seattle's central core, HomeStreet increased its construction lending for new homes and was instrumental in developing the area's very first shopping center, Northgate. Built in the midst of a fairly unpopulated area with no major highways, Northgate was a bold move that truly put HomeStreet in the spotlight, not only in the local community, but nationwide as well.

During the 1950s and 1960s, HomeStreet developed University Village, Aurora Village and Westwood Village shopping centers. The company expanded its single-family construction lending to create new suburban communities. In the late 1960s, HomeStreet was actively serving Seattle's "inner city" with special loan programs to develop those communities. While both residential and commercial lending steadily increased, they were strongly affected by Boeing's employment cycles.

When the national recession started in late 1969, Seattle experienced dark times once again. Boeing's layoff of almost 100,000 workers added to the gloomy economy. Although the area's unemployment situation had a drastic effect on HomeStreet, as many borrowers experienced financial failure or left the area, the company was able to weather this period.

HomeStreet looked forward to better economic times, and in 1970 it moved to new offices in downtown Seattle's Pacific Building. By 1972 the local

Northgate Mall in its early days — the mall was developed by HomeStreet Bank.

economy was starting to improve and the company opened a branch in Tacoma.

Over the next several decades, more branch offices were opened throughout the Northwest and in Hawaii. HomeStreet continued to experience steady growth. Although the company could have expanded to markets beyond the Northwest, it chose to retain its regional focus and continue to provide affordable housing in its own communities. In 1989 the Mortgage Bankers Association of America honored HomeStreet for providing construction loans and mortgages for hundreds of homes and apartments for families of modest income.

In the mid-1980s, in the midst of mergers, acquisitions, and failures of banks and thrifts, HomeStreet decided that its customers deserved great banking services to complement the real estate finance services. In 1986 HomeStreet's consumer banking services were started on the ninth floor of the Pacific Building. The new bank soon proved that the high level of service and competitive rates were what the community wanted, and it grew very quickly.

In 1996 the company was named Washington's "Family Business of the Year" by the *Puget Sound Business Journal.*

Groups of HomeStreet Bank employees often volunteer on community projects.

In spring of 2000, the company changed its name to HomeStreet Bank to better reflect its commitment to home and community. It also began offering business banking products and services, building on the same foundation of exceptional customer service that has distinguished all of its ventures.

Today, HomeStreet Bank has more than 500 employees, many of whom have been with the company for several decades. It encourages its employees to provide leadership to community groups such as the University of Washington Business and Economic Development Program, Greater Seattle Chamber of Commerce, and The Housing Partnership, and to volunteer with programs such as the Community Home Ownership Center, City of Seattle Affordable Housing Advisory Council, and the Columbia City Revitalization Board. To encourage further community involvement, HomeStreet Bank sponsored a house with Seattle Habitat for Humanity and employees have been given paid days off to work on the construction of this house.

To this day, HomeStreet Bank is committed to finding new ways to finance affordable housing. It offers programs such as the Location Efficient Mortgage available to Seattle homebuyers, and a special program that provides discounted loan services to employees of the City of Seattle, Seattle School District, University of Washington and others. It has also expanded its consumer banking services and developed other products that go far beyond home and commercial loans.

With more than 30 banking and mortgage branches in the Pacific Northwest and Hawaii and with assets totaling more than $1 billion, HomeStreet Bank believes more than ever that its success lies in serving the people and businesses in its communities.

HomeStreet Bank chairman and employees work on a Seattle Habitat for Humanity house.

NOWOGROSKI RUPP INSURANCE GROUP

Nowogroski Rupp Insurance Group, located in the Northgate business district of Seattle, is the 25th-largest insurance agency in the Puget Sound area, having been in continuous operation for nearly 60 years.

Committed to a client-centered business ethic, the agency provides comprehensive protection programs for its clients. This primary objective is realized through careful risk analysis and management coupled with the acquisition of well-designed and cost-effective insurance policies. Nowogroski Rupp honors the timeless values of integrity and creativity while embracing and celebrating change and technology.

Nowogroski Rupp uses a team approach in which every employee makes a clear contribution to the company's most important product — its relationship with its clients. This approach contributes to another key part of the company mission — to encourage each employee to experience joy in his or her work while continuously learning and developing both professionally and personally. The result is a workplace where employees feel not only valued

but also invested. In return, employees treat clients with respect and clients' interests with as much care as they would their own interests.

Ed Nowogroski, a University of Washington All-American football player, began his career in insurance working for General Insurance Company of America (now SAFECO) under the tutelage of H.K. Dent. He founded his agency in 1942 and sold it in 1973 to Don Rupp, CPCU.

Don Rupp began his insurance career in Hays, Kansas, in his father's agency. After graduating from Fort Hays State College, where he was a member of Phi Beta Kappa and listed in Who's Who Among College and University Students, Rupp worked for Cimarron Insurance Company, became a special agent for Great American Insurance Company in Albuquerque and then joined a brokerage in Greeley, Colorado. While in Greeley, he was active in city politics and community organizations and taught insurance at the local university. Unfortunately, the brokerage deteriorated and Rupp's non-compete agreement prohibited him from practicing

The welcoming lobby of Nowogroski Rupp Insurance Group

insurance within a 50-mile radius. Thus he began a search for another city in which to relocate his family.

After falling in love with Seattle, Rupp moved his family there in 1973. Besides managing Nowogroski Insurance Associates, as it was then known, he taught classes to fellow professionals, sat on the agents' committee to revise the State Insurance Licensing Exam, sat on many companies' national advisory committees and was active in the minority business community. He served as coach and mentor, nurturing many businesses to greater success.

After Rupp purchased Nowogroski Rupp, he bought other outstanding agencies while growing the company. The owners of The Wiltsie Agency, M.G. Brown Agency, James M. Cain Agency and Stanley R. Olson Company approached Don Rupp to purchase their agencies as they retired, which he did. The owners wanted their clients handled as these owners had serviced them and they knew that Nowogroski Rupp would do so.

Don Rupp, deceased in 1988, is remembered as an extremely knowledgeable insurance person and a man of great integrity. The Independent Agents and Brokers of Washington named him Insurance Person of the Year in 1987 and he received the City of Seattle Small Business Award in 1988. The Greater University District Chamber of Commerce continues to honor him with an annual Don Rupp Memorial Small Business Award.

Don Rupp loved the American way of life — he was compassionate, generous, nontraditional and politically tolerant. He instituted "casual Friday" before anyone had ever heard of it, gave his employees bus passes to encourage use of public transportation, and valued education and service above all other aspects of professional life. His influence and legacy are strongly felt at Nowogroski Rupp even today. It was said that "he never forgot what it was like to be an employee."

After his untimely death, Don Rupp's widow, Joan, continued to own and work in the agency. In 1991 Michelle Rupp, daughter of Don and Joan Rupp, rejoined Nowogroski Rupp after working several years in Manhattan. She began her insurance career working part time in her father's agency throughout high school. To gain a greater insurance industry perspective, Michelle

Rupp worked in the Surety Department of SAFECO for several years. After receiving a bachelor of science degree in finance from the University of Denver, she joined Nowogroski Rupp Insurance Group.

In 1993 a buyout issue between Michelle and Joan Rupp and several employees became contentious, leading to the departure of three senior employees. They took with them information concerning almost the entire commercial lines' book of business owned, produced and serviced originally by Don Rupp, and converted the business to their own to use.

After five years of litigation — in Ed Nowogroski Insurance, Inc. vs. Darwin Rieck, Jerry Kiser, Mike Rucker and Potter Leonard and Cahan — Nowogroski Rupp won its case before the Washington Supreme Court in 1999, which set an important precedent in the area of trade secret laws. The decision provided a clear ruling and signal to all that ex-employees who use their former employers' confidential customer lists are liable for damages, whether a physical list or memorized information is taken. This protracted litigation was pursued not only for Nowogroski Rupp's financial benefits, but also for the benefit of all business owners who expend capital, take risks, make sacrifices and work hard to create a valuable business asset.

Under Michelle Rupp's guidance, Nowogroski Rupp is considered to be on the leading edge in automation nationwide. She has been featured in many trade press articles highlighting her marketing, operational and technological expertise. She continues the Rupp legacy of community and industry involvement by serving on several local and national boards. She has also shown her commitment to the Northgate area as a founding member of the Northgate Chamber of Commerce and has helped the community envision its opportunity as a designated Urban Village.

The agency's long-term goal is to continue to be recognized as an ethical, technological and innovative leader in its industry. In this and its other endeavors, Nowogroski Rupp strives to manage the business effectively and create wealth for its customers, employees and shareholders. The Nowogroski Rupp Insurance Group is succeeding admirably.

> NOWOGROSKI RUPP HONORS THE TIMELESS VALUES OF INTEGRITY AND CREATIVITY WHILE EMBRACING AND CELEBRATING CHANGE AND TECHNOLOGY.

WASHINGTON MUTUAL

In the natural order of civic progress, a city's growth means growth for its business community. In some rare cases, however, a far-sighted business exceeds the pace of civic expansion and helps lead the growth of a metropolitan area instead of merely following it. For Washington Mutual, the combination of truly visionary leadership and a commitment to bettering the communities it serves has not only made it the fastest-growing bank in U.S. history, but also transformed Seattle into a major financial services hub.

In 1880 Seattle was a small town with a population of approximately 4,000. By 1889 it had grown tenfold. The end of the decade also brought two landmark events: a great fire that devastated much of the city, and the founding of Washington National Building Loan and Investment to help finance the rebuilding of Seattle. With Edward O. Graves as its first president, the new institution issued the first monthly installment home loan on the Pacific coast in 1890, establishing from the outset an innovative financial approach that would help Washington Mutual earn the

The Washington Mutual Tower in downtown Seattle serves as the company's corporate headquarters.

title of the largest savings institution in the United States a little more than 100 years later.

Washington National Building Loan and Investment eventually evolved into Washington Mutual Savings Bank in 1917. After surviving the Great Depression, it expanded repeatedly through acquisitions and mergers in the 30s, 40s and 60s, setting what would become another important precedent in the company's history. In the 1980s Washington Mutual continued to grow, achieving growth internally by adding insurance, brokerage, investment and other services. The 80s also marked the start of a renewed and unprecedented period of acquisitions and mergers — 26 between 1983 and 2000 — that propelled Washington Mutual into the top ranks of American financial institutions.

The growth that was achieved in the 1990s under the leadership of chairman, president and CEO Kerry Killinger was nothing short of phenomenal and dwarfed everything that had come before. A pragmatic man with a boundless vision, Killinger joined Washington Mutual in 1982 and was elected president in 1988. When he became CEO in 1990, the company was a small, Seattle-based thrift with $6.5 billion in assets and several dozen branches scattered throughout Washington state. A decade later, largely due to bold moves orchestrated by Killinger — the merger with Great Western Financial Corporation in 1997 and the acquisition of H.F. Ahmanson in 1998 — Washington Mutual had become a diversified financial services company with assets of $190 billion and operations from coast to coast.

A multifaceted company, Washington Mutual provides services through five principal lines of business. The Consumer Banking Group provides a comprehensive line of retail financial products and services to individuals and small businesses in eight states including Washington. Approximately 4.9 million households are served by more than 1,000 free-standing and in-store banking locations, more than 1,500 automated teller machines, and 24-hour telephone and Internet banking.

The Mortgage Banking Group serves more than 1.2 million households throughout the United States, making Washington Mutual the leading adjustable-rate mortgage lender and the fifth-largest mortgage lender in the nation. It is the No. 1 overall home lender in seven major states, including Washington.

The company's third subsidiary, the Commercial Banking Group, consists of two business lines: commercial banking through WM Business Bank and Western Bank; and commercial real estate lending operating under the Washington Mutual brand. Together, the programs offer a full range of commercial banking products and services to individuals as well as small and mid-sized businesses.

The Financial Services Group offers services that help make Washington Mutual much more than a standard bank. It is divided into three lines of business: WM Financial Services, Inc., a licensed broker-dealer with approximately 500 financial consultants; WM Group of Funds, a mutual funds complex; and Washington Mutual Insurance Services, Inc., a full-service insurance agency.

The Consumer Finance Group consists of Washington Mutual Finance Corporation and Long Beach Mortgage. Washington Mutual Finance makes consumer installment loans and real estate secured loans. Long Beach Mortgage originates, purchases and sells specialty mortgage finance loans.

Not only is Washington Mutual one of the most diverse and efficient financial services organizations in the country, but it also prides itself on employing the latest technological advances without sacrificing the personal touch. The bank's more than 6.6 million customer households know and appreciate that Washington Mutual takes an approach to service that differs from most of its competitors. Through simple courtesies, such as not charging fees for talking to tellers or using ATMs, or through the more complex transaction of taking the time to tailor a mortgage to a customer's needs, the bank strives against industry trends and remains an approachable organization with a human face.

The same philosophy that motivates Washington Mutual to retain a personal touch in service also moves the company to maintain a deep civic commitment that dates back to its founding. At Washington Mutual, community involvement is more than just an empty slogan; it is a promise supported by money and time that are freely given. Through the Committed Active Neighbors program (CAN!), employees are given up to four hours paid time off each month to participate in organized charitable events. The company also made a historic pledge in 1999 to make $120 billion in loans and investments over the ensuing 10 years through a variety of ongoing community support programs, including monetary grants, community sponsorships, in-kind donations and outreach efforts that focus on two causes that are close to its heart: affordable housing and K-12 education.

Washington Mutual's School Savings Program has taught children the benefits of saving since 1923.

If the growth of the 1990s is any indication of what is to come, the Washington Mutual communities will reap even greater benefits as the company continues to grow. Having expanded through acquisitions, Washington Mutual is now poised to unlock the potential of the franchise it has built, finding new and innovative products and services to meet its customers' needs more efficiently and profitably — and with a personal touch.

Washington Mutual's innovative Occasio financial centers are revolutionizing the way its customers conduct banking.

DAIN RAUSCHER

Dain Rauscher®, one of the nation's largest regional, full-service investment firms, has its roots in a small investment company founded in 1909 in St. Paul, Minnesota, called Kalman & Company. While Oscar Kalman was building his offices, across the river in Minneapolis, James Dain was starting his own investment company, focusing on municipal bonds. Throughout its history, Dain Rauscher has had numerous mergers, buy-outs, acquisitions and name changes, expanding its reach from the main office in Minnesota to offices across the nation.

In 1933 Texan John Rauscher and colleague Charles Pierce bought the bond department of the Mercantile National Bank in Dallas when Depression-fueled legislation forced the bank to divest its investment business. A 1968 merger brought Refsnes, Ely, Beck & Company on board, and in 1980 that company became known as Rauscher Pierce Refsnes Inc. Meanwhile, J.M. Dain and Company joined forces with Kalman & Company in April of 1967, becoming Dain, Kalman & Quail.

After nearly a century of experience, including several merges, acquisitions and agreements, the company became Dain Rauscher on January 2, 1998. Each name change, each marriage along the way, has brought new experts and a new wealth of experience and knowledge to the firm. Although Dain Rauscher is headquartered in Minnesota, the regional offices are community based and relationships with clients and communities are for the long term.

In July of 1982, the Seattle office was opened by Gordon Krekow. Born in Gray's Harbor, Washington, he knew the regional culture and was intent on preserving it in his work. It was Krekow's goal to expand Dain Rauscher's reach into the Pacific Northwest. Throughout his career, Krekow opened 18 offices in this region, nine in Washington, five in Oregon, two in Nevada and two in Utah.

In March of 1999, Karl Leaverton came to Seattle to take over Krekow's position. As the Dain Rauscher representative in the Pacific Northwest, Karl Leaverton has some fairly substantial shoes to fill. Based out of downtown Seattle, Leaverton is the regional director of Washington, Idaho, Oregon, Utah and Nevada. With his considerable experience in investment services, and backed by Dain Rauscher's commitment to helping clients achieve their financial goals, Karl Leaverton is continuing Dain Rauscher's tradition of excellence.

Dain Rauscher supports local community involvement and philanthropy. The firm believes building strong, working relationships involves more than the employee-client relationship; it includes committed service in the community. The Seattle office reinforces this belief by working with such organizations as Childhaven, Northwest Harvest, the Boys and Girls Club and the Milk Fund.

It is Dain Rauscher's primary concern to provide the best possible financial services for its clients. The company is nonproprietary (it sells no in-house manufactured investment products and therefore is unbiased) and recommends only "best-in-class" investments: this ensures that Dain Rauscher employees are representing the client first and foremost. Clients are investing their savings to fulfill a future need — a child's education or their own retirement — and Dain Rauscher's task is to help ensure those goals are achieved.

The downtown Seattle office of Dain Rauscher
Photo by Patricia Narciso

The Dain Rauscher headquarters in Minneapolis, Minnesota
Photo by Bill Eckloff

International Trade

As a center of international trade, Seattle's port and related industries
manufacture, market and transport consumer goods worldwide.

EXPEDITORS INTERNATIONAL OF WASHINGTON, INC.

Webster defines an "expeditor" as someone employed to accomplish, perform quickly and hasten progress. In the case of Expeditors International of Washington, Inc., the word fits well.

From a single 2,000-square-foot office in May 1979, Expeditors has grown into a global logistics powerhouse whose 200,000-square-foot Seattle high rise serves as headquarters for a network of more than 163 offices and 7,500 employees — numbers that have continued to rise every year. Expeditors grew this big this quickly by moving goods from one country to another as expeditiously as possible. When it comes to international cargo, Expeditors delivers.

Co-founder, Chairman and Chief Executive Officer Peter J. Rose says the company has succeeded because of its state-of-the-art information management systems, its excellence in customer relations and its skilled and loyal personnel. "We are technology-driven for sure, but when it comes down to it, you still have to move the freight," Rose observes. "You can't just hit a button and have the cargo show up. It takes consistent execution by trained professionals and strong relationships with carriers. It's all about the people."

Expeditors does much more than just "move the freight," of course. As a full-service global logistics company, Expeditors satisfies the increasingly sophisticated needs of international trade through services that include customs brokerage, insurance, cargo management, distribution and warehousing, duty drawback, export consulting, licensing, international letters of credit, consular legalization, packaging and other value-added global logistics functions. All of these services are in addition to acting as a non-asset based carrier expert in international air and ocean freight. Expeditors' customers include many of the major names in retailing, wholesaling, electronics and manufacturing around the world.

When Rose and co-founder James L.K. Wang, now the company's president-Asia, hatched the idea that became Expeditors "over a few beers one night on Lantau Island" in Hong Kong, they had no idea that they would be creating a billion-dollar enterprise. They only knew that they were frustrated working for another freight forwarder and felt certain that things could and should be better. Looking back, Rose describes it as "the winter of our discontent." Soon thereafter, Wang was instrumental in opening offices in Taiwan and Hong Kong, and Rose opened San Francisco and attracted the individual talent necessary to open offices in Seattle and Chicago. Included in this group was Glenn M. Alger, now Expeditors' president and chief operating officer.

They began with a lot of trepidation, Rose admits, but within three months they knew they were onto something big. "We had only one way to go," Rose says. "We took on an air of confidence as we realized we could do something here."

Expeditors International of Washington's world headquarters occupies this Seattle high rise.

(Far right) Expeditors' Web-based tracking software exp.o™ provides an unsurpassed level of control and detail.

Expeditors is a global logistics firm with offices on six continents.

In retrospect, Rose, Wang and Alger probably couldn't have picked a better time or better business model. The world was emerging from a recessionary mode and the present global economy was beginning to take shape. At that opportune moment, Expeditors provided something new in the cargo industry. By choosing Expeditors, customers could move cargo door-to-door from Asia to the United States and deal with just one company. It was the first time high-quality customs brokerage services had been integrated with a strong export-oriented forwarder.

While the company got its start transporting cargo from the tiger economies of the Far East to the import-hungry United States, measured expansion steadily shed Expeditors of its roots as a "niche forwarder." Rose comments, "We may have started as a niche player, but it was a heck of a niche." Australia and New Zealand offices were added in a joint venture created in 1983. In 1986 Expeditors added a London office, the first company-owned location in the Old World.

Going public in 1984 as a NASDAQ company trading under the ticker symbol EXPD contributed significantly to elevating Expeditors' public profile. The Expeditors team was able to leverage this increased stature into further growth. Company-owned offices, which had reached China and the Middle East in the early 90s and Latin America by the middle of the decade, were opening in Eastern Europe before the dawn of the new century.

Today global logistics is said to be a $100 billion-a-year growth industry. This has attracted the interest of some of the world's largest corporations, resulting in a series of high-profile mergers and acquisitions. Even so, Expeditors has managed to remain independent and ahead of the competition. Over the past decade, its net revenue has increased at a compound annual growth rate of 21 percent, reaching a 2000 total of over a half-billion dollars. Net income growth for the same 10-year period was an attention-getting compound rate of 24 percent. Not only did Expeditors grow, it grew more efficient over time.

Rose also recognizes that the way to grow is to maintain and nurture employee loyalty. He notes that the way to do this is to keep the company together, and as a result he is decidedly anti-merger. "They are dangerous to the employee," he explains. "After a merger, consolidation is inevitable, and consolidation costs jobs, which is not good in a service industry."

Many volatile factors influence international trade, including economic and political conditions in the United States and abroad, currency exchange issues, tariffs and other trade restrictions, to name just a few.

In addition to forwarding air and ocean freight, Expeditors' services include distribution and warehousing, customs brokerage, insurance, cargo management, duty drawback, export consulting, licensing, packaging and other value-added global logistics functions.

In this environment, flexibility has served Expeditors well. The company does not own assets that fly, float or roll, instead purchasing the space its customers need from the entities that operate airplanes, steamships and trucks. Thus, Expeditors can give each customer optimal, customized service without having to worry about filling its own fleet. And by maintaining good working relationships with customers, employees and suppliers, Expeditors stays ahead of the curve around the world.

"If you always treat customers, employees and vendors fairly, and let them know you're treating them fairly, then you really won't have problems," Rose says. "As long as you don't get greedy, don't forget where you came from and remember what got you here, you should be fine."

Expeditors now operates in so many different economies, Rose adds, that he feels the company has hedged itself against much of the volatility that a business operating in just one or two global markets would face. But that doesn't mean Expeditors will rest easy. The company is continuously updating and diversifying its services and looking for expansion into new markets. The CEO stresses that Expeditors' personnel work hard to keep up with new technology and techniques in the industry. Expeditors' strengths are its expertise and its people. In global logistics, both have no equal.

Although it started as a paper business with handwritten ledgers, the company anticipated the electronic

Expeditors Information Systems department maintains a full-time staff of more than 200 people worldwide to keep its cargo-tracking software systems running smoothly.

revolution and began to computerize by 1983. Its leaders had the additional foresight to create a networked and distributed data processing mini-computer environment rather than a centralized mainframe system. Even before the Internet, this allowed Expeditors' branches around the world to share systems and data and yet control their own operations and manage their customers' information.

Today Expeditors' Web-based tracking software (exp.o™) provides its employees and its customers with an unsurpassed level of control and detail. Through a real-time window, every aspect of the position, condition and status of goods in-transit can be displayed with the click of a mouse. Expeditors' information management systems communicate efficiently because they adhere to standards that enable seamless operation on a global scale. The software's high degree of compatibility allows Expeditors to deploy customized processes for customers worldwide, with a full-time staff of nearly 200 people around the world available to keep systems running smoothly and tend to upgrades, service and maintenance needs.

Technology alone is not the key to Expeditors' success, however. At Expeditors' core is its highly trained, professional staff. When Rose, Wang and Alger began the company, their original goals were to do well for themselves, to do an excellent job for their customers and to do something positive for all their employees. Despite its record of rapid growth, Expeditors can still call itself a family, and management knows how important it is to take care of family first.

That's why company policy and culture provides that each individual office distribute a bonus pool, calculated as 25 percent of the pre-tax earnings, to the employees critical to the success of that branch. The district manager decides how to distribute the bonus among key employees of that branch. The district managers are the heart of the company, Rose says, and he wants to reward them and

While Expeditors is a technology-driven company, it still has to move the freight.

have them, in turn, assure the loyalty of their local staff by including the key contributors in the bonus distribution. A district manager who keeps the whole share isn't much of a manager, Rose points out. "We tell them that if you're going to keep everything, pretty soon you'll have 25 percent of nothing."

Rose is proud that so many of Expeditors' top management and an increasing number of employees have remained with the company for 10 years or longer. "We award lapel pins to employees based on years of service," Rose comments. "Each service pin is distinct and easily recognized — silver after three years, gold after five years, gold with a ruby after 10 years and gold with an emerald after 15 years. We haven't got anyone who is up for the 20-year pin (gold with a diamond), but enough people are close enough that we've already ordered the pins."

In addition, Rose sends a personally signed letter, most containing some handwritten comment or observation, to every employee throughout the world who receives a pin. "Sure it takes a lot of my time to sign these letters, but it is the one thing that I can do as the CEO to promote that small-company atmosphere that we so value, in what has become a rather large company," he explains. "The fringe benefit to me, of course, is to be able to see how the ranks of employees and senior managers who are real believers in Expeditors continue to grow."

Expeditors also shows respect for its staff by achieving much of its growth organically. In most instances, Expeditors has selected the places to which it wants to expand, sent its own personnel there and found the right local people for the task, and opened a new branch itself. Expeditors has also opened new markets by developing a close relationship with local agents, fostering and nurturing

the Expeditors culture there, and then buying or merging with these businesses when synergies are clearly present. In these transactions, Expeditors seeks to keep the original team in place to continue to service the customers. Offices in Lebanon, Greece, Turkey, Ireland, Japan and Australia, for example, began this way.

By growing from within and through strategic acquisitions, Expeditors has already opened offices on six continents, but it still looks for new frontiers. Rose says the company would consider a branch in any market that has the right people with a desire to succeed and a sufficient client base. If a particular market is ready, the company's well-established strategies will work; most new branches are profitable within their first nine months of operation.

While adding to its reach geographically, Expeditors' horizons are expanding internally as well. Its newly established consulting business, Expeditors Tradewin, LLC, provides clients with expertise and assistance with customs compliance matters. Duty recovery programs, which help Tradewin™ customers recover duty payments, represent another growing facet of Expeditors' business. Future expansion will come in many ways, Rose says, as long as the company adheres to its stated mission: "To set the standard for excellence in global logistics through total commitment to quality in people and services, with superior financial results."

Entering the 21st century, Expeditors International of Washington, Inc. remains proud, feisty and independent — like its CEO Peter Rose. And Expeditors is likely to stay that way. Rather than through buyouts or mergers, Expeditors will most likely continue to expand organically, with sustainable annual increases in net revenues and earnings. "Expeditors will stay ahead by sticking to the basics," Rose vows. "That's what got us here."

Expeditors Chairman and CEO Peter J. Rose

Expeditors President and Chief Operating Officer Glenn Alger

MARINE RESOURCES COMPANY INTERNATIONAL

The history of the United States is also the history of the pioneering spirit that drove early European settlers ever westward. Once the geographic frontiers had been largely explored, that spirit carried on in new avenues of expression. During the last quarter of the 20th century, pioneers turned their attention to the exploration of cyberspace. Most of corporate America scrambled to followed suit, but Seattle-based Marine Resources Company International (MRCI) chose a different frontier and pioneered a unique commercial relationship in one of mankind's most time-honored enterprises.

At the height of the Cold War, few Americans could have envisioned a successful commercial enterprise with

MRCI was the first joint Russian-American venture to engage in large-scale fishing operations in the American waters of the North Pacific Ocean.

Russian partners. The idea, the brainchild of James Talbot, president of Bellingham Cold Storage, was perhaps even more foreign to citizens of what was then the U.S.S.R. But in 1976 MRCI was founded as one of the first Russian-American joint venture companies, and the first to engage in joint, large-scale fishing operations in the American waters of the North Pacific Ocean. It was also the first company to have an office in the Russian Far East that was staffed by an American.

MRCI's primary goal was to harvest and market underutilized fish resources off the coasts of California,

Oregon, Washington and, eventually, Alaska. The way in which it accomplished that goal was unique: the American fleet provided the catcher boats, and the Russian partners provided the processing fleet, which the Americans did not yet have at the time. The manner in which the operations were funded was also unique: U.S. fishing crews delivered low-value, high-volume species to the Russian processing ships for Russian markets; in return, MRCI received high-value, low-volume products such as salmon, crab and finished frozen products, which were then marketed around the world.

In the last decade of the Cold War, as tensions remained high between the United States and the U.S.S.R., Marine Resources Company International not only weathered the political storm but actually continued to grow. In the early 1990s, having survived the dissolution of the Soviet Union and the accompanying political, cultural and economic upheaval, MRCI entered a new era with a change in leadership and focus. Anthony P. Allison, a trade expert with an understanding and affinity for the Russian language and culture, was named general manager in 1990.

A change in the company's business focus became imperative in 1990 with the culmination of a long-range plan by the U.S. government to develop American fisheries in the North Pacific — a plan that had helped give birth to MRCI 15 years earlier. No longer dependent on the foreign processing fleet, the United States eliminated resource allocations for joint ventures like MRCI, and Russian-American fishing ventures ended in the American section of the North Pacific.

MRCI continued to operate under joint Russian-American ownership, but the dynamics of the partnership changed. Whereas prior to 1991, MRCI's focus was on pioneering fisheries in the American 200-mile zone, it now used the expertise it had gained through years of cooperation with Russian fishing organizations to concentrate instead on developing fisheries in the Russian 200-mile zone in the North Pacific. Coinciding with the beginnings of Russian capitalism, these new efforts flourished. In the 1990s MRCI's yearly sales grew to more than $100 million.

The company's main enterprise continues to be the development, maintenance and operation of Russian fisheries by means of a wide array of services provided. The most important of these is the marketing of Russian seafood — crab, shrimp, salmon and whitefish — to American, Asian and European markets. MRCI also provides operational services through technical and logistical support for the Russian fleet, arranging fueling and service on the high seas, and providing supplies, spare parts, packaging and transportation of product. Since 1991 the company has functioned as a general contractor, installing state-of-the-art turnkey fishing and processing systems for the Russian fleet through a primarily Seattle-based repair and refit program. It also represents American manufacturers in Russia, selling marine technology, equipment and supplies, as well as representing timber-related companies.

In addition to its Seattle headquarters, MRCI has Russian branch offices in Vladivostok, Petropavlovsk-Kamchatsky, Yuzhno-Saklahinsk and Moscow. It is one of the 150 largest private companies in the state of Washington and has approximately 30 Russian and American employees. One of the keys to MRCI's success is that many of its employees have been trained in the Russian language and culture. "There is more involved than just having knowledge about fisheries," Allison explains. "Success requires an understanding of the culture and language that we are bridging every day as part of business. You can't really separate the cultural aspect from the commercial in international commerce." Operating an enterprise that has few precedents to guide it, MRCI has a definite competitive edge because of the bilingual and bicultural abilities of its staff. In 1996 this unique reputation led the U.S. Russia Investment Fund to provide MRCI with $6.25 million in financing for the continued expansion of the joint American-Russian venture.

MRCI also does not separate bicultural considerations from its community involvement. Each year, together with its Russian partner, Binom Company, and with support from the state of Washington and the Foundation for

A crab vessel managed by MRCI in Russian waters

Russian-American Business Cooperation, MRCI helps to organize an endeavor that is close to the company's heart: an exchange of junior and senior high school baseball players from the state of Washington and Sakhalin Island in Russia. Allison describes the company's involvement as "enormously rewarding," and adds that "the experience goes way beyond baseball."

Marine Resources Company International operates in a business environment that is as dynamic, ever-changing and unpredictable as the oceans that make it prosperous. The adaptability and foresight of its leadership, employees and goals have steered it through succeeding decades of chilly diplomatic waters, political and social upheaval and an unusual array of business opportunities and challenges. No doubt the future will continue to bring new opportunities and challenges to this unique company.

A Russian vessel is refitted in a Seattle shipyard.

PACIFIC MARKET INTERNATIONAL

As a successful pioneer in Asian trade, Seattle-based Pacific Market International (PMI) has brought innovation and market savvy to global sourcing of consumer goods for nearly two decades. The company grew from a vision formulated by founder Rob Harris. While working with importers, he studied their successes, failures, methods and results and sought better options. In 1983 he founded Pacific Market Services — today's PMI — and formed alliances with select trading partners worldwide.

Harris recognized that myriad products could be produced offshore at compelling savings. He also understood the dangers that awaited the unwary. He concluded that long-term success depended on smoothly integrating every step of the process and delivering products that answered the needs of his clients and their customers. Today, that vision is the heart of PMI's mission. Dynamic, rapidly growing, obsessed with quality, and focused on serving its customers, PMI continues to be a pathfinder by designing, developing and manufacturing break-through products that appeal to consumers with active lifestyles.

As its global and domestic markets evolved and PMI grew, the company learned to adapt quickly to change, anticipate new trends and respond. It narrowed its focus and concentrated on select product areas where it could deliver exceptional value, quality and service. At the same time, the company added in-house specialists in product development, design, engineering, sales, marketing, client services, logistics and operations management. PMI opened an office in Shanghai, invested in key production facilities in China, and reduced its reliance on outside suppliers for products, materials and services. From inception and design through production and delivery, PMI today relies on its people and strengths to ensure success.

PMI manages product categories for major retailers, brands and corporate accounts worldwide, among them such icons as Nike, Starbucks, Eddie Bauer, Costco, Wal-Mart, Target and L.L. Bean. It works closely with clients and vendors to develop custom-designed products, both branded and private-labeled, in two categories: drinkware and carrygear. The drinkware division concentrates on unbreakable stainless steel and thermoplastic mugs, tumblers, and bottles featuring a revolutionary vacuum double-walled construction that maximizes heat retention. Carrygear specializes in soft goods such as daypacks, briefcases, shoulder bags, sports bags, wallets and travel accessories.

In 1998 PMI launched its own brand-name division — MiGo™ — dedicated to creating a unique set of products that appeal to "on-the-go" consumers. The product line grew from PMI's expertise and incorporates advanced technology, fresh colors and ergonomic designs.

By corporate directive, PMI actively recruits positive-minded individuals from diverse backgrounds to join its team of world-class professionals. Through comprehensive mentoring and training, the company introduces new members to the business of consumer products and international trade, encourages their creativity and enables them to become active contributors to PMI's success.

PMI shares that success with the community, actively supporting Northwest Harvest, the United Way, area Boys and Girls Clubs, and the Asian Counseling and Referral Service, and it participates in many international trade organizations. In addition, the company offers internship programs in partnership with local colleges and universities.

PMI believes the global market offers boundless opportunities as the company continues to successfully create great products with strong business partners. PMI is energized by the possibilities the future holds for success.

PMI's design process involves teamwork, creativity and vision that leads to the creation of high-quality, unique products for consumers around the world.

PORT OF SEATTLE

Since Henry Yesler built a 1,000-foot pier in the 1850s, the Port of Seattle has grown into the fifth-largest container port in the United States, handling 1.5 million 20-foot containers a year. On average, three freighters a day call on the Port, and about two dozen different steamship lines use Seattle's natural deepwater harbor.

Frustrated that railroad companies and other private interests controlled the commercial waterfront with no thought to overall port planning, the people of King County voted to form the Port of Seattle in 1911. It acts independently of state, county and city authority.

Today, Seattle, closer to Asia than any other major U.S. port, is an international hub for imports and exports. Only 12 miles south of the harbor is Seattle-Tacoma International Airport, serving 100,000 people every day.

In 1948, after community leaders asked the Port of Seattle to address the city's growing demand for air travel, the Port completed Seattle-Tacoma International Airport on 907 acres of forested land. In the early 1970s, the Port completed a major $44 million renovation of the airport, providing a facility that could handle 25 million passengers a year. Thirty years later, the airport handled nearly 28 million passengers annually, making it the 18th-busiest airport in the country, and began extensive expansion and renovation.

The Port gambled in the early 1960s by investing millions of dollars in containerization, the transport of goods in self-contained "boxes" transferable from ships to railroad cars or trucks. Using part of a $10 million bond voters approved in 1960, the Port purchased property and constructed the Terminal 5 container berth, despite no interested users. The risk paid off with the arrival of Sea-Land in 1964. After the Port dedicated more than 100 acres to container facilities over the next two decades, its foreign trade tripled, from 2.2 million tons in 1960 to 6.5 million tons in 1974.

In 1998 the shipping line APL opened the new, modern Global Gateway North at Terminal 5, the second-largest container shipping terminal on the West Coast, after a $270 million cleanup of environmental hazards on an old waste site.

The impact of trade is far-reaching. The Port's trade and transportation infrastructures are responsible for tens of thousands of direct jobs and hundreds of thousands of jobs related to its activities. In fact, one in four jobs in the state is related to trade, making Washington the most trade-dependent state in the country. In addition to shipping, the Port is home to the North Pacific fishing fleet, a new cruise terminal on Seattle's downtown waterfront, and Shilshole Bay Marina, the premier sailing center of the Northwest.

By 2010, $4 billion will have been spent in the first decade of the new century updating and improving the seaport and airport, allowing the Port of Seattle to meet the growing demands of tomorrow. The Port also is launching an aggressive eBusiness strategy that will provide eBusiness solutions to travelers and global trading partners.

The Port of Seattle seaport looking northeast from Terminal 46

Seattle-Tacoma International Airport

Manufacturing & Distribution

In addition to producing exceptional goods for individuals and industry, Seattle manufacturing and distribution companies provide employment for area residents.

ISERNIO SAUSAGE COMPANY

If Isernio Sausage Company is any indication, the combination of an Old World work ethic and an Old World recipe can create an exquisite and almost irresistible force. It can also create a truly American success story. Drawing on a humble but powerful foundation of family, neighborhood, tradition and quality, Isernio Sausage has gained the allegiance and culinary affection of an ever-expanding circle of devotees.

The company is the brainchild of native Seattle entrepreneur Frank Isernio. Born to Italian immigrants who farmed the land where Boeing Field now stands, Isernio grew up in the Beacon Hill neighborhood during the years when Seattle was a blue-collar seaport town. He never had to walk more than a few blocks to school, and in an interesting twist of fate, young Frank played in the very same neighborhood where one day his sausage company would stand.

Frank Isernio, founder of Isernio Sausage Company

The path that led Isernio to founding his own business had several hard-working stops along the way. After serving in the U.S. Army, he took a job in a macaroni factory, and worked as a pipefitter in the shipyards. Spending long hours in the bowels of a ship was difficult work, but it paid well. It also brought Isernio, who had adopted his family's traditional work ethic, the simple satisfaction of knowing he was doing what needed to be done. His next career stop as a route driver and salesman for Coca-Cola provided the marketing fundamentals he would later find very useful. After nine years at Coca-Cola, Isernio began to dream of starting his own company.

Throughout the years that he worked for other people, Isernio had pursued a love that was as much heritage as hobby: making sausage. In many parts of the country there were well-established Italian-American communities where Italian sausage was readily available. In Seattle, however, most grocers did not stock genuine Italian sausage; instead, they sold bland sausages made to appeal to a wide — and mostly non-Italian — audience. As a result, many Italian families made their own sausage at home. In the Isernio family, young Frank had been doing that since his early 20s. "Just as some people make wine for themselves, I made sausage," Isernio recalls. "I made it for my family, and I also made it to give to other people as presents. They loved it and kept saying that I should sell it." In 1980 he was finally convinced to start his own business, and accepted an offer to share the working quarters of a neighboring family who ran a stuffed pasta operation in their home.

To make his business successful, Isernio set an ambitious course for himself. He returned to the shipyards, working on the second shift. After getting home around midnight, he slept for four or five hours, then got up to make sausage. When that was done, he lined the trunk of his car with ice, loaded it with freshly made sausage and went from restaurant to restaurant, trying to convince the owners to use his sausage in their pasta dishes. Their reception surprised him: owners raved about his sausage but were reluctant to buy it because they feared it would not be appreciated by a clientele that was accustomed to mediocre sausage. Isernio was discouraged, but with his dream hanging in the balance, he refused to give up. Quality, he knew, would eventually be rewarded. He finally persuaded a few restaurant owners to give his sausage a try, and before long Isernio sausage was a favorite staple with a growing number of Seattle restaurants.

Whereas most new businesses spend their first year struggling to find customers, the challenge for Isernio Sausage was to keep up with demand. "Every day was exciting during that first year," Isernio reflects. "I was working 80 hours a week, and I had to hire a part-time person, then two people, and then more people. Soon we were expanding into most of the space in my friends' home, using the upstairs bedrooms for offices and the downstairs to make sausage and pasta." Next the company added two refrigerated trailers in the back yard, and Isernio quit his night job at the shipyards to focus all of his energy on Isernio Sausage.

That same year, with his belief in his product validated, Isernio turned his sights on the retail business. If his all-natural, authentic Italian sausage was popular in restaurants, he reasoned, it should also be successful in grocery stores. Since the only places that sold authentic sausage in the city were a few small mom-and-pop stores, the retail market was largely untapped. Ever the consummate salesperson, Isernio not only convinced one supermarket chain to test his sausage, but also personally demonstrated the product to the store's customers on weekends. Initially, consumers were reluctant to buy, believing that all sausage was high in fat and chemical additives. When Isernio proudly explained that his product was both low in fat and additive-free, the customers agreed to a sample. And after tasting it and getting recipe ideas from Isernio, they bought it. Soon the sausage was a staple in the supermarket chain.

Over the next five years, Isernio Sausage expanded into other supermarket chains. Using the system Frank Isernio had learned from Coca-Cola, the company hired route salespeople to sell, deliver and merchandise its product in retail stores. After starting out with two types of sausage (hot and mild), the company added a breakfast link, then more varieties. By 1985, as the number of customers and product lines continued to increase, the company outgrew its shared space and built its own new facility on Seventh Avenue.

More than 20 years after its auspicious debut with Seattle restaurants and supermarkets, Isernio Sausage continues to hold fast to the family recipe and principles that made it successful. Its sausages are made only from prime, lean cuts of meat, with natural casings and seasonings — no chemical preservatives or cereal fillers are used. And it is still made to order, mixed in small, carefully controlled batches, and delivered fresh. Isernio sells more than 650 tons of sausage every year to more than 700 grocery

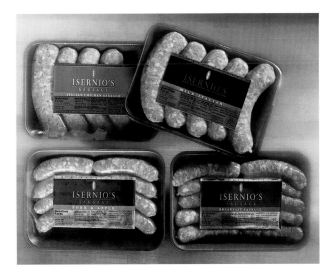

Isernio Sausage specialties: Italian Chicken, Mild Italian, Pork & Apple, and Breakfast Sausage

Authentic, flavorful Isernio Sausages are a favorite in Seattle homes and restaurants.

stores, restaurants and delis. Having branched out beyond Seattle, it serves Washington and Oregon customers along the Interstate 5 Northwest corridor, and has also expanded to Alaska and Hawaii. Under the continuing leadership of owner Frank Isernio, the company has grown at a yearly rate of 25 percent and now employs 22 people. Its spotless 15,000-square-foot facility is state of the art, and two additional sites are used for refrigerated storage.

Isernio now makes 15 core products including Italian Mild Sausage, Italian Hot Sausage, Gourmet Breakfast Links, Italian Chicken Sausage, Apple and Pork Links, Herbed Lamb Sausage and British Bangers. In the late 1990s, when the company looked for ways to grow, it launched a line of prepackaged pastas and risottos called Isernio's Fresh Italian Classics. The classics come in four varieties: Penne Pasta with Italian Chicken Sausage and Roasted Pepper Sauce, Rotini Pasta with Italian Chicken

Sausage, Pasta Fagioli with Italian Chicken Sausage, and Risotto with Italian Chicken and Mushrooms. In keeping with the Isernio tradition, they are all-natural and a delight to the palate, using only the most savory seasonings and premium ingredients. Because of Isernio's hot-fill, quick-chill process, they have a shelf life of 50 days without preservatives. They are popular not only with consumers but with industry critics as well: in 1999 three of Isernio's Fresh Italian Classics were honored with the American Taste Award of Excellence from the National Board of the American Tasting Institute. Isernio's Quick Italian Classics have also allowed the company to expand into airline food service as a tasty alternative to traditional airline meals.

As Isernio Sausage has grown, so has its involvement in the community. Born of a tradition firmly rooted in family, the company gives back to its neighbors in a variety of ways. In 1999 alone it sponsored and co-sponsored more than a dozen major charitable and cultural events, including the West Seattle Help Line Benefit, the

Northwest Women's Show, the MS 150 Bicycle Challenge and the Easter Seals Golf Tournament. Isernio contributes on a regular basis to charitable causes such as Cancer Life Line, City of Hope and Children's Orthopedic Hospital.

The company also supports the Seattle Public Schools and a host of Catholic organizations and charities.

For Frank Isernio, the history of Isernio Sausage Company's success is a personal one, the classic story of "Local Boy Makes Good." It is also a story about the success of an immigrant family and its Beacon Hill neighborhood. More than anything else, it is a tribute to the work ethic and quest for quality handed down through generations of the Isernio family. Frank Isernio explains it simply: "At the time we started selling our sausages to restaurants and retailers, people called it 'gourmet food.' But it's really just a throwback to quality. And as we continue to grow gracefully in the coming years, we will always make sure that the quality, consistency and integrity of our products remain true to the traditions we have established."

Isernio's Fresh Italian Classics are convenient and healthy.

Isernio sausages are made from only the freshest prime ingredients at a state-of-the-art production facility in the same neighborhood where Frank Isernio grew up.

INDUSTRIAL CRATING & PACKING, INC.

A box may just be a box to most people, but not to Palmer Arzo, founder of Industrial Crating & Packing, Inc. To Arzo, the box — his unique patented box — was the touchstone to his amazing success as one of the nation's largest and most versatile industrial packers.

Arzo's firm started out modestly in 1950, a short time after he graduated from the University of Washington with a degree in accounting. With his drive, enterprise and ingenuity, it wasn't long before he surfaced as one of the leading packers in the United States.

Since its beginning, Industrial Crating has served as a diversified packaging resource for corporations, government, military and freight forwarders handling both large-scale and sophisticated shipping projects. It was the company goal to give customers exemplary service at the best possible price. Based on this premise, during the past 50 years Industrial Crating has packaged massive cargo shipments needed to support the Korean and Vietnam wars, supported the North Slope's Prudhoe bay oil fields, and packaged all of the equipment and buildings necessary to develop large wheat farms in North Africa, among other projects.

The firm has also packaged one-of-a-kind artwork, mothballed U.S. Navy vessels and built special containers for air shipments of cattle, ostriches, alpacas, goats and other livestock to large-scale breeding programs located throughout the world. The smallest shipment Industrial Crating has handled was a tiny gear measuring less than one-eighth of an inch in diameter — it had to be weighed to be counted. One of the largest shipments consisted of a rare, perfectly restored Lufthansa Ju 52 aircraft which The Boeing Company flew to numerous air shows in the United States before being packed and shipped back via ocean freighter to Germany.

Handling several thousand individual shipments a year, Industrial Crating relies on the proven experience and innovation of its personnel, many of whom have been with the company for more than 20 years. With advanced training in military and hazardous materials packaging, Industrial Crating's key personnel are well-equipped to solve any packaging need that their customers encounter. The company's complete wood and corrugated box manufacturing divisions were designed to fulfill the need for small to moderate quantity orders requiring short lead times.

Ever mindful of its commitment to remain a family-oriented business, Industrial Crating has always considered the health and well-being of its employees and the community as its primary concern. The company contributes to the community by donating packaging services and supplies to schools and nonprofit organizations that send items such as computer equipment and disaster relief supplies to Third World countries.

Because of the aggressive role of the Port of Seattle in Pacific Rim countries, shipments to the Far East have grown steadily over the years and have become a major portion of the company's business. With a location convenient to both the Seattle and Tacoma ports as well as Sea-Tac Airport, Industrial Crating & Packing is anticipating that doing business during the next 50 years will be as rewarding as the last.

A pumping station destined for an offshore oil rig in Singapore is being prepared for shipping.

Aluminum roofing panels measuring 126 feet long are being packed for transport to a remote job site in Alaska.

DIVISION FIVE

In every construction project manual or plan book, specifications for the metal trades are listed under Division Five. As a result, Laurie and Jim Hagedorn picked that as the name of their steel fabrication company, knowing construction industry professionals would recognize it. Division Five, which calls itself "the" steel fabrication company, can make just about anything that is called for in structural and miscellaneous steel construction.

Division Five assembles steel into whatever products its customers design. The company's work can be seen in Bellevue Square Mall, the new Boeing headquarters in Renton, a Microsoft museum and store in Redmond, Seattle's Union Station, several Wal-Marts in Alaska,

condominiums in the Seattle suburbs, Starbucks' Kent roasting facility and the Family Fun Center in Tukwila, among many others.

Before the Hagedorns incorporated Division Five in 1994 and began operations in 1995, they had already been planning their steel fabrication company for more than a decade. Seattle native and Army veteran Jim Hagedorn, company vice president, estimator and project manager, says having a written business plan before they started and sticking to it were the most important elements in making the Tukwila fabricator successful. With Jim handling project management and his wife, Laurie, running the business as its controller and president, Division Five surpassed its billing projections almost immediately and exceeded its goal of a 10 percent annual sales increase each year.

The Hagedorns did not do it alone. "Silent partners" in Division Five are Laurie's parents, Bill and Harlene Robbins; not only did they invest in the company, but in its early days both also helped out with electrical work, bookkeeping, client introductions, purchasing and babysitting.

Even as the company grows, Division Five retains that family atmosphere. The Hagedorns' 1-year-old son James holds title to expediter, and 5-year-old daughter Caly is known as the little boss. Oldest daughter Leslee Van and her husband Chung (Joe) work for Division Five as well.

The close-knit, family feeling extends to other team members. Chief Estimator Chuck Cowley, Superintendent

Main stairway in Family Fun Center, Tukwila — Division Five assembles steel into whatever products its customers design.

(Far right) Steel awning over main entrance to Boeing headquarters in Renton — Division Five products look and work the way they're supposed to.

The Division Five crew — "Our team does whatever it takes to get the steel out."

(Far left) Vice President, Project Manager and Estimator Jim Hagedorn goes over plans with Chief Estimator Chuck Cowley — "Design may get more complicated, but ultimately it will still be about steel. Division Five knows steel."

Office Manager Leslee Van, daughter of company founders Jim and Laurie Hagedorn — even as the company grows, Division Five retains a family atmosphere.

Bill Sellers and Fitter/Welders Allan Erstad and Justin Hagedorn have been with Division Five since the beginning. And for almost as long, Phan Duong, Carl LaFontaine and Curtis Etris have also belonged to the crew. The Hagedorns speak with pride of the hard work and devotion their staff has provided to get the company up, running and meeting major deadlines on time and on budget. "Our team does whatever it takes to get the steel out," Jim says.

Recently the fabricator has expanded its client base, and its 1999 relocation to a 12,000-square-foot shop in Tukwila with a 20,000-square-foot yard will enable Division Five to set its expansion goals even higher. Additional Project Manager Michael Dodd joined the Division Five team in 2000 to further expand the scope of the company's construction activities. The immediate goals, however, are to stay competitive on bidding, to computerize additional office functions and to further develop the company's Web site.

Division Five will also remain active in business and civic affairs. Laurie Hagedorn is the first woman to sit on the board of the Pacific Northwest Steel Fabricators Association, while Jim is a board member of their local community club. The company belongs to the Better Business Bureau, the Greater Seattle Chamber of Commerce, Washington Employers Association and Master Builders Association, and it donates to Tukwila Community Center, Tukwila Police Department and Church By the Side of the Road.

For Division Five, success as a steel fabrication company is all about its experienced work force and ability to communicate with clients. "We try to cultivate relationships and teamwork with our customers and the designing architects and structural engineers, so we can make products that look and work the way they're supposed to," Jim Hagedorn explains. "Now that computers design things, design may get more complicated, but ultimately it will still be about steel. Division Five knows steel."

Project Manager Michael Dodd joined the Division Five team in 2000 to expand the company's construction activities.

THE LUCKS COMPANY

It's a sweet business. In 1910 Oscar J. Lucks decided to close his seven-year-old wholesale cigar distribution company, Oscar Lucks Cigar Company, and go into the business of selling supplies and utensils to bakeries under the name Oscar Lucks Company. After World War I, Oscar's son Carl entered the business and guided the company through the Depression and the years of World War II, selling a limited line of baking ingredients and equipment throughout parts of Washington and Alaska.

William Lucks, grandson of Oscar Lucks, entered the business in 1954 and led the company into expanded sales of equipment. The change was prompted by the growing market for equipment in supermarket in-store bakeries. He also moved the company into manufacturing in the 1960s by introducing a dry cereal mix and specialty ingredient manufacturing plant, initiating the production of some of the equipment the company already sold, and starting the manufacture of edible food decorations. In the 1990s Lucks

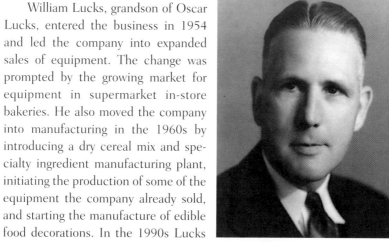

Carl W. Lucks, son of the original owner, guided the business through the Depression and World War II years.

William G. Lucks, grandson of Oscar Lucks and current CEO of The Lucks Company

acquired a plant to produce frozen dough and fruitcake. With its ability to service so many aspects of the baking business, The Lucks Company (so named in 1983) has a long history of bringing smiles to food lovers.

It was Oscar Lucks' religious beliefs that prompted a shift from tobacco in the early part of the 20th century, and for over 85 years the company sold baking ingredients and utensils. In the early 1950s, concern that the company was losing its market provided impetus for change. Small bakeries, confectioners and drugstores with soda fountains — Lucks' primary customers — began disappearing as new shopping centers drew shoppers from downtowns and "Main Street." William Lucks believed that the company had a great deal of unrealized potential, and this prompted him to move into manufacturing. The move to manufacturing meant new markets and a larger customer base. A major change in the baking industry was the introduction of in-store bakeries. These bakeries, housed inside large supermarkets, gave Lucks a whole new market opportunity for all its product lines. As The Lucks Company grew, it became necessary to divide the business into three divisions: Lucks Bakery Supply Company, Lucks Food Equipment Company and Lucks Food Decorating Company. The Bakery Supply Company furnished bakeries with ingredients, manufactured mixes, paper products and frozen dough products, and was sold in 1998.

The manufacturing of equipment began when a Lucks employee, hired to help with the installation of equipment, decided that he could build a better donut fryer than the ones that Lucks was currently buying. The fryer he built used gas/infrared technology and was considerably more efficient than traditional gas models. The design was extremely popular and Lucks began producing the fryers in its own factory. The Food Equipment Company evolved from there, building a tradition of innovative equipment design that has been a hallmark of the company ever since. Along with donut fryers, the Lucks Food Equipment Company manufactures a wide range of large commercial ovens for baking and roasting, and other dough-preparation equipment. It can provide any piece of equipment necessary to run an in-store, retail or small wholesale bakery. The Food Equipment Company also supplies baking and roasting equipment to commissaries, hospitals, hotels, schools and prisons — any food-service operator that does large-volume, centralized preparation of food.

A dominant player in the U.S. baking equipment industry, The Lucks Food Equipment Company has seen substantial expansion, selling its equipment in the United States, Canada and Mexico. A glass-backed oven that allows customers to view breads and pastries as they bake is a particularly successful item, and one unique to Lucks. The manufacturing plant is located in Kent, Washington.

The Lucks Food Decorating Company began with icing roses. In the mid-1960s William Lucks found Jack McPherson and his icing rose machine at a trade show and hired him the next day. Lucks then got into the production of molded-sugar decorations, or Dec-Ons®, when complications with its current supplier in Los Angeles developed. Thus the Lucks Food Decorating Company was born.

The demand for icing roses and molded sugar decorations grew steadily. In the1980s Lucks began testing a new idea that would extend its product line still further: the Edible Image®. Printed on an edible base, an Edible Image® is a picture that can be applied directly to the top of a cake: scary monsters for Halloween or sprays of roses for Valentine's Day, athletic themes for sports fans, and much-loved cartoon characters and comic book heroes for children's birthday parties. Initial response was excellent, and the Edible Image® was introduced to the marketplace in October 1994. Bakeries can order Edible Image® sets ready to be placed on waiting cakes. Edible Image® Print-Ons™ allow decorators to create personalized decorations. Using digital printing systems, a scanner, a computer, edible ink and the special Edible Image® Print-Ons™ base, decorators can reproduce the photograph of a customer's choice and have a photographic-quality, edible picture to decorate any cake. Edible Images® and Print-Ons™ have helped make the Lucks

Sweets for the sweet — some products from The Lucks Food Decorating Company

Food Decorating Company truly international, and The Lucks Company now supplies its food-decorating products to bakeries all over the world.

Whimsical or romantic, playful or personal, cakes that are individualized make any special occasion seem sweeter. The Lucks Food Decorating Company continues to expand its product lines to include the most popular licensed characters and to give customers more choices. The Lucks Food Equipment Company is also continually expanding and updating the equipment it manufactures. Providing the best customer service is a high priority at Lucks, and so The Lucks Company continues its tradition of innovation. Whether it's building a better donut maker or developing a way to put a picture of the winning team on the celebration cake, taking bright ideas and developing them into successful product lines makes The Lucks Company a sweet success.

An Ovation oven with curved-glass back allows consumers to see products being baked or roasted.

Marketplace

Seattle retail establishments, restaurants and service industries offer
an impressive variety of choices for Seattle residents and visitors.

BEST WESTERN EXECUTIVE INN

The success of a crucial business trip or a long-dreamed-of vacation often hinges on one key element: the hotel chosen by the traveler as a home-away-from-home. An uncomfortable room, an inconvenient location, or a staff that is ineffectual or indifferent to service can mar the most carefully planned and otherwise successful trip. A good hotel, on the other hand, can not only salvage a trip but also provide the traveler with a reason to return to the area on another occasion. In downtown Seattle — literally in the shadow of the world-famous Space Needle — the Best Western Executive Inn is known for giving guests a reason to return.

Built in 1979, the Executive Inn has been a Best Western franchise from the day it first opened its doors. The hotel is locally owned by Clise Properties, a property development and management company, which has been a Seattle business institution for more than 100 years. Although not the original owner of the Executive Inn, Clise Properties had long owned the land on which it was built, leasing it to the original developer. After the hotel fell on hard times in the late 1980s, Clise purchased it in the fall of 1991.

The new owner immediately made two major changes to set the Executive Inn back on the road to respectability and profitability. It invested $2 million in extensive renovations and has continued to reinvest in the

The warm and inviting lobby sets the tone for the rest of the hotel.

hotel ever since. Clise also brought in a new management team who not only oversaw the renovation of the hotel's physical amenities but also cultivated a hospitable and helpful staff to complement it.

With 123 guest rooms, 10 meeting rooms totaling 6,500 square feet, and a staff of almost 100, the Executive Inn is a full-service hotel. It boasts 38 executive king rooms that are perfect for business travelers and 85 rooms with two double queen beds to accommodate guests who are part of tours or groups. As an added bonus, many rooms offer a spectacular view of the scenic Seattle skyline. The hotel's decor is classic Northwest: warm and inviting, with comfortable, overstuffed furniture and an emphasis on wood that reflects the Puget Sound's beautiful forested terrain. Its facilities can also accommodate those with special physical needs, and include rooms that are specifically designed for guests who are physically challenged. The hotel features a restaurant that specializes in Northwest cuisine and a lounge that serves the best in Northwest microbrewed beer and vintage wines. The hotel's Seafair Ballroom can seat up to 250 people for business or social functions, including catered banquets for companies, organizations and weddings; the Executive Inn also caters certain events at the nearby Seattle Center.

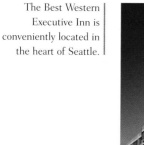

The Best Western Executive Inn is conveniently located in the heart of Seattle.

Not surprisingly, the hotel runs a high rate of occupancy year-round. Because of its reputation, location and rates designed to serve the broad economic middle, it is a popular vacation base for tourists, who comprise 40 percent of its yearly business. Large cities can pose logistical problems for out-of-towners, making it difficult to get around to attractions that are scattered throughout the area, but that is not a problem for guests who stay at the Executive Inn. Many of Seattle's most popular attractions are only a short, leisurely walk away: the Space Needle, a wide variety of arts and entertainment events at Seattle Center, the Seattle Art Museum, Paramount Theatre, and the Washington State Convention Center. Sonics NBA basketball at Key Arena and the Seattle Center Amusement Park are also very close by. And for those who want to shop in Seattle's bustling downtown, explore the famous and eclectic Pike Place Market, or experience the fine dining and picturesque views of the Puget Sound waterfront, the Seattle Monorail is only a few blocks away.

Conveniently located at the edge of the downtown commerce district, the Executive Inn draws a considerable number of business travelers, providing not only comfortable accommodations but invaluable services such as copying and faxing facilities. It also hosts meetings for a wide range of local and regional groups, including the Seafair Boat Club, which is involved in organizing Seafair, Seattle's biggest annual summer celebration for the last 50 years. A respected union establishment, the hotel enjoys a strong business relationship with labor organizations as well, hosting meetings and conventions for approximately 40 different unions on a regular basis.

The Executive Inn has won numerous awards from Best Western and received recognition for its excellence from an eclectic range of satisfied guests. It was honored for its service and professionalism by the U.S. Secret Service, who set up a command and communications center in the hotel during a visit to Seattle by President Clinton. It has also received awards for housing members of the U. S. Coast Guard while their vessels were in dry dock for repair. A prime contractor with all branches of the military since 1994, the hotel has received numerous commendations and annual recognition as one of the best providers of temporary military housing. Each year approximately 11,000 Army, Navy, Air Force and Marine recruits enjoy the hospitality of the Best Western Executive Inn for the two

Many rooms have a spectacular view of the nearby world-famous Space Needle.

days it takes to process their enlistment papers and receive their first assignments.

No matter what part of the country a hotel is in, its fate will always rise or fall because of three key factors: location, perceived value and quality of service. High marks on all three translate to almost certain success, but if even one is lacking, the others may not matter. Offering an unrivaled location in the heart of Seattle, eminent affordability and a seasoned management and staff who are dedicated to providing the best possible service, the Best Western Executive Inn is not only a safe bet for travelers but also a wise investment.

The Executive Inn features a full-service restaurant that specializes in Northwest cuisine.

BUDGET RENT A CAR

In one of its earliest incarnations, Budget Rent a Car's downtown Seattle location boasted a mere three employees and barely enough space to park five cars. Its airport customers picked up their vehicles at a gas station across from the airport and were asked to drive to the downtown office at their earliest convenience to sign the rental agreement. The trust the company placed in its customers was refreshing, but the practice was hardly convenient by Budget's present standards.

A Convergence of Companies

Seattle's Budget Rent a Car is the result of an amicable convergence of two car rental pioneers, Seattle U-Drive and Budget Rent a Car. Founded in 1928, David Litvin's Seattle U-Drive changed names and locations several times until it was sold to local business legends John Cain and Josef Diamond in 1961. A Seattle native and owner of a busy downtown Shell station, Cain had been renting cars to customers while theirs were being repaired. Diamond was a high-profile Seattle attorney with a flair for spotting good business opportunities. Under Diamond and Cain, the new Seattle U-Drive flourished.

A few years earlier in Los Angeles, Morris Mirkin had issued a challenge to the car rental industry by starting Budget Rent a Car, a company that rented vehicles for only $5 per day and 5 cents per mile — almost half the going rate. The Budget Rent a Car Corporation was established two years later, in 1960, for the purpose of franchising Mirkin's concept around the world. A Seattle franchise opened in 1961, the same year that Cain and Diamond acquired Seattle U-Drive.

In 1963 Cain and Diamond purchased Budget's Seattle franchise, merged the two competitors and adopted the Budget name. They opened a small office at the original Budget location on the corner of Westlake and Virginia and soon after leased the property across from the airport which eventually became Budget Airport Parking. The company expanded with the purchase of the Oregon franchise in 1973 and continued to grow by opening more Puget Sound locations throughout the 1970s. That same decade also marked the establishment of a car sales lot and a long sought-after rental counter at SeaTac Airport.

The 1980s brought even more changes that further strengthened the company. In 1983 Budget merged with

Budget Rent a Car's original location at 2001 Westlake Avenue, c. 1963

American International Rent-a-Car, owned by Jerry Costacos, making it the largest car rental operation in the state of Washington. Five years later the franchise was purchased by the Budget Rent a Car Corporation, which in turn became a wholly owned subsidiary of Budget Group, Inc. (BGI) in 1997. BGI's parent company was formerly Budget's largest franchise operator, Team Rental Group.

(Far left) Josef Diamond helped make Budget Rent a Car a fixture in Seattle.

John Cain, one of Seattle's car rental pioneers

Budget Rent a Car Corporation

Under the leadership of BGI chairman Sanford Miller, Budget Rent a Car Corporation has become the largest car and truck rental company operating under one name worldwide. With a network of corporate-owned and franchised locations at nearly 825 airports and 2,400 downtown, neighborhood and suburban locations, it has a presence in more than 120 countries and territories around the world. Budget was the first to rent luxury vehicles such as Lincoln Continentals and Town Cars and continues to offer the most exciting fleet in the industry, with more than 125,000 vehicles in the United States alone. As a BGI subsidiary, Budget is an important part of a multifaceted corporate network that also includes Budget Car Sales, Inc.; Budget Airport Parking, Inc.; Van Pool Services, Inc; and Ryder TRS, Inc.

Budget Rent a Car — Seattle

With offices in the Josef Diamond Building, Budget has 16 Puget Sound locations, including one solely dedicated to car sales. It also operates a large parking operation less than one-quarter mile from SeaTac Airport, offering air travelers economical parking in 1,500 stalls on three large lots. Through Budget, Seattle-area customers not only benefit from the company's 250 dedicated employees, but they also have easy access to a worldwide reservations and information network. The company's motto — "Get Out of the Ordinary" — is reflected in the attitude of its staff, its management philosophy and in the varied, high-quality fleet offered to customers.

Having earned a reputation as an industry leader in offering great selection and rates, Budget has also made a concerted effort to take the hassle out of renting a car through a new service that is especially beneficial to its most valued customers — frequent renters. Fastbreak is an enhanced express rental service that provides paperless transactions, faster service and greater choice. The program offers two options, depending on the Budget location. Fastbreak Choice gives customers more selection and the fastest, most convenient way to rent a car at many major U.S. airports. Customers can confirm their reserved car class on monitors at the Choice canopy, choose any car in that class from a wide selection of colors and styles, and then simply present their driver's license and a hang tag from the car's rearview mirror as they exit the lot. No time is lost while waiting in line or filling out forms. The second Fastbreak option, Fastbreak Counter, is offered at more than 134 airports where Fastbreak Choice is not available. It provides the same paperless transaction and selection, with a brief stop at the counter to pick up the vehicle's keys.

With increasing frequency U.S. companies talk about "thinking out of the box" — stepping outside the parameters of business as usual to find new ways of providing products or services. Budget Rent a Car and its Seattle forebears have been doing just that for more than 40 years. The "out of the box" thinking that brought together Seattle U-Drive's Diamond and Cain and inspired Morris Mirkin to start Budget Rent a Car is the same business mindset that gave birth to innovations like Fastbreak. For Budget in Seattle that is not a new trend, but merely the latest manifestation of its founding philosophy.

ELEPHANT CAR WASH

For residents of Seattle and Greater Puget Sound, that big, pink elephant is almost as much a symbol of home as the Space Needle or Mount Rainier. Since 1951 Elephant Car Wash's rotating, neon elephant has been a Seattle landmark; elephants now grace eight Elephant Car Wash locations in Seattle and surrounding areas. The Battery Street elephant, the most well known of them all, has been on television shows and in magazine articles, commercials and countless tourist photographs. Anyone who has ever been through an Elephant Car Wash knows that the elephant is also a symbol of long-standing quality and service.

The first Elephant Car Wash was opened in 1951 on Fourth Avenue and Lander Street in downtown Seattle. This elephant was the first "automatic" car wash — while most car washes relied entirely on plastic bristle brushes and human labor, original Elephant owners Archie, Dean and Eldon Anderson invented hands-free machines that cleaned cars more safely and reliably. A second location opened in 1956 on Battery Street in the heart of downtown Seattle, another in 1963 in Tacoma, and five more Puget Sound locations (Federal Way, Bellevue, Auburn, Puyallup and Burien) in the years to follow as Elephant's reputation for quality service spread and grew. Elephant car washes now exist in Eastern Washington, Arkansas and California.

In 1982 Bob Haney bought the Elephant Car Wash chain from the Anderson brothers. The car washes have long since abandoned the plastic bristle brushes in favor of high-tech, hybrid-blend cloths and high-pressure water cleaning. These washing systems produce a shine superior to hand washing but with minimal risk of scratches. Elephant was among the first car washes in the country to make the switch to cloth. Very little of the wash is actually done by hand — only those areas which are difficult to reach by machine. Around 90 percent of the wash is automatic, and each car is towel dried at the finish. Elephant is one of the few "full-service" car washes in the area. Customers can have their cars washed and waxed, the interiors vacuumed and the carpets shampooed. Automobile owners get a professionally cleaned vehicle without going through the time and expense of having it detailed.

People might think that operating a car wash would be difficult in rainy Seattle. After all, most car washes shut down on rainy days. Not Elephant Car Wash. In soggy Puget Sound a car wash that only operated on sunny days would quickly go out of business. Customers still come to Elephant to have their cars cleaned, even on wet days. Elephant offers interior cleaning as well as exterior, so it has plenty of business, whatever the weather.

Elephant's reputation for service extends far beyond Puget Sound. Celebrities, sports figures, high-ranking public officials, foreign diplomats, and candidates vying for political office all have their cars professionally washed at Elephant Car Wash whenever they are in Seattle. Even United States presidents have had their limousines washed at Elephant, a process that requires a security clearance for Elephant Car Wash, and concludes with FBI agents checking under the cars with mirrors.

Elephant Car Wash's relationship with Seattle and Puget Sound extends beyond just providing great service at a good price. Elephant owners and employees are also concerned about protecting the local environment,

Perhaps the best known Elephant Car Wash is in downtown Seattle on Denny Way.

especially the waterways. For many years Elephant Car Washes have reclaimed the water they use; this conserves water and also reduces the risk of pollutants making their way into streams, rivers or Puget Sound itself. Elephant Car Washes are very active in the Puget Sound Car Wash Association and do extensive work with the Charity Car Wash Program, a program designed to minimize waterway pollution from charity car washes.

Elephant Car Wash has always been a leader in advances in the car wash industry. Computers now operate the washes, the pH factor of the dirt build-up on cars is analyzed and the soap solution is adjusted accordingly. Cleaning equipment is replaced about every three years to ensure that Elephant has the best and most modern equipment available. Environmental issues are also a factor in how vehicles are cleaned and how wastewater is reclaimed at Elephant. Close attention to these details, along with a genuine commitment to good service, has kept Puget Sound customers loyal. Elephant Car Wash owners know that customers come back, and frequently even redeem Elephant discount coupons that have been at the bottom of someone's sock drawer for decades. Elephant always honors its coupons, even when the coupon is older than many of the employees.

It's not only the customers who are loyal to Elephant Car Wash — many employees have been with Elephant Car Wash for years, moving up through the ranks. Their knowledge extends to include every aspect of the business, and that is a large part of Elephant's success. Employee longevity, unusual in the high-turnover car wash industry, is attributed to the fact that the employees and owners make the business fun. Every employee is carefully trained to provide the high-quality service customers expect from Elephant Car Wash.

The pink, neon elephant that has been featured in movies and music videos may be whimsical, but Elephant Car Wash is serious about cleaning vehicles and protecting the local environment. Those who know the elephant also know Elephant's reputation for service, which has earned the company "Best Car Wash in Seattle" by readers of *Seattle Weekly* magazine consistently since the poll began. Expertise, dedication and attention to detail are as much trademarks of Elephant Car Wash as the pink elephant. These qualities have assured Elephant's continuing success in Puget Sound and beyond.

As much an icon of Seattle as the Space Needle, the big, pink elephant has been in movies and on television, in advertisements and on postcards.

The elephant at night

HAPPY GUESTS INTERNATIONAL, INC.

The title on Gerald R. "Gerry" Kingen's business card reads "Head Coach & Dishwasher" at Happy Guests International, Inc. Kingen also happens to be the founder, president and CEO, and a man with enough talent, ambition and innovative ideas to have succeeded in many different careers. However, he chose to channel his relentless energy and creative restaurant concepts into the food and entertainment industry, becoming an icon in the Pacific Northwest — a one-of-a-kind visionary who has, time and again, taken an idea that has worked elsewhere in the world and integrated it into the local culture. Kingen became successful in the eatery business by exceeding the expectations of millions of people, had fun doing it and made a lot of money, but his success story is not over. Thirty-seven years after he opened his first business, Kingen is busy launching a new casino-restaurant-entertainment concept.

Kingen grew up in his parents' restaurant business, where "child care" meant a mountain of dishes for Kingen to wash and dry. He went to Washington State University and Central Washington State College to become a dentist but found it stifling and headed instead to a major ski resort where he ran the food operation. He was not yet 21 years old, but he had 85 employees under him, served 16,000 lunches daily and profited financially in this mountaintop resort.

His success in this venture encouraged him to try his hand in the restaurant industry elsewhere. In 1965, at age 21, he bought a bar that he renamed the Climax Tavern, becoming the youngest Washingtonian ever to obtain a liquor license. He transformed it from an industrial tavern into a popular nightclub frequented by university students. In 1969 he purchased the original Red Robin tavern in Seattle's University District and pioneered the "gourmet hamburger" concept of a fun atmosphere, a unique menu and great service. To meet the liquor board's requirements of an 80 percent food/20 percent liquor operation, Kingen devised a menu that offered 28 different kinds of burgers. The sheer number of burgers sold is mind-numbing, says Kingen, who soon saw Red Robin's gross income grow from $12,000 to $100,000 a month. In the 70s and 80s Kingen expanded the Red Robin chain to more than 50 restaurants.

Over the next few years Kingen purchased or opened additional eateries, including Blue Moon Tavern; Warehouse Tavern and Nightclub; Boondock's on

Gerry Kingen and his dad, Robert Kingen, with their halibut catch off Bell Island

Broadway, where he introduced a 30-page menu and exhibition kitchen; The Great American Food & Beverage Company, which entertained guests with costumed waiters who broke into song every five to 10 minutes; Lion O'Reilly's and B.J. Monkeyshines, a New York steak and lobster house with a bar that was rated one of the country's top 100 by *Esquire* magazine in 1982; and the Lake Union Café featuring one of the first wood-fired pizza ovens in the Northwest.

In 1979 Kingen began franchising Red Robin, which he had transformed into an adult McDonald's and a poor man's Trader Vic's operation, with the first opening in Yakima, Washington. In 1984 Skylark Corporation, a Japanese restaurant company, bought 50 percent of Red Robin and later purchased an additional 40 percent, with Kingen retaining a 10 percent interest. In 1996 Kingen refocused on Red Robin International and was elected CEO and chairman of the board of the now 177-unit chain.

In 1980 Kingen embarked on another creative restaurant concept, Salty's. The first one opened in Portland as the debut of Kingen's chain of waterfront seafood eateries. Salty's at Redondo Beach in Des Moines, Washington, followed in 1981. In 1985 Kingen purchased the Beach Broiler, which was doing $1 million in business; he transformed it into Salty's on Alki Beach, which did $9.6 million in 2000. Salty's on Alki is one of the top three restaurants in its market by volume. In 1999 it was listed as No. 70 in the top 100 largest-volume restaurants in the United States, according to *Restaurants and Institutions* magazine. The popular restaurant seats 240 in the main dining area, and every seat in the house

has a view of the scenic Seattle skyline. The downstairs banquet facility seats 225 diners, allowing Salty's to compete with area hotels. Because it offers ample parking and is a quick drive from downtown across the West Seattle Bridge, Salty's has a thriving lunchtime trade.

Kingen married Kathryn Hilger, a graduate of the University of Washington, in 1982 and took a 10-year hiatus to devote himself to family life. In 1992 Kingen came out of retirement and reorganized his operations under the corporate umbrella Happy Guests International, Inc.

Kingen is currently creating a new concept called Funsters Grand Casinos, which will occupy 22,000 square feet of a 72,000-square-foot building near Sea-Tac International Airport. Kingen visualizes Funsters as a safe, stimulating, exciting sanctuary for people who want to temporarily escape from the cares of daily life — especially Baby Boomers — and a venue that also offers great food, fun games and Las Vegas-style entertainment. The name comes from a 1940s term, "You're quite the funster!"

Regardless of the nature of his endeavors, the common ingredients found in each concept Kingen has developed are commitment to cleanliness, fresh food and teamwork, guest satisfaction and enjoyment, great entertainment and fair value. This has been flavored by Kingen's irrepressible sense of fun and spiced by his complete fearlessness in trying something new. To Kingen, everything is a work of art. When working on a new eatery concept, the question always before him is simply, "Do people like it or not?" From all accounts, the public's answer to Kingen is a resounding "yes."

Diners at Salty's on Alki Beach enjoy a breathtaking view of Seattle and Elliott Bay while also enjoying world-class cuisine. Salty's is credited as one of the world's great view restaurants by a local journalist.

Gerry and Kathy Kingen with the original Red Robin mascot in Gerry's antique car at the annual Seafair Torchlight Parade

NORDSTROM, INC.

Arriving in New York City with just $5 in his pocket and unable to speak more than a few words of English, a 16-year-old boy named John W. Nordstrom had left his home country of Sweden for America in 1887. The first years in the land of opportunity were difficult. To make ends meet, he labored in mines and logging camps as he crossed the United States and settled in Washington. In 1897 he decided to try his luck in the Klondike gold rush in Alaska. The labor was hard and there was an oversupply of eager workers, but within two years Nordstrom had earned $13,000 in a gold mine stake and returned to Seattle. Eager to invest his money, he went into partnership with his friend Carl Wallin. The pair opened their first shoe store, Wallin & Nordstrom, in downtown Seattle in 1901. With first-day sales of $12.50, this was the humble start of what would become the retail legend Nordstrom, Inc.

From the beginning, John Nordstrom's business philosophy was based on exceptional service, selection, quality and value. Customers appreciated efforts to stock an extensive range of shoe sizes, and in 1923 the partners added their second store. In 1928 the second generation of Nordstroms assumed the reins.

Soon the company grew to be the largest independent shoe store chain in the United States. By 1960, Nordstrom had eight stores in Washington and Oregon, and the downtown Seattle store had become the largest shoe store in the country. Meanwhile, the company was looking for new ways to spread its wings. Venturing into the clothing market, Nordstrom purchased Best Apparel, a Seattle-based clothing store, in 1963. For the first time, customers were greeted with a selection of both shoes and fine apparel under a new store name: Nordstrom Best.

In 1968 the company was passed to the third Nordstrom generation, and in 1971 it went public. Just two years later, Nordstrom sales passed the $100 million mark and the company was recognized as the largest-volume West Coast fashion specialty store. The name was formally changed to Nordstrom, Inc. the same year. In 1975 the company expanded into Alaska while the first Nordstrom Rack was opened in Seattle as a clearance center for full-line store merchandise. The company moved into the competitive California market in 1978 and made the big move to the East Coast in 1988 with the opening of its Tyson's Corner store in Virginia.

Throughout its nationwide expansion, Nordstrom focused on catering to customers' needs. Instead of categorizing departments by merchandise, Nordstrom created fashion departments that fit individuals' lifestyles. Today, led by the family's fourth generation, Nordstrom is one of the nation's leading specialty retailers, offering a large selection of quality apparel, shoes and accessories for the entire family in a wide range of prices and sizes. Merchandise ranges from classic to contemporary as well as exclusive couture designs.

The shoe store in 1910 with central displays bordered by stock

(Far right) Carl Wallin and John Nordstrom at the original shoe store in 1901

John Nordstrom in 1925

In addition to the full-line stores across the country — which offer amenities such as concierge services, complimentary wardrobing, makeup consulting, cafes and espresso bars — there are Nordstrom Rack stores offering significant savings. Nordstrom also operates Façonnable boutiques throughout Europe and the United States. These shops feature men's and women's apparel and accessories from Nice-based designer Albert Goldberg, which are available in the full-line stores as well. There also are two free-standing shoe stores in Hawaii and one clearance store in Arizona. In addition, Nordstrom serves customers by mail-order catalogues and online through its Web site.

Nearly 47,000 employees nationwide — including about 7,000 in the six Puget Sound-area stores — work hard to take care of customers one at a time. The company's policy of empowering its staff to use their own best judgment provides a work environment that is supportive and entrepreneurial. In fact, Nordstrom has been named several times to *Fortune Magazine*'s annual list of 100 Best Companies to Work For. Other reasons cited are an extensive employee benefit program and a long history of promoting from within — a fact best illustrated by the significant number of corporate employees and store and regional managers who began their careers on the selling floor.

Naturally, a company with such a commitment to its shoppers and its employees also cares about the communities where it does business. Nordstrom is committed to preserving the health and vitality of those communities through financial support and involvement. While employees participate in annual United Way fund drives and volunteer in many regional charitable activities, the company supports outreach programs, special events and contributions targeting education, human services, the arts and community development.

In Seattle, its hometown, Nordstrom sponsors several community events. Fashion shows — especially the Designer Preview show each fall — benefit various nonprofit organizations, and diversity celebrations honor unsung community heroes. One of the largest fund-raisers is the annual Beat the Bridge race, attracting over 8,000 participants and earning more than $775,000 for the Juvenile Diabetes Research Foundation.

Nordstrom also contributes to the Seattle-area community by never forgetting its roots, even as it continues to expand across the country. While moving into the future, it retains local traditions. When the flagship downtown Seattle store moved recently — a $100 million relocation project that involved renovating a historic

The flagship store — Nordstrom downtown Seattle

Nordstrom renovated a historic landmark to relocate its downtown Seattle store just blocks from the original shoe store site.

landmark — it stayed downtown, in fact still within a few blocks of the original shoe store established in 1901. Today, 100 years later, the Nordstrom philosophy is no different from the one John Nordstrom set for his first shoe store: offering the best possible service, selection, quality and value.

PIKE PLACE MARKET

A favorite of residents and tourists alike, the Pike Place Market is downtown Seattle's heart and anchor. Officially opened in 1907, the 7-acre market was designed to cut out expensive middlemen and streamline the way farmers in Puget Sound got food to consumers. Lined up along Pike Place, farmers sold their fruits and vegetables straight off the back of their horse and buggy "trucks." Later, horse stables turned into permanent stalls where vendors could sell their goods and meet the public directly. Pike Place Market is the oldest continuously operating market in the United States.

who sell along the low stalls must produce what they sell. Virtually unchanged since the turn of the 20th century, Pike Place Market is a living institution touching on three centuries. In the 1960s, Victor Steinbrueck and a group of concerned citizens saved the market from the wrecking ball, and since then it has spearheaded a renaissance in the design and purpose of public markets. Full of the best fresh produce, seafood, breads, flowers, restaurants, cafés, arts and crafts and unique specialty shops, Pike Place Market is a taste of the best that Puget Sound and the world have to offer.

Co-owner Sandee Brock enjoys the food and the view at the Pike Place Bar and Grill.

One of Sarah Clementson's most popular paintings of the Pike Place Market

Pike Place Bar and Grill

Owners Gordy and Sandee Brock claim they have a "corner on the market." And it's true — the Pike Place Bar and Grill occupies the corner of Pike Street and 1st Avenue. Now one of the most popular restaurants in Seattle, Pike Place Bar and Grill was known as The Mint when it opened in 1962. The Mint's primary clientele were merchant seaman up from the docks for good food and cold beer. Today the restaurant is refurbished and renamed to reflect its close connection with the market. The Grill's fare is often bought at the market only hours before it is served, and market workers are among the restaurant's most devoted customers.

Piroshky Piroshky

The smell coming from Piroshky Piroshky has been known to draw in customers from clear across the market. Piroshkies, a typical Russian lunch food, are pastries stuffed with smoked meats, rich sauces, fat mushrooms and sweet fruit. Owners Vladimir and Zina Kotelnikov came to Washington from their native Estonia in 1989, and by 1992 they had set up shop in the market and were selling more than 30 kinds of piroshkies and pastries. Among the most popular foods in the whole of Pike Place Market, favorite piroshkies include the

Pike Place Market has evolved beyond its local heritage and now offers food and goods from all over the world. However, its patrons still meet producers in person — those

smoked salmon pate with cream cheese, onion and dill, the apple-cinnamon roll, the garlic and cheddar cheese, and the beef and onion. Vladimir Kotelnikov says his shop is blessed by a good wind — it blows the scent of his piroshkies around the market and then blows his customers in.

Studio Solstone Ltd.

Studio Solstone began in 1979 at the market. Owners Michael Yaeger and Sarah Clementson had recently returned from Europe and liked the European feel of the market. They began by selling tiny paintings and quickly broadened their inventory to include goods such as wooden puzzles, games, books and calendars. Clementson is a professional artist whose portraits of Pike Place Market have come to identify this landmark in many people's minds. Studio Solstone now sells her limited edition prints, note cards and original paintings. Yaeger, who began a lifelong love affair with the market at age 5 and has written books on the market, today serves as its Honorary Mayor.

Sur La Table

Although now a nationwide phenomenon, Sur La Table is one of Pike Place Market's "originals." Shirley Collins founded the original cookware shop in the market in 1972 to address Seattle's need for hard-to-find kitchenware. The Behnke family purchased Sur La Table in June 1995 and opened a second store that fall. The company has continued to expand its retail, e-commerce and catalog business ever since, becoming famous worldwide. A premier supplier of kitchenware, Sur La Table provides everything a cook could want: high-quality bakeware, gadgets, nearly a thousand different cookbooks, even an exclusive line of copper cookware. For beginner to *cordon bleu*, Sur La Table has the equipment to make every meal — and every chef — extraordinary.

Three Girls Bakery

For those looking for a tasty, affordable sandwich or a wide variety of fresh breads, Three Girls Bakery is the place. The oldest business in the market, Three Girls Bakery

A cook's view of paradise — inside Sur La Table at the Pike Place Market

was founded in 1912. Jack Levy became enchanted with the market while working at his father Leo's produce stand and in 1979 bought Three Girls Bakery to continue the family tradition at the market. Three Girls caters to Seattle's working crowd, who flock to the bakery for an excellent lunch. Offering food that is both exceptional and affordable kept the business alive during the Depression and two world wars and keeps Three Girls Bakery humming with customers now.

The original Three Girls Bakery and two of the original girls

MARKETPLACE

BALLARD BLOSSOM

When Mrs. Wiggen and Mrs. Keizer opened their flower shop in Ballard in 1927, they weren't aware that they were creating a piece of Seattle history. Although Ballard Blossom was small, it was long on charm and customer service, and it did well, surviving the Great Depression when many other businesses floundered. Ballard Blossom has grown considerably since then, though it still stands on the same city block. The shop has become a Ballard landmark, and Ballard Blossom is now the largest florist in Seattle.

By 1945 Mrs. Wiggen was ready to retire and she sold Ballard Blossom to John Martin. Martin, who had previously owned a business that sold groceries, baked goods and flowers, decided he wanted to focus entirely on flowers. At that time Ballard Blossom had only one employee besides Martin himself. Even with such a small staff, Ballard Blossom provided customers with excellent,

New owner John Martin looks over some flower arrangements, 1945.

The Ballard Blossom building on NW Market Street

highly personalized service. This tradition continues today and is a large part of Ballard Blossom's success.

Ballard Blossom offers more than just the freshest flowers delivered daily to the shop: clients can select from among chocolates, vases, pottery, ceramics, plush toys, greeting cards and balloons. And Seattle's largest and most experienced design and delivery staff will put together the perfect arrangement. Thanks to its size, Ballard Blossom can handle just about any special occasion — and because it delivers to a wide geographic area, customers all over Puget Sound can enjoy Ballard Blossom's beautiful flowers, outdoor plants and original floral arrangements.

Ballard Blossom's flowers are always beautiful, but its festive holiday arrangements make special occasions even more special. Christmas is particularly important at Ballard Blossom. The first or second week in November, Ballard Blossom is decorated top to bottom for its annual Christmas Open House. Customers are invited to eat cookies and drink coffee as they tour the shop, checking out the holiday arrangements, the decorated trees and the wreaths. Santa attends, and arrangements, trees and wreaths are given away as prizes in a drawing. The open house has taken place every year since the early 1960s and has become a Ballard tradition.

A tradition of providing excellent customer service is a significant part of Ballard Blossom's longevity and success. Although the flower shop may have grown large enough to handle 1,300 deliveries on one particularly busy Mother's Day, customers can still expect individual attention from Ballard Blossom employees. And staff members are just as loyal as the customers— at one point, three generations from the same family all worked at the shop.

Ballard Blossom has certainly expanded its product line and service area, but its ties to Ballard and Greater Seattle are strong. Ballard Blossom does considerable charity work in the area, making contributions and donating arrangements to help raise money for the community, including the local orthopedic hospital.

Ballard Blossom has had many opportunities to turn the single shop into a chain, but John Martin has always resisted that idea. The flower shop continues to be unique — unique in its commitment to its customers, in its range of flowers and gifts, and in its ability to design arrangements to suit any taste, any occasion.

BAY PAVILION

Walking into Seattle's waterfront Bay Pavilion is like a trip into the city's gold-rush past. Nearly torn down in 1968, the once-dilapidated pier that houses the shops and restaurants of Bay Pavilion has been lovingly refurbished — the original pilings, heavy timber and massive wooden beams all stand just as they did in 1897 when a ton of gold arrived by boat just north of Seattle's Pier 57, and the Alaskan gold rush was on.

Hal Griffith, the owner of Bay Pavilion at Pier 57, started the movement to save Seattle's historic waterfront when the City Council was preparing to tear it down and build a promenade. Several piers were threatened; all were in bad shape, having been neglected for decades. To lose the waterfront, Griffith thought, would be to lose an important piece of Seattle's past. He started the Waterfront Parks Association, an alliance of merchants who owned businesses along the water. The association went to the City Council to petition the removal of the piers. Access to the water would be more difficult without the piers, and the preserved buildings would provide an excellent tourist attraction. The Council was convinced, and the piers were renovated instead of destroyed.

One of the saved piers now houses Bay Pavilion. In order that visitors would be able to enjoy an authentic piece of gold-rush Seattle, Griffith installed his shops and restaurants carefully, gently setting them inside the existing structure. With its historic building and painstakingly preserved rustic feel, Bay Pavilion provides some of the most unique eating and shopping experiences in Seattle. The restaurants re-create gold-rush period cuisine: alder-smoked salmon, made using ingredients and methods devised by American Indians of the Northwest, is a specialty of The Salmon Cooker. At The Crab Pot, diners sit at tables covered in paper and piled high with cooked crabs. All the seafood served in Bay Pavilion's four restaurants is delivered fresh by boat to the pier. A bakery in Bay Pavilion serves sourdough bread made according to an old Alaskan recipe. Sourdough was a gold miner's favorite since new batches of bread could be started with leftover dough and thus didn't require fresh yeast. Bay Pavilion even boasts a carousel that is an exact replica of a much older machine. Each horse is like artwork, licensed and numbered, a faithful re-creation of an original carousel horse.

Bay Pavilion is more than just a place to eat great food and buy unique souvenirs — it is also a place to learn about an important part of Seattle's past. It is Griffith's continuing mission to preserve the history of the waterfront and maintain the character of the area. While all the businesses in Bay Pavilion are aimed at satisfying customers' needs, a deeper need is also satisfied — a connection with a time when miners left Seattle's waterfront piers with pickaxes, sourdough bread and dreams of gold.

Lobster and sourdough bread are favorites at The Crab Pot.

With a view across Puget Sound to the Olympic Mountains, dinner on the deck at The Fishermans is a treat for the eyes as well as the taste buds.

CANLIS RESTAURANT

Who would have imagined that 50 years after opening its doors to the Seattle public, Canlis Restaurant would still be setting the pace for fine dining in the 21st century?

If he were here today, founder Peter Canlis would not be surprised in the least. After all, he established Canlis to fulfill his lifelong dream to create a restaurant renowned for exceptional food, fine wines and unprecedented attention to service. Indeed, Canlis' vision encompassed a level of dining elegance that had never been achieved in Seattle.

His timing was ideal. The city was hungry for just such a place, and in 1950 Canlis opened at the eastern base of Queen Anne Hill.

It did not take long for Canlis to find its niche. Everything about the place, from its Frank Lloyd Wright architectural style to its extraordinary cuisine, epitomized the changing pace and culture of the city. Boldly setting new standards, Canlis offered selections like Ahi tuna long before many people had even heard of this tropical Pacific Ocean fish. In this way, Canlis essentially pioneered a new culinary bill of fare, Pacific Northwest Cuisine.

As Seattle's long-established families continued to shape the landscape and economic direction of the city, the restaurant itself experienced a number of changes. By the 1970s, it was about to witness another, as the reins to the now well-established Seattle landmark were handed off to son Christopher and his wife, Alice, when Peter Canlis passed away from lung cancer.

The next generation began to move quickly into the national forefront. For the first time, Seattle-based businesses like Microsoft and Starbucks, among others, were setting trends, not just participating in them. Seattle had emerged as a world-class city, offering a dynamic blend of cultures, opportunities and lifestyles.

For Chris and Alice Canlis, this presented new challenges. The two set out to reinvent Canlis in their own style, one that merged the restaurant's traditional level of sophistication with a more relaxed atmosphere. Their new approach strived to make people feel comfortable by treating them as if they were guests in their own home. To this day, the Canlises make a point each night to visit every table, talking with their guests and learning what occasion has brought them to Canlis. This level of attention continues to pay off. In 2000 Canlis experienced its most successful year ever.

Canlis — the most award-winning restaurant in Seattle and a beautiful excuse to dine

The Canlises are committed not only to superb cuisine, but also to the local community. For example, they hosted a $5,000-a-plate New Year's Eve 2000 gala, with all monies donated to selected arts, education and music organizations. The event raised $500,000, benefiting the YMCA and Seattle University, among others.

Year after year, Canlis continues to receive high accolades in the Seattle region and abroad. Such recognition includes *Wine Spectator*'s coveted Grand Award, and a recent Four-Star review from the *Seattle Post-Intelligencer*.

Now in its 50th year, Canlis still stands proudly on its original site, continuing to delight residents and visitors alike, and making all who enter feel very much at home.

DUNN LUMBER CO.

In Trenton, New Jersey, the renovation of an old high school gymnasium has hit a snag: builders need some fairly unusual materials in order to refurbish the roof. Rather than scour the countryside for the hard-to-find supplies, the renovators put in a call to Dunn Lumber Co. As always, the staff at Dunn Lumber is able to help, locating the necessary materials at an Oregon sawmill.

From its creation by founder Albert L. Dunn in 1907, Dunn Lumber Co. has always found innovative ways to remain competitive. Originally the company was located in Rhinelander, Wisconsin, and functioned as an intermediary, brokering deals between Pacific Northwest sawmills and Wisconsin lumber dealers. Albert Dunn realized that since many of the lumber and shingle mills he represented were located in the Northwest, Washington state was a better base for his operations. In 1910 Dunn moved his family and his business to Seattle for good.

With the addition of a retail lumber operation in 1927 and the purchase of larger premises in 1931, Dunn Lumber Co. continued its tradition of successful innovation. The new location came equipped with a rail siding — an important advantage as most of the company's supplies came by train. Although many other businesses failed during the Depression, Dunn Lumber thrived, thanks to the adoption of a "cash only" policy for sales. In July 1938 a massive fire completely destroyed the Seattle site, wiping out the lumber sheds, stock, trucks and offices. It took 68 carpenters only 12 days before the facility was rebuilt and open again for business.

In the last 10 years the emergence of large, national chains has changed the face of the retail building-materials market, forcing many independent lumber companies out of business. Dunn Lumber's response has been to focus even more effort on offering exceptional materials and service to clients. The staff works hard to establish and maintain one-to-one relationships with customers, offering expert advice and suggestions to help homeowners and professional remodelers finish their projects on time and under budget. Also, Dunn Lumber has put considerable emphasis on providing materials for the restoration of older houses. The recent boom in Seattle's housing market means that many older homes are being renovated, and these projects frequently require the kind of special knowledge and materials that Dunn Lumber can provide.

Dunn Lumber's Seattle roots run deep. Although it sources and ships materials across the United States and internationally, the majority of Dunn's customers are local; between 1948 and 1995 Dunn added nine more sites in and around the Seattle area. As one way of giving back to the community, Dunn Lumber contributes materials to United Way's annual Day of Caring campaign.

With the addition of a Web site for selling products and answering customers' questions, Dunn Lumber has found yet another way to provide better service to clients and remain competitive in the marketplace. Although Dunn Lumber Co. is the largest retail lumber operation in the greater Seattle area, it has remained a family business, and perhaps this explains why the resourceful, entrepreneurial spirit of Albert L. Dunn has prevailed for so long.

The lumber yard at Northlake and Latona in the 1930s

GARY QUINN'S PHOTOMAGIC

Gary Quinn, a "native" of the Pacific Northwest, is an award-winning photographer who has been guided by his creative spirit throughout his life. He was born an artist and in his school days explored his talent at every level, becoming first a musician and songwriter, then a photographer. His artistic bent has provided him with considerable versatility throughout his career, and he believes that if he can succeed in one area, he can also succeed in another. It is this approach to his career that allows him to feel as much at ease photographing a building interior as a CEO or a favorite pet.

In college Quinn majored in communications and broadcasting, then went to work for a Seattle record distributor. This experience led to the Hollywood music scene where a business associate persuaded him to buy a professional camera. Later, while an ad salesman for a local newspaper, one of his photographs appeared on the newspaper's front page, marking the beginning of his career as a photographer. His early work included beauty pageants, award banquets, bands, products, corporate executives and weddings. He had so much work that he never got around to establishing a niche specialty, but in the long run it allowed him to continue working with a wide spectrum of clientele and subjects. In 1985 he returned to the Northwest and established Gary Quinn PhotoMagic in Seattle.

Today Quinn's work focuses on architectural, event, food and product photography; performers, actors and models; studio portraits and portraits on location. His architectural photography for developers, builders, interior decorators and property management companies is used primarily to attract lessees or create high-end marketing pieces. His product photography is likewise used for a variety of purposes. For Qwest Dex, a major client, he photographs virtually any subject that can be put into a Yellow Pages advertisement, from attorneys or other service professionals to moving equipment and vacuum sweepers. For Vee Gee Scientific, Inc., another continuing client, he photographs microscopes, lab equipment and glassware for use in brochures, catalogs and a trade show booth background.

Much of Quinn's work revolves around performers, actors and models. Some clients use his photographs for publicity purposes only, while bands use them in press kits; talent agencies, for casting; model agencies, for fashion shows and print magazines; and performers, for press releases, publicizing performances or promoting compact disks. Quinn also excels at executive portraiture, whether in his studio or on location, for clients who want to evoke a particular mood through an outdoor environment such as a lake or a mountain meadow.

Calling upon his creative versatility, Gary Quinn is well versed in most aspects of digital imaging. Providing his clients with cutting-edge imagery is what keeps the creative juices flowing. With the "photomagic" ability that his business name implies, it is not surprising that he has received numerous awards from various photography associations and that some of his work is on permanent exhibit at the Los Angeles County Fair.

Quinn's photo shoot for Orca Beverage reveals an example of painstaking attention to detail and provided his client with a superior advertising medium.
Photo by Gary Quinn*PhotoMagic

(Far right) A self portrait by GaryQuinn*PhotoMagic — thanks to digital wizardry, you, too, could look 10 years younger.

Gary Quinn's portrait of Matt Eisenhauer, Seattle teacher and orchestra conductor, illustrates the effective people photography that can be made in studio or on location.
Photo by Gary Quinn*PhotoMagic

GLANT PACIFIC COMPANIES

In a city inundated with high-tech ventures, many of which go from boom to bust before their first birthday, Glant Pacific Companies is a business of a different sort. The family-owned scrap-metal and fabric company is one of the oldest in the city and is, by its very nature, a decidedly low-tech operation. The Glant companies have endured for three generations and are likely to be around for many more, as brothers Doug and Bruce Glant and their sister, Wendy, proudly continue what their grandfather began more than 80 years ago.

Founded in 1917 by Jules Glant, Pacific Iron & Metal Company initially sold recycled metal, cloth and paper domestically and overseas. In 1931, though mired in the Depression, Glant borrowed a hefty sum of money and built a larger plant on Fourth Avenue South, where the company still resides.

With room to expand, the company grew with the economy. Jules Glant's son, Earle, came to work for his father and in 1957 opened a fabrics division. It seemed an incongruous addition, but two very different and economically counter-cyclical businesses proved an efficient way to insulate the company against hard times.

The Glants had fun with their unconventional business mix. They played up their zany array of merchandise and drew hoards of bargain hunters to such high-profile events as "Pacific Iron & Metal's Annual Bathing Suit Sale" and "Pacific Iron & Metal's Fabric Division's Grocery Sale."

In 1974 Doug Glant took his grandfather's place as company president and CEO and reorganized the business into three distinct divisions. Pacific Iron & Metal, Pacific Fabrics & Crafts, and Pacific Iron Building Materials operate under what is now Glant Pacific Companies.

The fabric business in particular flourished. What began as an outlet for secondhand yardage sold by the pound, grew into a full-scale retail operation offering first-quality material. During the 70s the company operated as many as 18 home-sewing stores throughout the region. In later years, as industry giants faltered and fell

due to changing demographics, the Glants deftly pared that number to seven, keeping the division healthy and primed for growth.

The scrap recycling business also went through some changes, shifting focus from iron to nonferrous and precious metals. Bruce Glant, who serves as president and COO, moved sales efforts toward the Far East, making Japan, Korea, Taiwan and finally China some of the company's biggest markets. He also expanded the product line to meet the needs of both domestic and international consumers.

Describing the family's intrinsically low-tech business, Doug Glant laughs, "New Economy? We're not even old economy; we're prehistoric."

True, says Bruce, this is primarily a metal-bending industry, but in his effort to move the company into the modern world, he has installed cutting-edge management systems, processing equipment and information technology to secure the company's place as an industry leader and move it into the new century.

Service and quality have always been at the heart of Glant Pacific Companies, and whether the business passes to a fourth generation of family leadership or to professional management, the Glants are confident the company their grandfather began more than eight decades ago will remain a stalwart pillar of its community.

By 1974 a third generation of Glants had assumed leadership of the company. Today Doug Glant (right) is chairman and CEO, Bruce Glant was recently named president and COO, and sister Wendy is also an owner.

GEORGE WHITE LOCATION PHOTOGRAPHY

For George White, what makes location photography so fascinating is the endless variety of assignments, each with its own unique lighting, situational and people challenges. White has photographed everything from the sewers of Renton, Washington, to the Palmilla Hotel beach resort of Mexico's Cabo San Lucas, to aerial views of the Kingdome's implosion in downtown Seattle.

Geology, not photography, was his first career. But in 1981, after a decade as a soils engineer, White made the leap to professional photography.

Initially, he did mostly aerial photography. Today, however, White's location photography services also include corporate portraits and facilities work, architectural photography, plus an extensive and constantly growing library of stock photographs.

White's client base is as varied as his assignments. He's worked for several of billionaire Paul Allen's companies; documented park facilities for the City of Bellevue; and provided stock photographs to leading book publishers Harcourt Brace, Houghton Mifflin and McGraw Hill as well as *Parents* magazine, *Diversion* magazine and several airline in-flight publications. Other clients include *Bowler's Journal International*, Fidelity Investments, *Landscape Architecture*, the U.S. Postal Service and Opus Northwest.

A member of the distinguished American Society of Media Photographers, White brings to Seattle an accomplished and diverse talent.

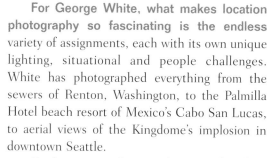

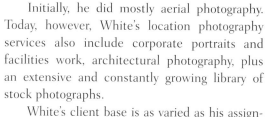

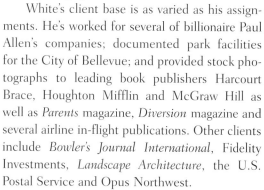

METROPOLIS

Located in the Phinney Ridge neighborhood of Seattle, Metropolis is one of those unique stores that has charm, faithful customers and a 20-year history. Owners Terry Heiman and Roger Aase went into business together in 1981. Heiman was the property master for Intiman Theatre and the Seattle Rep after moving from Oregon; Aase was an English teacher in Edmonds. Needing a change, they opened an antique store called The Prop Shop. Terry and his assistant, Linda Kenworthy, ran the store while Aase taught. Wanting in on the action, Aase opened his own space in the store and called it The Back Room Antiques & Collectibles. After a short time, Heiman and Kenworthy decided to get out of the antiques and collectibles business. The Prop Shop was dissolved, and Aase and Heiman took another space next to an old movie theatre and re-opened The Back Room. As cinema-goers waited in front of the store for their movie to start, they would notice — and come in to buy — some of the movie nostalgia postcards and greeting cards that The Back Room offered. One day a greeting card salesman came in, and as Aase and Heiman looked over the cards, they decided to make a major change. They were no longer going to offer antiques and collectibles but instead would become *the* greeting card store in the Phinney Ridge/Greenwood area.

They quickly outgrew their space next to the theatre and moved down the street to the corner of 72nd and Greenwood. Capturing a second corner at 73rd and Greenwood, the two opened a kitchen store and called it In and Out of the Kitchen. The card store grew quickly. When the Wallingford Center was nearing completion and looking for tenants, Aase and Heiman thought it would be a good location for another greeting card store. In July 1985 they opened their store in Wallingford Center and named it Metropolis. The kitchen shop closed and the card store moved to 73rd and Greenwood. The adjacent storefront became available, and Aase and Heiman turned the two premises into one big shop named Metropolis.

From the beginning, Metropolis was customer-focused and fun. Aase and Heiman wanted their shop to have a friendly, neighborhood feel and felt it very important to know the names of regular customers. They built their business on this premise of friendly customer service and award-winning window displays. In 1987 Metropolis was honored with the mayor's award for being one of Seattle's top 10 small businesses.

Heiman and Aase live on Phinney Ridge near their store and have been active in the local business community. Aase was the president of the Greenwood Chamber of Commerce for two years running, and Heiman made it his task to start an annual Christmas tree-lighting in their neighborhood, a ceremony which continues to this day.

With today's easy access to home computers and e-mail, Heiman likes to impress on customers that it's OK to e-mail, just don't forget to write. Nothing beats getting a hand-written card in the mail — it is still the best way to give and receive thoughtfulness and love.

Nothing beats a hand-written card to send someone your thoughts.
Photo by Gary Quinn*PhotoMagic

Candy and candles and cards, oh my!
Photo by Gary Quinn*PhotoMagic

PIKE PLACE FISH

When John Yokoyama purchased Pike Place Fish in 1965, it was just a quiet little stand, one of many at the historic open-air Pike Place Market in Seattle. Yokoyama was an employee of the fish market at the time, spending most of his $150-a-week salary to pay off his 1965 Buick Riviera. In 1990 Yokoyama and his staff made a decision to become world-famous, and in the years since they've been profiled in *People* magazine and made appearances on NBC's "Frasier" and ABC's "Good Morning, America." They've been in a Levi's commercial and even formed a business consulting team. People come from all over the world to watch them throw fish and banter with the crowd. The energy and wit of the fish market staff and their delight in interacting with their customers and passers-by make them not only one of the most popular tourist attractions in Seattle but also one of the most sought-after training teams in business.

A sign above the fish market stall reads "Caution — Low Flying Fish." Pike Place Market's famous "fish flingers" draw a crowd of passers-by: when a customer purchases a fish, the employee working out front heaves the fish to a waiting staff member behind the counter who — almost always — catches it. Originally intended only to save steps, this fish-throwing exercise is a sure-fire crowd pleaser. But Pike Place Fish is not only a high-energy, dynamic show, it's also a good place to buy some of the best seafood in the Pacific Northwest.

The antics of the Pike Place Fish staff are based on a philosophy that any business anywhere can and should work to improve the quality of life for others. The fish market employees direct their energies into positively impacting the lives of their customers and others who visit the market. They're spreading their message worldwide through two corporate training videos, "Fish" and "Fish Sticks," developed by Charthouse International Learning Corporation. The videos have been translated into five languages and distributed to a global market.

Fat crab and flying fish at the world-famous Pike Place Fish

Additionally, Pike Place Fish has been featured in *Fast Company* magazine, and Yokoyama and his staff frequently make appearances at special business events, demonstrating their unique work environment and showing others how to make work a place to both have fun and be productive. Employees of the fish market believe they should choose their own attitudes and come to work excited to be there. Their enthusiasm and energy is good for the visitors, good for Pike Place Fish, and ultimately, it contributes to the continuing health and success of Pike Place Market. Despite never having spent a dime on advertising, Pike Place Fish is truly world-famous.

A seafood feast for eyes and palate in downtown Seattle

Yokoyama trusts his well-trained staff to run the show, and he supports his team as they expand and grow. The business has taken off in unexpected directions with corporate training and business videos, but Pike Place Fish staff never forget the basics: provide the best product available, have fun and work to ensure that others have fun, and don't throw anything that has spines.

THE PINK DOOR

When Jacqueline Roberts, owner of The Pink Door restaurant, came to Seattle in 1976, few people in Puget Sound knew what arugula and fennel were. She saw it as her duty to educate the public about the Italian way to eat, drink and celebrate food, wine and fellowship.

The Pink Door is about the "full occasion of the table," as Roberts terms it: patrons are served the best meals and wine while also enjoying sights and sounds as rich and varied as the menu. Some of nearby Pike Place Market's most interesting public performers trade their skills for a free meal — a tarot-card reader tells fortunes, a balloon maker makes thought-provoking balloon shapes to inspire conversation. Every Tuesday through Saturday, a cabaret entertains the public for free. Performers such as these are not background, they are an integral part of the meal. Roberts feels that good conversation is as essential to a meal as the best ingredients. All of this adds value to the dining experience and ensures that customers come back again and again.

The Pink Door feels like one of Seattle's best-kept secrets. Because the restaurant is on the side of a hill, customers descend as they enter the dining room, giving the place an "underground" feel. But the view from the deck is spectacular, looking out over Puget Sound and the Olympic Mountains. The restaurant seems particularly secretive as it has no sign to advertise its presence — just a pink door. When Roberts opened the business in 1981, she intended to place outside a large neon sign of a chef twirling pasta on a fork. At the time, one of the Pike Place Market's governing bodies would not allow neon signs in the historic market. So Roberts decided her restaurant would have no signs at all. Since customers enjoyed feeling privy to the secret, says Roberts, she's continued the tradition. Besides, when customers have to really look for the entrance, it whets their appetite.

The Pink Door is famous for more than its absent advertising: the food is legendary. The lasagna, made with spinach noodles, béchamel and pesto and topped with a marinara sauce, is a big favorite with customers. Originally Roberts designed the dish because the colors were the red, white and green of the Italian flag. Now the lasagna is so popular that Roberts isn't allowed to take it off the menu. Another favorite is the *ciuppin* — a fish soup made with rich broth and locally caught clams, mussels, squid and snapper. To complement any meal, The Pink Door offers a range of wines. It is Roberts' philosophy that wine should be a pleasure, not an intellectual exercise, and so employees are always happy to make suggestions.

At The Pink Door, customers can be certain of several things: excellent food and wine and a truly convivial atmosphere in which to enjoy their dining experience. The Pink Door is a restaurant in the best Italian tradition — a celebration of *la dolce vita*!

The below-street feel of The Pink Door makes for an intimate dining experience.
*Photo by Gary Quinn*PhotoMagic*

PORCELAIN GALLERY

Graceful ladies in sweeping ball gowns, eagles and egrets in flight, stunning porcelain dinnerware and luminous crystal stemware: this is the Porcelain Gallery in Seattle's Magnolia Village district. A quiet business begun in 1973, the Porcelain Gallery has grown in size and reputation to become one of the most renowned porcelain retailers in the United States.

Since its opening, the Porcelain Gallery has become one of the most famous and respected galleries in the country. Careful selections of unique lines of handcrafted dinnerware, stemware, flatware, crystal and figurines give every buyer the opportunity to own exactly the right pieces. The Porcelain Gallery sells worldwide to collectors, brides and grooms, corporations, and porcelain and crystal lovers of every kind. The Porcelain Gallery's reputation has so far exceeded the family's original expectations that now word of mouth has become their best advertisement. Today the gallery is called upon to outfit corporate dining rooms, yachts, private jets and even dude ranches.

Beautiful tables and porcelain figurines are not just for the rich, however. The Porcelain Gallery offers selections to fit all tastes and budgets. Most customers are not interested in buying faddish styles or impractical pieces for their tabletops;

The Gyrfalcon — one of only 50 produced by Albany China, the falcon is hand-painted porcelain on a walnut, mahogany and iroko wood base, inlaid with bronze tiling.

they choose carefully, adding to collections over time. The Porcelain Gallery stocks timeless styles and chooses items for continuity and quality. It is important to be able to provide customers with additional pieces or replace broken items, so the Lundhs choose style lines that will last.

The idea of mixing and matching different styles of tableware was introduced to Seattle by the Porcelain Gallery. At first people were reluctant, but now the concept is very popular. And it's practical, according to the Lundhs — buyers often inherit or find incomplete sets at antique shops or in family attics, and pieces from other sets can "finish" the table. Most people do not have room in their homes for more than one full set of formal tableware. Mixing sets allows them to enjoy several designs and patterns and textures without the expense of buying — and the problem of storing — multiple sets.

The Porcelain Gallery takes great pride in offering its customers only the best — Lladro figurines from Spain; Royal Copenhagen, Meissen and Rosenthal porcelain from Europe; Herend porcelain from Hungary; and Baccarat and Lalique crystal from France are among the most popular brands. The Lundhs have many limited edition pieces, some so rare there are only a handful of them left in the world. The gallery also offers special occasion goods for the birth of a new baby, a wedding or an anniversary. The Lundhs believe that the most fundamental events in life are the most worth celebrating.

For the Lundhs, few things in life are as enjoyable as a good meal, shared with friends and family, set at a beautiful table. Nowadays, people have little quality time, often eating on the run while hurrying to the next thing. An elegant table setting helps bring people together, making dinner an occasion and every meal a celebration.

The treasure trove: inside the Porcelain Gallery

RAY'S BOATHOUSE

Like the red 50-foot "RAY'S" sign near its front door, Ray's Boathouse has become a Seattle icon that has changed the way the Northwest eats seafood. What began as a dockside café known for its home-cooked meals has become a must-visit restaurant with a majestic view of Puget Sound and rugged Olympic Mountains with a rare mix of dining elegance and hospitality. Its international reputation for seafood draws raves from publications like the *New York Times, Gourmet Magazine, Chicago Tribune* and *Food & Wine.*

In 1939 the original owner, Ray Lichtenberger, moved his growing boat rental and bait house to the current location and in 1945 opened a coffee house. By 1952, he'd built the neon sign that flashes "RAY'S" in bold, red letters on the dock overlooking Shilshole Bay at the crossing point to Puget Sound and the Harold M. Chittenden Locks leading to Lake Washington.

Through the 1960s Ray's operated as both a casual fish-and-chips café and boat rental. In 1973 Russ Wohlers, Earl Lasher and Duke Moscrip bought Ray's Boathouse and quickly refurbished the structure, transforming it into a nationally respected seafood restaurant while maintaining its cordial, glad-to-see-you atmosphere. While Moscrip left to pursue other restaurant ventures, Elizabeth Gingrich joined the owner team in 1975 and former Seattle Sonic Jack Sikma joined in 1986.

Under Wohlers' guidance, Ray's built its reputation on seasonal dishes prepared simply to highlight the flavors of impeccably fresh seafood and the freshest locally grown produce. Ray's became part of what has been called a food revolution in the Pacific Northwest, helping to introduce a fashionable and distinctive regional cuisine built around Northwest products, microbrews and wines. Ray's was the first to reintroduce to Seattleites Olympia oysters, the region's only native oyster, and heralded Northwest delicacies such as singing scallops, Loughbrough Inlet spot prawns, Copper River Salmon, Bruce Gore "frozen at sea" salmon and the concept of red wine with fish. Ray's was also the first local restaurant to purchase its own wholesale fish buyer's license, allowing it to buy directly from the fishermen, ensuring the freshest catch.

On May 26, 1987, at the height of its popularity, Ray's Boathouse burned to the pier. The four-alarm fire was reported by major newspapers across the country and footage of the fire appeared on national newscasts. Seattleites responded overwhelmingly to rebuild the landmark and a new Boathouse opened in April 1988.

Over the years, the restaurant's reputation has continued to grow, and it is now considered one of the 10 best seafood restaurants in the country. Ray's Boathouse was one of the select few enlisted to cater a gathering of over 200,000 people in Washington, D.C., prior to Bill Clinton's 1993 presidential inauguration. Its chefs have been guest cooks for Julia Child and the James Beard House, and have been invited to prepare Ray's cuisine in Beijing, Singapore, London, Paris and Stockholm, as well as many cities across the United States.

Ray's is committed to its community, being a prominent participant in Seattle's annual Taste of the Nation event and Children's Hospital's Auction of Northwest Wines, as well as numerous auctions to benefit AIDS research, children, seniors, homelessness and hunger.

Ray's isn't just a place to eat, it's a place where people meet. A longtime staff, many of whom have been at the restaurant 15 years and longer, help create a special place where friends come to enjoy a memorable meal, an unforgettable location and a slice of history by the water's edge.

Ray's Boathouse has become one of the most popular seafood restaurants in the country.

ROCK BOTTOM BREWERY

Located in the heart of the Seattle business district is a popular casual dining establishment where people come to have a great time and relax, eat a hearty meal, partake of handcrafted ales and enjoy extraordinary service. Rock Bottom Seattle, one of 22 Rock Bottom Breweries nationwide, is designed around a working brewery. Although the mainstay clientele is the high-energy 25- to 45-year-old crowd, Rock Bottom serves everyone from infants to centenarians and receives considerable business from the theater and convention center trade.

Rock Bottom Seattle embraces the Southern concept of lagniappe, meaning "that extra something special that is all the sweeter because it is unexpected." The philosophy of lagniappe at Rock Bottom begins with its hiring practices, in which two or three people from each department conduct interviews to ensure that an applicant will help retain an ongoing sense of community at the restaurant. It continues with crewmembers being empowered to make their own decisions, and finally translates into Rock Bottom's ability to provide professional, creative service for a variety of hospitality needs from audio video to floral services.

A distinct menu offers a cornucopia of gastronomic delights including appetizers such as spicy spinach dip, entrees ranging from Chicken Genovese to sausage and pepperoni pizza with roasted garlic, fresh basil and Rock Bottom's own pale ale-marinated Italian sausage, and desserts such as chocolate derby pie.

Rock Bottom's unique microbrewed ales are unparalleled in Seattle. Each Rock Bottom establishment makes its own beers and each brewer has autonomy to create personalized styles of beer. Catering to the ale cognoscenti — Seattle is located in "hops country" and local residents appreciate good beer — Rock Bottom Seattle carries such names as Faller Wheat Ale, Brown Bear Brown Ale, Flying Salmon Stout Ale, Pea Shooter Pale Ale and Rain City Red Ale as well as "barrel select" ales, which are made inside whiskey barrels to provide unusual flavors. The brewery also creates seasonal pilsners, ales and lagers — Roctoberfest in October, a naturally carbonated

> ROCK BOTTOM'S UNIQUE MICROBREWED ALES ARE UNPARALLELED IN SEATTLE. EACH ROCK BOTTOM ESTABLISHMENT MAKES ITS OWN BEERS AND EACH BREWER HAS AUTONOMY TO CREATE PERSONALIZED STYLES OF BEER.

and hand-tapped English-style firkin beer in summer, and Fire Chief Ale in March, a percentage of whose profits are donated to the local fire department to aid its charities. In 2000 Rock Bottom began working on a barley-wine beer that will take a year to produce.

Rock Bottom can host any event, from an intimate get-together to a dinner for 200 people, in one of its three venues. The beautiful wood-paneled, soundproofed Board Room, equipped with audiovisual capabilities, allows up to 50 guests to enjoy extraordinary food and delicious, award-winning beer in total privacy. The Pool Room, with four championship billiard tables, accommodates up to 48 people, and the Upper Dining Room, surrounded on three sides with picture windows, is available for parties up to 200.

With live entertainment on weekends and numerous live sporting events via DirecTV throughout the week, great food and drink, friendly and attentive service and a comfortable atmosphere, Rock Bottom is likely to remain a popular gathering place in Seattle for many years to come.

The popular Rock Bottom Brewery, located in Rainier Square, attracts the 25- to 45-year-old crowd and serves everyone from infants to centenarians.

SORRENTO HOTEL

High atop Seattle's First Hill stands the Sorrento Hotel, a city landmark for nearly 100 years. The dramatic architectural design, mission-style towers, Italianate fountain and canopied carriage entrance all reveal to arriving guests that an extraordinary experience awaits them.

In 1908 clothing merchant Samuel Rosenberg commissioned Harlan Thomas, the first dean of architecture at the University of Washington, to design the hotel. Thomas fashioned the building after the Italian Renaissance characteristics that inspired him during a visit to Sorrento, Italy. Interestingly enough, Rosenberg later traded the hotel during hard times for Bear Creek Orchards near Medford, Oregon. The exchange was once characterized as "trading a lemon for a pear," as Rosenberg's sons, Harry and David, managed to turn the orchards into a multimillion-dollar business.

In its early years, the hotel was visited by such prominent personalities as President William Taft, the Vanderbilts and the Guggenheims. Between 1930 and 1960, one of the signature hotel features was its "Top of the Town" prime rib restaurant where the popular Betty Hall Jones entertained nightly and, in 1942, a full-course steak dinner cost $1.50.

Through good economic times and bad, the hotel has maintained its reputation for style and elegance, always paying close attention to details. Old World charm combined with modern comforts give the Sorrento its distinctive appeal. Original woodwork in rich Honduran mahogany conveys a European ambiance to the lobby area and Fireside Room, and fresh flower arrangements are graced throughout. Also prominent is the Sorrento's commitment to exceptional service. Hotel staff are trained to remember guests' names from the time of arrival and stand prepared to respond to any request, large or small.

This traditional sophistication extends to the guest rooms and suites, which offer custom furnishings and original artwork along with goose-down pillows, bathrobes and oversized bath towels. Each night, the Sorrento's signature turndown service brings guests relaxing comforts, even hot water bottles during chilly winter nights.

However, while the Sorrento maintains its historic presence in the city, it also recognizes the ongoing need to incorporate modern luxuries. In 1981 the hotel underwent a $4.5 million restoration, which transformed the original 150 rooms into 76 individually styled rooms and suites, all with two-line cordless phones with data ports, in-room coffee makers, and twice-daily maid service, among many other amenities.

Today the Sorrento remains Seattle's oldest-operating luxury hotel. It is an oft-chosen spot for marriage proposals (the hotel averages 20 per year), and the hotel's infamous Hunt Club, recently honored as one of the nation's best restaurants by the readers of *Gourmet,* is a popular dining choice for Seattleites and out-of-town visitors alike.

For presidents, royalty, business-persons and discerning travelers from all over the world, the Sorrento Hotel remains, for many, the preferred "home away from home."

Sorrento's Fireside Room transforms from traditional tearoom by day to a lively gathering spot at night.

Inspired by its Italian namesake, The Sorrento Hotel is Seattle's oldest-operating luxury hotel.

STARBUCKS COFFEE COMPANY

In 1971 Starbucks Coffee opened its first store in Pike Place Market. Since that time, Seattle's enthusiasm for specialty coffee has made Seattle the coffee capital of the world. The founders of Starbucks shared a love of fine, dark-roasted coffees and wanted residents to have the best.

In 1983 Howard Schultz, then director of retail operations and marketing for Starbucks, took a business trip to Italy. On the streets of Milan, inspiration struck Schultz as he observed the rich culture of the Italian coffee bars. The experience marked the beginning of an extraordinary personal and professional vision — to bring the flavors and traditions of espresso beverages and coffeehouses to the United States. Schultz realized he had found his passion and immediately set his plan in motion. By 1987 he was able to purchase Starbucks with the support of local investors. His concept of offering

This is where it all began. The original Pike Place Market Starbucks opened in 1971 and began selling fresh-roasted whole beans to delighted coffee lovers. Now a Seattle landmark, the store attracts both tourists and locals as they wander the market.

Many people come to Starbucks for a refreshing time-out, a break in their busy days, and a personal treat. Starbucks coffeehouses provide an inviting and enriching environment in which people can sit down and connect with one another.

high-quality coffees and espresso drinks to American consumers quickly gained popularity and momentum.

Over the years, Starbucks Coffee Company has held true to its original mission — to establish itself as the premier purveyor of the finest coffee in the world while maintaining uncompromising principles during its growth. The company did not set out to build the great brand it is today, but rather a great company, one that values the authenticity of its product and the passion of its people.

Starbucks is dedicated to supporting the communities in which it does business by supporting local organizations that benefit literacy, children's welfare, AIDS outreach and environmental awareness. Starbucks is also involved in a variety of community focused cultural events, including jazz and film festivals.

Valuing employees (called partners) remains at the forefront of Starbucks philosophy. Starbucks is one of few companies to offer full benefit packages, including Bean Stock, stock option grants through the companywide stock option plan, to both full- and part-time employees.

Superior quality is another area where Starbucks will not compromise. The world's finest *arabica* beans are sourced from around the world and carefully roasted to perfection at the Starbucks Kent Roasting Plant in Kent, Washington, and York Roasting Plant in York, Pennsylvania.

Starbucks Coffee Company is the leading retailer, roaster and brand of specialty coffee in the world. The company offers more than 30 blends and single-origin coffees, handcrafted espresso and blended beverages, teas, specialty merchandise and more. Starbucks currently operates in 41 U.S. states, five Canadian provinces and 20 international markets.

Today, the name Starbucks has become synonymous not only with a delicious cup of coffee, but also with a way of life. Every store strives to give customers the unique Starbucks Experience.

"You get more than the finest coffee when you visit a Starbucks," says Schultz. "You meet interesting people, experience first-rate music and enjoy a comfortable, upbeat meeting place."

From the aroma of rich coffees and fresh pastries, to being part of each community around the world where it does business, Starbucks is proud of its Seattle roots and will carry the city's spirit and energy with it as it grows globally.

STARWOOD HOTELS

In Puget Sound, business is booming and that means people are traveling, bringing both conventioneers and vacationers to Seattle. And the Emerald City is well prepared to welcome these travelers at its two luxury Starwood properties. The Sheraton Seattle Hotel and Towers and the Westin Seattle provide world-class accommodations and services to the business and leisure traveler.

Founded in Seattle as Western International Hotels, the Westin Hotels and Resorts brand recently celebrated its 75th anniversary. The flagship Westin Seattle property was built in two phases, the first tower completed in 1967 and the second added in 1984. It remains the only downtown hotel with spectacular unobstructed views of Puget Sound and the surrounding mountains. The Westin's unique circular towers have long been a Seattle landmark and have hosted many famous guests, including all recent United States presidents. The Westin Seattle is proud of its role in Seattle's illustrious history and continues its commitment to the local community through support for Seattle Symphony, Pilchuck Art School, and the Junior League of Seattle. Each year, it plays host to a glittering array of charitable fund-raisers including The Virginia Mason Dreambuilder's Ball and the Harborview Gala.

With 891 rooms, 43,000 square feet of meeting space and the largest ballroom in the Pacific Northwest, The Westin Seattle is equipped to handle international conventions and local social events with equal skill. Its downtown location is convenient for business and pleasure, just a short walk from Nordstrom, Pike Place Market, the waterfront, and a wide array of excellent shops and restaurants. The hotel has recently embarked on a $12 million renovation of the lobby, meeting rooms, guest rooms and suites.

The Sheraton Seattle Hotel & Towers was constructed in 1982 and became one of the most sought-after convention spaces in the Northwest following a $7 million renovation of the lobby, guest rooms and suites. The Sheraton features 840 rooms, 25 meeting rooms and 44,000 square feet of meeting space, including a 14,000-square-foot ballroom that can accommodate up to 1,750 people. The hotel's proximity to the newly expanded Washington State Convention and Trade Center makes it a prime location for meetings and conventions.

Sheraton's owners are especially proud of the beautiful second-floor ballroom, which hosts several annual charity auctions. The Sheraton Seattle Hotel and Towers is a proud partner in raising both money and awareness to benefit such worthy causes as the Fred Hutchinson Cancer Research Center, Cystic Fibrosis Foundation and Juvenile Diabetes Foundation. These galas are renown as the only charity events in the United States to raise in excess of $3 million dollars in a single evening!

Starwood Hotels and Resorts is proud to continue providing traditional Seattle hospitality at Sheraton Seattle Hotel and Towers and The Westin Seattle.

The Westin Seattle Hotel

The Sheraton Seattle Hotel and Towers

13 COINS

Seattle has faced many changes over the last few decades. The Kingdome no longer rules the downtown skyline and the city has become more known for software and coffee than salmon and timber. One tradition, however, has stood firm in an age of cookie-cutter cafes where image too often rules over substance. That tradition is 13 Coins restaurant.

Since 1967 (and 1973 for its sister restaurant near the airport), 13 Coins has remained an old-style corner-stone of metropolitan character, serving up hearty fare in an upscale atmosphere. Dark, polished wood and high-back chairs characterize the restaurant while along the walls, booths with high, leather-padded walls rise all the way to the ceiling. This creates a dining experience that is both quiet and private. This 24-hour eatery maintains the strictest code of comfortable discretion, drawing celebrities and sports stars into its confidence. Diners shouldn't look for autographs or 8-by-10 glossy photos, though. The staff is charmingly tight-lipped about who slips through the doors.

The name 13 Coins is taken from an old tradition. It is said in Peruvian legend that a poor man loved a wealthy girl but all he had to offer was 13 coins. The man assured the girl's father that his wealth was greater than these coins because he would offer the girl his undying love, care and concern. The father was so touched that he assented to the man marrying his daughter. To symbolize such care and concern toward the diners at the restaurant, there are 13 coins embedded in each of the tables, each a gleaming promise of a good meal.

Lunchtime is populated by business folks wheeling and dealing over chicken *cordon bleu* or the famous eggs benedict. Just as likely, though, are people escaping their work-a-day grind and indulging in the legendary cheesecake. The dinner and late-night crowds can be somewhat more eclectic: after-hours artists, audiences, insomniacs and romantics are all drawn into 13 Coins.

Recommendations are easy to get, and every patron swears that their favorite on the 130-plus item menu is surely the best. Everything is prepared in an open kitchen giving counter-side diners a show of fast-action food, live called orders and flaming sauces that have earned the cooks the nickname "pyro-technicians." Every mode of preparation is represented: grilling, scrambling, flipping, tossing, sautéing, frying and flaming, all at speeds that have made not only the Coins, but its cooks, famous. There is something for every palate, mood and occasion. Mounds of custom fettuccini, steaming pesto clams and hearty steaks are produced in mouthwatering arrangements alongside oyster stews, traditional prime rib and the Coins' own smoked salmon.

Every hour of every day, 13 Coins offers everything from a quiet escape to a venue for parties. Traditional yet innovative, both of the Coins restaurants are truly Seattle landmarks, and when betting on getting a good meal, 13 is a lucky number.

13 Coins offers diners a front row seat while their food is being prepared.

WORKSITEMASSAGE^{SM}/ OPTIMAL PERFORMANCE, INC.

WorksiteMassage^{sm}/Optimal Performance, Inc. found a way to help companies reduce tension and stress while keeping their employees on the job. Energizing For Success^{sm} is the message and WorksiteMassage^{sm} is the fitting name of the service. A licensed massage practitioner with a specially designed chair goes directly to the workplace and gives employees what might be called a mini-massage — usually about 20 minutes a week per person — to refresh them and reduce their health care expenses. It is based on the premise that the healing art of massage is no longer a luxury but a vital

link in the daily coping process for busy working people and successful businesses. While job performance can suffer as a result of debilitating muscle aches, tight shoulders or neck, or headaches or back pain, a massage can energize and revitalize employees, enabling clearer thinking, increased alertness, heightened creativity — and happier, healthier employees.

WorksiteMassage^{sm} was the first service offered by the company, which was founded in 1988 by Oshen Schiweck. He had been the lead massage practitioner at a resort in the San Juan Islands off northwest Washington. The guests — many of them Seattle-area executives — liked his massages so much that they encouraged him to set up a business they could use in Seattle. At the same time, a portable massage chair was developed that was perfect for carrying around to various sites. With that chair and his list of executives as prospective customers, Schiweck started the company, which now has about 30 practitioners visiting more than 60 work sites on a regular basis.

Building on the success of WorksiteMassage^{sm}, the company opened a chair massage service in early 1998 in the bustling atrium of the Bank of America high-rise tower in downtown Seattle. This operation allows the many thousands of people who work in or near the building to schedule a 10- to 40-minute massage right there at their convenience. Dozens of people each day take advantage of this opportunity, weekly appointments are common, and repeat customers come back as often as three times a week. In fact, this service met with so much enthusiasm that in 2000 the company opened a similar service in Rainier Plaza in the nearby city of Bellevue, and plans to open in many other high-rise buildings in the future.

Meanwhile, the company's MassageConcierge^{sm} service also evolved from the flourishing WorksiteMassage^{sm} business in 2000. It brings table massage to homes, hotels, offices, yachts, or anywhere customers have enough space and want the convenience of their own full-body table massage.

Each massage delivers an energizing lift that helps promote well-being, increases morale and enhances productivity. This is how the company helps the business community take care of the work force and lives up to its name by *optimizing* the *performance* of all who take a break for massage.

WorksiteMassage^{sm} energizes customers at more than 60 locations.
*Photo by Gary Quinn*PhotoMagic*

WorksiteMassage^{sm} vans advertise the company's services as they transport practitioners and equipment to office buildings. Running the company are (left to right) Harleigh Pesch, operations manager; Oshen Schiweck, president and founder; and David Yeoman, vice president of marketing and sales.
*Photo by Gary Quinn*PhotoMagic*

Networks

Seattle's media, energy and transportation companies keep
information, people and power moving throughout the region.

ALASKA AIRLINES

What makes a great and lasting team? Complex strategic planning? Strong leadership? Plain old hard work and determination?

All that is part of the equation. But truly outstanding teams are a testament to the power of people working together in common cause for something bigger than the sum of the parts.

Business is the same way. Teamwork is key. To achieve it, though, there must be a unifying set of beliefs.

For nearly 70 years, Alaska Airlines and its people have been guided by a shared commitment to integrity, caring, resourcefulness, professionalism and spirit. Even the airline's name — Alaska — exemplifies a place where neighbor-helping-neighbor attitudes are ways of life. The result of such teamwork includes a long list of aviation milestones and countless stories of people going out of their way to help others, both in the course of business and in the support of organizations that make their communities better places to live.

In the process, Alaska has grown from a small regional airline to one of the most respected major carriers in the nation. Carrying more than 12 million customers per year, Alaska's route system spans 45 cities and three countries. Its fleet of 93 Boeing jets is one of the youngest in the nation. And its reputation for outstanding service, delivered by 12,000 dedicated employees, consistently earns best U.S. airline recognition from the likes of *Travel & Leisure* and *Condé Nast Traveler* magazines.

"In many ways, I think we're a reflection of the communities we serve," says the airline's president, Bill Ayer. "Friendly, professional, reliable and willing to go the extra mile to help out. The end result is a very loyal following of customers."

Storied Roots

The airline has come a long way since its origins in 1932 when Mac McGee started McGee Airways, flying his three-seat Stinson between Anchorage and Bristol Bay, Alaska. Finances were tight, but perseverance ruled the day. A merger with Star Air Service in 1934 created the largest airline in Alaska. And after several more mergers and a couple of name changes, they found a name that stuck — Alaska Airlines.

Alaska moved its headquarters to the Seattle area in the late 1940s — first to Everett's Paine Field and then to Sea-Tac Airport. This marriage of airline and community has been mutually rewarding, with each playing a significant role in the other's growth and prosperity.

With beautiful Mount Rainier in the background, one of Alaska's Boeing 737-400s arrives at Seattle.
Photo by Don Conrard

About the same time the airline was moving its head-quarters south it began using surplus military aircraft to branch into worldwide charter work. This thrust Alaska into the middle of two historic events — the Berlin Airlift in 1948 and the epic airlift of Yemenite Jews to Israel in 1949, known as Operation Magic Carpet.

In the late 1960s, Alaska strengthened its operating base by merging with Alaska Coastal-Ellis and Cordova Airlines, two legendary Southeast Alaska carriers owned by aviation pioneers Shell Simmons, Bob Ellis and Mudhole Smith. Alaska's world now stretched from Fairbanks to Ketchikan and down to Seattle. Not only that, in some of the coldest days of the Cold War, Alaska made headlines with regular charters to the Soviet Union.

A New Era

When Fairbanks businessmen Ron Cosgrave and Bruce Kennedy came on board in 1972, the airline was in a financial fight for its life. They went to work setting goals and bringing people together. Their efforts won back the trust of creditors and improved on-time performance. They had one big break — the construction of the Trans-Alaska Pipeline, which required carrying supplies, equipment and workers to and from the region. This gave Alaska Airlines the boost it was looking for.

During this new era of success, customer service became the top priority, laying the foundation that would position the airline well for the deregulation of the industry in 1979.

For many carriers, deregulation was the end of the road. For Alaska, it was a new beginning. The airline expanded methodically throughout the West, offering nonstop service from Seattle and Portland to destinations in California and later Mexico. Alaska also joined forces with two carriers similarly committed to outstanding customer service — Jet America and Seattle-based regional carrier Horizon Air. By the end of the 1980s, Alaska's fleet had increased fivefold, its route map included scheduled service to Mexico and Russia, and the marriage with Horizon proved outstanding.

Continuing the Legacy

For Alaska, staying in the forefront continues to mean evolving with the times. Alaska is still differentiating itself, offering more flights than any competitor in almost every market it serves and investing heavily in quiet, fuel-efficient new aircraft. The airline continues to provide a superior level of customer service and maintains a leadership position in the development of technologies that improve on-time

The human touch: Alaska is the only major carrier featuring a person on its tails.
Photo by Don Conrard

performance and expand safety margins. And the awards just keep on coming.

Every time the history of commercial aviation is written, people ask how an obscure little airline in America's hinterland survived and thrived while once-proud giants disappeared? It's a good question. Hard work and sound planning are no doubt part of the answer.

But more than anything, the answer is the people.

"I've always felt that Alaska Airlines is like a big family," says John Kelly, the airline's chairman and CEO. "Our people care — about each other and our customers. They possess a unique blend of integrity, ingenuity and professionalism that makes our airline a little different and, we think, a little better. It's all about people, the right people, working together day after day, year after year."

Out of it all comes a spirit — the unique spirit of The Great Land where the airline was born — that enables Alaska Airlines to soar as one of the nation's last great airlines.

KING 5

On a rainy Thanksgiving afternoon in 1948, a high school football game played in front of 13,000 people at Memorial Stadium took on historic significance, a significance greater than the game's outcome. With two cameramen positioned in the stands, the first television station north of San Francisco and west of the Mississippi made its first telecast that day.

Dorothy Bullitt, gathering with family and friends in her Seattle home, was one of 1,000 television owners in the city curiously watching the flickering images of a West Seattle high school football team play Wenatchee to a 6-6 tie. Just eight months later, Bullitt bought the fledgling station for $375,000, and a new era in communication in the Northwest began.

Changing the call letters of the station from KRSC to KING, Bullitt, who only a year earlier had bought an FM radio station, daringly ventured into a new medium many thought wouldn't last. Over the next 45 years, Bullitt, a broadcast pioneer and visionary, would help turn what was considered a risky venture into a powerful medium, shaping political thought and stirring the direction of a city.

Not long after King Broadcasting was founded, a friend of Bullitt asked Walt Disney to draw a logo for the fledgling company. For $75, Disney drew "King Mike," the microphone with legs, smiling face, a robe and crown that became the station's symbol. In 1947 Bullitt, whose husband, Scott, had died of cancer in 1932, bought radio station KEVR FM. She then bought the call letters

KING from another radio operator, a freighter. She liked KING because it referred to the surrounding King County and it suggested market dominance.

In September 1951, KING's first evening news telecast began with a 15-minute segment at 6:45 p.m., five nights a week. The local news report was presented by 29-year-old Charles Herring, who would sit behind a desk and smoke a pipe as he read in somber tones stories from that day's newspapers. The news department consisted of Herring and a cameraman. Herring's first breaking news story was a huge fire in the small logging town of Forks, 100 miles west of Seattle. Herring's report was shipped to New York and aired on national television.

KING-TV broadcast the 1951 hydroplane races on Lake Washington, an event that drew 250,000 people. To cover the race, station engineers developed the country's first 100-inch camera lens, which was designed to capture close-ups of the hydroplanes. The lens would eventually be used by other stations across the country. Not long after this, KING engineers transformed bread trucks into remote broadcast trucks to carry bulky equipment.

Basing advertisement rates on the number of televisions sold and antennae counted, KING-TV initially charged $32 a minute. By 1954, with 250,000 homes in the area now with televisions, KING was clearly in

Seattle for good. But it came at a high price for Bullitt, who had sold much of the holdings from her husband's real estate company, and even her own jewelry, to keep her broadcast company afloat. That same year, KING moved into a converted furniture store on Aurora Avenue.

For the station's first five years, it remained the only television station in the Northwest, allowing it to carry programs from NBC, ABC and CBS. In 1953 KING became an ABC affiliate and in 1959 it changed to NBC. On July 1, 1954, KING broadcast the first color program in the Northwest. Under the guidance of then-program director Lee Schulman, in 1955 KING began two long-running series of children's programs that starred Stan Boreson and Ruth Prins, who was known to her young viewers as Wunda Wunda. The first documentary produced in the Northwest, "Lost Cargo," aired on KING 5 on June 25, 1959, creating so much discussion that the Port of Seattle re-examined its mission.

In the 1960s, with Bullitt's son Stimson as company president, KING continued to champion innovative television programs, including the first live two-continent, three-nation debate via Early Bird Satellite. The program was called "Vietnam: World Opinion" and was broadcast in 1965. By then, Bullit's company had expanded to include KREM-TV in Spokane and KGW-TV in Portland.

After Bullitt died in 1989 at age 98, her three children sold the company to Providence Journal Company in 1992. Then just five years later, A.H. Belo Corporation acquired Providence, making Belo the third-largest independent television group in the country. Belo is now a media giant, owner of newspapers including the *Dallas Morning News* and 18 television stations that reach 14 percent of the country's television household.

In 1951 KING engineers developed the nation's first 100-inch camera lens, giving the camera a long-distance range.

King Broadcasting made television history again in 1995 when it launched NorthWest Cable News, a 24-hour cable news channel serving Washington, Oregon, Idaho and northern California. In 1997 King Broadcasting debuted KONG-TV, a station that aired 1960s television reruns and later introduced a 10 p.m. edition of the day's news, giving KING over 35 hours of local news each week.

In November 1998, 50 years after that first fuzzy broadcast of a high school football game, KING continued its legacy as a pioneer in television when it began broadcasting High Definition Television (HDTV). It was one of the first stations in the country to broadcast the sharp image of the new high definition cameras.

KING crossed another milestone in March 2000 when it became the first Seattle station to make video news reports available on its Web site. Besides live local news broadcasts, both "Evening Magazine" and "Northwest Backroads" became available at the Web site.

Over the years, King Broadcasting has been active in community projects. In 1998 KING was involved in a relief project for victims of the Hurricane Mitch that devastated Central America. Working with World Vision, KING helped supply 30 tons of rice and beans, 5,000 blankets and $129,000 in cash donated by viewers. Other community service programs KING has teamed with are the Summer Reading program, Northwest Bookfest, Northwest AIDS Walk and Race for the Cure.

With the same commitment to quality programming that Bullitt had when she founded King Broadcasting, the station's legacy of excellence continues.

Beginning in 1953, children could tune in at noon on weekdays to watch Ruth Prins in "Wunda, Wunda."

KOMO 4 TELEVISION

For almost 50 years now, viewers have invited KOMO 4 Television into their homes.

They've watched as events from around the world and in their own backyard have touched their lives and shaped their futures. Local viewers spent hours with news anchor Dan Lewis as the tragic story unfolded at Columbine. Viewers shared in the joy and triumph as news anchor Kathi Goertzen reported the historic crumbling of the Berlin Wall. The eruption of Mount St. Helens, the first walk on the moon, the election of presidents and the mourning of those lost — triumphs and tragedies, victories and celebrations — all were brought into their homes through television.

And when the next big story breaks, KOMO 4 is more prepared than ever to bring the news to Northwest viewers. New technology and great people are all in place at the station's new home.

Home for KOMO 4 is now Fisher Plaza, a state-of-the-art, completely digital facility. It is one of the best-equipped communications complexes in the country. Fisher Plaza is a sophisticated gateway to the information superhighway with hundreds of miles of cable conveniently hidden under the floor. The facility is designed to create and distribute news and information through multiple digital platforms. In addition to cable, fiber optic, Internet and wireless technology, 10 satellite antennas are positioned on the roof, ready to deliver information to the Northwest and to the world.

All the high-tech tools are helping KOMO invent new ways of delivering local and world news. Right now, if a viewer needs local news, KOMO makes it available instantly on the cell phone or on the Web. Viewers will soon find KOMO 4 news on Quick Source kiosks in the busy places they visit such as the airport, shopping malls and office buildings. It is all part of a new pledge to make information available whenever the public needs it, wherever they need it, anywhere and anytime.

These high-tech tools have created a true pioneering spirit for the staff at KOMO 4 Television as it uses technology in innovative new ways to create and deliver information. With the breaking of new ground, KOMO promises not to break with one tradition — to be comprehensive, complete and always first for local news.

At the heart of that tradition is the anchor team of Kathi Goertzen and Dan Lewis. The duo have been on the air together longer than any other team in the market. When a big story breaks, KOMO is very proud that viewers turn to the team they can trust. That trust is built from the consistency that comes from night after night of telling compelling and compassionate stories. Kathi's nightly "Health Watch" stories and Dan's "Working World" segments are another step in making the day's news relevant to daily life.

When it comes to news that affects daily lives, weather is at the top of the list. The KOMO weather center is equipped with all the bells and whistles to track and show its changing weather systems. Steve Pool uses the tools and his own special explanations to make the forecasts on KOMO clear, concise and accurate.

And the newscast is not complete without bringing home the sports. Eric Johnson covers

Anchors Kathi Goertzen and Dan Lewis, Steve Pool with weather and Eric Johnson with sports deliver the KOMO 4 promise to be first for local news.

the hometown teams and the big news from across the country and adds his own popular series, "Eric's Little Heroes."

The KOMO tradition of great storytelling continues during the award-winning "Northwest Afternoon." Since its premiere in 1984, "Northwest Afternoon" has been the region's top-rated local talk show. Hosts Elisa Jaffe and Kent Phillips delve into issues and topics that speak directly to the needs and interests of Northwest women. This unique program also features Cindi Rinehart with a daily dishing of the scandal from daytime dramas for the soap opera crowd. From top authors and Hollywood stars to ordinary people with extraordinary stories to tell, "Northwest Afternoon" is a compelling hour of great stories every weekday afternoon.

Whether it's "Northwest Afternoon" or the local news, it doesn't make it to the television without the behind-the-scenes work in the control room. In a television station, the control room is command central. It is where voice, pictures, video from reporters in the field, video from the set, graphics and music all come together and make their way to the televisions in people's homes. While most control rooms are dark, windowless spaces with a maze of monitors, the control room in Fisher Plaza sits in natural light with video inset into futuristic plasma boards.

But what does this technology and forward thinking mean for people at home watching television? Across the country, television stations are preparing to take the giant leap into high definition broadcast. And while others are preparing, KOMO has already jumped into broadcasting in high definition. In fact, KOMO was the first television station in the world to broadcast a local daily newscast in high definition. For viewers at home it means a different shape screen that is wider and a picture that is infinitely clearer. It's like having the quality of a movie film on a television.

All of this focus on the future hasn't diminished KOMO's historic connection with the community. From broadcasting live local events like the 4th of July fireworks show to the Children's Hospital telethon, KOMO is an active partner in Northwest events.

From creating a free festival for families called KOMO KidsFair to a 13-year public service campaign focused on families named For Kids' Sake, KOMO is an active advocate on issues that matter to its community.

Dan Lewis and Kathi Goertzen have been together as an anchor team longer than any others in the market.

Since its first broadcast in 1953, KOMO has been a leader in the broadcast industry. Nearly 50 years later, KOMO television, an affiliate of the ABC Television Network, remains under the ownership of Fisher Broadcasting, making it the only locally owned television station in the market. Today, Fisher is committed to being a world-class, high-performance media and communications company with 26 radio stations, 12 television stations, a satellite and fiber transmission service, and an entertainment division.

Technical crews work in a new high-tech control room with video inset in plasma screens.

SEATTLE CITY LIGHT

Seattle City Light customers take for granted their ample electricity, dependably delivered at some of the lowest rates in the country. But without the vision, genius and zeal of J.D. Ross, the picture would have been much different.

In the first third of the 20th century, the battle between private and public utility companies was intense. To the dedicated capitalist, a municipally owned utility like the Seattle Lighting Department was nothing less than socialism. The battle over who would provide electricity to Seattle was one of the region's defining political struggles.

At the turn of the century, power in Seattle was produced and distributed by as many as 17 small, privately held neighborhood companies and cost 20 cents a kilowatt hour. In 1902 Seattle citizens approved a $500,000 bond issue to develop a hydroelectric facility on the Cedar River, the nation's first municipally owned hydroelectric project. A young Canadian, J.D. Ross, was hired to oversee its construction.

In 1910 the Seattle City Council created a separate Lighting Department, which would become known as

When City Light was battling Puget Power for control of Seattle's service territory, its advertising featured an endorsement from none other than Chief Seattle.

J.D. Ross, pictured in 1913, his second year as superintendent of Seattle City Light, also served as a member of the Securities and Exchange Commission and as the first administrator of the Bonneville Power Administration.

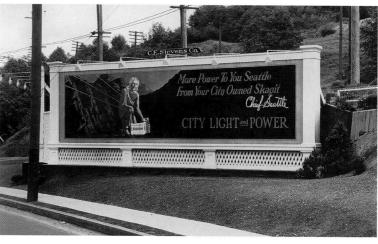

Seattle City Light. Ross was appointed superintendent in 1911. He was given the green light for his vision for the Skagit River — a series of three dams that would supply all of booming Seattle's electrical needs. But private power also was interested in the Skagit. Several companies claimed development rights, but none could raise enough capital to begin construction.

Then Stone and Webster, a wealthy, Boston-based utility holding company that owned the Puget Sound Power, Light and Traction Co., gobbled up development permits that tied up the entire Skagit River. Stone and Webster ultimately decided that the Skagit project was too expensive, but held onto its development rights anyway. Finally, in December 1917, when the country needed electricity to support the war effort, Ross was awarded rights to develop the Skagit.

Ross was a self-educated engineer and is now remembered as the Father of City Light because it often seemed that only his indomitable will kept the Skagit project moving. Selling bonds to finance the dam was difficult and costs skyrocketed as difficult terrain, bad weather, lack of roads and even a forest fire threatened the project. He didn't have enough customers for the projects. He would have to steal them from private power companies.

Ross also fought with a succession of city hall administrations, city councils, waxing and waning public opinion and a hostile press. Ross, however, was a believer and an indefatigable promoter — a self-taught engineer with great political skills. He organized weekend excursions for Seattle citizens to see the Skagit firsthand. He knew that the awe-inspiring scenery would sell his vision better than words could. Ever the showman, he added spectacular lighting, music, landscaping, even a zoo. These tours quickly became the rage and public opinion began to turn in his favor.

The first Skagit dam, Gorge, was dedicated in 1924, but the battle between Ross and the private Puget Sound Power and Light for the city's power business remained as brutal as ever. Seattle streets were lined with parallel wires of both utilities. In 1930 the private companies tried to make public ownership of electrical utilities illegal, but the plan was defeated in a statewide vote.

In 1931 Mayor Frank Edwards, supported by *The Seattle Times*, fired Ross. But the University of Washington Student Body President, Marion Zionchek, who would go on to become a member of Congress, launched a recall campaign against Edwards. In a remarkable testimonial to Ross' popularity, Edwards was ousted by a 36,000 to 22,000 vote. The new mayor, Robert Harlin, reinstated Ross, and City Light was never again seriously challenged by the private power companies. *The New York Times* summed it all up:

"Mr. Edwards is out. Mr. Ross is restored to utility control. The power trust has a flea in its ear, and the Moscow papers have a good story."

In November 1950, by a slim 754-vote margin, Seattle voters approved a buyout of all licenses held by private power companies in Seattle, giving the city a unified power system wholly owned and operated by its citizens. Seattle City Light is directly accountable to the public. It is governed by elected officials, guided by the public interest and supported by customer revenues.

Ross was devoted to the public interest and that remains the guiding principle for Seattle City Light. He would hardly recognize his city now. City Light's service area encompasses more than 131 square miles and 350,000 customers. Early on, Ross was planning for the density that now exists in the downtown core. Ross felt that reliability of electrical service was crucial to business development and began installing a special distribution system for the growing downtown. The Downtown Network is now an underground system that provides highly reliable power via a series of redundant supply connections. This high-quality power connection provides support for the constant demands of today's communications systems.

Seattle City Light also takes its stewardship of the state's natural resources seriously. Its energy conservation program is internationally recognized and continues to

The Skagit tours romanticized the new power plants that were rising out of the north Cascades. The trip took two days and was successful in building political support.

develop and encourage new ways of reducing energy consumption, particularly with its commercial and industrial customers. Since 1977 Seattle has saved enough energy to provide service to its customers for 18 months. City Light is committed to meeting its customers' energy needs without contributing to global warming. This means a growing reliance on green energy strategies such as wind, solar and geothermal power. The utility is also deeply involved in projects to protect fish and wildlife on the Skagit River and elsewhere. Its "fish-first" policy has helped revive chinook, pink and chum salmon runs.

In the workplace, City Light has developed strong partnerships with its labor unions. An apprenticeship program helps the utility attract and retain highly skilled technical workers in a tight labor market.

J.D. Ross died in March 1939, a month after the first concrete was poured for Ross Dam, the final jewel in the Skagit River crown. His vision of energy in the public interest continues to guide Seattle City Light today.

Ross touted Seattle as "the best-lit city in America." He spoke from knowledge. He designed the streetlights himself.

SEATTLE PUBLIC UTILITIES

When Seattle Mayor Robert Moran addressed a letter to the Common Council on September 24, 1888, suggesting a gravity water system with a source at the Cedar River, he could not have imagined that 112 years later another Seattle mayor and other state and federal officials would sign agreements declaring the entire 90,546 acres of the Cedar River Watershed an ecological reserve.

Although the Cedar River had been considered in the past as a source for Seattle water, Mayor Moran was the first elected official to express the vision of a municipal water supply.

The Cedar River was considered a potential source of water as early as December 25, 1880, when the *Fin-Back,* a regional weekly newspaper, predicted its use. At the time, the population of Seattle was 3,500. Although City Surveyor F.H. Whitworth gave consideration to this prediction, many felt that the current water system of springs and pumps was adequate.

By the end of the 1880s, the population of Seattle had blossomed to more than 40,000 people. At that time, the largest water system was the Spring Hill Water Company, which had been established in 1881. Despite improvements to the system and an increase in the water storage capacity from 200,000 gallons in 1883 to 2.5 million in 1889, the system was strained by the increase of users. In 1888 Mayor Moran submitted his proposal to the Council, which turned it over to the city's Fire and Water Committee. The committee recommended a special election, calling for a citizen vote authorizing a $1 million bond to construct a water system from Rock Creek, a

tributary of the Cedar River. One week before the election, Mayor Moran discovered an error in the ordinance that made the call for election illegal. The Council postponed the election until July 1889.

On June 6, 1889, one month before the scheduled July election, flames swept through downtown Seattle, leaving much of it in ruins. The Spring Hill Water Company pump, located along the shore of Lake Washington, was strained to the limit and flames spread quickly, consuming everything in their path. Realizing that the growing city could no longer rely on private water supplies, voters overwhelmingly authorized the construction of the Cedar River Water Supply in the July 8, 1889 election, 1,875 in favor and 51 against. However, process and economics delayed construction of the pipeline until 1899.

On June 4, 1890, Seattle voters, by a nearly unanimous vote, approved the purchase of the Spring Hill Water Company and established a public water system. Mayor Moran and the Common Council hired Benezette Williams, a hydraulics engineer from Chicago, to prepare the water system's plans. After surveys showed that Rock Creek did not permit a large enough supply, Williams recommended the Cedar River source.

In 1892 J.T. Ronald was elected mayor of Seattle and appointed R.H. Thomson (1856-1949) as city engineer. Assisted by George Cotterill, Thomson began the arduous task of determining how to build the gravity system. A

Seattle's watersheds gather and store rain and snowmelt for more than 1.3 million people in the greater Seattle area. More than 160 million gallons of clean, reliable and inexpensive water are delivered daily from the protected boundaries of the Tolt River and Cedar River watersheds.

After a fire swept through downtown Seattle on June 6, 1889, residents authorized the establishment of a public water system by a nearly unanimous vote.

nationwide economic collapse in 1893 made his job even harder. Realizing how expensive the Cedar River supply could become, many Seattle residents and officials began looking for other options.

Although money was scarce, Thomson fought hard to achieve the Cedar River system. Concurrently, he began construction of a citywide sewer system, another drain of financial resources. The expenses incurred by these projects and paid for by the electorate turned public opinion against him, but Thomson's Cedar River supply eventually won out. Today, more than 100 years later, Seattle Public Utilities (SPU) manages the Cedar River Watershed, which supplies two-thirds of the drinking water for 1.3 million customers.

In 1997 it wasn't a major fire but different challenges facing the growing Puget Sound region that caused a new group of civic leaders to form SPU by consolidating the Water and Engineering departments to include Engineering Services, the Solid Waste Utility, the Drainage and Wastewater Utility and Water Utility. The consolidation was designed to maximize citizen resources and give Seattle residents "one-stop shopping" for all water, sewer, drainage, garbage and recycling utility services.

The new organization was tested on its very first day of existence as a powerful winter storm ripped through the metropolitan area. Adding to the already unprecedented wet season, snow, heavy rainfall and high winds resulted in downed trees and landslides that caused damage to homes, local roads as well as major arterials and bridges.

SPU's response, coordinated by new Managing Director Diana Gale, set the standard for the vigorous new agency that has grown to more than 1,300 employees. SPU quickly became the organizing department, drawing on expertise from its newly absorbed engineering and drainage staff, as well as enlisting the important support of the Department of Construction and Land Use, SEATRAN and the Parks Department to form an interdepartmental Landslide Committee. The committee's charge was to identify, prioritize and remediate the damage from this 100-year storm. Working with the mayor and the City Council, the Landslide Committee directed work that stabilized the affected areas, developed a two-year work plan for the less critical slide-prone areas and began a comprehensive public information program to help prevent conditions that could produce landslides in the future.

A quality water supply, sewer and drainage system, solid waste collection and disposal all in one place; seamless, single contact for utility services; protection of the infrastructure so businesses can continue to do what they do best; environmental stewardship and protection of natural resources for the region and the world; simply put, this is what Seattle Public Utilities is all about. It is a long-term commitment to its citizens and ratepayers.

(Top)
Seattle Public Utilities is restoring portions of Seattle's creeks through the Urban Creeks Legacy Program. While restoring habitat for salmon and other wildlife is the primary goal of the effort, the works will also improve drainage, prevent erosion and flooding, and improve community open spaces and trails. Volunteer creek stewards pick up trash, plant trees, remove weeds, build trails and have fun!

(Below, left)
Seattle is committed to bringing back healthy salmon runs. Seattle Public Utilities and other city departments whose daily operations can impact the environment are working hard to make the region friendlier for fish and wildlife.

(Below, right)
The new Tolt Treatment Facility is a 120 million gallon per day (MGD) filtration and ozonation plant for treatment of Seattle's Tolt River source of supply, which provides about one-third of the water for Seattle and its 26 regional wholesale customers.

SOUND TRANSIT

Explosive growth both in population and commerce during the 1980s and 90s transformed Seattle from a sleepy city tucked away in a corner of America into a bustling hub of technology, trade and culture. However, this massive growth quickly met, then exceeded the capacities of the transportation infrastructure of the region and made Seattle famous for a reason beyond its salmon, coffee, software and airplanes: traffic. Newspaper headlines proclaimed Seattle to have the third-worst bottlenecks in the nation with rush hour traffic averaging only 25 miles an hour and slowing.

The problem of traffic was clearly beyond the scope of local authorities and voters called for a regional solution. In March 1992 the state Legislature created an 18-member board made up of elected officials from King, Pierce and Snohomish counties, officially called the Central Puget Sound Regional Transit Authority. This body became Sound Transit.

The 3,000-horsepower, 132-ton, GM Electro-Motive locomotive and Sounder train en route through the Green River Valley

The new Sound Transit faced an awesome challenge. Early reluctance to adopt regional transportation measures had let many opportunities slip past. In the late 60s, the federal government would have paid for 80 percent of the cost of a regional transit system. Unfortunately, citizens at that time did not foresee how clogged the area's transportation arteries would become and how much more costly a future project would be.

Sound Transit moved quickly to coordinate dozens of local authorities, communities, the concerns of business leaders and the expectations of voters. The first plan, a 16-year project, was defeated by popular vote in 1995. A year later, however, a new 10-year plan was adopted. While the new plan was 40 percent less expensive and somewhat reduced in scope, nearly six out of 10 voters in the three counties clearly expressed their support through the adoption of a local .4 percent sales tax and a .3 percent increase in vehicle excise taxes.

In a choice that suited its mission, the Regional Transit Authority became based in the old Union Station in downtown Seattle. The mammoth, neoclassical structure had been built in 1911 and closed after the last train left the station in 1971. When the building's multimillion-dollar restoration was completed by Sound Transit, local billionaire Paul Allen turned the structure over to Sound Transit for one dollar. Now infused with new life, Sound Transit's Union Station headquarters heralded the ambitious return of rail transportation.

Before focusing on rail, however, Sound Transit implemented the first segment of its program, ST Express bus service, featuring 18 new regional, limited-stop routes for commuters traveling longer distances. By the fall of 2000, service on 13 of those routes began with 154 buses, many of them with added features such as air conditioning, bike racks, reading lamps, overhead storage racks and high-back cloth-upholstered seats. For extra convenience, agreements were also made between the region's transit agencies allowing riders to use a single pass for each of the five agencies in the area. Also, 35 new transit centers, park-and-ride lots and direct access ramps to high-occupancy vehicle lanes were included to make ST Express service even more convenient, swift and reliable.

Even more ambitious were the light rail and commuter train services. The first of these projects, commuter rail, launched its operations in fall 2000. When running at full capacity, 30 trains will provide comfort and relief from crowded freeways along an 82-mile corridor of some of the worst traffic congestion in the country. The Sounder commuter train route runs along existing rail tracks from Everett in the north to Lakewood in the south. During peak commuting hours, the air-conditioned Sounder trains run every 30 minutes, providing clockwork convenience. The air-conditioned passenger cars are equipped with overhead compartments, power outlets for laptop computers, bicycle storage, onboard restrooms and even cup holders for that ever-present latte. In an age of constantly shrinking leisure time, the Sounder trains restore precious hours of relaxation during which its passengers can nap, read, socialize or just watch the forests and waters of Puget Sound whisk past. Each of the station designs also reflects the character of the community in which it stands. Ranging from a traditional, European-style station in Tacoma to a structure designed to resemble a hops kiln in Sumner, each of the stations includes public art and serves as a hub for local transit as well.

Seattle Mariners fans leaving the Sounder's special Home Run train from Tacoma to Seattle

The last piece in this vast puzzle is the Link light rail system. The electric rail is one of the most exciting and controversial elements of the Sound Transit plan. The light rail was originally conceived to serve the urban center, with a transport capacity of a 10-lane freeway but at only one-third the cost. However, a system to cover such a large and diverse area had to consider an equally large and equally diverse number of opinions on where the system should run. While every leg of the rail system represented additional cost, every segment not built also represented a potential loss of tens of thousands of riders. Roughly one-third of the system lies below the streets in tunnels, another third will run on the surface streets and the remaining sections will be on elevated tracks. Some communities were concerned that surface tracks would divide their neighborhoods and disrupt commerce. However, the cost of an entirely underground system would have rocketed the price up by hundreds of millions of dollars when compared to a mixed surface/tunnel system. Statewide initiatives from special interest groups also wreaked havoc on planned budgets for the entire system.

One initiative cut vehicle license tabs, creating a loss of hundreds of millions of dollars for transit and transportation projects. While Sound Transit's funding remained firm, it impacted valuable partnerships with the state and transit agencies and forced Sound Transit to fill the gaps. Another proposed initiative which was defeated aimed to devote 90 percent of all transit moneys to simply building more roads through already crowded communities. Experts and lawmakers continued to forge ahead, however, pointing out that the bulk of the area's voters clearly supported Sound Transit's initiatives and the simple "building more roads" approach would be nearly impossible given the areas many waterways.

The Sound Transit project gives the Seattle metropolitan region a fully integrated system where light rail, express buses and commuter trains link the region's business centers, universities and shopping districts. For example, the Link light rail system alone can carry more than 120,000 passengers a day to their destinations, making it the one of the most heavily patronized light rail systems in the nation. Starting from behind, Seattle has quickly moved to clear its clogged transport arteries and add a new credit to its fame: a world-class, urban transportation system. Clearer roads mean cleaner air and Puget Sound citizens can all take a deep breath of relief thanks to Sound Transit.

THE SEATTLE TIMES

The Seattle Times is the largest daily newspaper in Washington state and one of the most respected newspapers in the United States. Year after year, this Pulitzer Prize-winning paper produces the best, most relevant and timely articles and is consistently recognized as one of the nation's finest for its in-depth reporting and award-winning photography and design.

Colonel Alden J. Blethen founded *The Seattle Times* in 1896. A schoolteacher and attorney from Maine, Blethen left his home state and settled in Seattle where he bought a four-page paper, the *Seattle Press-Times*. He renamed the paper the *Seattle Daily Times* and within six months had doubled its circulation to 7,000. The Colonel passed away in 1915, leaving a paper that had increased tenfold in circulation and was read by 70,000 on weekdays and

The North Creek production facility where the majority of *The Seattle Times* and *The Seattle Post-Intelligencer* papers are printed

Publisher Frank A. Blethen, Senior Vice President and Executive Editor Michael R. Fancher and Managing Editor Alex MacLeod

82,000 on weekends. Four generations and more than a century later, the paper is still owned by the Blethen family, and the success started by Colonel Blethen continues. The Seattle Times company is the largest locally and family-owned and operated newspaper chain in the United States, producing more than 1.25 million copies daily.

The continued success of *The Seattle Times* rests on its commitment to quality journalism. In 1997 *The Times* won two Pulitzer Prizes, bringing its total to seven and becoming the only paper in the Northwest to possess more than one. The paper also has won recognition from The Society of American Business Editors and Writers for its exceptional Business section, and its focus on education garnered accolades from the National Awards for Education Reporting. Acclaimed for the quality of its photographs, the paper was selected for an Award of Excellence in the "Best Use of Pictures" category in the annual Pictures of the Year competition. The Society for News Design ranked *The Seattle Times* among the 16 best-designed newspapers in the world.

Writers for *The Seattle Times* know the impact an article can have on a community. A recent article on the war-torn Thai-Burma border won the paper numerous journalism and human rights awards; more importantly, it prompted donations in the amount of $24,000 from readers to a clinic that provides medical assistance to Burmese refugees. The paper is also concerned with issues of public safety and the environment, pursuing polluters and publicizing widespread use of contaminated industrial wastes in fertilizer.

Taking an active role in the community and working hard to keep connected to its readers is important to *The Seattle Times*. The Front Porch Forum is an innovative public journalism partnership between reporters and readers. Through public meetings and message lines, journalists at *The Seattle Times* and a local public television and radio station stay abreast of the topics that most concern readers. The paper provides a forum for public discussion of those issues.

Connection to the community takes many forms at *The Seattle Times*. The paper is a significant online information provider with two of the Northwest's most visited Web sites — one dedicated to providing newspaper-generated information, and the other a community destination site offering various information about

Seattle. Online news is updated several times daily, giving readers immediate access to the most current information. Other features help readers find the movies they want to see, new restaurants to try, apartments to rent and sports events to attend. Archives dating back two years are a valuable research tool. InfoLine is a telephone service that assists more than 15,000 information-seekers a day. Callers request information such as stock quotes, weather, soap opera updates, horoscopes and even recipes.

The Seattle Times is committed to excellence in all aspects of its business, and that includes being a good citizen of the community it serves. The company supports numerous programs that focus on education, literacy, diversity, youth and human services. The paper contributes to education scholarships and also provides educational experiences such as the Urban Newspaper Workshop for minority students and the Newspapers in Education program.

In 1990 *The Seattle Times* was instrumental in bringing about a cooperative public service media campaign designed to educate people about the reasons the United States celebrates Martin Luther King Jr.'s birthday. Thanks to *The Seattle Times*, newspapers, television outlets, radio stations and advertising companies have come together to promote Dr. King's message and help keep his dream alive. The company makes it a practice to promote diversity within its walls as well. The national Association for Women in Communications awarded *The Seattle Times* the first-ever Ruth Weyand Award for outstanding contributions in advancing women in the workplace. Publisher Frank A. Blethen has been honored as a leader in promoting racial and gender equality.

Even the paper that *The Seattle Times* is printed on is never taken for granted. To protect the resources and preserve the beauty of the Northwest, the paper uses newsprint that is more than 80 percent recycled. All the newspaper waste is reused, even the ink. The Washington State Department of Ecology and King County have recognized the paper's extraordinary efforts to protect the local environment.

The Seattle Times is good for the business environment as well. The Sunday paper, which reaches more than 1 million readers, provides an excellent medium for local businesses wanting to advertise. The paper has extensive in-house capabilities with creative, advertising and market-research services, professional copywriters and designers. Voted Newspaper

The 1997 Pulitzer Prize-winning team

Marketer of the Year from *Advertising Age* magazine and the Newspaper Association of America, *The Seattle Times* not only provides advertising opportunities in print, but the online edition — the most visited newspaper Web site in the Northwest — serves an additional 3 million pages a month to readers online.

Thanks to the exceptional quality of its writing and photography, *The Seattle Times* is the most widely circulated paper in the Northwest. But the paper doesn't stop at reporting on the issues of the day, it acts on them. Efforts to promote women and minorities in the workplace, emphases on education and environmental protection, dedication to remaining connected with readers and the communities they live in — all of these are part of *The Seattle Times*' excellence and continued success.

The Seattle Times corporate headquarters

UNITED AIRLINES

United Airlines has been operating for nearly three-quarters of a century, and it all started in the Pacific Northwest. In April 1926 Varney Air Lines, an early predecessor of United, inaugurated the nation's first scheduled contract airmail service. The 460-mile route was from Pasco, Washington, to Boise, Idaho, and on to Elko, Nevada. The airplane was a 1926 Swallow biplane that held 300 pounds of cargo and cruised at a speed of 90 mph.

Varney Airlines, along with Pacific Air Transport and National Air Transport, later merged with Boeing Air Transport, which was part of a group of companies that included Boeing Airplane Company and engine manufacturer Pratt & Whitney. United Airlines was organized in 1931 as the management company for the airline division. Three years later the merger broke up and its divisions became separate business entities.

Since that Swallow biplane soared into the sky in 1926, United Airlines has been adapting successfully to ever-unfolding historical events. It reorganized in 1934, following the cancellation of U.S. government airmail contracts. It served during World War II, modifying airplanes and training crews for the U.S. Army and Navy, as well as transporting more than 156,000 military personnel, 8,600 tons of freight and 9,200 tons of mail. And it responded to the strong postwar demand for air travel with an extensive expansion program and the purchase of its first jets in the 1950s.

During the same years, its innovations — including the world's first flight attendant service in 1930, the first airline flight kitchen in 1936, and the first nonstop coast-to-coast U.S. flights in 1955 — contributed to the growth of commercial aviation.

The airline's size increased significantly in 1961, when Capital Airlines merged with United. Capital had begun operations in 1927, carrying mail between Pittsburgh and Cleveland. The merger added about 7,000 employees and increased United's route system by 7,250 miles.

United's scheduled service outside North America began in the Northwest, too, with nonstop service between Seattle and Tokyo in 1983. Since then, United has become one of the largest international carriers in the world, carrying nearly 9 million travelers on 70,000 international flights each year.

Today, United Airlines serves more than 130 cities on five continents. Its primary hubs are in Chicago (the airline's corporate headquarters), Denver, San Francisco, Los Angeles and Washington, D.C. Its fleet is comprised mainly of Boeing aircraft, and United is Boeing's largest customer, having purchased more than 1,000 airplanes from the famous Seattle aircraft manufacturer.

Employing more than 99,500 people worldwide, including about 10,000 pilots and 23,500 flight attendants, United operates nearly 2,400 flights a day. It carries more than 87 million passengers a year.

United made its first official landing at Seattle-Tacoma International Airport (Sea-Tac) in October 1944, when the airport was still under construction. Now it is one of Sea-Tac's largest airlines, carrying approximately 6,000 passengers a day on 50 nonstop flights to many domestic and international cities. It also offers direct flights from Sea-Tac to many other cities on the airline's route system, as well as a network of conveniently scheduled connecting flights to Pacific Northwest cities on the regional carrier United Express. Nearly 800 passengers a day board the 65 daily United Express flights from Sea-Tac to these closer destinations.

United Airlines also handles almost 21,000 metric tons of cargo a year at Sea-Tac — anything from a small package or bundle of

1926 Swallow mailplane, United Airlines' first aircraft

mail to a beluga whale! In fact, it shipped three beluga whales — two from Chicago to Seattle, and one from Seattle to Chicago — facilitating a trade between Tacoma's Pt. Defiance Zoo and Chicago's Shedd Aquarium.

At Sea-Tac, United has about 1,200 employees. Another 600 work at the airline's reservations center in downtown Seattle, and 200 manage United's ticket offices in Seattle and the nearby cities of Bellevue, Issaquah, Lynnwood and Tacoma.

United Airlines employees participate actively in the local community. In fact, the airline's philanthropic wing, the United Airlines Foundation, sponsors and supports charitable organizations as well as service and cultural programs and activities wherever its customers and employees live and work.

In Seattle, United makes donations to such organizations as the Fred Hutchinson Cancer Research Center, Cystic Fibrosis Foundation, Children's Hospital & Regional Medical Center, Seattle Art Museum, Paramount Theatre, Corporate Council for the Arts and several others.

In addition, the airline's Seattle employees volunteer in several noteworthy activities that are part of United's service efforts worldwide. One of the most rewarding is the airline's "Fantasy Flights." At Sea-Tac, employees host magical "flights" that take disadvantaged or seriously ill children to Santa's workshop, which is actually one of the airline's gate areas specially decorated to look like the North Pole. Clowns, magicians and elves entertain the children, who also receive presents to take home for the holidays.

One of the airline's fund-raising activities is the annual AIDS Walk sponsored by the Northwest AIDS Foundation. Employees volunteer to help raise money for the local AIDS cause by organizing teams to participate in the 5-kilometer walk. Typically these teams raise $3,000 - $4,000 per walk, and United also recognizes its employees' volunteer spirit by making grants of up to $1,000 to the walks.

An annual activity that helps in a different way is "Take Your Community to Work Day." On that day, United employees introduce economically disadvantaged youth from the local community to career possibilities in the field of aviation. The employees explain their jobs, involve the students in carrying out work responsibilities and discuss career possibilities.

Finally, United contributes to the educational and cultural richness of the communities it serves by donating aircraft it no longer uses to universities and museums. In Seattle the beneficiary is the Museum of Flight, which proudly displays to the public that historic 1926 Swallow biplane that marked the real beginning of United Airlines.

710 KIRO

As a pillar of the Seattle community, for seven decades Newsradio 710 KIRO has stayed current, moving with the times and seasons in the Northwest. Other stations have come and gone, but 710 KIRO has remained at the same place on the radio dial, bringing the community the best of newsradio. KIRO belongs to Entercom Communications Corp., the fifth-largest radio broadcasting company in the United States, which acquired the station from Bonneville International Corporation in 1997.

In 1927, radio station KPBC (which would become KIRO) was founded by Moritz Thomsen, owner of the Pacific Biscuit Company. It operated at 100 watts. In 1933 Saul Haas, a newspaperman, active Democrat and

Internationally acclaimed journalist Edward R. Murrow (right) with his parents and a KIRO reporter, c. 1940s

KIRO Vice President Saul Haas (left) with CBS journalist Lowell Thomas, c. 1938

director of U.S. Customs, purchased shares in KPBC. In 1935 Haas and business partners purchased the remaining KPBC stock from the Thomsen family, changed the call letters to KIRO and transformed the station into a profitable enterprise.

The Federal Communications Commission (FCC) authorized KIRO Radio to operate as a full-time station and in 1936 increased its power to 1,000 watts. Haas wanted to make KIRO the most powerful and influential voice in the Pacific Northwest, and in 1937 his goal was achieved when the station became the official Seattle outlet for Columbia Broadcasting System (CBS). Through his strong political affiliations Haas acquired a special FCC license enabling KIRO to operate at 50,000 watts. In June 1941, with war looming, the FCC halted any further frequency development, making KIRO the most powerful radio signal (and voice) north of San Francisco and west of the Mississippi River.

During World War II Edward R. Murrow, a prominent radio broadcaster, began reporting live from Europe. In the process, radio assumed a new role in its listeners' lives as they relied on KIRO to keep them accurately informed. KIRO also recorded all CBS nightly 15-minute newscasts, which now constitute the most comprehensive library of World War II newscasts in the world.

In 1948 television came to Seattle. The new medium made increasing inroads into the one substantial night-time radio audience. KIRO competed for Channel 7 and the FCC ruled in its favor. Other applicants appealed and the FCC ordered the case remanded to the examiner for a second hearing. KIRO prevailed. In June 1957 it received a construction permit to build a television antenna, and in 1958 KIRO Television was born. In January 1964 Bonneville International Corporation purchased KIRO.

KIRO has twice received the highest national honor for radio — The Edward R. Murrow Award of Excellence — for outstanding broadcasting achievement, in 1982 and 1989. KIRO's mission, stated in 1928 as providing the community with quality, entertaining and informative radio, is still valid today. KIRO remains a Seattle mainstay due to its talented, dedicated staff: KIRO's talk show hosts provide compelling points of view, interesting programs and involve their listeners, and sports remain a programming priority.

KCTS

A society is defined by its culture and by the aspirations inherent in that culture. To be realized, those aspirations need to be nurtured, refined and celebrated. In the culturally rich Puget Sound, that effort is championed by one of the most accomplished and creative public television stations in the country, KCTS.

Since 1954 KCTS has been providing an essential service to a diverse community by creating and distributing commercial-free programs that inform, involve and inspire. It is the largest public television station in the Pacific Northwest and the fourth-most-watched station of its kind in the country. KCTS owns and operates sister station KYVE in Yakima and is available via cable and satellite throughout Canada, reaching more than 2 million viewers in Washington and British Columbia. As a creator of numerous high-quality programs for the Public Broadcasting Service, cable and commercial networks, KCTS has an influence that is not only regional but national and international as well.

During the 1990s the station received nearly 200 awards in recognition of its production accomplishments. It pioneered the development of aerial high-definition television (HDTV) and is an international leader in the production of HDTV and the introduction of digital television. By 2000 KCTS had produced more than 20 HDTV programs, including "Chihuly Over Venice" (the first HDTV program distributed by PBS) and "The Seattle Symphony Orchestra: Live from Benaroya Hall" (the first live HDTV symphony broadcast in North America).

One of the station's greatest contributions is its legacy of promoting learning among viewers of all ages. KCTS Kids & Family services help preschool and school-age children acquire educational skills by broadcasting 11.5 hours of children's programming each weekday — more than 3,400 hours of nonviolent, uninterrupted educational and entertaining programs each year. The station launched a cable service dedicated to children's and arts programming in 1997, and has provided three channels of digitally broadcast educational programming since 1999.

Each year it also holds one of the most successful Reading Rainbow Young Writers and Illustrators contests in the country for children in kindergarten through third grade, and distributes thousands of books to area children in the First Books program. KCTS also provides 360 hours of instructional TV programs each year to 210,000 students and 13,000 teachers through the Learning Services Cooperative; and, through its Web site, provides lesson plans, classroom projects and a database that allows teachers to find programs by grade level and subject. Reaching beyond the classroom, KCTS partners with public and private organizations to provide community service outreach materials that address such issues as women's health, youth violence, diversity and substance abuse.

Progressive and committed, KCTS contributes to the community every hour of every day through a wide array of programming and services. Whether it is celebrating the arts, exploring important issues, illuminating history, showcasing the world or teaching a child the ABCs, KCTS raises public television — and television in general — to a higher level. It also preserves and nurtures the best in an ever-changing culture, laying the groundwork for a more enlightened future.

KCTS Kids & Family nurtures positive learning experiences for children, teachers, caregivers and parents.

Nonprofit Organizations

Seattle's nonprofit organizations provide medical assistance
education, food, clothing and shelter for Seattle and the world.

CHILDREN'S HOME SOCIETY OF WASHINGTON

Imagine a World...

A world where every child is happy and able to achieve his or her full potential is not just a dream, it's a possibility. A world where every child is cherished and every family is strong is not a mere ideal, it's an achievable goal. It is this world, a world where every child and every family succeeds, that Children's Home Society of Washington (CHSW) strives toward.

For more than 100 years CHSW's programs have served a critical mission: "To help children thrive by building on the strengths of children, families and communities." In pursuit of that mission, the Society is turning hope into reality for all of Washington state.

A Vision for Every Family

Every family needs help from time to time. For many, friends and relatives become a family's circle of support. For families without that safety net, however, formalized support can be the difference between triumph and tragedy, between the ability to raise a healthy, happy child and one marred by abuse or neglect. Through parent education and peer support, family counseling, residential treatment and foster care programs, adoption support, family support centers and numerous other services, today's CHSW helps families weave a critical net of community-based support.

A History of Caring

When the Rev. Harrison D. Brown and his wife, Libbie Beach Brown, arrived in the Pacific Northwest in 1895, they brought with them profound compassion and a conviction that children should not be raised in institutions. In fact, the Browns described their Northwest mission thus: "To find a family home for every child." They facilitated their first adoption in 1895, placing an orphaned Portland girl named Gabriel with a Seattle family. A year later, Washington's Children's Home Society was incorporated, subsidized in its infancy by the Browns' meager pastoral income and donations from friends and church communities. As the number of children in need of homes grew, the Browns turned to a legion of volunteers — beginning a tradition of volunteerism that continues to be the organization's bedrock today. Early leaders recognized the value of family support. Where poverty threatened the well-being of children, they stepped in to provide needy families with food and other practical help. The mission to find a home for every child, then, expanded to include supporting children in loving birth homes challenged by hard times.

From day one, the Society's founders made social justice for children an organization priority. They helped craft the first laws in Washington to protect children from abuse and were instrumental in the creation of Washington's first juvenile court in 1905. CHSW continues to advocate a wide-ranging child- and family-focused legislative agenda today.

In the latter part of the 20th century, the Society's adoption focus has shifted toward a broader model of family support, abuse prevention services, and specialized foster care

and residential treatment for children with severe emotional or behavioral problems. Since 1896, CHSW has supported tens of thousands of children in adoptive homes. Thousands more children and families have found the assistance they need to not only survive, but thrive.

Today's CHSW

Children's Home Society is Washington's oldest and largest statewide, private nonprofit organization committed to improving the lives of children. It offers a range of programs and services at 38 sites statewide. Supported by public and private contributions, the Society touches 22,000 individuals each year through:

• Early childhood education programs, helping families make the most of early developmental years

• Involvement in 13 Family Resource Centers across Washington, offering families "one-stop" connections to social services and family-building programs, including parent education and peer support

• A Foster Care to Adoption Program, connecting families well prepared to adopt with foster children most likely to need a permanent home

• Counseling services and other mental health programs

• Specialized foster care and residential treatment programs, helping highly challenged children and families acquire positive coping and parenting skills

• Adoption Resource Centers, providing information and resources to those touched by adoption.

Building Community

Children's Home Society of Washington, according to an 1897 editorial in the *Seattle Post-Intelligencer*, "will endure forever because it is built in the hearts of the people." It has grown to become Washington's flagship child and family advocacy organization thanks to the generosity of thousands of donors, volunteers and supporters.

These visionary community partners know that every penny given, every minute volunteered is an investment in a child's future.

As the Society moves further into its second century of service, its success depends on an expanded foundation of support. "Families bear the primary responsibility for raising children, but they cannot do it alone," says Sharon Osborne, CHSW president and CEO. "It will take all of

us working together — staff, volunteers, donors and other public and private partners — if we are to continue to improve outcomes for kids. All of us are necessary and indispensable to building a community of support vital for the children of the 21st century."

A Vision for the Future

The CHSW vision encompasses all of the state's children, wishing for them a future bright with opportunities and teeming with potential. For more than 100 years, CHSW has fostered partnerships among individual families, their communities, local and state policy makers, and its own staff, volunteers and donors. Such partnerships have made Washington a good place for children and families. A continued commitment to partnership at all levels will make it an even better place in the future.

"In our second century, the Society is building upon a strong foundation of comprehensive services designed to support children from birth and give them the best possible start in life," says Osborne. "Similarly, our support to parents is focused on self-sufficiency so that they too can be successful as loving, nurturing, capable caregivers and providers.

"Both are integral if we are to succeed in supporting the next generation of kids to productive adulthood."

SEATTLE'S UNION GOSPEL MISSION

Seattle's Union Gospel Mission has seen dramatic changes since it opened its door on August 21, 1932. In the midst of the Great Depression, the mission was conceived and brought into existence by a group of business- and clergymen in response to the plight of the city's destitute. The mission's goal: to reach out and touch lives. Its message: to break destructive cycles and rebuild lives through faith in Jesus Christ.

More than "Soup, Soap and Salvation"

In its humble beginnings, the mission served essentially as a haven for "soup, soap and salvation." Many people still think of the mission primarily as a soup kitchen and a refuge for homeless men. But times have certainly changed. Responding to Seattle's ever evolving social and economic needs, today the mission has grown to serve the community through its men's shelter, women's and family shelter, drug and alcohol recovery programs, youth center, dental clinic, senior ministry, legal aid clinic, prison ministry, and family service department.

Executive Director Reverend Herb Pfiffner

The mission served more than half a million meals in the year 2000.

Over the years, the mission has directed its overall vision and programs toward healing the "whole person" by addressing physical as well as spiritual needs. This long-term approach enables people to build self-confidence and a sense of purpose through the teachings of the Gospel while, at the same time, attending to real-world issues like developing good work habits, managing legal matters and health and dental concerns. The mission has some of the finest, most comprehensive educational programs in the city — all designed to guide men, women and children toward making more positive life choices.

However, most worthwhile goals in life require commitment. In no place is this truer than at Seattle's Union Gospel Mission. Those who participate in programs must abide by the mission's rules and values. They also attend chapel services and Bible studies.

According to Herb Pfiffner, executive director since 1989, "For all the positive benefits that financial donations bring to the mission, it is people's increased hunger for the Gospel that turns their lives around," he says. "When people respond, they stay responsive."

Of course, practical, day-to-day matters are also important. Everyone has a job assignment — the basic philosophy being "work is therapy." For many, this type of structured responsibility is their first step toward bringing discipline and order to their lives.

Yesterday and Today

Seattle's Union Gospel Mission continues to face many challenges, as evidenced by some of the staggering demographic statistics of the people it serves.

For example, just 25 years ago, the average profile of an individual coming to the mission was 55 years old and male. Today, that average has dropped to about 26 years of age. Thirty years ago, the women's shelter consisted of 14 beds, of which about half were occupied on any given night. Today, nearly 40 percent of the homeless are women and children. The mission's women's and family shelter can now accommodate up to 41 families.

Why the dramatic change? According to Pfiffner, one of the reasons for the rise of homelessness in this country is due to the breakdown of the family unit and, consequently, the sharp rise in single parenthood. Use of drugs and alcohol as well as the unfortunate reality of abuse in the home only compound the problem. Pfiffner believes that the fastest-growing homeless population in the future will be the working poor — not by choice but by economic necessity. He maintains that people need jobs closer to home, not an hour or two away, in order to maintain a stable family life. That translates into a need for more affordable, low-income housing within the city — a need that Seattle's Union Gospel Mission recognizes and strives to build awareness of throughout the community.

Youth Reach Out Center — "Changing our world, one child at a time"

Despite the statistics, it is not all gloom and doom. Youth programs, for example, offer some of the most encouraging success stories. Each year the mission sponsors summer day camps that attract 600-700 children and teen-agers — camps that provide much needed guidance and valuable life skills through group activities, outings, Bible studies and fellowship.

According to Scott Urie, a long-standing member of the board of trustees, the mission is helping more youngsters than ever. The staff is starting to see many positive changes, not just in the kids but in their parents as well.

How does Seattle's Union Gospel Mission continue to meet the needs of so many? Though it receives generous donations from corporations and organized groups, the true foundation for its survival has consistently come from the faithful individuals who give $5-$10 each month. Clearly, every little bit does count.

Hope for the Future

Year after year, Seattle's Union Gospel Mission has consistently risen to the call of those in need. From those early years during the Depression and continuing up to the present, one thing is certain — there has never been a shortage of human compassion or words of hope. With over 150 full-time staff members, the mission takes pride in the fact that approximately 35 percent of them came through the doors originally seeking help — a statistic that clearly demonstrates the organization must be doing something right. Amid social and economic challenges, Seattle's Union Gospel Mission remains an oasis, helping people to rebuild their lives through education, discipline and, most of all, the words of Jesus Christ.

Executive Director Pfiffner knows the plight of troubled souls all too well. But he is rarely discouraged. With the support of an exceptional staff and a strong community, he looks ahead with hope, knowing that Seattle's Union Gospel Mission will continue unfalteringly to reach out and touch lives — one person at a time. Says Pfiffner, "I get paid to see miracles happen every day."

The Old Ace Hotel, serving as the Men's Shelter since 1951, provides 1,300 meals and shelters over 300 men per day.

THE MILLIONAIR CLUB CHARITY

On a cold rainy day in 1921, Martin Johanson looked out his office window to the street below and witnessed a scuffle in a bread line. He realized then that the homeless needed more than food; they needed jobs to get off the streets and regain their dignity.

With help from his friends, Johanson set up shop in a borrowed basement on Main Street in Pioneer Square, near Seattle's original Skid Road. He sought to "provide jobs for the unemployed" and "food for the hungry men and women out of work." Johanson called his new organization the Millionair Club Charity because he believed that people who helped others would feel like millionaires. He dropped the "e" from "Millionaire" so nobody would confuse the organization with an elite social club or feel that wealth was required to lend support.

Several years later the Millionair Club moved to Belltown — a neighborhood now known for expensive shops, restaurants and condominiums with panoramic views — and eventually purchased its Western Avenue location in 1942 for the grand sum of $7,000. Here with its own breathtaking view of the Puget Sound and Olympic Mountains, the Millionair Club has dispatched homeless men and women to over 670,000 day labor jobs and has served nearly 9 million meals.

Through the years, services expanded to include job search training, forklift and flagging certification courses, emergency financial and referral assistance, a thrift store,

The Millionair Club's day labor program allows homeless workers to earn money as they build an employment history. Workers can be hired for a variety of jobs including yard work, housework, painting and moving.
Photo by Dean Wenick

Martin Johanson swept the steps to the organization he founded to provide "jobs for the unemployed" and "food for the hungry men and women out of work." Eighty years later, the Millionair Club has provided more than 670,000 jobs and served nearly 9 million meals.
Seattle Post-Intelligencer Collection, MOHAI

hygiene center and eye clinic. Yet the Millionair Club remains dedicated to changing lives through jobs, providing, as its mission states, jobs and direct temporary assistance to people in need to encourage self-sufficiency.

The day labor dispatch program matches employers who have a job to fill with Millionair Club workers who possess the right skills for that job. Employers are private businesses, contract workers and residents throughout the Seattle area who need help with specific projects — from general labor, yard work, housework, painting and moving to construction and masonry. Workers earn money and build an employment history, while business and community members get the help they need.

Dispatching over 500 workers a week, the Millionair Club opens its doors at 6:30 a.m. every morning, Monday through Saturday. Employers are required to pay a prevailing living wage directly to the worker for at least four hours of work each day. Unlike commercial labor suppliers, the Millionair Club does not charge employers for using the dispatch service and does not take a percentage of workers' wages. As a nonprofit, tax-exempt organization without government funding, the Millionair Club relies solely on donations from private individuals, companies, foundations and corporations.

While the day labor program remains the cornerstone of the Millionair Club, the organization offers a number of other vital support services. More than 12,000 hot, nourishing meals are served each month, three times a day, Monday through Friday. The meal program is open to everyone, with priority given at breakfast to workers waiting to be dispatched. On Saturday breakfast is served to those working in the day labor program. The Millionair Club also cooperates with Northwest Harvest, Food Lifeline and food banks, ensuring that no donation ever goes to waste.

In addition to the meal program, the Millionair Club's thrift store distributes free clothing and household items to the homeless through a voucher system. Day labor program participants receive work clothes and work boots at no cost, and job search program participants receive interview attire.

Unlike traditional clothing banks, the Millionair Club does not select clothing for their voucher clients, who choose their own items just as paying customers do. This practice is in keeping with the founder's philosophy of restoring a person's dignity. The thrift store is also open to the public Tuesday through Saturday, and offers some of the best buys in Belltown. All proceeds benefit the Millionair Club's programs.

Opened in 1998, the Donald Lofquist Hygiene Center provides a safe, clean place for day laborers and job search participants to shower and do laundry. The hygiene center also provides storage lockers so the homeless can store their belongings before going to the job site or to job interviews. The hygiene center is one of only nine such facilities available to Seattle's more than 5,000 homeless men and women.

The Job Search Program was created to secure permanent employment for Millionair Club workers. Working one-on-one with the Millionair Club's resource specialists, participants learn to write resumes, generate job leads and prepare for interviews. Priority goes to day labor program participants, who earn money as they search for permanent employment. The job search center also provides access to computers, telephones, fax machines and other reference materials. Free voice mailboxes allow potential employers to contact workers, who may also use the Millionair Club's mailing address for correspondence. Once employed, job search graduates receive rental assistance for up to six months.

Serving more than 12,000 meals each month, the Millionair Club's meal program is open to everyone, with priority given at breakfast to those waiting to be dispatched to work.
Photo by Michele Norris

The Millionair Club's thrift store is more than a clothing bank, using a unique voucher system that allows the homeless to shop clothing racks as retail customers do, selecting the items they want.
Photo by Dean Wenick

The Millionair Club also offers monthly forklift safety and flagging certification training, courses that would not otherwise be affordable to clients. This certification complies with industry standards and is required by law if a worker wishes to operate a forklift or join a road crew. The Schultz Vocational Training Program, established by a bequest, covers the cost for clients to attend local vocational schools and community colleges.

In cooperation with the Lions Sight and Hearing Foundation, the Millionair Club provides a free vision care clinic each week. Local optometrists and opticians, who donate their time, conduct free exams and fit homeless and low-income clients with glasses.

Since 1921, the Millionair Club has provided jobs and other essential services to people in need without cost or obligation. Martin Johanson believed in providing assistance with kindness and concern, not at the expense of a client's self-respect. Although the organization's programs have grown, the Millionair Club's philosophy remains the same: "Dignity in work and charity without embarrassment."

THE SEATTLE FOUNDATION

"From what we get, we can make a living; what we give, however, makes a life."

In 1946, 15 community leaders founded The Seattle Foundation with a mission to address present-day problems not only in Seattle but also in the Puget Sound area, and to establish resources for an unknown future. The founding trustees were Paul P. Ashley, Frank S. Bayley, Leo D. Black, Mrs. A. Scott Bullitt, Kenneth B. Colman, George K. Comstock, George Donworth, Richard E. Fuller, George H. Greenwood, Henry J. Judson, Richard E. Lang, Reginald H. Parsons, Nat S. Rogers and Dietrich Schmitz.

The charitable endowment the founders created — made up of gifts from many sources — accomplishes the foundation's goals by supporting local community organizations and efforts and enabling donors to leave a dynamic legacy for themselves or their families. The foundation began with $289,000 in assets and made its first grants totaling $8,000 in 1947. By 1999 its assets had increased to over $235 million, and more than $18.2 million in grants were given to 1,100 nonprofit organizations that year. In 2000, total assets reached almost $325 million and continue to grow. Grants — totaling over $39 million in 2000 alone — support organizations working to improve the quality of citizens' economic, physical, intellectual, emotional and cultural well-being in Puget Sound.

Over the years the chairman of the board of trustees has always been a community leader and voice for philanthropy. The Seattle Foundation honors its former chairmen of the board: Dr. Richard E. Fuller, Nat S. Rogers, A.R. Munger, Michael Dederer, William G. Reed, Sr., Willard G. Wright, Walter Wyckoff, Volney Richmond, Jr., D.E. Skinner II, Willis L. Campbell, William Schnatterly, Charles Osborn, Kenneth R. Fisher, Robert Hitchman, W.J. Pennington, David E. Ellison, Frank A. Dupar, Jr., Kate B. Webster, P. Cameron DeVore, Samuel Stroum, Christopher T. Bayley, Elaine Monsen, Ph.D., Brooks Ragen, Kemper Freeman, Jr., Roger Eigsti and Kerry Killinger. Anne Farrell has served as president and CEO of The Seattle Foundation since 1984.

Donors reflect this area's diversity and come from all age groups, income levels, ethnic backgrounds and spiritual traditions. Their philanthropic interests range from education to micro lending and they support a broad range of activities from alleviating hunger to building playgrounds. They contribute for different reasons: to honor a friend or loved one, to give back to the community or to support issues they care about. No matter what type of assets are donated, the giving options available through the foundation can provide long-term income and/or tax benefits while championing organizations and causes for years to come. As contributions are pooled together and invested, every donation, no matter the size, makes an ongoing difference in the community.

In a dual role as partner with donors and community resource, the foundation is able to address the broad needs of the area. Although some issues remain constant — the physical necessities of food, clothing and shelter or the intangible desire for art, music, dance and companionship — the methods for meeting those needs change. The Seattle Foundation keeps informed of community developments and evaluates recipient organizations to ensure funds are used in the most effective ways.

Once each quarter, The Seattle Foundation awards Community Grants to organizations working to improve social or human services, education, arts, culture, conservation and health services. Highest priority for these grants is given to requests for specific capital projects, equipment to meet infrastructure needs and funds to strengthen organizational capacity. The foundation seeks to support organizations that address a community issue in a unique way or that might not be able to raise funds elsewhere.

Each year the foundation recognizes two Community Grant recipients for their outstanding efforts and honors them with the Chairman's Award and the Leadership Grant. A recent recipient of the Chairman's Award was Eastside Baby Corner, an organization that collects and distributes food and clothing to children from birth to age 12. The 2000 Leadership Grant was awarded to the Refugee and Immigrant Parent Support Network, a coalition of 18 community-based groups that have come together to work with the Seattle Public School District to address barriers to effective education of immigrant and refugee children. The coalition also works to increase parent participation in school activities and decisions that affect their children's education.

Nonprofit organizations look to the foundation for its leadership and its ability to bring people together to discuss new ideas and collaborations. The foundation has supported a number of cooperative efforts, including the Northwest Giving Project, which inspires and educates new philanthropists, and the Nonprofit Assistance Center, a management and consultant resource working to build the capacity of grassroots nonprofit organizations in low-income areas and communities of color.

As a facilitator, The Seattle Foundation helps donors and nonprofit organizations explore innovative ways to help their neighbors and celebrate the human spirit. No matter what the reason or issue, The Seattle Foundation offers a way for donors to give through its various funds.

• *Advised Funds* allow donors to bring specific grant requests (for example, an alma mater or favorite charity) to the foundation for consideration. Thus givers enjoy ongoing involvement with the distribution of gifts from their funds.

• A donor may prefer to establish an *Area of Interest Fund* that targets issue areas such as the environment or health, or groups of people such as children, the elderly, homeless families or residents of a particular town, country or region.

• If a donor wishes to be even more specific, he or she may establish a *Designated Fund*, which goes to one or more specific charities named to benefit from the gift. If the charity ceases to exist, the foundation reallocates the gift to another agency that most closely reflects the donor's original intent.

• *Scholarship Funds*, the fastest-growing type of fund, are important "votes of confidence" for deserving students.

Regardless of their diverse heritages and lifestyles, The Seattle Foundation's donors share a common desire to add meaning to their lives through giving, to forge strong connections with their neighbors and to positively impact the community for years to come. The foundation's role supporting both donors and nonprofit organizations ensures that donors find philanthropy satisfying and grant recipients are able to work more effectively in the community.

WORLD VISION

The first child helped by Bob Pierce, founder of World Vision, was a young Chinese girl named White Jade. She had been beaten for listening to Pierce's evangelistic message and becoming a Christian. After running away from home she had nowhere to go. Pierce gave money to a missionary to provide for White Jade and promised that he would continue to send money for her room, board and education. Neither White Jade's nor Pierce's lives would be the same again after their encounter.

From that one experience Pierce founded World Vision — a Christian relief and development organization committed to changing the lives of those in greatest need. With money donated by generous people from around the globe, the child sponsorship program that began in 1950 now reaches into nearly 100 countries, helping 1.7 million children as well as their families and their communities escape poverty and find hope.

World Vision is quick to respond in the face of a crisis, whether a natural or man-made disaster. From emergencies such as the famine in Ethiopia in the 1980s to Hurricane Mitch that devastated Central America in 1998, World Vision can be counted on to be there, helping people to rebuild, finding solutions, and providing medicine, food, care and comfort. Although responding to an earthquake or civil conflict

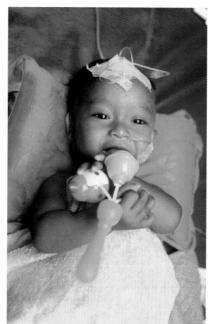

A Cambodian girl who is HIV-positive receives treatment at a World Vision clinic.
Photo by Sanjay Sojwal/World Vision

may be the initial reason that World Vision enters a country, its workers stay as long as they are needed.

In the mid-1980s, the people of Ethiopia were looking death in the face. Famine and drought killed thousands and brought many more to the brink of starvation. World Vision was there to feed the desperate masses but then stayed to help develop long-term projects that would prevent such disasters from happening again. In the Antsokia District, World Vision worked with local farmers to develop sustainable agriculture. An integrated farmers' association encouraged neighbors to share resources, and today, in spite of a lingering drought in the horn of Africa, families in the area have food to eat.

Today a crisis of unprecedented proportions is breaking in the developing world. Each day more than 1,300 children die of AIDS and another 1,700 children are infected with HIV. In Africa there are now more than 10 million children — four Seattle-sized cities —orphaned by parents who died of AIDS. Again, World Vision is fighting this battle on the front lines, providing compassionate care for the sick and grieving. Its sponsorship and child-survival projects in Africa, Eastern Europe, Asia and Latin America are helping communities support child-headed households through education, food, clothing and other services for the children, while teaching populations how to prevent the spread of the disease.

World Vision supplies the needy with five essential resources: food, basic health care, education, a clean water supply and microenterprise development (MED). While it is necessary to provide food, water and medicine during times of crisis, building people's capacity to help themselves reaps more rewards. Believing that it is better to teach a man to fish than to feed him for a lifetime, World Vision doesn't want to just save lives — it wants to change them for the better. And World Vision always works directly with recipients, asking communities to identify needs and then cooperating to find the best solutions.

Actor Blair Underwood (left) meets an Ethiopian family that received food through World Vision.
Photo by Catherine Bauknight/World Vision

When World Vision came to a neighborhood in the slums of Bangkok, Thailand, families barely earned enough to stave off eviction and starvation. Children could not go to school because families could not afford the tuition. With money provided by sponsors, World Vision was able to support children's education, providing uniforms, books, shoes and other necessary supplies. In addition, World Vision helped the women of the community form a savings group where they could borrow money to establish small businesses. Today, families are able to provide for themselves and send their children to school, allowing World Vision to move on to help another community.

People who pledge to sponsor a child develop lifelong relationships with the children and families they support. Sponsors know that their donations help to feed, clothe and educate children. Although the focus of the program is the children, the children's communities are also helped. It is, after all, better to provide teachers or build a school for an entire community than to send one child to school. Health clinics and schools; homes and community centers; training in better agricultural practices; lessons on nutrition, hygiene and sanitation; and microenterprise loans to families mean greater prosperity for all. World Vision assists communities to build, implement and manage these improvements — which ultimately improve children's health and well-being — with the funds supplied through sponsorship.

World Vision not only works overseas, but also helps find solutions for impoverished communities in the United States. Programs here focus on helping children, at-risk teens and families in areas such as Appalachia and distressed urban neighborhoods in Chicago, Los Angeles, Seattle/ Tacoma, Minneapolis-St. Paul, New York and Washington, D.C. Gift-in-kind items such as food, clothing, school supplies or building materials help meet immediate needs while services such as financial counseling, employment readiness, tutoring or mentoring help people gain skills that lead to self-reliance.

Former sponsored child Ronald Rodriguez (left) leads a World Vision medical team to help Hurricane Mitch survivors.
Photo by Jon Warren/World Vision

World Vision, through its many services, provides healing not only for the body, but also for the heart and the spirit. Motivated by faith in Christ, World Vision staff are dedicated to living and working according to their Christian principles. Bob Pierce once wrote on the flyleaf of his Bible, "Let my heart be broken with the things that break the heart of God." World Vision is dedicated to healing hearts: one child, one family, one community at a time.

World Vision's KidREACH program connects tutors from the Christian Reformed Church in Tacoma, Washington, with students from Boze Elementary School.
Photo by Todd Bartel/World Vision

CENTER FOR CAREER ALTERNATIVES

The Center for Career Alternatives (CCA), founded in 1979 by Alan Sugiyama, is a private, nonprofit agency designed to help those who want to help themselves. CCA assists people in learning skills, finding employment and achieving their goals. It accomplishes this task through job training and placement, educational services, and citizenship and English as a Second Language courses.

When CCA began in 1979, Sugiyama was told that his desire to serve the neediest would work against him. His success rate, he was told, would be low. Better to pick and choose those who could be helped most easily; this would generate better statistics. But Sugiyama's idea was to open a center that could meet the needs of those who most required help. He set up office in Seattle's Rainier Valley and targeted low-income areas, the unemployed, educational drop outs, and immigrants and refugees whose lack of familiarity with the language and culture of the United States were major barriers to success. The community needed an agency that would serve such a diverse population, and CCA was prepared to take on the challenge. In 1986 CCA expanded into low-income areas in Snohomish County and opened an office in Everett.

The center offers courses for both youth and adults. Any 16- to 21-year-old who was unable to finish high school can take the GED course or earn credit towards high school graduation. A middle school re-entry program provides academic and behavioral instruction to youngsters who have been expelled. A mentorship program matches at-risk youth with adults who assist the teen-agers and model successful behaviors. Summer Youth Employment is designed to give young people paid work experience and all the confidence and maturity that go along with a first job. Community service teaches responsibility as well as job skills.

Adults can learn a trade in the manufacturing, transportation and office technology sectors, or they can learn skills necessary for jobs in health-related fields. Foreign-born residents can take classes to improve their language skills and prepare to be citizens of the United States. Direct job placement helps the job-ready find employment; a yearlong follow up helps participants stay there. CCA doesn't just prepare participants to find a job, it helps them learn to be productive citizens. Behavior and attitude training help lower barriers to success, while service activities and field trips to cultural events connect participants with the larger community.

CCA's multiethnic approach to serving the community was unusual in 1979 and still is today. Instead of targeting a specific ethnic community, the center serves everyone, regardless of race, ethnicity, educational background or native language. The diverse, multilingual staff delivers training and assistance of the highest quality, and it is justifiably proud of its record. CCA has won many local and national awards, including two presidential awards. Any member of CCA's staff will attest that recognition is nice, but helping a disadvantaged person achieve real and lasting success is the best reward of all.

CCA participants celebrate their graduation from the GED program in front of family and friends.

Executive Director Alan Sugiyama (left) with two of his many successful adult program participants

CHILDHAVEN

The damaging effects of abuse and neglect last well beyond childhood. In Washington state alone, over 80 percent of today's prison inmates were abused as children. Childhaven ends this cycle of abuse and neglect through early intervention, giving children under the age of 5 a second chance.

In 1909 the Rev. Mark Matthews of Seattle First Presbyterian Church established The Seattle Day Nursery, one of the first 50 child-care centers in the country. Childhaven's Broadway Branch is now housed in three structures built in the Central District in the early 1900s. By 1959, the first staff was hired to replace a volunteer board, and the agency led the community in developing programs, including Head Start and the Model Cities Child Care.

Patrick Gogerty became the executive director in 1973. Under his leadership Seattle Day Nursery changed its name to Childhaven in 1985 and became one of the most progressive child-care agencies in the country. In 1977, two years before the Washington state Legislature mandated the reporting of child abuse, Childhaven created the Therapeutic Child Development (TCD) Program, first in the country to focus on early intervention and treatment for abused and neglected children birth to 5 years.

Nationally recognized as a model program, TCD operates from four centers in King County and has been replicated in nearly 40 communities throughout North America. Services include transportation to and from TCD centers; nutritious meals; medical supervision; individualized speech, physical and play therapy; loving, stable emotional support; and parent education and support groups. The innovative Childhaven Client Profile, a computerized behavior-rating and record-keeping system,

provides an efficient clinical report of each child's daily physical, emotional and behavioral status.

When Patrick Gogerty retired in 1998, Laura Sheehan was appointed executive director and now oversees four pioneering programs in addition to TCD. The Drug-Affected Infant Program, also first in the state, treats children affected — either in utero or environmentally — by their parents' substance abuse. The Crisis Nursery Program is King County's first and still

In Childhaven's safe environment, children form positive bonds with adults by interacting with a highly trained staff and dedicated volunteers.

only 24-hour crisis prevention program for children at risk of abuse and neglect. Other programs are Developmental Therapies (e.g., speech/physical therapy) and Creative Therapies (e.g., art/music).

Research shows that Childhaven's early intervention works. From 1980 to 1982, children under 2 years of age were randomly chosen from Child Protective Services referrals. Half the children went to Childhaven; the other half received standard care from Child Protective Services. An independent, 12-year follow-up study revealed that only 3.7 percent of the Childhaven group were later arrested for serious or violent crimes, compared to 23.8 percent of the control group. Children in the control group were more aggressive, violent and twice as likely to abuse drugs. The results support medical and social research proving that early intervention is critical.

For over 90 years, Childhaven has nurtured and protected society's most vulnerable children. Partnerships with the private and public sector have seen thousands of children grow into healthier adults. The community currently joins Childhaven in building a state-of-the-art center on its original site, thereby enabling the organization to change the world one child at a time.

Every day, Childhaven's services help 268 children overcome the devastating impact of abuse and neglect.

LIFELONG AIDS ALLIANCE

Lifelong AIDS Alliance was founded in January 2001 through the merger of Chicken Soup Brigade and Northwest AIDS Foundation. Both organizations were founded in 1983 with the long-term goal of providing valuable support to people in the Seattle community who are living with or affected by HIV and AIDS. More people are now living with HIV and AIDS than ever before, and as a result, AIDS service organizations need to evolve along with the disease. Lifelong AIDS Alliance is a new organization for this new era of HIV and AIDS.

As a single, new organization, Lifelong AIDS Alliance continues to diversify, but its underlying commitment of supporting the living and comforting the dying has not wavered. Lifelong AIDS Alliance provides case management, financial advocacy, insurance continuation, emergency grants, and housing assistance for people with AIDS in the Seattle community. The organization also provides fresh meals and healthy groceries to people living with AIDS in King County. Clients consult Lifelong's nutritionist to ensure that the food complements their medications to best address their nutritive needs. Trained volunteers help clients maintain clean, comfortable home environments

Walkers at the annual Northwest AIDS Walk, a $1 million fund-raiser to benefit Lifelong AIDS Alliance

by making beds, cleaning bathrooms, and doing laundry and other household tasks. These volunteers also offer companionship, breaching the social isolation that often occurs when living with HIV and AIDS.

Lifelong AIDS Alliance also provides rides to ensure that people living with the disease receive the necessary professional therapies. Clients can request vouchers redeemable at all three agency thrift stores to meet basic household and personal needs. Auxiliary services include loaning microwave ovens, coordinating free haircutting services, and providing a free ticket program to cultural events.

The organization actively works to prevent the spread of HIV and increase AIDS awareness through a variety of education programs, including group education workshops, one-to-one outreach, workplace training, a volunteer speakers' bureau, and safer sex campaigns.

Lifelong AIDS Alliance educates policy-makers about the realities of HIV and AIDS and advocates at the state and national levels for meaningful health care reform, adequate government funding and sound public policy. The agency makes annual grants to nonprofit AIDS service organizations across Washington state, helping to ensure that a range of necessary services remain available to people with HIV and AIDS.

In July 1999, Chicken Soup Brigade launched a pilot project, which is continued by Lifelong AIDS Alliance. This aims to improve the health of people living with chronic or terminal illnesses other than HIV or AIDS. Volunteers deliver meals and groceries each week, enabling caregivers to take a break from the day-to-day, meal-to-meal stresses.

The launch of Lifelong AIDS Alliance is only possible because of a dedicated corps of volunteers and donors. From delivering loaves of bread to reaching more than 50,000 people each year with prevention education messages, this organization is making a difference in the fight against HIV and AIDS.

A Lifelong AIDS Alliance volunteer prepares vegetables for a nutritious meal.

MARCH OF DIMES

The March of Dimes story began with President Franklin D. Roosevelt, who established the organization in 1938 to save America's youth from polio. Believing people could solve any problem if they worked together, he created a partnership of volunteers and researchers; and within 17 years the Salk vaccine was developed and polio was on the run. After that, the March of Dimes turned to preventing birth defects, infant mortality and premature birth. Today the organization's Washington state chapter is one of 55 saving the lives of millions of babies by funding innovative programs in research, advocacy, community services and education.

Currently, the research includes finding the causes of premature births (premature babies are 12 times more likely to die in their first year of life than full-term babies) and the causes, treatments and prevention of birth defects — the leading killer of infants in this country. Since most birth defects are genetic, the focus is on gene therapy.

Advocacy is the March of Dimes way to encourage federal, state and local governments to improve public policy and invest in effective programs to improve the health of mothers and babies. The community service programs address urgent infant and maternal health needs, especially targeting women and men of childbearing age and new mothers and fathers. The education programs are directed at many different audiences and complement the March of Dimes Resource Center, which provides answers and information to millions of people by toll-free phone, fax, Web site or e-mail.

The March of Dimes Washington state chapter is headquartered in Seattle, where some lifesaving scientific breakthroughs have occurred — including the discovery that specific birth defects are linked directly to alcohol consumption by pregnant women. Related community efforts aim to reduce and prevent substance abuse during pregnancy. The Washington chapter also helped to successfully lobby for and obtain free or low-cost health insurance for tens of thousands of children in Washington state who formerly were not considered eligible, and it is working to make sure families learn about and sign up for

these health care benefits. The chapter also educates health care professionals about the latest advances in maternal and child health and shares vital information through television, radio, community education kits, brochures, videos, and seminars and curricula at worksites and schools.

All these projects are supported by donations of time and money to the March of Dimes as well as many fund-raisers, especially the annual WalkAmerica. This event is held in more than 1,400 communities nationwide. In Washington about 10,000 walkers and runners, mostly in teams from companies, clubs, schools and other groups, participate in 11 cities, raising well over 1 million dollars. The second-largest money-raiser is the annual black-tie Star Chefs Gala, which features nationally and locally known executive chefs who personally serve their signature dishes.

At the core of the organization is an army of dedicated volunteers from medical, media and corporate experts to countless other workers. All of them believe in saving babies together — ensuring that all mothers receive regular, early and adequate prenatal care and that no baby is born so small that it has to fight for its life. The March of Dimes has a remarkable track record of success and is determined not to stop until every baby is born healthy.

Dr. David B. Shurtleff, University of Washington School of Medicine, treated many young patients with birth defects. With the help of a March of Dimes grant, he discovered that delivering babies with spina bifida by Caesarian section may reduce the risk of paralysis.

Seattle-area WalkAmerica

SENIOR SERVICES OF SEATTLE-KING COUNTY

United Way planners showed great foresight when they created the nonprofit agency Senior Services and Centers in 1967. Today Senior Services provides support to more than 70,000 older adults, their families and caregivers throughout King County through a network of 11 core programs, nine centers and six adult day health centers. The agency receives funding from United Way, corporate and foundation grants, individual contributions and local, state and federal government.

The mission of Senior Services — to support the independence of seniors — is carried out in many ways. The Centers are sites for nutritious meals, recreation, social interaction, peer support and counseling, a variety of classes and activities, and health education. Adult day health centers provide care and support for less independent individuals — such as those with Alzheimer's, stroke or other disabilities that require daytime assistance — providing a therapeutic program and respite to families and caregivers.

Senior Services' nutrition programs serve more than 600,000 meals annually to older adults. Meals on Wheels delivers nutritious frozen meals to homebound seniors. Weekly deliveries of reasonably priced grocery items are available through Mobile Market. Seniors enjoy a delicious hot meal and positive social interaction with their peers through the Congregate Meal Program, available at 37 sites in King County. Homesharing, an intergenerational program, supports older residents' desires to stay in their own homes. Seniors who need help with household chores or modest rental income are matched with carefully screened compatible persons who are looking for an affordable place to live. Minor Home Repair handles smaller plumbing, electrical and carpentry repairs for low-income homeowners of all ages.

Senior Information & Assistance provides easy access to more than 3,700 community services and one-on-one telephone follow-up from specially trained advocates. Seniors who have concerns surrounding legal, consumer and health issues receive information from trained volunteers through Senior Rights Assistance. The Elder Law Clinic sponsors a no-cost legal clinic for seniors, held twice monthly.

Senior Wellness Project is an innovative health promotion and disease management program for older adults. Partially funded through the Robert Wood Johnson Foundation, the program includes health enhancement, lifetime fitness exercise classes and a healthy life workshop.

Specialists identify older African Americans who need services and provide personal support and assistance through the African American Outreach Program. In response to a growing, ethnically diverse population, Senior Services' Volunteer Transportation program prints brochures in seven languages to educate more people about their services and also attract more ethnic volunteer drivers. Drivers provide frail seniors with personalized, private transportation to and from essential medical and other appointments.

Senior Services could not function effectively without its faithful volunteers, some 5,500 strong, who devote their time, energy and talents to support all the programs and centers.

In September 2002 Senior Services celebrates completion of its comprehensive capital and endowment campaign. A permanent home; low-income senior housing; an upgrade of programs, services and centers; and funding of a healthy endowment will give Senior Services the ability to meet a huge increase in demand for service as King County residents grow older.

Respect, Dignity, Independence

Professional Services

Professionals in Seattle provide consulting, networking, promotions, public relations, law and other essential services to the area's businesses and individuals.

MARSH & McLENNAN COMPANIES

Marsh & McLennan Companies (MMC) is a leading global professional services firm to whom many of the world's largest corporations turn for risk and insurance programs, investment management and business consulting. Dedicated to exceptional quality and innovative technology and products, MMC has served the state of Washington since 1919, when it opened an office to handle claims for salmon canneries, steamships and the lumber business. In the ensuing years, MMC's initial modest presence has grown into the largest risk control staff in the Puget Sound area.

Children's Hospital

Founded by two pioneers in the insurance industry, Henry Marsh and Donald McLennan, MMC traces its roots back to the aftermath of the Great Chicago Fire of 1871. Early on, the company became known for being at the forefront of insurance product development. Henry Marsh introduced the concept of brokers acting as buyers of insurance representing the client, instead of acting as a seller. He also pioneered the concept of risk management. Donald McLennan established what became the industry research standard for assessing risk.

After decades of broadening its base internally and through high-profile mergers and acquisitions, the company became known as Marsh & McLennan Companies in 1969. A period of intense international expansion followed in the 1980s. In the next decade MMC's position in the industry was further bolstered by the acquisitions of Johnson & Higgins in 1997 and U.K.-based Sedgwick Group in 1998. As a result of these acquisitions, Marsh & McLennan solidified its position as the premier firm in its field and now has more than 50,000 employees and clients in more than 100 countries. Through the Seattle offices of three of its leading companies — Marsh Inc., Marsh Advantage America and William M. Mercer — MMC serves such high-profile clients as Boeing, Starbucks, Children's Hospital, Nordstrom and REI. The important PortAdvantage™ program is administered from Seattle as well.

Marsh Inc.

Marsh Inc. is the world's foremost risk management consultant and insurance broker for corporations and high net worth private clients. Marsh was formed as a new holding company for MMC's risk and insurance services in 1999 after integrating the three respected traditions of Marsh & McLennan, Johnson & Higgins and Sedgwick.

The Seattle Mariners

Marsh Inc. provides a complete range of services to identify, value, control, transfer and finance risk for business, public entity and professional service organizations. Having developed an impressive array of industry specialty practices, it serves its Seattle-area clients in the fields of aviation, high technology, biotechnology, health care, higher education, real estate, retail, energy and more. Marsh Inc. also counts among its local clients two of Seattle's professional sports franchises, the Mariners and Seahawks.

A trendsetter in applying new technologies to its operations and service, Marsh has been honored by *PC Week* with a high ranking on its "Financial Services Fast-Track 100" list of IT innovators in 1999. The company's proprietary risk management information system, STARS 5.0, was named the 1999 Enterprise Risk Management System of the Year by *Risk & Insurance Magazine*. Marsh Inc. in Seattle has a staff of more than 290 professionals dedicated entirely to client service and support.

Seahawk Stadium

Marsh Advantage America

In 1982 MMC consolidated its insurance program management business (then known as Marsh McLennan Group Associates) into a separate entity in Seattle. In 1990 the company was renamed Seabury & Smith, in honor of two of its former chairmen. Now known as Marsh Advantage America, the company designs, manages and administers health-care, property and casualty, and many other services for small companies, associations, affinity groups, and educational and nonprofit institutions.

Nationally, Marsh Advantage America has more than 52 offices and approximately 4,500 employees who service more than 40,000 clients throughout the United States. The Seattle office — with clients in the areas of technology, health care, biotech, food service, entertainment, social services, construction and retail — is staffed by nearly 75 professionals. In each client's field, Marsh Advantage America offers a full range of solutions to help its clients stay abreast of industry changes.

William M. Mercer, Incorporated

William M. Mercer, Incorporated is the human resource consulting subsidiary of MMC. Starting as the corporate benefit department in 1937, Mercer has become a global leader in consulting with offices in more than 40 countries. Its services and expertise include health care and retirement benefits, communication, performance and rewards, executive compensation, sales effectiveness, human resource operations and investment consulting. Mercer employs more than 12,000 people worldwide, with 250 employees in Seattle serving employers and organizations throughout the Pacific Northwest.

REI

From serving the insurance needs of the great clipper ships of the 19th century, to managing the complex risks associated with e-commerce today, only a handful of U.S. companies have a history as long or as rich as Marsh & McLennan Companies. Even fewer have the foresight and expertise to anticipate and meet the ever-changing needs of a diverse client base. With so many people around the world — employers, employees and their families, members and beneficiaries of associations and organizations — relying on the expertise of Marsh Inc., Marsh Advantage America and William M. Mercer, Incorporated, Seattle's MMC companies are committed to meeting the challenges and opportunities of the coming years and doing so in a way that lives up to their legacy of stability and service.

MCKINSEY & COMPANY

Anyone who hires McKinsey & Company expects high-quality work — deep research, comprehensive analysis and critical thinking brought to the most important business issues its clients face. That is a given and has long been McKinsey's passion. However, its commitment to entrepreneurial leadership and diversity — especially in Seattle — is also strong.

McKinsey's Pacific Northwest office, based in Seattle, was founded in 1995 through the passion of its founding partner and director, Atul Kanagat. A 13-year veteran of the firm and Chicago office, Kanagat was eager for new challenges. The firm, a private partnership that emphasizes individual professional development, encouraged him to start a new office in any region with the underlying business fundamentals to support it. That same philosophy had built the firm from a single office 75 years ago to a network of 82 offices in 43 countries today. Kanagat chose Seattle for its dynamic, diverse business leaders and innovative, inclusive culture. He was joined by partners Steve Shaw and Jim Robb from San Francisco and Endre Holen from Scandinavia. The office now numbers almost 50 people who were drawn by the opportunity to be entrepreneurial and at the same time serve a wide array of leading companies.

Friday lunch presentation
*Photo by Gary Quinn*PhotoMagic*

The Firm

In 1926 James O. McKinsey founded McKinsey & Company in Chicago. His distinct approach of working

A typical team meeting
*Photo by Gary Quinn*PhotoMagic*

side-by-side with senior management to solve major business problems quickly established the credibility of the consulting field. After his death in 1937, Marvin Bower stepped up as leader, raising standards of professionalism, performance and client focus.

In the years that followed, McKinsey consultants have had an enduring impact on some of the most visible organizations and areas of the world. McKinsey designed the original organization of NASA; developed the Universal Product Code; advised on restoring and reintegrating East Germany's economy after the fall of the Berlin Wall; and led the first study examining Russia's economy from the ground up. Its 1,000-plus clients include 100 of the 150 top global companies as well as emerging growth companies, high-tech startups and family-owned enterprises. McKinsey's work with governments and institutions around the world has helped reshape economies; its pro-bono work has forwarded humanitarian goals.

More than 10,000 people worldwide make up the McKinsey team, including 800 principals (junior partners) and directors (senior partners) who own the company. A closer look at the McKinsey team reveals an extraordinary collection of cultural diversity, intellectual capital and expertise. Its 6,000 consultants represent more than 80 nationalities. While their academic and professional backgrounds vary widely, their individual records of accomplishment are uniformly strong.

The Pacific Northwest Office

Similarly, the professionals in the Seattle office have unique backgrounds and expertise, yet all experienced a particular attraction to the Pacific Northwest. Associate Principal Dilip Wagle, who grew up in Bombay, first came to Seattle as a Microsoft employee but stayed because he and his wife love the area. "It is deeply friendly," says Wagle, who also notes the area's world-class theater. Bob Felton, a director recently transferred from Seoul after years of globe-trotting for McKinsey, shares Wagle's feelings: "I grew up in Washington and always wanted to come back here." Katie Bain is a Connecticut native who came to the University of Washington to do graduate work in oceanography after finishing her degree at Princeton. She fell in love more with the city than an oceanography career and returned to Seattle to join McKinsey after earning an MBA at Columbia.

Derek Kilmer grew up in Port Angeles, a small town northwest of Seattle. As a Marshall Scholar (McKinsey is the largest employer of Rhodes and Marshall Scholars in the world), Kilmer did his graduate work at Oxford University. He finds that his work fulfills his aspiration to work on complex topics and achieve positive public outcomes. Kanagat, a vice chair for the Seattle Symphony board, has led several pro-bono studies for the organization. The office has also done pro-bono work for the Chamber of Commerce and KING-FM, among others. The firm has always stressed being part of the local community.

Every McKinsey office has a distinct personality while adhering to the firm's values and structure. In Seattle that personality mirrors Wagle's "deeply friendly" description of the city. "I find the civility of the culture very attractive," Kanagat adds. "Other cities often find ways to exclude people, but Seattle finds ways to include people. We've been lucky and thoughtful about building the culture of our office. Our people reflect the city."

"While our work is always interesting and challenging, the office is more focused on people than content," says Dennis Oldroyd, an Associate Principal from Los Angeles whose wife grew up in the Seattle area. Allen Webb, an associate who came to Seattle after graduating from the University of Chicago's Law School, finds the city and his clients vibrant, young and creative. Katie Bain adds, "People in Seattle are into their activities. When people ask you what you do, they mean what activities, like boating or snow skiing."

While the office culture may not stress marathon work hours or cutthroat business ethics, that doesn't mean the consultants don't work hard. "It's more about being creative and flexible with your clients," says Wagle. Because the office is also a center for the firm's work with clients throughout Western Canada and the Rocky Mountain states, consultants rarely focus exclusively on a narrow area of expertise. Regardless of their location, McKinsey clients have access to a global network of top-notch talent and resources. From a client's perspective, McKinsey brings a unique depth and breadth of industry-specific and functional knowledge to solving tough, ambiguous and business-shaping problems. "We are serving the cutting-edge companies in their field on the critical issues facing their businesses," says Holen. "It's a very exciting and forward-looking business community here."

"McKinsey is more like a professional society than a business," Kanagat explains. "Thus, the numbers follow, they don't lead." Felton feels the company's community involvement and pro-bono work is defining for him and important in providing consultants broadening experiences. Kilmer agrees but stresses that there's a Pacific Northwest flavor. "We're just not a cynical office," he explains.

Some members of the leadership group
Photo by Gary Quinn*PhotoMagic

BENSUSSEN DEUTSCH & ASSOCIATES, INC.

Hard work, adaptability and an unabashed enthusiasm for the promotional products business catapulted Bensussen Deutsch & Associates, Inc. (BD&A) onto success's fast track.

In 1984 two young men started Sports Marketing, Inc. with a $2,000 investment. At the time, Eric Bensussen was a 20-year-old college student and 17-year-old Jay Deutsch was in high school. They grew up together in Seattle buying and selling sports collectibles.

With their first venture, the production of 1,000 Seattle Seahawks sweatshirts, Sports Marketing, Inc. was born. As more sports promotions followed, they found that concepts they were using to promote sports were also applicable to corporate promotions. Their corporate division started when The Boeing Company ordered 24 sweatshirts.

In 1989 they changed the name to Bensussen Deutsch & Associates, Inc. Their slogan, Your Merchandise Agency℠, emphasized the customized approach they took toward offering complete merchandise-based marketing solutions that tied together with a company's advertising and public relations. In 1997 they developed BD&A's licensing division, highlighted by the creation of their retail toy division, Toysite.

Eric Bensussen and Jay Deutsch

National promotions started in 1992 with college photos of top professional basketball players on trading cards in Kellogg's Raisin Bran boxes. Beginning in 1994, BD&A was recognized as one of Washington state's fastest-growing, privately held companies. In 1996 BD&A ranked 379th among *Inc.* magazine's list of the 500 fastest-growing firms in the nation. Additionally, *Washington CEO* magazine named BD&A the No. 1 fastest-growing private company in 2000.

By 2000 BD&A employed over 400 people and occupied an 85,000-square-foot building that included corporate offices and a warehouse. In addition, regional sales and marketing offices were located in San Francisco, Indianapolis, Charlotte, Austin, Dallas, Los Angeles, Atlanta and Denver. Revenue jumped from $56 million in 1998 to $109 million in 1999.

As the nation's 8th-largest promotional products company and the No. 1 sports promotion company, BD&A provides merchandising for Major League Baseball, the National Football League, National Basketball Association, National Hockey League and over 70 college teams. Microsoft, Pepsi Cola, Bank of America, Delta Air Lines, Amazon.com and Nintendo are among its business clients.

BD&A's many services make it unique and are helping to redefine the promotional merchandise industry. BD&A develops and supports promotional campaigns, events, sales promotions, and catalog and e-commerce programs by creating a vast array of branded merchandise from toys and clothing to electronics and sporting goods. It also helps corporations concentrate on producing their respective products and services by managing company stores for The Boeing Company, Bank of America, Eli Lilly and others.

Bensussen Deutsch & Associates, Inc. headquarters

BD&A plans to continue opening more branch offices. It supports local organizations wherever its offices are located, and has established a tradition of doing business with companies owned and operated by women and minorities. In the Seattle-Woodinville area, BD&A supports Northwest Harvest, Marsha Rivkin Center for Ovarian Cancer Research, the Jewish Federation and local chambers of commerce.

Both partners insist they don't necessarily want to be the biggest, just the best. Jay Deutsch said, "One of the biggest things we've learned is adaptability. We have never gotten stuck in one way of thinking. We're constantly trying to improve with our people, our innovations, and our creative work in delivering quality products and services."

BUSINESS NETWORK INTERNATIONAL

Business Network International (BNI) is designed to help people succeed. Connie Hinton, Executive Director of BNI Northwest, a subsidiary of BNI, is in the enviable position of making sure that happens — every day.

BNI is a referral organization of professionals that draws on the collective value of its members' reputations. It provides a supportive environment in which people can develop personal relationships with other professionals to expand their businesses. The core philosophy of the organization is "givers gain," which translates simply to, "Let's help each other."

"BNI is a structured system to help people build their businesses through word of mouth," says Hinton. "It can be any business — but the idea is to teach other members who to talk to in order to be more successful."

Business Network International is the brainchild of Dr. Ivan R. Misner, who in 1985 acted on the conviction that there were better alternatives than cold calling to generate new business for his San Dimas, California, consulting company. Misner, who had a doctorate in organizational development, conceived the idea of getting a few business friends together to form a "networking" program. The concept flourished. Some 15 years later, BNI now claims over 33,000 members in 11 countries. In the United States alone, there are currently 1,200 chapters established in 45 states.

Like Misner and many BNI members, Hinton has found networking to be the most important factor in helping to further her own business achievements. New to the Seattle area in 1995, Hinton began operating a secretarial service from her home. Like many new business people, she harbored the common misconception that as soon as she opened shop, the phone would start ringing. It didn't. This quickly inspired her to get out and network. That is when, by chance, she met a member of BNI who encouraged her to attend one of the organization's weekly breakfast sessions. One experience was all it took to entice her to join. Hinton's business tripled in the first three months. And, things have not slowed down since.

Energized and refocused, Hinton had been a member of BNI for only a year when she became the assistant director of western Washington. She was a natural at networking and, as she discovered, mentoring others in the art as well. Through her BNI involvement, she has helped scores of people improve their communication skills and increase business sales.

"By doing presentations on a regular basis, people get more comfortable in structuring their thoughts," says Hinton. "Nobody networks better than BNI people because we practice every week."

In 1997 Hinton seized the opportunity to purchase the BNI franchise for western Washington. Over the course of the next two years, she purchased additional franchises for eastern Washington, northern Idaho and southern Idaho. Hinton now oversees a management team that covers a large portion of the Pacific Northwest region — a territory that currently consists of 29 chapters and 535 members.

BNI is truly a success story for businesses and individuals alike. As members will tell you, word-of-mouth advertising is the best advertising there is.

Executive Director Connie Hinton speaks at a BNI chapter meeting.

MWW/Savitt

When MWW/Savitt opened its offices in November of 1993, founders Kathy Savitt and Rosanne Marks were determined that it not be just another public relations firm. The agency founders saw the opportunity to build a truly national public relations practice in the burgeoning Seattle economy. And in order to build that national practice, they felt that a more strategic and business-oriented focus was required. MWW/Savitt was founded with the mission to be the world's leading company in solving complex business problems through strategic communications. In other words, simply getting press coverage wasn't good enough.

MWW/Savitt focused on gaining a depth of understanding about its clients' businesses and delivering advice, counsel and media coverage that helped its clients meet their bottom-line objectives. With creative approaches to public relations and strategic communications that take advantage of new and emerging technology as well as the social trends that change how people communicate, MWW/Savitt has pioneered a new way of practicing public relations.

MWW/Savitt's growth has mirrored that of its hometown. When the firm was founded, the local economy was in the early stages of a technology-driven expansion. Microsoft was beginning to spawn small software startups — the Baby Bills. MWW/Savitt represented a number of these software companies and related technology companies as they launched, established a market and, ultimately, often sold to a larger company. At the same time, MWW/Savitt also represented some of the local premier brands — QFC, The Ackerley Group, Starbucks — that were seeking to expand their businesses beyond local borders and appreciated a communications partner with a more national approach and viewpoint.

As the Internet boom occurred in Seattle, MWW/Savitt also contributed significantly to the dialogue and thinking around the new world of communications. The company represented some important Internet pioneers and venture capital firms. Additionally, in a world where relationships and the endorsement of powerful opinion leaders actually created valuation for companies, MWW/Savitt pioneered a practice in influencer relations. This practice involves identifying the cadre of 50 to 200 people who can contribute to the success of a company and then developing communication messages and strategies to help transform these people into supporters and evangelists for the company. MWW/Savitt owes much of its own success to the implementation of an effective influencer relations strategy for its own business.

As Seattle ends the first 150 years of its pioneer history and looks forward to its next phase of growth, MWW/Savitt looks forward to new frontiers of its own. In November 2000 the firm and its parent, MWW Group, were bought by PR giant Golin/Harris and its holding company, the Interpublic Group. As a result, MWW/Savitt clients can now explore the frontiers of public relations counsel in Europe, Asia and South America. The company is retaining its own culture and identity while enjoying new opportunities for itself, its clients and its employees.

MWW/Savitt President Kathy Savitt

Staff members demonstrate their creativity on the Team Wall in the MWW/Savitt lobby. Photo by Fritz Dent

OFFICELEASE

Finding an ideal office space in the Seattle area is no small feat. Companies face an ever-changing real estate environment, while even more daunting are negotiations with landlords and their leasing agents. Tenants must also coordinate the efforts of architects, project managers, attorneys, moving companies and other information and communication technology specialists. To confront these formidable tasks, companies seek help from OfficeLease, an independent tenant representative providing strategic real estate planning, lease and purchase negotiations, and financial analyses to corporate clients throughout the Puget Sound.

Recognizing the need to provide tenants with resources already available to landlords, Paul Suzman founded OfficeLease — originally named Business Space Resources — in 1981 and coined the phrase "Tenant Representative" in the Pacific Northwest. For over 20 years the company has exclusively represented commercial space users, maintaining its independence from property owners, developers or listing brokers. OfficeLease professionals monitor the pulse of the real estate market to keep clients informed of the latest trends. Anticipating the shift toward e-commerce, Suzman bought the OfficeLease Web domain in 1995 before changing the company name.

As the Seattle partner of International Tenant Representatives Alliance (ITRA), a group of exclusive tenant representatives in over 40 cities, OfficeLease works with its national partners to pool knowledge of local markets for the benefit of national and regional clients. Membership in ITRA, by invitation only, is limited to licensed single-agency tenant representatives with proven experience that successfully complete a rigorous application and screening process.

OfficeLease has no trouble exceeding ITRA standards. The firm's principals, Suzman, Don MacLaren and Larry Pflughoeft, have used their combined 60 years of skills, knowledge and experience to negotiate over 5 million square feet of facilities for prominent local companies including Nordstrom, PaineWebber, Microvision and Frank Russell Company. Still, OfficeLease does not measure success simply in terms of square footage, but by the quality of the relationships it facilitates. According to Suzman, facilitating a lease agreement is akin to arranging a marriage — both are long-term partnerships.

Tenant clients can expect exclusive representation; nationwide access to timely and objective information; expertise in analyzing and structuring transactions; skilled, diplomatic third-party negotiations; and comprehensive real estate advice on property acquisition and leasing. Clients are encouraged to consider key variables such as how a building's design, telecom and cabling systems, accessibility and neighborhood amenities might attract and retain talented employees. In other words, is the facility an asset from which a client can expect an Internal Rate of Return?

Satisfied tenants offer praise for OfficeLease's abilities. Thom Emrich of Mithun wrote: "Your thought-provoking questions during our search for space... captured the essence of our firm culture. Your connections within the real estate community opened doors to spaces that offered unique opportunities... Your ability to understand our nature provided us with an outside voice of reason in which we could trust. Your focused, direct support of our position during lease negotiations minimized our long-term financial exposure. In short, you provided a type and quality of service more than a cut above the typical 'full service' real estate broker." When it comes time to negotiate, OfficeLease extends a hand to link tenants and landlords in successful long-term partnerships.

OfficeLease identified Pier 56 as the perfect home for Mithun Architects.

OfficeLease identified the Lake Union Steam Plant for Zymogenetics' new home.

PRESTON GATES & ELLIS LLP

Too bad Harold Preston isn't around to see what has become of the Seattle law firm he founded in 1883. Now called Preston Gates & Ellis LLP, this full-service firm of more than 350 lawyers has offices in five states as well as Washington, D.C., and Hong Kong. Preston Gates attorneys play a prominent role in the business and civic life of each of the communities where the firm's offices are located, and are deeply involved in the new economy.

For decades Preston Gates has been known for its municipal bond expertise. The firm began doing bond work in 1912 when Harold Preston formed a partnership with Oliver Bernard (O.B.) Thorgrimson. Thorgrimson was known as the best bond lawyer in the Northwest and the only one whose legal opinions Eastern bond buyers

Managing Partner B. Gerald Johnson oversees over 350 Preston Gates attorneys in 11 offices across the United States and Hong Kong.
Photo by Richard Morgenstein

Partner Gary Kocher leads the Emerging Business Practice Group for Preston Gates along with Partner Connie Collingsworth.
Photo by Richard Morgenstein

trusted. They still trust these opinions, which is why Preston Gates annually handles more than half the bond issues in the Northwest, including high-profile financings such as SAFECO Field, the Seattle Mariners ballpark that opened in 1999.

In recent years, Preston Gates has also become one of the country's leading technology/intellectual property law firms, serving a broad spectrum of high-tech clients, from e-commerce startups to industry giants. For these and its many other business clients, Preston Gates offers a full complement of legal services, such as advice on business structuring, financing, alliances, licensing, acquisitions and global commerce.

Additionally, the firm has one of the largest, most experienced groups of environmental lawyers on the West Coast. It also has a substantial litigation department and a highly qualified team that manages large volumes of paper and electronic documents for clients and other lawyers.

In addition to quality legal work, the lawyers at Preston Gates are known for their civic achievements. In the 1950s, now-retired partner James R. Ellis conceived of and led the drive for METRO (the Municipality of Metropolitan Seattle). A decade later, he helped implement Forward Thrust, a program that produced the Kingdome and the Seattle Aquarium. William H. Gates, another highly regarded Preston Gates lawyer, found time while he was practicing to serve as a trustee, officer or volunteer for more than two dozen Northwest organizations and numerous bar associations, inspiring others to do the same.

In every Preston Gates office, lawyers annually devote many hours serving on nonprofit boards, providing legal services to the needy and otherwise making their communities a better place to live and work. The firm's commitment to civic service is memorialized in a statement of shared values to which all Preston Gates lawyers and staff subscribe.

It's a commitment Harold Preston would surely understand. Despite a busy law practice, Preston served as a Washington state senator (1897-1901). He also drafted the state's first workers' compensation law. Were he still alive, Preston would be proud that the law firm he founded over 100 years ago is continuing the tradition of civic service he began. And he'd be amazed at what a legal powerhouse the firm has become both regionally and nationally.

SHAPIRO AND ASSOCIATES, INC.

Environmental consultant Shapiro and Associates was founded in historic Pioneer Square in 1974, when the environmental industry was in its youth — Earth Day was 4 years old, the National Environmental Policy Act was 5, and the Clean Water Act would not be established for another three years.

Recognizing a need in this new industry for thorough, objective and clearly written environmental documents, Shapiro was established to provide natural resources, land-use planning, and regulatory assistance to agency decision makers and private clients. Under the leadership of owners Sue Sander and Marc Boulé, who have been at Shapiro for 26 and 25 years respectively, the company has provided environmental documentation for regionally significant projects, including several that have addressed regional issues and shaped the personality of Seattle.

Shapiro prepared environmental documentation for the Seattle Municipal Civic Center, which will create a governmental center for the city; Harbor Steps, a development project that was the final link connecting the city from Interstate 5 to the waterfront; and Elliott Bay Marina, the last large-scale marina built on Puget Sound. Shapiro also contributed to the South Downtown Waterfront Master Plan and Seattle Commons Environmental Impact Statement (EIS), and has prepared transportation studies for several construction and renovation projects under Seattle Schools Building Excellence Program.

Soccer Stadium & Exhibition Center
Home of the Seattle Seahawks

From a regional transportation perspective, Shapiro prepared the EIS for the proposed second Tacoma Narrows Bridge, which was the first public-private initiative approved by the state Legislature; EIS sections and wetland mitigation plans for Seattle's First Avenue South Bridge; and environmental documentation that allowed Burlington Northern Santa Fe Railway to re-establish passenger rail service between Seattle and Vancouver, B.C. Shapiro also worked with the Port of Seattle on the EIS for a new Sea-Tac Airport Master Plan and third runway, and with Boeing in preparing wetland mitigation plans and permits for its Customer Service Training Center, where training is conducted for Boeing's 777 crews.

Water quality is another major regional issue. Shapiro wrote the EIS on the Tolt Filtration Plant and continues to provide environmental documentation for various segments of the Tolt Pipeline. With the listings of several fish species under the Endangered Species Act, Shapiro has been involved in assisting King, Pierce and Snohomish counties with an urban issues plan. The company also works with developers, builders and private waterfront landowners to comply with ESA regulations.

As people work harder, recreation becomes more important. Shapiro prepared EISs for the Mariners' Safeco Field, the Seahawks' Stadium and Exhibition Center, and Emerald Downs Racetrack. These projects were on accelerated schedules to allow a rapid start to construction. Shapiro also prepared environmental documentation for improvements to Woodland Park Zoo and a TrendWest destination resort in Cle Elum.

Shapiro's commitment to the environment extends beyond its core business. Staff members partner with the national Student Conservation Association on a variety of restoration projects at sites throughout Puget Sound.

Expanding to include offices in Portland, Oregon, and Boise, Idaho, Shapiro's clients range from federal, state and local jurisdictions, to business and industry and individual landowners. Shapiro's mission remains constant as it strives to help clients achieve their planning and development goals while responding to dynamic environmental regulatory demands.

Shapiro prepared a fast-track EIS for the new Seattle Seahawks football stadium and nearby exhibition hall being constructed on the site of the old Kingdome in Seattle's historic Pioneer Square/International District.

Under an innovative design-build, public-private partnership, Shapiro conducted environmental studies, wrote the EIS and provided permitting assistance for construction of a second Tacoma Narrows Bridge.

Quality of Life

Educational, medical and religious institutions as well as
retirement, recreational and community organizations contribute
to the quality of life enjoyed in Seattle.

CHILDREN'S HOSPITAL & REGIONAL MEDICAL CENTER

For more than 90 years Children's Hospital & Regional Medical Center has been the premier pediatric referral center for children throughout Washington, Alaska, Montana and Idaho. Children's has become nationally recognized for its various specialties and involvement as a pediatric teaching hospital associated with the University of Washington School of Medicine.

The hospital began in 1907 as Children's Orthopedic Hospital, due to the vision of one person: Anna Clise. Following the death of her 5-year-old son, Willis, from inflammatory rheumatism, Clise devoted the next nine years of her life to researching and establishing a hospital dedicated solely to children. Her cousin, Dr. John Musser, president of the American Medical Association, advised Clise, "There is nothing so important to be done as service to children. Look about and see what is being done for them in your state. Find out what is *not* being done that is necessary and worthy, and do that."

Nineteenth-century Seattle had hospitals serving charity cases and the growing middle class. There were even facilities to treat deaf, mute or blind children. But medicine wasn't a particularly profitable business during this era. With only 67 doctors listed in the 1900 city directory, medical care was confined mostly to either those in critical need or those who could pay.

On January 4, 1907, Anna Clise gathered 23 of her friends together and explained they would be opening a hospital catering to children suffering from tuberculosis, osteomyelitis and malnutrition. These ladies were the wives of Seattle's movers and shakers and became trustees of the fledgling hospital. They were encouraged to participate in

Trustees and children pose on the back porch of the Fresh Air Cottage.

the endeavor by using their time and energy in a constructive manner. The first year's budget of $480 was raised at the same meeting.

Surgeons Dr. Caspar W. Sharples, Dr. Park Weed Willis and Dr. Frederick Fassett were recruited as staff physicians. With the trustees' approval, the doctors proposed that payment from patients would be contingent on a family's ability to pay, with the poor or indigent having first preference for admission. In February of that year, the Children's Orthopedic Hospital Association Ward was opened at Seattle General Hospital. In October, Madeline, a 14-year-old African-American girl who suffered from tuberculosis, was admitted and the trustees voted to accept any child regardless of race, religion or the parent's ability to pay.

By June 1, 1908, the trustees were able to build the Fresh Air Cottage on Queen Anne Hill at the corner of Warren and Crockett streets. In those days, fresh air was seen as the way to hasten recovery from disease, so the Children's 12-bed hospital featured outdoor porches, decks and patios. Classroom instruction for patients began that fall with trustees serving as teachers.

Today, recognized by *Child Magazine* as one of the top three pediatric hospitals in the country, Children's Hospital continues the mission begun by Anna Clise so long ago, residing at the Laurelhurst property gifted to the hospital in 1950. With over 200 beds and a staff of 2,500, including a medical staff of 1,000, Children's continues to have a positive impact on the surrounding community. Over 900 dedicated volunteers contribute nearly 125,000 hours of service each month.

The 12-bed Fresh Air Cottage, 1907

Affiliated with the University of Washington School of Medicine, Children's operates as a private, nonprofit hospital. Not only do resident, intern and nursing students do their training here, they extend their training to the entire Pacific Northwest service region of the hospital. This means that Children's Hospital & Regional Medical Center services the largest geographical area of any similar facility in the country.

Treuman Katz, president and chief executive officer of Children's, says that philanthropy has always been a major part of the hospital. "The biggest achievement from my perspective is that we have remained true to our mission: our philosophy of not turning any child away due to the parent's inability to pay remains intact."

Children's success is due in large part to support from a generous community as well as sound financial management. The responsibility for raising private funds is shared by the Children's Hospital Foundation and the Children's Hospital Guild Association. More than 50 percent of the approximately $25 million raised annually is unrestricted, meaning this money can be directed toward maintaining the hospital's main mission. The remainder goes to research, capital improvement and patient care. Over $20 million in care is allocated each year for patients whose parents can not pay for some or all of the cost of their medical care.

Children's provides the highest-quality medical care, combining the latest medical research with compassion and understanding for the special needs of children and their families. More than simply a world-class medical facility, Children's has a well-deserved reputation for being a caring, child-friendly environment where doctors and staff truly know children. This is because they only treat children. Families are also very involved and are part of the care team.

Partnerships with other leading medical and research facilities ensure patients will receive exceptional care, both now and in the future. In an effort to speed the development of new treatments for cancers and provide integrated cancer care, the Fred Hutchinson Cancer Research Center, the University of Washington and Children's have formed the Seattle Cancer Care Alliance (SCCA). Other new partnerships with health care providers throughout the Puget Sound area and a number of regional specialty clinics exist to provide a broader range of medical treatment to children throughout the Pacific Northwest.

Nephrology patients with Dr. Sandy Watkins

With over $13 million from external grant funding and nearly 40 internal research endowments, research will remain a major focus to carry Children's Hospital far into the future. Since 1990, research projects have more than doubled at Children's and funding has increased by over 160 percent. Doctors and scientists have been working on a broad spectrum of pediatric health issues with special emphasis in infectious disease, virology, audiology, gastroenterology, oncology and cystic fibrosis.

The hospital also serves as an advocate for the health and well-being of all children. Such a high level of patient care would not be possible without the tremendous support from donors, volunteers and guild members. This commitment has led the hospital to join campaigns for safety standards on things such as drowning prevention and bicycle helmets. Children's has also taken great strides in understanding the causes and helping to prevent Sudden Infant Death Syndrome and Shaken Baby Syndrome.

The Main Campus of Children's Hospital & Regional Medical Center

If Anna Clise were alive today, she would be happy to see how the hospital has continued to grow. After losing her sight in 1914, following unsuccessful surgery for glaucoma, she moved to California but her interest in the well-being of the hospital and its patients never ended. Her vision and hard work are still seen in the success and renown of Children's Hospital & Regional Medical Center. She would find comfort in the fact that "No one knows children like Children's," and the mission is still intact.

ECONOMIC DEVELOPMENT COUNCIL

When the aerospace industry took a dramatic nose dive in the late 1960s, The Boeing Company laid off 86,000 workers over three years, gripping the Seattle region with a recession and triggering a migration of people out of the city in search of work.

A billboard along Interstate 5 read, "The last one out, please turn out the lights."

Faced with one of the region's worst recessions, a desperate business community developed a plan to revitalize the Puget Sound region. They would band together, forming an organization that would recruit and retain businesses. Out of that economic downturn in 1971, the Economic Development Council of Seattle and King County (EDC) was born. Originally called the Puget Sound Economic Development Council, the organization's intent was to avoid a similar recession in the future.

Today, the EDC is a private, nonprofit organization funded by a coalition of business, government, education and community interests joined by a common goal: the health of the county's economy. In general, when the economy is good, the organization's primary focus is on retention; when the economy goes into a downward spiral as it did in 1971, the emphasis is on recruitment. For the most part, the EDC works directly with visiting or local businesses in providing siting, permitting and financing assistance and selling King County as a great place in which to live and do business.

With a membership of 134, the mission of the EDC is to build an economically vibrant and globally competitive region that helps local businesses thrive while attracting innovative new companies to King County. The EDC's six-member staff actively coordinates its job creation efforts with local organizations, including chambers of commerce. Its recruitment process includes finding a facility for a potential company and acting as the liaison between the local jurisdiction and the company, helping to cut through the red tape. Oftentimes, expediting the process means the difference between a company coming to King County or going elsewhere.

The EDC responded to over 800 inquiries in 2000, representing over 11,000 potential jobs for King County. EDC successful clients provided up to $48 million in annual new wages and $32 million in annual retained wages. In 2000, EDC client companies were located in 25 states, with a majority of them in Washington, Oregon, California, Texas, Pennsylvania and New Jersey.

Retention efforts by the EDC have often kept businesses from moving out of King County. That was true when Honeywell nearly pulled out of Redmond. The EDC intervened, documenting the reasons why the company should stay. As a result, 800 jobs remained in Redmond and the company relocated 400 new jobs from Florida. "We often act as middle person between business and government," says Richard Chapman, EDC vice president. "If we didn't step up in Redmond, those jobs would most likely be gone."

The EDC also works with King County businesses to find new sites. When the Port of Seattle expanded its operations to Harbor Island, 50 businesses needed to relocate from the Seattle location. The EDC met

The objective of the Economic Development Council of Seattle and King County is to maintain economic prosperity for the area. *Photo by Don Wilson/Port of Seattle*

with every business owner to inform them about government and community programs available to help in the relocation process. All along, EDC emphasized the importance of staying in King County. Out of the 50 businesses, 46 remained in the county.

In the 1970s and 80s, the EDC's primary function was to diversify King County's business makeup, making it less susceptible to the downturns of one specific business — Boeing. The success of the regional diversification strategy was evident when Boeing laid off 30,000 workers in 1999. The job-growth rates slowed only from 4.5 percent the previous year to 2 percent in 1999 and 1.7 percent the following year. The continued economic growth was due to the success of Microsoft and the software industry as well as Immunex and the biotechnology industry.

One of EDC's big success stories of the 1990s was the recruitment of Capital One, the Fortune 500 financial services and credit card company. In its search to locate its West Coast regional office, Capital One had a long list of prospects. EDC convinced Capital One executives that Federal Way was the ideal site because of relatively inexpensive commercial real estate, affordable housing prices, a good K-12 school system and a capable work force. Convinced, Capital One bought 20 acres and plans to employ 1,000 people by 2002.

The EDC is not only an advocate for coming to King County, but it also informs companies offering employees less than $6 or $7 an hour to seriously consider locating elsewhere. The EDC knows that those wages won't be able to compete against the in-county companies already offering $10 an hour and higher. "We provide unbiased information by telling them point blank it may not be in their best interest to locate in King County and refer them to other parts of Washington state," Chapman said. "We're not going to convince a company to come here if it's not a good fit for the county and company. Our job then is to find a suitable area within the state for that company."

In 1995 the EDC redefined its role when the leadership of the business community asked that the EDC focus specifically on the attraction and retention of high-technology and manufacturing businesses.

The EDC realizes that prosperity is not guaranteed. That is why the EDC is the secretariat of the Action Plan

Photo by Don Wilson/ Port of Seattle

for Continued Prosperity for King County. The Action Plan is a vehicle for connecting the many entities, both public and private, that are actively engaged in the efforts to meet the economic development challenges facing

TODAY, THE EDC IS A PRIVATE, NONPROFIT ORGANIZATION FUNDED BY A COALITION OF BUSINESS, GOVERNMENT, EDUCATION AND COMMUNITY INTERESTS JOINED BY A COMMON GOAL: THE HEALTH OF THE COUNTY'S ECONOMY.

King County and the region as a whole. Future economic health depends on successfully responding to competition from other states, redevelopment and more efficient use of a limited land supply, meeting the demand for skilled workers, helping businesses obtain permits and solving transportation congestion. The EDC remains committed to the continued prosperity in King County through its coordinated business development efforts.

GREATER SEATTLE CHAMBER OF COMMERCE

From its first meeting in April 1882, the Greater Seattle Chamber of Commerce has been Seattle's most powerful and enthusiastic advocate, playing a part in nearly every major development affecting the city. In 1882 Seattle had only 4,000 residents and little in the way of infrastructure. Although Seattle enjoyed a diverse business community, a lack of organization and cooperation among its masters of commerce meant that Seattle was too dependent upon the more developed cities of Portland and San Francisco for supplies. The Greater Seattle Chamber of Commerce would quickly change all that.

The Seattle Chamber was formed to protect Seattle business interests, and the first battle was with Portland, Oregon. James Ludlow, a Seattle resident and Baptist minister, was planning to undertake an evangelical mission to the north, traveling through Washington, British Columbia and Alaska by steamboat. Seattle businessman John Leary realized that Ludlow's boat could carry mail as well as Bibles. When the Portland Board of Trade attempted to interfere, Leary urged Seattle's business community to form a chamber of commerce capable of handling such situations. Without organization, Leary argued, Seattle would continue to lose out to more established and powerful cities. The chamber was formed, the battle was fought, and Seattle retained the right to carry the mail to Alaska. It was an important first fight: not only did Seattle now have a functioning chamber, it had a crucial line of communication with Alaska — a connection that would prove vital to Seattle in the near future.

When the Great Seattle Fire of 1889 wiped out 60 acres of Seattle's downtown, destroying the business district and every pier on the waterfront, the Greater Seattle Chamber of Commerce was quick to respond. It encouraged businesses to reopen as quickly as possible. Using the fire to the city's advantage, the chamber pushed for planned rebuilding: this time Seattle would have wider streets, a better sewage system and fire-resistant buildings. Thanks in large part to the chamber's efforts, the Seattle that rose from the ashes was far superior to the one that had gone before.

Another of the chamber's most important victories was the railroad. Northern Pacific Railroad had built its terminus in Tacoma, and Seattle was unable to get a tie-in line. Passengers and cargo had to go between Seattle and Tacoma by ship, resulting in extra expense and time lost. Fortunately, another railroad magnate, James Hill of Great Northern Railroad, was interested in making Seattle his railroad terminus. With the assistance of chamber member Judge Burke, Hill managed to get the land for his railroad, and the Great Northern Railroad laid its rails in Seattle in 1893. It wasn't a moment too soon. The Panic of 1893 destroyed many businesses nationwide, but Seattle was able to continue exporting goods and raw materials by rail across the country. Seattle not only survived the depression, but was also perfectly placed to benefit from America's newest cash crop: gold.

In July 1897 the steamship *Portland* came from Alaska bearing a huge cargo of gold. The Greater Seattle Chamber of Commerce reacted quickly, knowing that the gold discovery could mean huge economic advantages for Seattle. It hired Erastus Brainerd to market Seattle as the logical jumping-off point for gold seekers: Seattle businesses could provide miners with all the equipment necessary for survival and success in Alaska. Brainerd marketed Seattle to the world, and miners flocked to

A newly completed Smith Tower dwarfs one of the city's older landmarks, the Seattle Hotel at First Avenue and Yesler Way, 1915.

(Far left)
The Columbia Center
and the Seattle skyline
at sunset
Photo by Brian Huntoon

Seattle, the Space
Needle and Mt. Rainier
viewed from Kerry Park
Photo by Brian Huntoon

The setting sun reflects
off buildings of
downtown Seattle.
Photo by Brian Huntoon

Seattle for pickaxes, camp stoves, saddles, blankets, even dehydrated food and evaporated milk.

Throughout its history, the Greater Seattle Chamber of Commerce has focused its time and efforts on issues that impact Seattle's economic prosperity and quality of life. To attract business, Seattle must be an attractive place to do business. To that end, the chamber addresses concerns such as education, the environment, recreation and traffic through its special and affiliated programs. Building and maintaining Seattle's infrastructure is essential, so the chamber is involved with a wide range of activities, including leadership training, housing development for moderate-income families, local sports franchises and nonprofit arts organizations. The chamber assists and advises minority business owners, works in partnership with local public schools and lobbies for business concerns with state and local government officials.

With the Puget Sound region on the list as one of the most congested areas in the country, transportation continues to be a top chamber priority. Together with other business groups and the Washington Transportation Alliance, the Seattle Chamber continues to advocate for the development of integrated, comprehensive, world-class transportation systems and the funding mechanisms needed to sustain them.

The Seattle Chamber also recognizes that educational quality and achievement are critical to the region's competitiveness in the global economy. Through its partner organization, the Alliance for Education, the chamber supports the Seattle School District's efforts to create a "world-class, student-focused learning system" that ensures every child meets state and district standards for academic achievement.

Serving Seattle frequently involves looking outside the borders of the city. With the chamber's support and encouragement, Seattle has built links to the greater global economy. The region was linked to and trading with Asia long before other American cities were; it was one of the first cities to reconnect with Japan after World War II. In the late 1800s, Seattle already housed several foreign consulates. To keep traffic between Seattle and the rest of the world running smoothly, the chamber has fought hard for improvements to Seattle's docks, airports and railroads.

Seattle has always attracted unconventional entrepreneurs. From the first settlers willing to go West, to miners searching for gold, Seattle citizens have a tradition of risk-taking. The Greater Seattle Chamber of Commerce has always celebrated and supported that spirit. Chamber members know that the diversity of talents and interests in the city is the key to Seattle's continued economic growth and vitality. The chamber's willingness to get involved in a broad range of issues and to participate in hands-on activities that directly affect the quality of life in Seattle ensures residents and business owners that Seattle will remain a great place to live and do business.

HIGHLINE COMMUNITY HOSPITAL HEALTH CARE NETWORK

Highline Community Hospital (HCH) is a non-profit, community-owned hospital located minutes southwest of Seattle in Burien, a friendly community on Puget Sound that feels more like a small town than a suburb. HCH opened in 1958 as Burien General Hospital and in 1978 became Highline Community Hospital reflecting a broader service area. Today, the Highline Community Hospital Health Care Network offers the people of southwest King County acute hospital care, inpatient specialty care, a network of health clinics, and approximately 200 physicians and health care providers.

Highline Community Hospital has 269 beds on two hospital campuses. In addition, the 27-bed Regional Hospital for Respiratory and Complex Care is a "hospital within a hospital" caring for the region's ventilator-dependent patients. Highline's acute care campus, located in Burien, offers comprehensive 24-hour emergency and trauma care, a state-of-the-art family childbirth center, inpatient medical/surgical care, intensive care, cardiac care and cancer care. The Specialty Center campus, located a few minutes east in Tukwila, offers geropsychiatry and rehabilitation services, synergos/head injury, recovery services/chemical dependency, home health/hospice and rehab restorative care. In 2000, Highline Community Hospital admitted 8,630 patients, delivered 1,272 babies and served 48,535 patients through the emergency departments.

In addition to a comprehensive array of acute and specialty care services, Highline has long been committed to providing the people of southwest King County with some of the most advanced diagnostic technology available. From high-resolution, magnetic resonance imaging to state-of-the-art stereotactic needle biopsy and highly advanced diagnostic cardiac procedures, Highline remains committed to ensuring that patients can receive the care they need right in their own community.

Highline is proud to be the only Planetree affiliate hospital in Washington state. The name Planetree comes from the legend that Hippocrates, the father of medicine, taught his first students under the sycamore or "Planetree" that caring for the sick included providing comfort and compassion and maintaining patients' dignity. The Planetree philosophy of care is dedicated to cultivating healing in a pleasant, caring and homelike environment while encouraging family involvement, providing easy access to health care information and embracing the healing arts. Because a patient's environment can play a role in the healing process, the patients' surroundings at HCH incorporate elements of Planetree. One example is the design of the Cedar Wing that opened in late 1998 on the Burien campus. This new wing is home to a state-of-the-art Family Childbirth Center, Medical/Oncology Unit, community health education center and an exercise facility for cardiac rehab patients.

The Cedar Wing added over 97,000 square feet to Highline Community Hospital and provides both the latest technology and comfortable surroundings for patients and their families. The Family Childbirth Center features private birthing suites equipped with TV/VCRs, stereo

Highline Community Hospital, Burien Campus

Highline Specialty Center in Tukwila

systems, private bathrooms, whirlpool tubs and sleeper sofas for support persons. Each suite has been uniquely designed with generously sized windows, finely detailed wood cabinetry, warm colors and unique wall coverings.

The new Medical/Oncology unit also features private rooms decorated in soothing colors with finely crafted woodwork, large windows and sleeping space in patient rooms for family members. This unit does not have a traditional nursing station; caregivers are positioned with work areas just outside each patient room, encouraging open communication with patients and their families. Both patient care floors in the new wing provide spatial alternatives to the customary family areas, as they are designed with a fully equipped kitchen, resource library and an open area for family and visitors.

In addition to the warm and comforting surroundings of the Cedar Wing, the Planetree Health Library and the Healing Garden also provide quiet spaces for families and staff. The library offers books, periodicals, medical texts, clipping files and a computer reference system that provides access to a vast array of information. The hospital's healing gardens on both the Highline and Specialty Center campuses provide peaceful sanctuaries for patients, families and staff.

Involvement of family or close friends as care partners in a patient's treatment plan is another key element of Planetree at Highline. A Care Partner is someone chosen by the patient to be involved in his or her care and treatment. This support is helpful in relieving a patient's anxiety and isolation. Care Partners are given tours of the patient care areas, patient/family lounges, kitchen areas and libraries so they will be familiar with their surroundings. The personal touch provided by a Care Partner promotes healing by lending emotional and spiritual support to the patient.

As part of the Planetree Patient Information Program, health and medical information is made available to patients while they are hospitalized. Each hospital unit has a resource library with an assortment of reference books and brochures. Information packets are also made available on specific medical conditions. Staff is trained to ask every patient about their informational needs. In addition, music, art aromatherapy, meditation, healing gardens and hands-on patient comfort measures, such as massage, are all part of the healing arts programs at Highline. These comfort measures help to enhance the healing process.

While the Highline network has grown over the years, the mission has remained the same. Highline works in many ways to meet the health care needs of the communities it

Birthing suite in new Family Childbirth Center

serves. A recent example includes the partnership between Highline Community Hospital and Health Care Network and the Seattle-King County Department of Public Health to open a health clinic in White Center. This clinic serves a diverse population with many barriers to obtaining traditional health care, including language, culture, transportation, unemployment and poverty. The clinic offers primary care, maternity care, pediatrics, and interpretive and maternity case management services to residents of White Center and surrounding communities. Since the clinic opened its doors in 1999, over 12,000 patients have been seen. In 2000 the HCH Health Care Network received the Washington State Hospital Association Year 2000 Health Care Leadership Award for establishing the Roxbury Clinic in White Center.

After more than 40 years of providing health care to the community, Highline continues to work hard to fulfill its mission of providing quality, compassionate, accessible and affordable health care that meets the needs of the people in the communities it serves.

Highline Community Hospital, Burien, c. 1959

PLANNED PARENTHOOD

In 1935 the nation was in midst of the Depression. There was little work to be found in Seattle, and most families were struggling to provide adequate housing, food and medical care. In a society where many children were once considered a blessing, the difficult times made the addition of even one more mouth to feed a heart-wrenching strain on family resources. Recognizing the need for affordable, medically supervised family planning, Mrs. Robert Percy, a registered nurse, began seeing women to dispense contraceptives and give referrals to doctors in Seattle. With the assistance of the Church of the People, Mrs. Percy was soon seeing all the patients she could handle in the basement of her home.

First family planning clinic in the United States, Brooklyn, New York, 1916

Caring, professional medical care
Saul Bromberger Sandra Hoover Photography

In 1939 a board of directors was formed and the agency received accreditation from Planned Parenthood Federation of America, a national, nonprofit organization founded in 1916 in New York by Margaret Sanger. A nurse and pioneer of modern family planning, Sanger was a fervent opponent of the 1873 Comstock law that banned the public dissemination of contraceptive information, which prevented women from making informed, safe decisions about their reproductive health. One of 11 children herself, Sanger saw her young mother die of tuberculosis, brought on by too frequent pregnancies. As a result of this traumatic experience as well as the distress she felt seeing women dying of self-induced abortions, Sanger established Planned Parenthood to provide a safe harbor of education, medical care and women's health advocacy.

The Seattle agency quickly grew due to the efforts of many concerned and committed volunteers. In 1940 its first clinic opened in a Broadway storefront. News of Planned Parenthood in Seattle spread largely by word-of-mouth and soon there were lines of women up and down the sidewalk, waiting to get in.

The early days were a struggle financially. The clinic had been built in an old laundry with rustic facilities and a burgeoning caseload. The privy facilities were in the back yard. The beds were old army racks and the dividers were sheets and cardboard, but still the women came. The clinic's meager resources were soon stretched to the breaking point.

In 1945 the Planned Parenthood board reluctantly went to the public for support. While the clinics nationwide had sometimes met with legal challenges and even had their staff members jailed, Seattle was more welcoming of the Planned Parenthood mission. The city's newspapers reported that "scores of socially prominent men and women... engaged in a drive to raise $10,000 for the Family Planning Center." Representatives of the organization were eventually invited to speak in area schools,

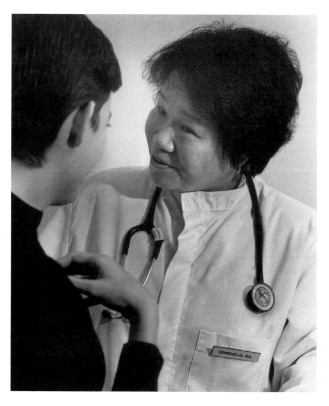

Scout and Campfire meetings, as well as with other groups. Often, the family planning information was the only education of its kind that students received. Former board member Lenore McIntyre remembers "a lot of parents didn't want family planning talked about... but the questions I would get from these students... were all about contraceptives."

Far from discouraging people from having children, Planned Parenthood encourages families to plan ahead and make every child a wanted child. Planned Parenthood provides federally approved birth control methods, including emergency contraception. Often confused with the unrelated prescription drug RU486, emergency contraception allows women to prevent pregnancy before conception, within a 72-hour window. With the advent of AIDS, Planned Parenthood added affordable HIV testing and counseling to its other essential services such as Pap smears, breast exams and STD treatment. The clinics also provide detection and treatment of cervical cancer and related disorders. All services are provided confidentially and include outstanding prenatal and adoption referrals. As part of its educational mission, the clinics also counsel young women on the dangers of using drugs like "ecstasy" and cocaine, which inhibit responsible decision making. Its Sex Information Line is the only resource between Seattle and California where someone can talk to a real person about issues related to sexuality. This range and accessibility of professional services have made Planned Parenthood the largest provider of women's health care in Washington state.

Planned Parenthood services focus mainly on women, but the group ardently encourages the involvement of men, both in the organization and in its family planning. Although 95 percent of its patients are women, men can get vasectomies, counseling, condoms and family planning information at any Planned Parenthood location.

During the organization's early years, men initially opposed the organization's goals. Original board member Emily Harris remembered that reproductive education was "a new idea, a cultural difference, so the men objected." Since then, however, the organization has recruited prominent male members of the community to its board. These include prominent businessmen like Ken Fisher and political figures like former mayor Norm Rice. Marillyn Watson, who was a board member from 1959-1992, recalled feeling that the agency needed the involvement of men, and this led to a recruiting effort on the part of the board.

Planned Parenthood has served the local community for 66 years.

Both the city of Seattle and the agency have experienced many changes over the decades and Planned Parenthood has continued to grow and meet the needs of the community. A constellation of clinics across the state advises and educates not only women but entire neighborhoods. Planned Parenthood educational efforts also helped the citizens of the state defeat both Initiative 471 (1984) and Initiative 694 (1998), which would have limited women's access to reproductive choices.

After three-quarters of a century of service, Planned Parenthood has provided Seattle with more than quality, affordable medical care, more than education and more than advocacy; it has empowered families to bring every child into life by choice, not by chance.

Community educators promote responsible decision making through reality-based sexuality discussions in schools and youth groups.

SEATTLE ACADEMY

Whether world-renowned scientist Jane Goodall is speaking to Seattle Academy students about starting a local Roots-and-Shoots chapter; whether the entire sixth-grade class is writing and publishing a professional-quality book on World War II or Seattle's love affair with water; or whether high school students and faculty are presenting, by invitation, at the Laptops Anytime Anywhere conference at the Seattle Convention Center, a Seattle Academy education takes students beyond the textbook and outside the classroom.

Located just above downtown on Seattle's Capitol Hill, Seattle Academy is an independent school that prepares students for college and life. Serving grades six through 12 with a demanding, college-preparatory curriculum, the school seeks to put students in real-world situations as an integral part of its program... not just an occasional field trip, but regular, in-depth application of what the students are learning so they may see how their lessons will help them participate effectively in modern society.

Seattle Academy's upper school is in the historic Vanderbilt Building at 12th and East Union.

Seattle Academy's satellite urban campus gives middle school and high school students a city college-style environment as they move from class to class and building to building through one of Seattle's most vibrant business and residential area communities. As a result, students develop confidence in discovering what it takes to be a citizen in a large metropolitan city.

All of Seattle Academy's graduates attend institutions of higher learning within two years of high school graduation, and they attend an impressive array of colleges, universities and conservatories, including the nation's most selective. A few graduates defer college admission for a year while they travel the world, work for local or international humanitarian organizations, or get a head start into the business world.

And, they feel they are ready.

(Far right) Seattle Academy's engaging, hands-on curriculum frequently produces this reaction.

Students say, "At Seattle Academy, we don't just study science, we do science."

Meeting the challenge of integrating and applying skills and knowledge — whether in the classroom, on the athletic field or in the arts — expands personal horizons and fosters greater self-esteem, confidence and maturity. For example, a junior biology student may conceive, develop and orally defend a scientific hypothesis to a jury of parents and experts. In doing so, students put to use knowledge learned in textbook and laboratory, creative thinking learned in the art studio, presentation skills honed on the stage, and the courage to take risks developed on the athletic field.

This engaging, real-world approach begins in middle school at Seattle Academy. For example:

Exposure

learned the importance of commitment and accountability, who can cope with ambiguity and change, who can live with ease in a multicultural society, and who have developed an understanding of the sense of purpose that comes from responsible contribution to their community.

Support is generously given to affect each student's academic and personal goals. They are encouraged to participate, to have the courage to try, to fail and to succeed, and to respect and support others who are learning through the same risk-taking process. At a time when both middle school and high school students are grappling with important personal and social issues, the academy promotes both academic achievement and effective attitudes such as accountability, honesty, compassion and purpose.

Apparent from the first time one enters its doors, Seattle Academy is a community where individuals and families find good times, helpful support and close friendships. It is an inclusive community, not an exclusive one, respecting the integrity of each person and celebrating diverse definitions of success as beneficial to a healthy community.

The city of Seattle is Seattle Academy's campus. And, when graduates return to talk to current students about what it's like out there, they return to a central message: They were prepared — not only for college, but also for life.

A Seattle Academy education goes far beyond the classroom: witness its annual outdoor adventures to the American Canyonlands or the Arctic Circle.

• Sixth-graders take the roles of journalists as they interview subjects, write and rewrite feature articles and, ultimately, see them published in book form.

• Seventh-graders, working with professional scriptwriters and videographers, write, stage and produce a video based on events in Washington state history. The video is filmed at the Museum of History and Industry, and the museum uses the finished product to demonstrate to other schools how to use museum resources in the teaching of curriculum.

• As part of their human biology studies, eighth-grade students plan and present a full-day symposium on health issues relevant to teen-agers. They present their own workshops to sixth- and seventh-grade students and also arrange for visiting scientists and keynote speakers.

The emphasis on research and communication skills intensifies in high school with original DNA research, development of math models, mock-trial, and award-winning Youth Legislature and speech and debate programs. Advanced and honors classes are offered in many disciplines, including English, history, science, statistics, calculus, acting, dance, vocal music and visual arts.

Every high school student has a laptop computer that is used throughout the curriculum, not just for word processing. Specific, subject-oriented software further afford students the opportunity to apply what they're learning in a professional setting.

Just as important as helping students build successful futures is graduating young men and women who have

A parent recently said, "The word on the street is that if you want math, you go to Seattle Academy."

SEATTLE COMMUNITY COLLEGE DISTRICT

Crossroads of Education

If Seattle has a historic crossroads of education, it must be the corner of Broadway and Pine on Capitol Hill. For nearly 100 years, students have occupied this corner, which was the site of the city's first public high school and today is home to Seattle Central Community College, the first of three colleges — North, South and Central — which comprise the Seattle Community College District.

Ever since its first campus opened on Broadway in 1966, the Seattle Community College District has been changing with the city. It has developed into the largest community college district in the state, educating 51,000 students every year.

The demand for technology careers translates into new facilities such as the High Technology Learning Center at North Seattle Community College.

At the beginning, what was then called Seattle Community College operated as part of Seattle's public school system. The demand for higher education was great. News stories at the time reported that students waited in line all night to enroll in classes. After Gov. Dan Evans signed the Community College Act of 1967, establishing community colleges as a unique system of higher education in the state, Seattle's colleges, like others in the state, grew dramatically.

On the recommendation of an educational consulting firm, two new campuses were built equally distant from downtown Seattle. By September 1970, all three colleges opened together for the first time as a multicampus district. The dreams of the early planners materialized into colleges that have become focal points of their neighborhoods:

- Seattle Central Community College on Capitol Hill
- North Seattle Community College at Northgate
- South Seattle Community College in West Seattle.

Seattle Vocational Institute, in the city's Central District, joined the district in 1991 as part of the state's Work Force Training and Education Act. The district also operates six specialized training centers throughout the city: the Duwamish Education Center; NewHolly Learning Center; RetailSkills Center; Sand Point Education Center; Seattle Maritime Academy; and Wood Construction Center.

Growing With the Region

By design, the Seattle Community Colleges reflect the region's social and economic community. The first students, members of the postwar Baby Boomer generation, chose from a curriculum that included programs such as Gregg Shorthand and keypunch operation; a self-improvement course in "Tailoring for the Homemaker"; and electronics courses featuring vacuum tubes and transistors.

Today's generation of students chooses from an array of more than 135 academic and technical programs

Historic Broadway High School building at the corner of Harvard and Pine — the center section is still in use as the Broadway Performance Hall. *Seattle Public Schools Archives*

in sophisticated fields such as biotechnology, information technology, telecommunications, and Web design. The college curriculum has not only kept pace with regional changes, it has led the way as the Puget Sound area has moved from a manufacturing and resource-based economy to service and information-based industries. Today, high technology is incorporated into almost every program of study, from culinary arts to zoology, and it is the fastest-growing area of study — the region's newest frontier.

Instruction has also changed over the decades. In the 1980s, the Seattle Community Colleges earned national recognition for pioneering the Coordinated Studies program, in which students focus on a subject from a variety of disciplines, including the sciences and the humanities. A decade later, the colleges earned similar acclaim for adopting a curriculum of Applied Academics for students in technical fields. The Seattle Community Colleges developed the nation's first engineering and electronics curriculum that integrates standards of the American Electronics Association and also led the nation in developing skills standards for manufacturing technology and engineering technology.

The Community College Act of 1967 made community colleges responsible for providing an affordable "open door" to education for all who seek it. Technology has opened the door even wider, to a degree not even imagined at mid-century. Through Internet-based distance learning, the Seattle Community Colleges reach learners across the country and on other continents. A new college cable television station brings the classroom into the homes of the local community and also broadcasts educational programming over the Internet.

Colleges in the Community

As they have grown and changed, each of the Seattle Community Colleges has continued to mirror its community. Like the city itself, the college population is dynamic, with one of the most ethnically diverse student bodies in the Northwest. All of the colleges are comprehensive and offer programs in college transfer, professional technical training, adult basic education and continuing education. However, each one also offers unique professional technical training programs in response to local needs.

At Seattle Central Community College, for example, the legacy of the 1902-era Broadway High School buildings lives on at the Broadway Performance Hall. The modern theatre space hosts a full schedule of national and international performers, while students rehearse and take classes in its music performance classrooms. During the

The High-Tech Library at South Seattle Community College symbolizes 21st-century research and learning.

1990s, the college bought and renovated the nearby Masonic Temple building to house fine arts programs. North Seattle Community College, a landmark in its highly visible location near Interstate 5, has developed into the area's premier training ground for the Puget Sound electronics industry. A new regional High Technology Learning Center is complemented by several acres of environmentally sensitive wetlands used for instruction. South Seattle Community College overlooks Elliott Bay and downtown Seattle from its 87-acre campus in residential West Seattle. While its training programs continue to reflect the region's most important industries, its new high-tech Library and Learning Center is a model for current learning environments.

A five-member board of trustees is appointed by the governor to direct each of the state's college districts. Through the years, an impressive number of community leaders have served on the board and guided the Seattle district. A president administers each college, while overall operations of the district are the responsibility of a chancellor.

Into the New Century

In the words of current Chancellor Peter C. Ku, "We exist to provide a positive and enriching impact, both for individuals and, ultimately, the entire community." More than 1 million alumni of the Seattle Community Colleges are involved in every aspect of the city and range from doctors to executive chefs, engineers to accountants, and more.

With the new century, Ku says, the district "is poised to respond to accelerating changes in the regional economy, employment needs and demographics." The Seattle Community College District faces the future ready to educate and train new generations of learners.

SWEDISH MEDICAL CENTER

In the field of health care, bigger does not always mean better — unless the provider in question is Swedish Medical Center. A once-small hospital that has grown to span 25 square blocks and three campuses, Swedish is recognized as the region's premier medical institution. The hospital has been a nonprofit entity since its inception, allowing it to continually reinvest in improving care. As a result, it has earned a reputation for expanding and upgrading facilities, leading the way in vital areas of research, and attracting physicians and staff whose expertise is unrivaled.

A Humanitarian Mission Evolves

The hospital was founded in 1910 by Swedish immigrant Dr. Nils Johanson, a surgeon who saw a need for a high-quality, nonprofit medical facility in the area. Backed by 10 Swedish-American business professionals, he opened a small, 24-bed hospital in a remodeled apartment building on Seattle's First Hill. In 1912 the board of trustees acquired a neighboring 40-bed hospital whose founder had died suddenly as the facility was about to open. Because everything in it was mono-grammed with the initials S.H. (for Summit Hospital), the board decided to keep the initials and name the new facility Swedish Hospital in honor of its heritage.

Under Dr. Johanson and President J.A. Soderberg, Swedish Hospital immediately began setting a high standard

for care. Johanson traveled the globe, bringing back the latest medical techniques — and sometimes the physicians who pioneered them. He promoted the emerging field of medical diagnostics and established a training school for nurses. And he set another enduring precedent: never turning away a person in need.

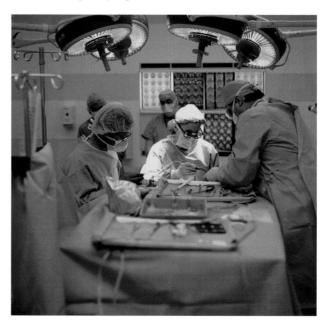

Johanson's legacy was carried on by his son-in-law, Elmer Nordstrom, who was an active board member for many years, and then by Dr. Allan Lobb, a visionary who became the hospital's first medical director in 1961. By the 1970s Swedish was a major medical center, and in 1980 it acquired Doctors Hospital and Seattle General Hospital. By the early 1990s, Swedish had become the region's largest, most comprehensive medical facility with 697 licensed beds.

In 1992 Swedish merged with Ballard Community Hospital, a full-service, 163-bed community hospital. The addition of Ballard brought a second campus and important programs, including an accredited Sleep Medicine Center, a Transitional Care Unit and a Family Childbirth Center. In July of 2000 Swedish forged a strategic alliance with Providence Health System-Washington, another health-care provider with strong patient-care programs and a rich history of community service. The alliance with Providence Seattle Medical Center gave Swedish Health Services a third medical center campus and a network of primary-care clinics located throughout King County.

Building on a Legacy of Excellence

With more than 1,400 physicians representing every major specialty, a skilled and caring nursing staff, state-of-the-art facilities, and the latest diagnostic, treatment and rehabilitation options, Swedish Medical Center is consistently rated by consumers as the area's most preferred hospital, according to independent research firm National Research Corporation. President and CEO Richard Peterson explains the reasons for such an enviable reputation: "Since its beginning, Swedish has had an unwavering commitment to excellence. This legacy describes our past, it defines our present, and it directs our future."

Today Swedish is a major regional referral center for numerous specialties. It began as a surgical hospital, and that focus continues. In 1999 alone, more than 30,000 surgeries were performed at Swedish by top surgeons in a wide variety of specialties. Swedish is a leader in areas such as orthopedic surgery, organ transplantation, neurosurgery and cardiac surgery and has garnered worldwide recognition for pioneering some of the latest procedures. With state-of-the-art operating rooms, highly skilled surgical teams and an experienced rehabilitation staff, it offers the Northwest's largest and most comprehensive surgery program.

The Swedish Heart Institute is also well recognized in the region. It performs thousands of procedures each year, including nearly 900 open-heart surgeries in 1999. From diagnostics and treatment to prevention and rehabilitation, the Heart Institute offers patients a full spectrum of the latest in cardiac care.

The Swedish Cancer Institute is a leader in oncology treatment and clinical research, providing treatment for more than 100 types of cancer. Founded in 1932 as the first cancer-care center west of the Mississippi, it now provides the latest in treatment options to more people than any other facility in the Northwest. And for neurological disorders such as epilepsy, Parkinson's disease and multiple sclerosis, the Swedish Neuroscience Institute offers exceptional care. Like the other Swedish institutes, it utilizes the most sophisticated technology, the most effective drug therapies, and a full range of rehabilitative services.

Swedish is also known for the number of babies it brings into the world. Over the years, more children have been born at Swedish than at any other hospital in the state. The Women and Infants Center offers the most advanced obstetrical care available, state-of-the-art birthing suites, and one of the region's few Level III neonatal units designed to care for the most premature and sick newborns. The Ballard campus also boasts a

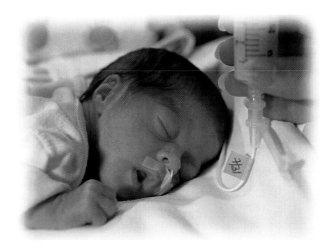

The Swedish Women and Infants Center offers one of the region's few Level III neonatal units designed to care for the most premature and sick newborns.

popular obstetrics program. In 1999 the Swedish/Ballard Family Childbirth Center received the Golden Bootie Award from the readers of *Seattle's Child* magazine for being "The Best Place to Deliver Your Baby in Seattle."

A Future Focused on People

Swedish Medical Center came into being because Dr. Nils Johanson saw a need and decided to meet it. Almost a century later, his hospital is holding fast to his humanitarian vision, committed to serving all members of the community, regardless of their medical or financial condition. Swedish provides more charity care than any other non-tax-supported institution in the state, and its foundations manage more than 40 nonprofit funds. Because it reinvests in the community, Swedish Medical Center offers a spectrum of services far exceeding traditional hospital care. By holding itself to a higher standard, it raises the bar for other medical facilities, and thus has the effect of improving care for the entire region.

More than 1,400 physicians practice at Swedish, representing virtually every medical and surgical specialty and subspecialty.

TRENDWEST RESORTS, INC.

Vacations. Those precious days each year when we cast work aside and head for the mountains, the ocean or some faraway land. Some of us go in search of adventure. Others seek peace and quiet. Some crave the comfort of the familiar, others the excitement of the unknown. But all of us want choice — the freedom to choose where we go, when we go and how long we stay. It's the American way, and perhaps no company understands that better than Trendwest Resorts, Inc.

Trendwest Resorts sells vacation-property timeshares with a twist. Instead of using the traditional timeshare model, which locks the buyer into the same week at the same resort year after year, the Redmond-based company sells "vacation credits" owners can use to "purchase" time at any condominium in the company's resort network. Owners can travel when they like, choose the size of their accommodations and vary their length of stay. The vacation-credit model gives the flexibility of public accommodations with the benefit of private ownership, and its appeal is heightened by the fact that nearly all of the resorts are an easy driving distance from major metropolitan areas where the company markets its product.

Trendwest is the only vacation ownership company of its kind, and its maverick course has proved fruitful. In just over 10 years the company has built a network of nearly 40 resorts in the Western United States, Missouri,

Hawaii, British Columbia, Mexico, Australia and Fiji. New condominium projects continue to sprout as the company extends its reach to the Southern and Eastern United States, and a staff of more than 3,000 employees serves a burgeoning membership of more the 114,000 owners. Company revenues crested the $300 million mark at the turn of the millennium, and Trendwest continues to grow at a rate of about 30 percent a year.

Those are impressive statistics for a company that began operations in 1989 with just two condominiums. Trendwest entered the market during a difficult time for the timeshare industry. During the 1970s, aggressive sales techniques and undercapitalized developments had tarnished the industry's reputation. In the 80s, government regulation helped curb risky and unethical activities, but still the product was difficult to sell. Trendwest's CEO, Bill Peare, observed that people liked the timeshare idea, but travel patterns were changing. No longer were mom, dad and the kids packing up for a week or two-week vacation somewhere far from home. Instead, the modern, dual-income family was taking shorter, more frequent excursions better suited to their busy lives. They needed the flexibility of nearby destinations and short-range planning; they wanted the security of ownership.

Trendwest's credit-based system caught on, and the company began to add new resorts to its inventory. Some were purchased, but most Trendwest has developed and built on its own. Upon completion, each resort is transferred debt-free to Trendwest's subsidiary, WorldMark, The Club. WorldMark is a nonprofit entity that operates separately from Trendwest, with its own board of directors and employees. WorldMark owns and operates the properties, Trendwest manages and develops them, and the owners' investments are protected from the uncertainties faced by for-profit corporations.

WorldMark also preserves value through a well-funded maintenance and refurbishment program. In addition to purchasing credits, owners pay an annual maintenance fee based on the number of credits they own. These fees fund ongoing preventive care to keep every condo looking like new.

(Left to right) Chief Financial Officer Tim O'Neil, Executive Vice President Al Schriber, President and Chief Executive Officer Bill Peare, Executive Vice President Gene Hensley, and Chief Operating Officer Jeff Sites

The company prides itself on exceptionally high standards of quality and service, and owners take comfort in knowing exactly what they can expect at each resort they visit. No matter where they travel, owners will find a condo in like-new condition complete with TV, VCR, CD player and fully equipped kitchen. The standard amenity package at each resort includes a spa, fitness center, swimming pool, children's pool and clubhouse — features designed to enhance comfort without inflating prices.

Affordability is key to Trendwest's success. The company has clearly identified its middle-income market and tailored its product to suit that demographic. Most owners are in their 40s or older, though the age is dropping. Most own their home and have worked at the same job for 10 years or more. Many are empty-nesters. And 16 percent of Trendwest owners are single. That figure is uniquely high in the industry, and due in large part to company efforts to offer single owners special group vacations and other benefits.

Trendwest owners own an average of 9,000 credits, valued at close to $13,000. The average stay at a resort is three days and most reservations are made 60 or fewer days in advance. These figures support Peare's theory on how Americans travel. But it's not just conjecture. In the past 10 years, Trendwest has interviewed 153 million people to find out how they vacation, and the company is always looking for new ways to offer more vacation options. Today owners can use their credits to book a small studio, a lavish penthouse or passage on a cruise ship. In addition, a partnership with Resort Condominiums International makes 3,300 RCI-affiliated resorts in 90 countries available to WorldMark owners.

Potential to offer owners new destinations is virtually unlimited, but prudently, Trendwest has tethered its growth, expanding only as quickly as it can find and develop the people to support that expansion. Staff development is a priority. The company offers in-house training through its Management University program and encourages employees to discover what they do well, develop their skills and reach their full potential.

Employees handle every function of the company, from resort construction and sales and marketing to legal services and house cleaning. Operations are

A spellbinding view from WorldMark at Depoe Bay on the Oregon coast

spread among several regional units, creating a vertically integrated company as flexible and dynamic as its product.

Looking to the future, Trendwest will be challenged to make the most of new technology as it reaches out to an ever-expanding customer base. The company's member-friendly Web site will be outfitted with e-commerce technology, and new marketing techniques will be designed to attract today's savvy consumers.

Innovation is critical, but even as the company moves forward, the people at Trendwest know it's their commitment to customer service and uncompromising standards of quality that secure the company's future and ensure that owners enjoy vacations to remember.

The Sea of Cortez sets the stage for WorldMark at Cabo.

BAYVIEW MANOR

More than a century ago, Captain George Kinnear broke ground on the sparsely populated south slope of Queen Anne Hill to build a mansion befitting a leader in early Seattle. The view from his home was as striking as the hill was steep — the Olympic Mountains to the west, Mount Rainier to the south and the Cascade Range to the east.

In 1956 the Captain's son, Charles A. Kinnear, bequeathed the property to United First Methodist Church for the care of older adults and children. The spirit of Kinnear lives on in the tall, sturdy tower of Bayview Manor, a retirement residence at the base of the busy and still very steep Queen Anne Hill. The neighborhood, one of Seattle's oldest, is home to Victorian-style homes, espresso stands, young professionals and musicians, and more than 230 residents who live at Bayview Manor. They are an active part of the local community: the Queen Anne Historical Society has an office in the Tower and several other community-based, nonprofit groups are provided with regular meeting space.

A member of the Queen Anne community since 1961, Bayview Manor's 10-story Tower includes independent and assisted-living apartments, many with sweeping views of the city. The 10th floor of the Tower provides a striking 180-degree perspective of the Seattle skyline and Elliot Bay, a view that makes a clear day in Seattle unforgettable. The Terrace building, which opened

in 1995, offers a Health Care Center that provides short-term, long-term and respite skilled nursing care.

Bayview Manor is committed to providing a holistic approach to wellness throughout the community. It provides easy access for residents as well as members of the Queen Anne area to participate in ongoing education, fitness and health promotion programs. The Senior Health Club is complete with strength training equipment, aquatics programming and an aerobics room sporting floor-to-ceiling mirrors and resilient floors. Computer classes and health lectures are also available.

> THE SPIRIT OF KINNEAR LIVES ON IN THE TALL, STURDY TOWER OF BAYVIEW MANOR, A RETIREMENT RESIDENCE AT THE BASE OF THE BUSY AND STILL VERY STEEP QUEEN ANNE HILL.

A popular and well-received Intergenerational Child Care program is located on site and provides the critical link between Bayview Manor residents and day-care children as the two groups participate in activities together. The spark of youth brings joy to the entire community. Through such innovative and creative programming, Bayview Manor has clearly succeeded in meeting the desires of Kinnear to serve members of both generations.

The future may bring more work with children. Ideas under construction include acquiring or managing existing child-care facilities. Other potential possibilities are to increase the number of assisted or independent-living units by acquiring existing buildings beyond the Tower, or integrating Bayview Manor's services to help older adults maintain their daily lives in their own homes. These approaches suggest a future in which Charles Kinnear's generous vision spreads far beyond his father's mansion, throughout the community.

CORIXA CORPORATION

Started in 1994 by Steve Gillis, Mark McDade, Ken Grabstein, Mac Cheever and Steve Reed, Corixa is a company with a mission to heal. Using a strong research foundation, Corixa is developing new products to treat or prevent disease by directing the body's immune system. The company focuses on novel therapies for autoimmune diseases, cancer and infectious diseases and is continuously developing new immune system-based technologies in the fight against a variety of illnesses in these areas.

The people who founded Corixa recognized the vast potential for a novel approach to treating disease called immunotherapy. The goal of immunotherapy is to stimulate patient immune responses through vaccination or antibody therapy to treat or eliminate disease. Current vaccines trigger the body to produce antibody responses to destroy invading pathogens. However, many diseases such as cancer or certain infectious diseases need more than just an antibody response. Corixa's vaccines have been developed to provide the boost needed to make vaccine approaches more effective. Corixa's staff, which has an impressive collective expertise in immunology, is developing new technologies that will trigger targeted immune responses that one day may treat and prevent illnesses including cancer, psoriasis, rheumatoid arthritis, allergies, multiple sclerosis and many others.

Corixa focuses on the following technology components: antigens, vaccine components that stimulate immune system responses; adjuvants, vaccine components that boost the body's immune response; antibodies, the first level of immune response to disease; and antigen delivery technology. Corixa uses each of these technologies as components of vaccines developed in-house or in vaccines produced by other companies. The goal is to produce therapy that will trigger specific and sufficient immune responses without permanently disturbing the body's normal immune system functions.

The timeline between discovery and regulatory approval of a drug is usually a very lengthy and costly procedure. In an effort to offset these costs, Corixa pioneered a "partner early and often" strategy in which it licensed some of its technologies to developers and marketers of pharmaceutical and diagnostic products. These partnerships continue to provide Corixa with considerable financial support, enabling the company to focus on development and research while amassing a product pipeline that currently includes 16 candidates in clinical trials. Any vaccines developed using Corixa components are marketed under the "Powered by Corixa™" brand, recognizing the company's contribution to safer, more effective treatments. As the company, its capital and capabilities have grown, Corixa has chosen to partner its technology only after considerable development has been successfully completed, thereby maximizing potential downstream rewards.

In addition to partnerships, an aggressive acquisition strategy gives Corixa a strong foundation. Acquisitions of Coulter Pharmaceutical, Inc. in 2000; Ribi ImmunoChem Research, Inc. in 1999; Anergen in 1999; and GenQuest in 1998 mean greater access to products, intellectual property, manufacturing facilities and technologies that complement Corixa's existing programs.

Some of Corixa's near-term product developments include Bexxar™, a treatment for non-Hodgkins lymphoma currently being reviewed for commercial approval by the FDA; Melacine®, a vaccine for malignant melanoma that is approved in Canada; and PVAC™, a treatment for mild to severe psoriasis. Committed to reducing human suffering through greater understanding and utilization of the body's natural immune system, Corixa is working to make immunotherapy an important new means of disease treatment for patients around the world.

Corixa's fourth-floor lobby on Columbia Street in Seattle

CATHOLIC COMMUNITY SERVICES AND THE ARCHDIOCESAN HOUSING AUTHORITY

A work begun with women sewing baby clothes in parish circles 80 years ago now addresses the roots of injustice, combining prophetic insight with a loving touch. Catholic Community Services (CCS) and the Archdiocesan Housing Authority (AHA) together are now the largest local, nonprofit provider of assistance to the poor and vulnerable in the Northwest. The eyes of their workers remain fixed on the faces of the poor, whom they serve regardless of race, ethnicity or creed and whose accounts of suffering reveal new rents in the social fabric and challenges to the human spirit.

CCS Family Centers

In CCS's 13 Family Centers, workers integrate all the services available in the communities they serve to nourish self-sufficiency. The goal is to achieve wholeness and well-being for every member of the family. Each year workers provide 141,000 hours of counseling and mental health services, almost 200,000 meals and emergency services and 140,000 bed nights to families in need.

The Archdiocesan Housing Authority

AHA provides a warm, safe refuge from the streets in emergency shelters where much more than a hot meal is offered to the homeless men, women and children who come in need. The agency annually provides 150,000 bed nights, access to medical attention, alcohol and drug treatment, job counseling and refugee assistance. And when shelter guests are ready, AHA will place them in one of their 1,300 units of permanent, affordable housing.

Long-Term Care Services

CCS workers come into the homes of the elderly and disabled who need daily assistance with the personal things they cannot do for themselves. For those who have no other income other than a Social Security check, CCS workers, who provide over 1.5 million hours of home services each year, offer affordable personal care to sustain them with dignity in the home they cherish.

Trying to do much with little requires that CCS and AHA continually reassess their work. Relying upon the information they receive from their people in the field, leaders consistently develop new programs to address a changing human services climate. CCS and AHA maintain the philosophy that wrapping its arms around those in need and addressing all the issues that put them in crisis, while using every resource available in the community, brings the greatest success in ushering the poor and vulnerable toward a fuller life.

The present archbishop of the Seattle Archdiocese, Archbishop Alexander J. Brunett, reminds people that if the poor are always with us, so too is the promise of hope.

"If the new millennium is to be the dawn of a golden morning, we must simply see it as another day in which we rise again in our continuous battle against the inequities and injustices we see. This enduring stance toward our society, in favor of the common good with a deep concern for the poor and vulnerable, must become a constant practice, a habit of the mind and heart, as natural as the air we breathe."

CCS & AHA work in solidarity with the poor and vulnerable to honor and dignify each life, healing pain with kindness and despair with hope.

ST. JAMES CATHEDRAL

When Bishop Edward O'Dea arrived in Seattle at the turn of the 20th century, his message was clear: the Catholic Church was here to stay. He purchased a city block on Seattle's First Hill, a dramatic setting overlooking the city, and began making plans for a great cathedral. In 1904 he hired the prestigious New York architectural firm Heins and La Farge, whose other project at the time was New York's Cathedral of St. John the Divine. The firm set out to build an immense structure — a 14th-century Neo-Italian Renaissance cathedral with a spectacular dome in its center and twin towers rising 175 feet into the sky. The building was completed just three years later and carried a staggering price tag for that time — $225,000.

St. James Cathedral opened in Seattle on December 22, 1907, with great anticipation. People walked across the terrazzo floor of the vestibule and read the words set in mosaic tile, *Domus Dei Porta Coeli*: "House of God, Gate of Heaven," which inspired the hope and purpose of the great church to all.

However, only eight years after its dedication, in the winter of 1916, the central dome collapsed under the weight of heavy snow, hurling wooden pews against the walls and blowing out windows. The cathedral seemed doomed, filled with a mountain of rubble and left with a large, gaping hole in its roof. Reconstruction was given to the capable hands of local architect John Graham, who reworked the interior and, in doing so, introduced four corner piers to support a new central dome — a dome that was never actually built.

The interior got another facelift in 1950 by Rambusch Studio of New York in collaboration with local architect John Maloney. However, it was not until 1994 that the cathedral underwent the most aggressive renovation since its construction, orchestrated by Bumgardner Architects of Seattle. The renovation incorporated the teachings of the Second Vatican Council (1962 to 1965) to direct the focus of liturgical action toward the midst of the assembly. To achieve this, the altar was moved to the center of the building, which many suspected had probably been the original intent of the architects in 1905. Additionally, thousands of painted acoustical tiles were replaced with detailed plaster coffers to bring resonance and clarity to music and the spoken word.

Today, St. James Cathedral unites contemporary Roman Catholic theology with original Renaissance architectural design. It demonstrates that major liturgical changes and functional improvements can be achieved without detracting from the historic integrity of the structure.

Though undeniably magnificent as a historic landmark, more importantly, St. James Cathedral has one of the largest and most active congregations in the Pacific Northwest. Through its many programs and services — The Catholic Worker Family Kitchen, Winter Shelter, English as a Second Language Program, and others — the church takes a very active role in the community. Inspired by Christ's example of mercy, the people of the many ministries of St. James continue their work to bring dignity and hope to the lives of the poor and vulnerable.

COVENANT SHORES

On any given day, visitors to Covenant Shores Retirement Community will find it abuzz with activity. The 23-year-old community is home to more than 300 residents who have come to enjoy a carefree retirement. Covenant Shores supports their active lifestyles with a host of amenities and a full spectrum of care, and residents take comfort in the security and peace of mind such a place affords.

Covenant Shores is one of 15 not-for-profit retirement communities established nationwide by Chicago-based Covenant Retirement Communities as a ministry of the Evangelical Covenant Church. Situated on 12 acres along Mercer Island's north shore, the retirement community offers residents a scenic setting and the opportunity to take full advantage of the city. Due in large part to its prime location and the support of a century-old religious organization, Covenant Shores has emerged as one of the region's most desirable and most comprehensive retirement communities.

Covenant Shores opened its doors in 1978. Eager to establish all levels of care for its residents, the organization was hampered only momentarily by city building restrictions. By the early 1990s, it had added 100 independent-living apartments and new assisted-living accommodations. In 1994 the community acquired state approval for a 43-bed skilled nursing center, and when that facility opened in 1997, Covenant Shores could offer residents the full continuum of care.

Covenant Retirement Communities also developed a substantial benevolent care fund. Income from this fund is used to assist residents who can no longer fully cover the cost of their housing and care. The organization

takes pride in the fact that no one has ever been asked to leave a Covenant Retirement Community due to inability to pay for care.

The decision to move to a retirement community can be a difficult one, but overwhelmingly, Covenant Shores residents have only one regret: that they didn't make the move sooner. This community has something for everyone. It offers a variety of living accommodations from cozy studios to spacious 1,800-square-foot apartments, many of which boast a view of Lake Washington and the community's own 51-slip marina. Activities abound both on site and off. Residents can exercise in the community gym, take classes in everything from painting to dancing to woodworking, and enjoy guest lectures on an unlimited number of subjects. Other opportunities include trips to museums, plays and restaurants as well as journeys farther afield to places such as Vancouver, Alaska and other destinations throughout the Northwest.

Covenant Shores serves dinner restaurant-style each evening in the historic Fortuna Lodge located on campus, and residents enjoy other amenities such as a wellness clinic, chaplaincy services and security features that enable worry-free travel.

Future plans for the community include a new four-story building, which will double the number of assisted-living units and increase the number of independent-living units. People are planning their retirements earlier, and inquiries come daily from those drawn to Covenant Shores' ideal location and environment, its foundation in Christian tradition, and the peace of mind such a community can offer later in life.

HORTON LANTZ MAROCCO

Horton Lantz Marocco (HLM) is a strategic creative agency — blending the artistry of a design firm, the communication resources of an ad agency and the interactive expertise of a Web company. Together, they provide calculated, well-crafted solutions that build brands and produce results.

The agency's philosophy is rooted in the belief that the best brands require strategy and execution, concept and craft, words and images. And it's a difference they believe is easily identified in their work. HLM has merged some of the best creative minds in the business: brand strategists, designers, copywriters, illustrators, media buyers, production artists and Web developers — and a diligent team of account and project managers.

HLM has had the good fortune to work with a wide variety of companies, all of which have a true passion for their respective businesses. HLM believes that passion is critical to the communication process. To begin with the human element of a product or service. To find the connection it has to every day life. To define its unique benefits and to share this brand personality with the world.

HLM has created successful consumer campaigns for clients such as: Starbucks, Voice Stream, Vail Resorts, Cinnabon, Seattle's Best Coffee, Sage Flyfishing, Restaurants Unlimited and the Professional Bowlers

| HLM office interior

| HLM lobby

Association. In the business-to-business category, HLM continues to deliver strategic, creative communications to the business decision-maker through its relationships with clients such as: Microsoft, Eddie Bauer, Flight Safety, Boeing, AEI Music and Ten Square.

Horton Lantz Marocco helps its clients reach the goals they desire using an integrated communications approach. From brand strategy and advertising, to direct mail and sales collateral, to trade shows and Web concepts, HLM has proven expertise in the marketing arenas. In six short years, its strategic, creative approach has helped HLM become one of the Puget Sound's largest design firms. The rest, as they say, is history-in-the-making.

MOUNT ZION BAPTIST CHURCH

Mount Zion Baptist Church, located at 19th and Madison Street in Seattle since 1918, is the oldest and largest African American Baptist church in Washington state. Founded in 1890, it is a church known for believing in and acting on God's word and for its vigilant advocacy on behalf of the least, the last, the lost, the locked up, the locked out and the left out in society. Ever true to the prophetic paradigm of holding in tension the need for both personal conversion and social transformation, Mount Zion has stood as a beacon of light to those of every color, race and creed who search for God's Kingdom and a truly just society.

Mt. Zion Baptist Church's African-flavored design has won national acclaim.

Mount Zion's grand history began over 100 years ago when a small group of people who wanted an African American Baptist church gathered at a storefront on 14th and East Madison. In 1894 the small but growing congregation became incorporated. It was not until 1906 that property was purchased and the congregation built its first facility. A simple one-room, wooden structure was erected at 11th and Union. It was partially warmed by a pot-bellied stove, and the members sat on backless wooden benches during worship services. In 1918 Mount Zion purchased an eight-room house and lot and underwent a two-year, $30,000 construction of the parsonage and sanctuary. Mount Zion quickly became the meeting place in the African American community for religious, educational, political, civic, social and other neighborhood-based activity.

The outbreak of World War II brought military personnel and their families to Seattle, increasing the population of the city overall and also increasing the membership of local churches. Mount Zion more than doubled to over 400 members during this era and once again looked to expand its facilities. In 1963 an education wing was added to the church, and in 1975 a new sanctuary was dedicated. The new state-of-the-art facility received regional and national acclaim for its uniquely Africentric design and décor.

The second half of the 20th century was a dynamic and progressive era for Mount Zion Baptist Church. The congregation received national recognition for its leadership in the arena of civil rights. Also, the church began to expand its outreach in the local community. Programs included the development of the Mount Zion Baptist Church Federal Credit Union, Mount Zion Pre-School and Kindergarten, an Educational Excellence Program, and a Saturday morning Ethnic School and Learning Center. A cocaine outreach and recovery ministry, weekly feeding ministries to the poor, the homeless and the shut in, and the building of the Samuel Berry McKinney Senior Housing Development were also added to the growing list of Mount Zion programs and services.

Mount Zion enters the new millennium as a historic yet growing and dynamic congregation of over 3,000 members. Sunday morning worship services attract people from all ethnic and social backgrounds. An award-winning Web site extends the ministry of Mount Zion to a global audience. Weekly youth ministry, Bible studies, tutorial programs, choir rehearsals, men's and women's ministries and much more continue to engage the hearts and gifts of faithful people still beholden to the simple proposition of personal conversion and social transformation.

Mount Zion Baptist Church is affiliated with the National Baptist Convention USA, Inc., the American Baptist Churches, USA, and the National Council of Churches.

Worship and music: the choir and congregation of Mt. Zion Baptist Church

NORTHWEST CENTER

In 1965 a group of parents shared a vision: to create a program in which their developmentally disabled children could realize their potential through education, rehabilitation and work opportunities. Northwest Center grew from this vision and has helped thousands of people with disabilities throughout the Northwest find continuing support and positive futures. Businesses have also found quality service through Northwest Center, which tailors its products and services to meet employers' changing needs.

Northwest Center began as four programs that merged into one when the Department of Education granted the founders the 7.5-acre former Naval Station on West Armory Way. Undaunted by the task of renovating the abandoned buildings, the parents mobilized the community, and armed with screwdrivers, paint and tools, a self-designated neighborhood task force refurbished the property in record time.

At its new site, Northwest Center established an activity program for children that expanded to include adolescent and adult services. The founders were also key writers of Washington state's 1973 Education for All Handicapped Children act, the model for the national law passed in 1974 that mandated all school districts to provide services to children with disabilities.

Northwest Center is now the largest, most comprehensive private organization for people with disabilities in the Northwest, and it encompasses both the groundbreaking programs its founders envisioned and quality enterprises to support the organization. With a mission to provide "education, rehabilitation and work opportunity," Northwest Center's core child and adult development programs are designed to meet the ongoing needs of people with disabilities and their families. Recognized as one of the top 10 early intervention programs in the country, Northwest Center's Child Development Center is the only mainstream, inclusive child-care center in King County — 40 percent of the children have special needs, while 60 percent are developing in a typical way.

Northwest Center also provides vocational and non-vocational Community Rehabilitation Services programs to help people with disabilities develop long-term work skills. By coaching its clients on an ongoing basis and staying in regular contact with employers and families, Northwest Center helps people with disabilities obtain and keep jobs. Employers come to realize that workers with disabilities are productive, motivated, dependable, and love to contribute to society as taxpayers.

These workers receive valuable training in Northwest Center's service-oriented commercial operations in Washington state, which are committed to providing quality services that support the organization's mission. Among these services are American Data Guard certified document destruction, Document Management Service, Northwest Center Industries, Packaging and Assembly, Sound Choice Janitorial, and a commercial laundry. Northwest Center's many enterprises provide top services at competitive prices.

Northwest Center is one of the largest unaffiliated, nonprofit organizations in the country to solicit and collect donations of used clothing and household items for sale. Collected goods are sold at Value Village Thrift Stores from Bellingham to Yakima, providing millions of dollars in income to Northwest Center every year.

Since 1965, when a group of parents came together with a vision to help their children with disabilities reach their fullest potential, Northwest Center has embodied the principles of caring, quality and entrepreneurship, creating a better community for everyone.

Northwest Center, located on West Armory Way, has been serving people with disabilities since 1965.

PILCHUCK GLASS SCHOOL

In the summer of 1971, Dale Chihuly, several fellow glass blowers and 18 art students gathered in a forested area 50 miles north of Seattle. Chihuly, who organized the gathering, envisioned a Pacific Northwest retreat where artists could work together creating art in glass.

Over the years, thanks to strong financial support from benefactors John H. Hauberg and Anne Gould Hauberg, Chihuly's vision became Pilchuck Glass School, the world's largest, most comprehensive educational center for artists working in glass.

Artist and Pilchuck Trustee Preston Singletary, assisted by Nadege Desgenetez, at work in the Pilchuck Glass School Hot Shop

Located in the Cascade foothills overlooking Puget Sound, Pilchuck's 54-acre campus includes an architectural award-winning lodge, several studios, and residential facilities for teachers, students, staff and artists in residence. A recent capital campaign funded numerous physical plant improvements, among them new casting facilities, cutting-edge studio equipment and additional faculty housing.

Every year from May to September, Pilchuck runs five sessions, each consisting of five two-and-a-half week classes. The classes are limited to 10 students and taught by renowned glass artists from around the world. Students learn technical skills such as blowing and hot-sculpting, casting, fusing, engraving and flameworking.

Founded in 1971 by artist Dale Chihuly, Pilchuck Glass School has helped establish Seattle as an international mecca for glass art.

But the emphasis at Pilchuck remains, as it has since the beginning, on artistic exploration and self-expression.

The admissions process for Pilchuck is highly competitive; some classes have as many as 90 applicants for 10 spots. And the student body is quite diverse. Some students are in their late teens, others in their 80s, and they come from all over the world. Twenty-nine different countries were represented in a recent summer session.

Like other glass-blowing studios, those at Pilchuck are expensive to operate because they consume large quantities of propane and batch — a silica, ash and lime mixture that is the raw material for glass. Student tuition covers only about a quarter of the school's operating costs. The rest comes from foundation and corporate support, private benefactors and organizations such as PONCHO and the Washington State Art Commission. An annual auction of glass art also provides significant funding.

To make Pilchuck accessible to outstanding artists regardless of their ability to pay tuition, the school has an extensive and growing scholarship program. During a typical summer, more than 100 of the 250 students receive scholarship assistance. Scholarships are awarded even to artists working in media other than glass because their presence enriches the creative process.

For years glass was viewed as a medium for craft rather than fine art. But that view is changing, in no small part because of Pilchuck. Evidence of the change was the appointment of Barbara Johns as executive director. Johns, who served as chief curator and twice acting director for the Tacoma Art Museum, provides a vital link between Pilchuck and the broader world of fine art.

To celebrate the school's 30th anniversary and honor the Haubergs and Chihuly, who is no longer involved in the school's day-to-day operations but sits on the board of trustees, a special totem pole was installed on campus in the summer of 2001. A cooperative effort by Alaskan native carvers and Pilchuck glass artists, the totem symbolizes the collaboration, creative experimentation and cross-cultural reach that have marked the school since its founding.

PLYMOUTH CONGREGATIONAL CHURCH

Since Seattle's early pioneer days, when loggers slid logs down "skid row" to Yesler's mill and the city's population was barely 1,000, Plymouth Congregational Church has been helping shape and form a city.

Even when other churches fled the downtown to the suburbs during the 1960s, Plymouth resisted the migration, finding instead its identity and purpose in the needs of the inner city. Today Plymouth Congregational Church, the second-oldest church in Seattle, remains a vibrant, working force, extending a helping hand to the needy while sharing God's message of hope.

With John and Caroline Sanderson, direct descendants of the Mayflower Pilgrims, leading the way, the Plymouth church in Seattle was established on October 16, 1869. Within a few months, the worship services moved from the Sandersons' home to a room above a drug store in the two-story Yesler Hall. Attendance averaged 100 for morning and evening services, a remarkable turnout considering the times and conditions. At a troubling time for the fledgling church, in July of 1876 the Reverend J.F. Ellis became pastor, offering leadership and a fresh vision for the church and the city.

As the city grew, so did Plymouth and its influence. In 1884 the church exhorted city officials and police to purge "Tenderloin," a section of the city where saloons, brothels and gambling halls thrived. All were closed and Sunday blue laws were enforced. In 1886 Reverend Harry Bates, then the church's pastor, marched with rifle in hand and with men from his congregation to quell a riot against Chinese laborers who had been accused of taking work away from others.

Over the years, Plymouth Congregation has built four churches, the first of which was completed in 1873 on the land between Second Avenue and Seneca that had been donated by Arthur Denny, a church trustee and one of the first to settle in Seattle. That wooden church survived the city's devastating fire of 1889 but was replaced by a stone church on Third and University in 1892. New churches were built at Sixth and University in 1911 and 1967, the second of which is home to the church's current membership of 1,200.

In 1980 the congregation began a low-income housing project called the Plymouth Housing Group, a not-for-profit organization that operates nine buildings and has 650 units. The church's most recent developments are the House for Healing, which provides housing for the mentally ill, and the founding of a new church on Beacon Hill. "When you look at a city, it's not just business and it's not just government that's important," said Anthony Robinson, Plymouth's senior pastor. "Religious communities and institutions also play an important role in the life of a city. We've had a part in that."

Amidst Seattle's changing skyline, from the wooden, two-story Yesler Hall of the 1860s to the towering, steel-girded skyscrapers of today, the Plymouth Congregational Church has remained a voice for the needy, fulfilling a pledge made by Sanderson and the rest of the congregation in those first meetings over 130 years ago.

After 130 years, Plymouth remains in the heart of downtown Seattle.

SEATTLE UNIVERSITY

Located on 46 acres of urban oasis in the First Hill neighborhood, Seattle University is the largest independent institution in the Northwest and one of the West's leading regional universities. Its eight schools and colleges, among them schools of law, nursing, education, and business and economics, offer more than 40 undergraduate and nearly two dozen graduate programs.

As a Jesuit Catholic institution, Seattle University is committed to the well-rounded development of each student, including a student's ethical, moral, religious and spiritual dimensions. The school prepares students not just for careers but for lifetimes of service, to enable them to contribute to the building of a just and peaceful community.

Seattle University is Catholic but welcomes a student body with diverse religious backgrounds. Approximately half of the 6,000 students are non-Catholics who represent over 15 different faith traditions.

The school was founded in 1891 by two Jesuit priests from Yakima and is one of 28 Jesuit colleges and universities across the United States. Established more than 450 years ago by Ignatius of Loyola, a Basque nobleman, the Jesuit Order has a well-deserved reputation for integrity, intellectual accomplishments and educational excellence. The Jesuit tradition of humanistic education grounded in the liberal arts and sciences is the cornerstone of Seattle University's undergraduate and graduate curriculum.

Along with its respected degree programs, Seattle University is widely recognized for its educational innovations. In the 1930s, the school (then known as Seattle

Seattle University's Chapel of St. Ignatius, built in 1997, is an award-winning design and a focal point for campus life.

Seattle University, founded in 1891, is one of the nation's 28 Jesuit colleges and universities. It is the largest independent university in the Northwest.

College) began admitting women, becoming the world's first coeducational Jesuit school. Seattle University also offered the nation's first graduate degree in software engineering in 1979 and the region's first executive graduate program in not-for-profit leadership in 1993.

In 1993 the university took an important educational step when it assumed sponsorship of a law school affiliated with the University of Puget Sound in Tacoma. Six years later, Seattle University School of Law moved on to the Seattle University campus and into Sullivan Hall, a spectacular, state-of-the-art building named after popular and highly successful Father Bill Sullivan, the university's president from 1976 to 1996.

In recent years, all the academic buildings on the campus have been rebuilt or entirely refurbished, providing first-rate facilities for study and research. The most remarkable campus building is the Chapel of St. Ignatius. Dedicated in 1997, it was designed by Steven Holl, an internationally recognized architect who also designed the new Bellevue Art Museum. The American Institute of Architects recognized the chapel with an Honor Award for Architecture and Religious Art & Architecture Design.

In addition to being a civic landmark, the chapel is a gathering place for individual and community worship. In that sense, it is a metaphor for Seattle University, where students and teachers come together to pursue truth and knowledge in the Catholic Jesuit tradition.

THE ART INSTITUTE OF SEATTLE

A dynamic energy is in the air and nowhere is it more prominent than at The Art Institute of Seattle. Located on Seattle's beautiful Elliott Bay waterfront, The Art Institute is part of a thriving neighborhood with a variety of high-tech companies and design firms as neighbors. Visitors who step into a class at The Art Institute immediately sense an energetic and creative environment.

The school was originally founded in 1946 as the Burnley School for Professional Art located on Seattle's Capitol Hill. At that time, the school's offerings were limited to commercial art courses. The school joined The Art Institutes in 1982 and became The Art Institute of Seattle. At that time, enrollment numbered just 95 students.

In 1985 the school moved into new facilities along the Puget Sound waterfront to accommodate its growing student body. Today, The Art Institute boasts an enrollment of nearly 3,000 students from around the world who are interested in pursuing professional arts and culinary careers. Students can work toward one of three diplomas and 12 associate of applied arts degrees with classes offered in graphic design, fashion, culinary and media arts. Yet, no matter the student's focus, the school's curriculum also addresses another important aspect of today's rapidly changing technology.

"The ability to communicate thoughts and ideas to other members of the team is absolutely critical for success in today's business environment," says Timothy Schutz, president of The Art Institute of Seattle. "Our students learn that by incorporating the ideas of their team members, they stretch their own boundaries and end up with far better results."

This approach is evident in the school's curriculum, which focuses on group interaction through a variety of team-oriented projects. Numerous national awards won by The Art Institute students attest to the success of this approach and the strength of the school's instruction.

Many of The Art Institute's faculty are creative, skilled and experienced professionals who have a great deal of real-life experience in their area of expertise. This knowledge is imparted to students through classroom discussions and hands-on projects that allow students to experience a real-world taste of their future.

Another way students get a taste of the real world is by participating in the local community through art and design projects sponsored by nonprofit organizations such as Habitat for Humanity, March of Dimes, and The Point Defiance Zoo. The Art Institute and its employees set the example themselves by participating in nonprofit organizations such as Northwest Harvest, which collects and distributes food to approximately 280 hunger programs in Washington state.

Graduates of The Art Institute have contributed to a variety of art and design businesses in the greater Puget Sound area and beyond. These graduates enter the working world confident in their creativity and knowledge, so it's no surprise that the school is known for graduates who are assets to the companies that employ them.

(Far left)
Gallery shows feature the work of students, faculty and alumni, as well as artists from around the nation.
Photos by Zee Wendell

(Middle)
The Art Institute of Seattle has a reputation within the business community for graduates who are assets to the companies who employ them.

(Left)
Design concepts become reality at The Art Institute. Through hands-on training from industry professionals, students have the opportunity to develop skills and techniques necessary to succeed in their chosen field.

UNIVERSITY OF WASHINGTON

Founded in 1861, the University of Washington (the UW) has long been a leading institution of higher learning in the Pacific Northwest. The UW operates 17 schools and colleges on its Seattle campus (at its present site since 1895), and on newer campuses in Bothell and Tacoma. More than 38,000 students study under an internationally respected faculty of almost 3,600 instructors, earning degrees in a broad spectrum of programs that are among the best in the country — from aeronautics and theater to medicine, computer science and zoology.

Because the university is a major research institution, students enjoy the added benefits of faculty who are at the forefront of their fields, a dynamic curriculum, opportunities for direct research experience, and extensive library collections. The UW operates several state-of-the-art research centers, including Friday Harbor Laboratories, widely acknowledged as the world's leading center for teaching and research on marine invertebrate animals. Since 1974 the UW has received more federal research funding annually than any other public university in the country, and it currently ranks second among all private and public universities in the amount of federal research funding received — a distinction that reflects the quality and stature of the UW's faculty.

Thanks in part to its exceptional commitment to research, the UW has earned an international reputation as one of a handful of elite graduate and professional schools. *U.S. News and World Report* rates the programs in primary care medicine, rural medicine and nursing as the best in the country; other programs recently ranked in the top 10 include microbiology, computer science and engineering, dentistry, bioengineering, oceanography, public health and community medicine, psychology, creative writing and geography. Not surprisingly, the chance to work in the newest frontiers of scientific and scholarly research draws almost 8,000 graduate students to UW programs, which include more than 90 special research centers and 25 field sites.

The university also helps shape the cultural identity of the Pacific Northwest through its support of the arts and collegiate athletics. Faculty and graduates helped launch Seattle's now-thriving theater scene, and the university currently operates three theaters that stage almost 100 performances each year. It also boasts two museums, including one of the world's largest collections of aquatic life. For sports fans, there are NCAA football games at Husky Stadium and athletic events in 22 additional sports for men and women.

Each year 70 percent of the UW's 10,000 graduates remain in the state, adding high-quality workers to the labor force. The university also creates a significant number of jobs, directly employing more than 20,000 people and generating more than 35,000 additional jobs in the private sector through contracts for services, technology transfer and licensing of discoveries made in UW research facilities. Since 1960 more than 130 new companies have formed to commercialize UW-developed technologies, earning the university a crucial role not only in the educational and cultural well-being of the Northwest, but in its economy as well.

Denny Hall, built in 1895, was the first structure built on the present Seattle campus.

The Liberal Arts Quadrangle, framed by cherry trees, is the heart of the Seattle campus.

UNIVERSITY OF WASHINGTON ACADEMIC MEDICAL CENTER

The University of Washington Academic Medical Center consists of four institutions that embody the UW tradition of excellence and involvement in the community. The UW School of Medicine is widely recognized as a leader in biomedical sciences and the teaching of medicine. Harborview Medical Center, a respected provider of specialty care, offers the region's only Level 1 adult and pediatric trauma and burn center. University of Washington Medical Center (UWMC), one of the region's most renowned referral hospitals, provides leading-edge specialty care for the Pacific Northwest region. And University of Washington Physicians Neighborhood Clinics bring comprehensive primary care to many King County sites.

Founded in 1946, the UW School of Medicine excels in both scientific research and clinical training for more than 1,500 residents and fellows. With a prestigious faculty of more than 1,600 that includes three recipients of the Nobel Prize, it is consistently among the top five medical schools in both the amount of federal research funding received and in the transfer of technology. This commitment to advancing medical knowledge forms the foundation of outstanding primary and specialty medical care programs. The Association of American Medical Colleges ranks the school sixth in the nation in the number of graduates practicing in the primary care fields of family medicine, general internal medicine and general pediatrics, and almost half of its alumni are practicing or training in fields where physicians are in short supply.

The School of Medicine's faculty and physicians practice at Harborview Medical Center, UWMC and other affiliated facilities. Harborview is known for its pioneering work in injury prevention and research. It treats burns and trauma, and is a primary center of research on diseases and injuries of the brain and central nervous system, as well as for HIV/AIDS research and treatment. Harborview has also been a pioneer in the field of out-of-hospital emergency care (establishing Seattle's Medic One Program) and treatment for victims of sexual assault, earning it an international reputation for innovative programs.

University of Washington Medical Center ranks among the best hospitals in the nation and serves as a referral and treatment center for a wide array of specialized health care needs. UWMC has been a research-based medical center since 1959, pioneering numerous medical procedures to improve the lives of its patients.

University of Washington Physicians Neighborhood Clinics provide primary care in the fields of family medicine, pediatrics, general internal medicine, women's health and senior care. Working together, components of the University of Washington Academic Medical Center are making important contributions to the advancement and delivery of the highest-quality health care, the impact of which can be felt in the Pacific Northwest and around the world.

UWMC has provided breakthrough medicine and exceptional care since 1959.

Harborview Medical Center is the region's only Level I adult and pediatric trauma center.

WASHINGTON ATHLETIC CLUB

The Washington Athletic Club — locally known as the WAC — is more than just a place to work out. The WAC is a partner in the pursuit to attain mental and physical well-being. The Club serves the whole member: body, mind and spirit. The WAC's mission is to "enrich the quality of life" of those it serves, and it does so by providing the best and most diverse facilities, helping members set and achieve wellness goals, and being attentive to the changing needs of its members. It's a club that members feel passionate about, and there's a lot of club to love.

With 21 floors of athletic and conditioning facilities, restaurants, overnight rooms, committee rooms and ballrooms, the Washington Athletic Club offers its members the most elegant of surroundings in which to work and play. Since it opened in December 1930, the WAC has been *the* place for social and athletic activities in Seattle. To its clients, the WAC is a haven from the pressures of work and everyday life. Whether they sweat in the state-of-the-art athletic facilities, conduct business over a gourmet meal in one of the four restaurants or relax in the sauna, WAC members are in the hub of Puget Sound's business and social circles.

Now the largest city athletic club in America, the WAC has always been concerned about serving its members

completely, inside and out. Social activities unique to the WAC are part of that tradition: the Father/Daughter Banquet honors that special relationship, and the annual Jubilee is the Club's largest event, bringing in over 1,100 members for a black-tie evening of glorious food and music. It's a celebration of life and a toast to the spirit. The WAC is committed to wellness for a lifetime for its members, and to accomplish that, it offers something for everyone.

At the WAC, wellness means learning to live a life in balance, and this extends far beyond personal training or nutrition classes. Wellness includes programs ranging from quarterly cholesterol checks to customized nutriceuticals (vitamins, minerals and herbs chosen specifically for an individual based on that person's sex, height, weight and age). And since wellness involves emotional as well as physical health, the WAC is a haven of stress relief: book clubs, excursions to the theater, wine tastings or quiet places to sip fine cognac and meet with friends. The WeeWAC's child-care center tends to the needs of the littlest members, allowing parents some freedom and peace of mind.

The Washington Athletic Club's Athletic and Wellness Expansion project (or AWEsome) is one way the WAC is working to serve its members' needs. AWEsome is a response to the changing requirements of new and existing members: as Americans live longer lives and become more health- and fitness-conscious, there is an increased demand for athletic facilities and programs. To meet that demand, the WAC is expanding. The WAC is committed to providing the most up-to-date services, and the AWEsome project demonstrates the depth of that commitment.

Above all, the Washington Athletic Club is a place that satisfies and refuels the body and the mind. Members are proud to bring friends and business associates to the Club, proud to be a part of the tradition of excellence that is the WAC.

Sports & Recreation

Seattle's spectator sports teams entertain residents and visitors
and enjoy world-class media coverage.

Fox Sports Net

In the beginning, there were no fancy studios or large operating budgets, just a developing business strategy — and a love for the game.

That love has turned what started in 1988 as Northwest Cable Sports (NCS) and 100,000 subscribers into Fox Sports Net, a 24-hour network with a regional subscriber base of more than 2.5 million. With a clear passion for regional sports broadcasting including partnerships with the Seattle Mariners and University of Washington Huskies, Fox Sports Net has brought a whole new meaning to that common Saturday afternoon request — "Honey, hand me the remote."

Carl Malone, now executive producer at Fox, looked back on the early days of the network when resources were limited. "We cleared time on the Shopping Channel.

Weekend anchors of Northwest Sports Report — Angie Arlati and Brad Adam
Photo by Gary Quinn*PhotoMagic

One minute you would see a diamond necklace, and then up would come a volleyball game."

Humble beginnings for sure, but single sporting events slowly broadened into a much more exciting playing field. Through persistence and good marketing sense, NCS soon forged a relationship with Prime Sports Network, changed its name to Prime Sports Northwest (PSN), and secured a dedicated channel where it aired regional sports from 4 p.m. to midnight daily. It also scored big points when it clinched its first major advertiser, Rainier Beer.

Growing rapidly, PSN realized it was time to bring an experienced manager to Seattle. In 1990, Clayton Packard, who had been working in the regional sports business in Los Angeles, was hired as vice president and general manager. Packard had contacts outside the Pacific Northwest and quickly expanded PSN's programming strategy. Before long, the network became a household name to sports fans throughout the region with live coverage of the Goodwill Games and Pac-10 and Big Sky Conference football and basketball games.

While PSN continued to develop college sports, the network was also keenly interested in covering the professional teams dominating the region — primarily Seattle SuperSonics basketball, Seattle Mariners baseball and Seattle Seahawks football. It did not take long to reach that goal. In 1990, PSN made a major move forward by securing an agreement with the Seattle Supersonics to distribute 20 games that year.

PSN just kept on rolling. Every year brought another major achievement — an agreement with the Seattle Seahawks in 1993 (to telecast preseason games throughout Washington, Oregon, Idaho, Montana and Alaska) and another with the Seattle Mariners in 1994.

Prime Sports' star was rising and in 1996 the network had its most significant milestone to date — it was purchased by Fox Broadcasting along with eight other regional sports networks across the country. The newly formed Fox Sports Net regionals, including Fox Sports Net Northwest, were able to offer the best of both worlds — live, local sports programming and national-caliber production and programming standards. Today, Fox Sports Net's Northwest region is one of 21 regional sports networks affiliated with Fox Sports Net serving 71 million viewers throughout the country.

With national exposure, demand for more comprehensive sports coverage was on the rise. From a regional perspective, Fox Sports Net was ready to take some dramatic steps to meet the heightened expectations of its viewers. That meant producing original, in-studio programs.

To launch a successful show of this type, Fox needed a knowledgeable sports broadcaster to pull it off. They found the talent they needed in Tom Glasgow, who had spent 14 years with local KIRO News.

In early 1997, with Glasgow as host, Fox Sports Net aired "Pac-10 Tonight," a 30-minute program that was produced Monday through Thursday. Later, Fox changed the format and the name of the show to "Northwest Sports Tonight," which became the first regional sports magazine of its kind, offering viewers coverage of all the home teams in the Northwest. The program included special features, interviews with athletes, and sports news and events making headlines throughout the region.

"Our instincts were right when we decided to move into the studio business," recalled Clayton Packard. "Our strategy was to do live regional sports events surrounded by live news programming, and it has paid off."

Success in the studio gave the network the confidence to take its coverage of regional sports to the next level. In June 2000, Fox launched "Northwest Sports Report," a 30-minute comprehensive sports broadcast running nightly at 10 p.m. as a complimentary partner to "Northwest Sports Tonight." "Northwest Sports Report" is hosted by weekday anchors Tom Glasgow, Rod Simons and Bill Wixey. Angie Arlati and Brad Adam serve as the "Northwest Sports Report's" weekend anchor team. The show is enormously popular with sports fans who have become increasingly disenchanted with the lack of sufficient sports coverage on local news programs. "Northwest Sports Report" has plenty to cover as Fox Sports Net recently signed a multiyear agreement with the Seattle Mariners that expands Fox Sports Net's coverage to over 100 games a season.

From high school championship tournaments to professional sporting events, Fox Sports Net is on the scene capturing the region's most talented athletes — on the playing field, in the locker room and in the neighborhoods where they live.

Broadcasting sports is only part of the picture. Each year, the staff at Fox work hard to nurture and support regional and national athletic events like Special Olympics, the United Way and the Boys and Girls Clubs of America, to name a few.

Today, while millions of local sports enthusiasts throughout Washington, Oregon, Idaho, Montana and Alaska sit riveted to their televisions, Fox Sports Net continues to work in front of the camera and behind the scenes to make sure fans are getting comprehensive, high-quality coverage of their favorite teams and athletes. Given the network's increasing popularity and success, it appears that Fox Sports Net and its viewers will remain hopelessly in love with the game.

Weekday anchors of Northwest Sports Report — Rod Simons, Bill Wixey and Tom Glasgow
Photo by
Gary Quinn*PhotoMagic

Vice President/General Manager of Fox Sports Net Clayton Packard and Executive Producer of Fox Sports Net Carl Malone
Photo by
Gary Quinn*PhotoMagic

FULL HOUSE SPORTS & ENTERTAINMENT

Full House Sports & Entertainment, the business and marketing arm of the SuperSonics and Storm, was launched in 1994 by The Ackerley Group, the umbrella company that owns the Sonics and Storm. The creation of Full House was part of Barry Ackerley's vision to expand the SuperSonics' focus on excellence beyond the game itself, recognizing that the company couldn't survive if it attracted only avid sports fans. At the same time, a push led by the revitalized National Basketball Association (NBA) encouraged more aggressive marketing of the league's teams. The launching of Full House coincided with the Sonics' rebranding, which included a new logo, addition of new game features, and innovative halftime and in-game entertainment.

The Ackerley Group was accustomed to revolutionary ideas, which can be traced back to 1983 when it dramatically departed from its core business strategy of new acquisitions and purchased the Seattle SuperSonics. This

bold and surprising venture was all the more intriguing, considering that Barry Ackerley was new to sports management and professional basketball. A devoted Sonics fan, Ackerley purchased the team to ensure that it wouldn't leave Seattle. He then hired the most knowledgeable people he could find and let them do what they did best. Eventually, this style of management led to the acquisition of the Sonics' new home, KeyArena, in 1995, the team's advance to the NBA Finals in 1996, and the founding of the Seattle Storm, a WNBA team, in 2000.

Today, Full House manages all finance, marketing, sales, concessions, broadcast production, public relations and retail operations for the Sonics and Storm. In addition, Full House serves as the marketing agent for KeyArena by selling advertising and luxury seating for the facility.

The mission of Full House's 80 full-time employees is to provide quality sports and event management with a commitment to exceeding customer expectations. On game night, Full House strives to build and maintain an electrifying atmosphere for KeyArena guests and to amplify the NBA basketball experience. Full House's award-winning event production staff works in conjunction with the Seattle Center to carry out the elaborate production tasks of each special event. Full House also provides catering specialists for high-volume events, offering a diverse menu ranging from sports casual and picnic fare to fine dining.

Full House considers its customers among the most knowledgeable fans in the NBA and is committed to keeping the "Sonics faithful" in the loop. It does this by producing several online and print publications containing breaking Sonics news and information, providing every fan on game night with a copy of *Playball*, the Sonics' complimentary home game program, and publishing *The Official Sonics Yearbook*, which profiles Sonics players and coaches.

Expanded pregame shows and behind-the-scenes player features are just part of the coverage offered on SonicsTV by Full House. Full House sells and manages sponsorship for the Sonics, the Storm and its own charitable and community programs, which make possible several community events and promotions where Sonics players can reach out to fans at area schools, hospitals and other locations.

Full House Sports & Entertainment and the SuperSonics do not measure success solely on winning

Gary Payton and Michael Jordan square off in the 1996 NBA finals.

games. Giving back to the community has always been a priority. Full House created the T.E.A.M. Foundation to support charitable organizations throughout the Puget Sound region. Working closely with Seattle Public Schools, T.E.A.M. conducts programs to improve students' reading, writing and fitness skills. The Read To Succeed Challenge helps students make reading a priority in their lives by motivating them to read 20 minutes a day for 20 days each month. Students involved in the program receive complimentary reading materials provided by Full House. They also interact with Sonics players during school

The new Seattle Storm team unveils its logo.

assemblies and participate in the Sonics Read To Succeed Jam each year at KeyArena. Read To Succeed's aim is to get children excited about reading and help them learn that reading can empower their lives.

The Hip To Be Fit Challenge sends Sonics players to local schools to encourage children to achieve a high level of health and fitness. Each year, students who reach the nation's 85th percentile in five fitness areas receive a Hip To Be Fit T-shirt and an opportunity to be recognized as a fitness leader at a Sonics game.

Publish With Pride focuses on improving students' writing skills as well as introducing them to the many uses of technology. Publish With Pride encourages children to submit writing samples they've created using the latest computer technology. Finalists' work is posted on the Sonics Web page and each entrant has the opportunity to win a laptop computer, attend a Sonics shootaround, interact with players and file a Sonics game-day report.

Sonics team members take a hands-on approach to giving back to the community by rolling up their sleeves to help build houses for low-income families. Full House and the Fannie Mae Foundation have joined forces to help many local families achieve the dream of owning a home. Additionally, the Sonics and the Fannie Mae Foundation co-sponsor a home-buying fair presented each year at Seattle Center.

Full House and the Sonics support the Make-A-Wish Foundation's efforts to transform the dreams of children with life-threatening illnesses into reality. They also support Children's Hospital and the Fred Hutchinson Cancer

Research Center. Through NeighborHoops, Full House volunteers help renovate run-down basketball courts at local community centers and parks.

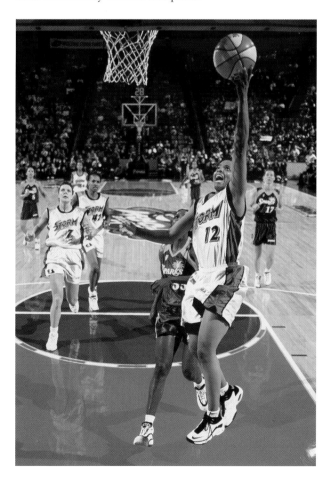

Edna Campbell in the Storm's inaugural season at KeyArena

SEATTLE SEAHAWKS

The Seattle Seahawks, the National Football League (NFL) team of the Pacific Northwest, share a special bond with loyal and passionate fans throughout the region, spanning Washington, Oregon, Idaho, Montana, Alaska and British Columbia.

Washington state's new football/soccer stadium and new home for the Seattle Seahawks, set to open in 2002

Head Coach Mike Holmgren, who is also Seahawks General Manager and Executive Vice President of Football Operations, leads the Seahawks.

The NFL story in Seattle began in 1974, the year the city was awarded an expansion franchise. Two years later the Seahawks played their first game in the Kingdome, their home for 24 seasons. The team was such an immediate hit with the public that a waiting list for season tickets was soon thousands of names long. The Seahawks' early years were highlighted by the passing combination of Jim Zorn to Steve Largent and by imaginative play calling that led to exciting wins. The team reached the playoffs for the first time in 1983, defeating Denver and then Miami before suffering a loss to the Los Angeles Raiders in the AFC Championship game. Playoff appearances were made again in 1984, 1987, 1988 and 1999.

Many fine players have worn the blue, green and silver over the years, including NFL Hall of Famer Steve Largent. In addition to establishing several NFL records as a receiver for the Seahawks, Largent displayed a strong commitment to community causes during and after his playing days. In 1989 he was elected as the first member of the Seahawks' Ring of Honor. Largent, the lone Seahawks player in the NFL Hall of Fame, was recently inducted into the Washington Sports Hall of Fame. He has also made his mark in national politics as a U.S. Congressman in Oklahoma's 1st District.

Jacob Green is another Seahawks' Ring of Honor member whose dedication to the community continued after his playing days were over. For 12 NFL seasons Green led a ferocious rush against opposing quarterbacks, becoming the Seahawks' all-time leader in quarterback sacks and in fumbles forced against the opposition. His leadership has since extended to the fight against cancer, with Green hosting a major annual golf tournament and gala/auction with proceeds going to Seattle's Fred Hutchinson Cancer Research Center.

Many other current and former Seahawks continue to have a positive impact in the Seattle area, devoting countless hours to motivate children in schools, comfort hospital patients and serve as celebrities for charitable fund-raising events. Their success in promoting community causes is a reminder that these players leave long-lasting impressions on the fans who have come to know them over the years.

The bond of the team to community was fortified when the Seahawks were acquired by Seattle's own Paul Allen in 1997. Allen stepped forward to purchase the Seahawks when the franchise was on the verge of relocation. He immediately strengthened the charitable commitment of the team and the Seahawks Foundation to ensure that the region fully benefited from keeping the team in Seattle. Through "Big Men, Big Hearts," the Seahawks' community outreach program, Seahawks players, former players, Sea Gals and "Blitz," the team mascot, make more than 1,000 charitable appearances each year. The outreach effort focuses on enhancing and promoting programs for youth in the areas of education, athletics and health.

One of the most notable and successful team-sponsored endeavors is the Seahawks Academy, an accredited, alternative Seattle public middle school of 120 students, many of whom had difficulty in traditional school settings. The Seahawks have partnered with other corporate sponsors to provide funding for extra teachers and counselors to work with the students. The continued success of the Seahawks Academy is also attributable to Seahawks players serving as mentors and advisers at the school, motivating the students to succeed in school and in life. Academy students are afforded tickets to Seahawks games as rewards for academic and behavioral accomplishments.

On December 26, 1999, the Seattle Seahawks played their last game at the Kingdome. The Kingdome was imploded on March 26, 2000, following voter approval in 1997 of a statewide referendum on a public/private partnership to build a new football/soccer stadium and exhibition center. The Seahawks played in Husky Stadium during the two-year interim period while construction was under way on the new world-class stadium being built in downtown Seattle on the Kingdome site. The new stadium is designed with a 68,000 seat capacity, with 4,000 additional seats available for special events. A roof will cover 70 percent of the seating area and fans will be positioned as close as possible to the field, with sideline seating a mere 52 feet from the playing field and end-zone seats just 40 feet

Pro Bowl defensive back Shawn Springs — on the field he takes on the best wide receivers in the NFL, and off the field he is actively involved in programs to educate and motivate children.

Seahawks players Maurice Kelly, Darrell Jackson and Charlie Rogers help students paint a new mural at the Seahawks Academy.

from the action. The new stadium will boast wide, comfortable seats and include 1,400 seats for fans with disabilities and their companions. The facility will also feature a dozen elevators and expansive concourses with an ample provision of concession stands and restrooms.

As the 20th century ended, fans were entertained by the play of Ricky Watters, Shawn Springs, Cortez Kennedy, Chad Brown and Walter Jones, and the Seahawks won the 1999 AFC West Championship. As the 21st century began, excitement was generated by the play of talented rookies such as Shaun Alexander, Chris McIntosh and Darrell Jackson under the leadership of Mike Holmgren. With a dedication to succeeding both on the field and in community endeavors, the Seahawks are soaring into the new century with the same enthusiasm they have shared from the start with their loyal fans.

SEATTLE MARINERS

In April 1977 the Seattle Mariners made their debut at the Kingdome. Community leaders had worked for years to secure a Major League Baseball franchise, and that season more than a million fans came to watch the team play. But throughout the early years of the expansion franchise, two questions loomed: Was Seattle really a "baseball town"? And were the Mariners there to stay?

Today it's clear the answer to both questions is an unequivocal "Yes!" Much has happened over the years to foster enthusiasm for the team, but the events of the last decade have made the Mariners a veritable Northwest institution.

SAFECO Field has gained a reputation locally, regionally and nationally as a terrific setting for baseball and a great place for baseball fans.

In July 1992 Mariners ownership changed hands for the third time. Japanese businessman and president of Nintendo Co. Ltd., Hiroshi Yamauchi, partnered with local investors and purchased the team for $100 million. The new ownership group quickly set about developing a strategy to build a winning baseball team. The first major move was to hire manager Lou Piniella, a revered leader known for his aggressive style. Then in 1995, after one of the most dramatic stretch runs in baseball history, the Mariners won their first American League Western Division Championship and came within two games of a trip to the World Series.

Fans went wild for the underdog team. The following year, home-game attendance rose from 1.6 million to 2.7 million. The marketing theme from 1996 to 1998 was "You Gotta Love These Guys," and people did. Ken Griffey Jr., Edgar Martinez, Randy Johnson, Jay Buhner and others became bona fide stars as fans increasingly identified with the players.

Ken Griffey Jr. in particular captured the fans' favor. Not only was he the son of the famous outfielder, he also came up through the Mariners' minor-league system and debuted in the majors at 19. As the team's first marquee player, Griffey single-handedly drew fans to the ballpark. And as the team improved, making post-season appearances in 1997 and 2000, the fan base grew, extending across eastern Washington into Idaho and Montana; south into Oregon; and north into British Columbia and even Alaska. In 2001 the Mariners added Japanese superstar Ichiro Suzuki, who along with Kazuhiro Sasaki, the all-time saves leader in Japan, helped expand the Mariners fan base into Japan.

The Mariners also made an impression off the field. Mariners Care was established in 1990 to encompass all of the team's charitable activities, and in recent years the organization has donated more than $1 million annually to various charities and community projects.

As the Mariners hit their stride, plans for a new ballpark took shape. In September 1995, King County voters narrowly defeated a proposed sales-tax hike to pay for the project, but the dream of a new outdoor park became a reality nonetheless as community leaders came up with alternative financing. Construction on SAFECO Field began in 1997. When it opened in 1999, baseball fans were awestruck by this classic ballpark complete with retractable roof, spacious concourse and panoramic views — a great place for fans to enjoy the national pastime for generations to come. In the ballpark's first full season in 2001, over 3 million fans came through the gates to experience Mariners baseball under blue skies and on green grass.

SAFECO Field is destined to become an enduring symbol of Mariners baseball, just as Fenway Park in Boston represents the Red Sox, Yankee Stadium the Yankees, and Chicago's Wrigley Field the Cubs. But it's the Mariners and their fans who have affirmed beyond a doubt that Seattle is indeed a baseball town and baseball is here to stay.

SEATTLE SOUNDERS

Since its inception in 1974 as a part of the North American Soccer League (NASL), the Seattle Sounders soccer team has achieved unrivaled success. With the Pacific Northwest's only back-to-back championships in professional sports history, the A-League's only back-to-back championships (1995 and 1996), and seven consecutive post-season appearances, the Sounders continue a great tradition of winning soccer.

Beginning in 1993, the Sounders started another tradition. That year, the Sounders announced that their operating charter had changed to that of a community-oriented sports organization which would donate to children's charities the greater of all profits achieved from operations or 2 percent of gate receipts. The Sounders are the only known professional sports organization in the world with this unique charter. As a result, the organization is committed to making a positive contribution to the community, specifically in the areas of grassroots soccer development and in using the game of soccer to provide young people with a healthy alternative to gangs, alcohol use, drug use and other negative social behaviors.

Through a relationship with a not-for-profit entity called Sounders Soccer Success Fund, the Sounders are developing the Sounders Club System. The Sounders Club System is the first soccer club model in America that provides a young person with the opportunity to climb from the youngest youth team all the way through to professional play within the same system. The Sounders Club System simulates European Soccer Clubs in that all activities and programs are available to all youth regardless of color, race or ability to pay. Unlike the European Soccer Clubs, however, the Sounders Soccer Club focuses equal attention on the development of female players.

The Sounders have enhanced the effectiveness of the Sounders Club System with an exclusive and expansive affiliation with S.V. Werder Bremen of the German Bundesliga. The relationship between the two clubs involves youth evaluations, clinics, camps, professional and amateur player exchanges and friendly matches between the Sounders and Bremen youth teams. This agreement is unique to any U.S.-based professional soccer club with a German Bundesliga club. The Sounders have also developed a relationship with the Frauen Bundesliga in Germany to provide equal opportunities for female players within the Sounders Soccer Club.

Forward Viet Nguyen
Photo by Corky Trewin

The Seattle Sounders are already known in soccer circles as one of the top developmental teams in the United States. The club has developed over 20 players who have been or are currently on Major League Soccer rosters and has placed several former players on European team rosters. The Sounders Club System programs will use that same player development expertise to obtain college scholarships for Sounders youth players while also providing an even greater number of quality players to the professional ranks.

In the coming years, the Sounders have ambitious plans. New facilities, expanded programs, expanded international relationships and more championships are on the horizon. Most importantly, however, is the plan to develop thousands of Puget Sound youth to be quality high school, college and professional players and to develop life skills that will continue to contribute to their success in the future.

Defender Scott Jenkins
Photo by Corky Trewin

Technology

Diverse businesses have gathered to make Seattle one of the
country's leading centers of technology innovation,
development, manufacturing and employment.

THE BOEING COMPANY

The young man who had earned his fortune in the timber business excitedly climbed down from an open cockpit biplane in 1914, thrilled by his first airplane ride and convinced he could build a better one. He was right.

William Boeing, the son of a German father who died when William was eight, turned a small, struggling business that built its first plane in 1915 into a mega-giant. By the end of the 20th century, 80 percent of the planes flying were Boeing jets carrying 675 million passengers a year, or nearly 12 percent of the world's population. The company that had sold only one plane in 1938 had become the world's largest builder of commercial airline planes.

While The Boeing Company is associated with historic planes like the B-17 Flying Fortress that helped win World War II and the 707 and 747 jumbo jets that revolutionized air travel, it is not limited to building planes. Boeing also built the first stage of the Saturn rocket that launched the Apollo to the moon, developed the Minuteman missile used to protect North America, and designed the Lunar Rovers astronauts drove to explore the moon surface. Boeing is now prime contractor in the building of NASA's space station.

This journey began with a chance meeting in 1910 between Boeing and Conrad Westervelt, a young Navy lieutenant. Neither had been in an airplane, but both shared a passion for flying. Another five years would pass before they'd both catch their first flight aboard a rickety Curtiss seaplane. It was then that Boeing and Westervelt first talked of how they could build a better plane. And that was the start of what was to become the world's biggest manufacturer of airplanes. Together, Boeing and Westervelt built their own twin-float seaplane, a two-seater with a maximum range of 320 miles. They called it the B & W. It was Boeing himself who made the first flight, taking off from the waters of Lake Union. Yet Westervelt, the designer of the plane, was soon transferred to the East Coast, ending the short-lived business relationship. Naturally, Boeing, who had came to Hoquiam, Washington, in 1903 to earn his fortune in the timber industry, was just beginning.

By the late 1920s, Boeing had ventured into the mail- and people-carrying business, spearheaded by the successful design of a cargo plane dubbed the Model 40, an all-metal, open-cockpit monoplane that leisurely cruised at 135 mph. To bolster its growing mail and passenger service, Boeing, buoyed by its delivery route from San Francisco to Chicago, purchased a number of small airlines and began expanding. At the same time, Boeing absorbed several engine and propeller manufacturers, merging it all under the name of United Aircraft & Transport Corporation. Several more mergers followed. United's first annual report in 1929 showed an $8.3 million profit and $27 million in assets. However, the government ruled it a monopoly and forced a breakup of the Boeing network of aircraft manufacturers and airlines, setting loose the company that is today United Airlines. Frustrated by the government's intrusion on aviation and his company, Boeing walked away from the company in 1934 at age 53, returning only briefly during World War II as an adviser. He died of a heart attack while aboard his yacht in 1956, just as the company he had founded was moving into the jet age with a revolutionary plane design.

In 1934, in response to the Army's request for a large, multiengine bomber, Boeing designed the model 299, a four-engine plane that was the prototype for the B-17 Flying Fortress, which filled the skies during World War II. With four Pratt and Whitney Hornet engines and a top

William Edward Boeing's intrigue in flying made him a pilot in 1915 and then an owner.

The B & W was the first plane built by Boeing. It was sold to a New Zealand flying school and was later used in the country's first airmail flight.

speed of 236 mph, it was far more advanced than other planes. While the Army initially bought only a few of these planes, Boeing still decided to pursue this route of building bigger planes. It was a big gamble at that time because the Douglas Aircraft Co. had a lock on the market. Boeing put a passenger fuselage on the XB-15 for Pan American Airlines, which wanted planes to fly across the Pacific. Boeing then introduced the first pressurized cabin, the Model 307 Stratoliner, allowing pilots to climb to 20,000 feet and out of rough weather.

Still, Boeing sold only one plane in 1938, the XB-15, an experimental bomber. When the United States entered World War II, Boeing halted its commercial transports production and began building warplanes. By 1944 the Seattle plant was rolling out 16 B-17s in 24 hours.

Following the war, Boeing designed the B-47, the first sweptwing jet. The five other design proposals offered conventional straight-wing planes, yet Boeing sold the Air Force on its more radical idea. The B-47 was a revolution in aircraft design, and all modern jet aircraft use the swept wing established. In the early 1950s, Boeing got back into producing commercial airplanes with the Dash-80, a jet transport that flew from Seattle to Baltimore at an average record speed of 612 mph. It eventually became the 707, the predecessor to the 747 and the plane that made commercial flying commonplace. Tex Johnston drew nationwide attention to the jet's capabilities by taking it into a barrel roll over the Seafair hydroplane course in 1954.

In the mid-1990s Boeing acquired the North American division of Rockwell International and merged with McDonnell Douglas Corp. By the end of the decade, Boeing was the world's largest manufacturer of commercial jetliners and military aircraft and the nation's largest NASA contractor.

Boeing, like the man who began the company, is low-key about its charitable involvement. While giving more than $50 million a year to education, musical associations, community centers and youth programs, it does so with little fanfare and publicity.

The company named after a man who never lost his curiosity for aviation continues to go against the grain and remains a leader in airplane manufacturing and space travel.

FRED HUTCHINSON CANCER RESEARCH CENTER

Since opening its doors in 1975, the Fred Hutchinson Cancer Research Center has made major progress in understanding and treating cancer and many other diseases. The Hutchinson Center's mission is "the elimination of cancer as a cause of human suffering and death," and to that end, the center engages in research and specializes in treatments that have earned it an international reputation.

Fred Hutchinson was a baseball player and one of Seattle's best-loved sports heroes. A major-league pitcher and manager, his career was cut short: he died in 1964 at 45, a victim of lung cancer. His brother, Dr. William Hutchinson, was then head of the Pacific Northwest Research Foundation, an organization that provided funds and laboratory space to physicians engaged in research. Dr. Hutchinson recognized a need for a center devoted entirely to the study of cancer. To fulfill that need and to honor the memory of his brother, Dr. Hutchinson founded the Fred Hutchinson Cancer Research Center.

Dr. E. Donnall Thomas, then director of oncology at the University of Washington, brought his research to the Hutchinson Center in 1974. Thomas was working to develop a procedure in which cancer patients are given lethal doses of chemotherapy and radiation to kill their cancer cells, and then "rescued" with the transfer of healthy bone marrow cells from a donor. The Hutchinson Center, an independent research institution, is the world's leader in bone marrow transplants. In 1990 Thomas was awarded the Nobel Prize for Medicine for his pioneering work on bone marrow transplantation.

Research has always been the focus of the Hutchinson Center's attention. Continued study of bone marrow and stem cell transplantation has led to new treatments for leukemia, lymphoma and many other diseases. Patients worldwide come for treatment at the center. To some extent, every patient seen at the Hutchinson Center is a study subject, a learning opportunity. Each bit of knowledge gained improves therapies. However, the work at the Hutchinson Center goes beyond the development of new therapies.

By looking at life at the cellular level, scientists increase their understanding of the origin and behavior of cancer cells. By looking at the lifestyles of patients and volunteers worldwide, scientists find environmental and lifestyle factors that contribute to the development of cancer. More than half a million people around the globe participate in cancer prevention programs run by the Hutchinson Center.

The Hutchinson Center frequently implements new strategies to continue improving treatment. One such initiative is a drive to increase interdisciplinary collaboration and communication between divisions. A dual mentorship program provides graduate students with advisers in two scientific disciplines. Staff can join the Interdisciplinary Club, a group which meets monthly for presentations on research being conducted throughout the center. Retreats and gatherings offer informal opportunities for staff and students to meet and chat. All of these activities help overcome language barriers between the disciplines and stimulate cross-divisional, collaborative research.

Over the years, the Hutchinson Center has had long-standing affiliations with the University of Washington and Children's Hospital & Regional Medical Center. These relationships support their missions of research, patient care and education. In 1998 they formed the Seattle Cancer Care Alliance (SCCA), which unites the oncology-related patient care services for all three organizations. Through the SCCA, patients will have access to the finest clinical care programs and state-of-the-art, patient-focused cancer care.

In addition to providing top-level patient care, the SCCA will collaborate with physicians and hospitals throughout the region to speed the sharing of research-based therapies and other new information that could improve diagnoses and treatments of cancer patients.

The Fred Hutchinson Cancer Research Center (in the foreground) against the backdrop of downtown Seattle and Mount Rainier

Greater collaboration between specialists will accelerate the research process, and new technology, discoveries and treatments will move more quickly from the laboratories and to the community.

The relationship between the Hutchinson Center and the greater Seattle community is symbiotic: because the center is nonprofit, it depends on grant money from the federal government and private sources. Fund-raisers and individual contributions help the center to provide fellowships for young scientists and scholarships for nurses; to purchase new equipment; to house and transport patients and their family members through the Family Assistance Fund; to continue to study leukemia, AIDS, breast and prostate cancer, and other cancers and related diseases. Money comes from hikers who pay to be led to the base camp at Mount Rainier or runners and walkers who pay to participate in races along the shores of Lake Washington. Bike rides, golf tournaments and celebrity events bring in additional revenue to support cancer research. In return the center provides its patients — most of whom are from the Pacific Northwest — with compassionate care and some of the most advanced treatments in the world.

Providing patients with care that is sensitive as well as effective is one of the Hutchinson Center's highest priorities. The Pete Gross House is one example of how the center strives to ease patients' lives during difficult times. The Pete Gross House, like the Fred Hutchinson Center, is named for a Seattle sports-related figure who died of cancer. Pete Gross was best known in Seattle as "The Voice of the Seahawks;" he was the commentator for the Seahawks from its first game in 1976 until the year he died. The Pete Gross House is a 70-unit apartment building that provides housing for patients who must travel to Seattle for treatment. School-age patients, their siblings and young children of adult patients are able to attend the Hutch School on the first floor. Children who are too weak or vulnerable to leave the hospital are provided one-on-one tutoring by Hutch School teachers.

The Fred Hutchinson Cancer Research Center is committed to excellence in all that it does: in research and patient care, in improving diagnostic skills and increasing treatment options, and in contributing new knowledge to

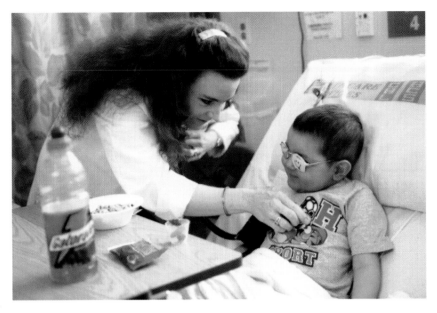

Theresa Ajer, infusion room nurse, checks the heart rate of patient Michael Aman Patrick, 4, of Greenleaf, Idaho.

the fight against cancer. The Hutchinson Center trains doctors and treats patients from all over the world and engages in studies that researchers hope will one day make cancer centers such as the Hutchinson obsolete. Fred Hutchinson was once quoted as saying, "The ones who work the hardest are the ones who make it, the ones who win." This is the philosophy that the Hutchinson Center has adopted, the legacy that Fred and William Hutchinson leave behind.

Sanjeev Datar is a MCB/MSTP graduate student in Dr. Bruce Engars' laboratory in the Basic Sciences Division. MCB/MSTP is the M.D./Ph.D program where the student obtains two degrees.

MICROSOFT

Few companies in history have affected the world the way Microsoft has. When Bill Gates and Paul Allen began Microsoft in Albuquerque, New Mexico, they had little more than an improbable vision: a personal computer on every desk and in every home. The Microsoft idea of a truly personal computer was revolutionary. In the mid-1970s, only a handful of people even knew what a personal computer was. As impossible as Gates' and Allen's dream may have sounded in 1975, they have come a long way toward turning it into a reality, making Microsoft a household name and an international phenomenon in the process.

Microsoft co-founder Bill Gates

As Bill Gates tells it, Microsoft truly began with a build-it-yourself computer called the MITS Altair 8800, which Gates and Allen had read about in a magazine. Although the computer didn't do much that was useful, the two young men quickly recognized the computer's potential. The Intel 8080 microprocessor that served as the "brain" of the Altair was tiny in comparison with the computers of the day, which required their own rooms. In order to be truly revolutionary, however, the computer would have to do more than sit on a desk and blink its lights: it needed software that would allow the machine to perform computing tasks and transform it into a useful tool. And so Gates and Allen developed a BASIC computer language for the Altair — the first programming language. They formed Micro-Soft and led the world's most radical technological transformation into the 21st century.

Microsoft moved to Washington state in 1979 and has since become the worldwide leader in software, services and Internet technologies. Microsoft's task now is to continue to explore and expand the possibilities of

personal computing, empowering customers to make full use of computers, software and new technological advances.

Since the beginning, Microsoft's focus has been on empowerment, on putting the most innovative and effective tools in the hands of business people, private citizens, teachers, students and charitable organizations. It is one of Microsoft's most fundamental beliefs that people can accomplish great things if they have the resources they

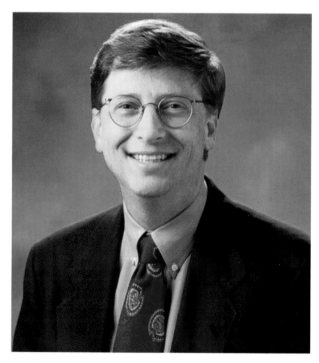

need. This belief fueled the creation of Microsoft Windows — an operating system so easy to work with, it opened the personal computer to a much wider audience of users. Windows allowed users to view unrelated applications simultaneously and to move information between applications. In 1983 Microsoft announced the first graphical user interface, Microsoft Windows, scheduled to ship in 1985. Microsoft's creation of user-friendly operating systems enabled even the least technologically inclined to make use of the power of the PC.

In 1986 Microsoft went public, selling for $21 a share. By the end of the 80s, there were more than 90 million PCs in homes, schools and businesses worldwide, and Microsoft's vision of a computer in every home and on every desk was well on its way to becoming a reality. In 1995 Microsoft launched one of the most anticipated

Founders Bill Gates, Paul Allen and the Altair PC

products of the decade: Windows 95. More than 1 million copies sold in four days, making it one of the best-selling computer products in history.

During the Internet explosion of the late 1990s, the number of users ballooned from 3 million to more than 200 million in a few short years. Microsoft embraced the Internet, releasing Internet Explorer in 1995. A truly effective tool for managing and maneuvering through the Net, Explorer gave users unparalleled access to the vast resources of the World Wide Web. As the Internet enters people's lives in more ways and through different and more sophisticated devices, Microsoft is already looking ahead to the next generation of Net uses. The Microsoft.NET Platform, announced in June 2000, is yet

The original New Mexico group responsible for Microsoft's first successes

> MICROSOFT WAS FOUNDED ON
> THE BELIEF THAT ALL PEOPLE
> SHOULD HAVE ACCESS TO
> PERSONAL COMPUTERS
> AND THE KNOWLEDGE
> TO USE THEM EFFECTIVELY.

another Microsoft innovation. This platform securely stores information on the Web, not on personal computers, providing access to information from any location. Users can tap into their brokerage accounts at the gym or send e-mails on any wireless device. Microsoft.NET will allow full exploitation of the interconnectivity of the Internet without the barriers of hardware.

Microsoft was founded on the belief that all people should have access to personal computers and the knowledge to use them effectively. To that end, Microsoft and its staff have donated millions of dollars and hours of technical support to provide people with PCs and training. Microsoft's aim is threefold: bring technology and its benefits to people and communities, support organizations in communities where Microsoft employees live and work, and support employees' decisions to become active in their communities by matching gift programs. Microsoft knows that children are the next generation of computer users, developers and programmers and believes that no child should be left behind. The company offers training and computer access through donations to schools and organizations like the Boys and Girls Clubs of America. Microsoft also works with Npower, a Seattle-

based, nonprofit group that donates technology and training to various charitable organizations in the Puget Sound area. Microsoft is committed to bridging the digital divide, and contributions of computers, software, money and time bring technology to those who would otherwise have limited or no access.

The first "general purpose" computer was developed by the University of Pennsylvania in 1946. It weighed 30 tons and cost nearly half a million dollars. Back then, computers that could sit on a desktop or lap or nestle in the palm of a hand were unthinkable. Fortunately, the leaders and staff of Microsoft are well versed in overcoming impossibilities, including limitations of the imagination. Today, personal computers are as commonplace as telephones, and vast amounts of information are instantly available at people's fingertips. And Microsoft isn't finished yet: as the Internet links people from around the world, enabling the transfer of information, from medical breakthroughs to dinner reservations, the possibility of a truly global community is becoming a reality.

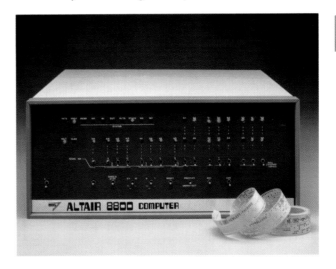

Helping people work with computers is a Microsoft mission.

ULTRABAC.COM

Computer hard drives crash. Operators make mistakes. Even the most thoroughly tested software can have one or more bugs lurking in a program. Any one of these scenarios can mean sudden catastrophe for information management systems unless steps have been taken to back up mission-critical data. As a premier producer of high-performance backup and disaster recovery software, UltraBac.com is one of the leaders in preventing and handling such computer crises. A small but growing, privately owned company, it stands out as a seasoned veteran in a field mostly populated by dot-com businesses that sprang up virtually overnight in the late 1990s.

UltraBac.com was founded in 1982 around a product named AUTODOC and $10,000 in seed money. For the first 10 years, the company — known as BEI Corporation until the late 1990s — developed and sold utility software for the Wang minicomputer market. It first became profitable with the development of a leading-edge spell checker for Wang WP, and eventually expanded into the backup software market with a new product it christened UltraBac. When the Wang market was gradually eroded by the increasing popularity of PCs, BEI used its backup expertise to reinvent itself by developing a completely new product, with the same brand name, for the fledgling

Windows NT market. Microsoft included a free backup program in its Windows NT software, but UltraBac was more sophisticated and powerful. After two years of development, the new UltraBac was launched in 1995. When Windows NT became a commercial success so did UltraBac. The only backup software developed expressly for Windows NT, UltraBac is also unique in that it is still sold and supported by the same company who created it.

Since its successful entry into the Windows market, UltraBac.com has primarily focused its development energy on the backup needs of small- and medium-sized networks, but began adding the necessary support for large networks in 2000. Unlike most software companies that divide their attention and manpower among numerous products, UltraBac.com has focused all of its expertise and resources on backup. The company stands out from most of its competitors by having developed its own software instead of acquiring it from other companies. Founder and CEO Morgan Edwards succinctly sums up the company's mission: "We live and breathe backup." As a result, UltraBac is the most compact, easiest to use and most flexible product of its type, and is consistently rated the fastest backup by independent reviewers. Industry product recognition in 1999 included the Editor's Choice Award from *Windows NT Magazine* for best backup product, and inclusion on the prestigious WIN100 List by *Windows Magazine* for Best Enterprise Backup product for Windows NT.

In 2000 UltraBac 5.5 was released, enhancing its fast, reliable tape and disk backups for customers ranging in size from a small single-user to companies employing large multiple-server and workstation environments. With the release of Version 5.5, UltraBac supports Microsoft's Cluster Server, SQL 7 Server, Exchange 2000 and includes options for RAID, Oracle, Locked File Backup, One Button Disaster Recovery and Windows 2000 support. Future releases will include remote device backup, comprehensive tape management, WAN reporting, Internet-based GUI control and LINUX.

UltraBac.com paid its dues during its first decade and began experiencing remarkable growth in the second half of the 1990s. Under the leadership of CEO Edwards and partner and Chief Technology Officer Paul Bunn, it has remained debt-free, funding operating expenses and growth exclusively through sales. Revenues have grown an average

Founder and CEO of UltraBac.com, Morgan Edwards

healthy share of the backup market and can boast an active customer base of more than 20,000 that includes such high-profile clients as AT&T, Harvard University, IBM, the Federal Aviation Administration, GTE, the U.S. Armed Forces and Dow Jones, Inc. Such success is due not only to the high quality and reliability of UltraBac.com's product but also to its hard-earned reputation for providing outstanding support — during business hours, the average wait to get technical help by phone is only 90 seconds, a feat virtually unmatched among the company's competitors.

UltraBac.com is a fast-growing, forward-looking company that is positioned to do almost anything it wants in the coming years. Edwards attributes that enviable position to being privately owned. "There's no one telling us what to do," he reflects, "and we don't have to worry about near-term profits, satisfying investors or industry analysts. When we decide we want to do something that might affect our bottom line for the year, we can do it without fear of market reprisals. We are independent, healthy and growing, and we have the dogged determination to make it work." For now, the company will maintain the focus that has made it successful.

This, however, does not mean UltraBac.com intends to stand pat. Instead, it will expand beyond Microsoft applications into other platforms; UltraBac versions for LINUX and UNIX operating systems are already on the horizon. Backup is a constantly evolving field, bringing new challenges every day. As one of the most adaptable, focused and innovative companies in this software field, UltraBac.com stands not only to reinforce its reputation but also to benefit from each new change the future brings.

of 20 percent each year since 1997, and the number of employees has more than tripled since 1998. In 1999 UltraBac.com was recognized by Deloitte & Touche as one of the 500 fastest-growing technology companies in the United States, and has been listed by the *Puget Sound Business Journal* as one of the 100 fastest-growing privately held companies in Washington state every year since 1997. UltraBac.com has also made *Software Magazine's* list of the 500 largest software companies in the world every year since 1998.

Although still relatively small, UltraBac.com competes successfully with much larger software companies due to a wide range of capabilities, including product development, technical support, marketing and sales. The company functions in a fluid, well-integrated, creative atmosphere that fosters a thorough understanding and dedication to the entire process, from concept and sales to customer service. As a result, it has carved out a

INFOSPACE, INC.

Behind every successful enterprise is a complex world of technology that constantly works to ensure a pleasant and satisfying customer experience. InfoSpace's vision is to fundamentally change how people communicate, access information, conduct commerce and otherwise manage their lives from any device at any time. One of the most prominent companies helping its clients offer these services to their customers is InfoSpace, Inc.

The Bellevue-based company was founded in 1996 by Naveen Jain when he noticed that the Internet failed to provide people with the useful and relevant real-world information they needed when and where they needed it most. Starting with just three employees, Jain quickly turned his "people and business finder" into a worldwide leader providing infrastructure services for commerce, communication and information to wireless carriers, merchants and Web sites. These services reach more than 90 percent of all Internet users on PCs and on wireless devices.

Naveen Jain, founder of InfoSpace, Inc.

Arun Sarin, CEO of InfoSpace, Inc.

InfoSpace went public in December 1998 and now employs more than 550 employees in offices worldwide.

InfoSpace is also the one company that bridges the gap between the online, offline and wireless worlds, thanks to its alliances with the world's foremost wireless carriers, regional bell operating companies, merchant banks and other local media networks.

These relationships make InfoSpace the leading provider of worldwide commerce capabilities that users can access from any location on their wireless devices. InfoSpace is one of the only companies to offer location-based services that enable mobile users to search for information such as restaurants or hotels in the area closest to where they are at that point in time.

InfoSpace's goal is to turn all wireless devices into true transaction devices. This will give mobile users the ability to press one key to make purchases from virtually any Web site and deliver online promotions to consumers on their wireless devices. Thanks to its forward-thinking philosophy, InfoSpace also supports any format, any platform and any device to make it easy for users to get their personalized information and services. This includes wireless devices such as a cell phone, wireline devices such as the PC or broadband devices such as the television.

While InfoSpace may have a global audience, the company is keenly aware of the impact it can have closer to home. InfoSpace's corporate philosophy includes giving back a percentage of its profits to the community through charities such as Northwest Harvest and United Way. Employee contributions to charities are also matched dollar for dollar by the company.

If InfoSpace's future could be summed up in one sentence, it would be that what they develop today will help busy people better manage their lives tomorrow. It's no small task, but with InfoSpace leading the way, communication can only get better.

In October 2000, InfoSpace merged with Go2Net, a Seattle-based company that is one of the Internet's leading providers of applications and technology infrastructure for both narrowband and broadband, bringing the total number of employees to approximately 1,200.

LizardTech, Inc.

Imagine going to a Web site that delivers media-rich photographs and perfect reproductions of scanned documents incredibly fast, even with a 58k modem. This is exactly what LizardTech does for thousands of companies in a myriad of industries worldwide.

Founded by John R. Grizz Deal in 1992, LizardTech develops imaging software and solutions that simplify and enhance the distribution, management and control of digital images and documents. Deal, who was formerly involved in product and technology development at Los Alamos National Laboratory (LANL), established LizardTech as a vehicle for commercializing imaging technologies.

Based in Seattle's Pioneer Square neighborhood, LizardTech has steadily grown since its inception and now occupies 50,000 square feet of office space for its 200 local employees. The company employs close to 200 professionals worldwide, has an additional office in Amsterdam, and — after Mitsubishi Corporation led $25 million in LizardTech's last round of financing — plans to open a new office in Japan.

LizardTech's technology products are on more than 30 million desktops and integrated into over 200 software applications and solutions. Imaging solutions include the patented MrSID® and DjVu® technologies and LizardTech™ Content Server. MrSID (Multi-Resolution Seamless Image Database) encodes photographs, maps, engineering drawings and other large files so they can be easily sent over the Internet or a company's internal network. LizardTech licensed Generation I of its patented MrSID software from LANL. The same team that created the FBI standard for storage and transmission of its large fingerprint image library developed Generation I of MrSID.

DjVu is an innovative scan-to-Web publishing technology that does for documents what MrSID does for photography. Documents can be sent at high speeds over the Web by reducing file sizes up to 1,000 times while retaining the image clarity of the original. LizardTech acquired its DjVu technology from AT&T Labs for the commercialization of products in the private sector.

The LizardTech Content Server is the fastest Internet application for delivering high-resolution photographs and perfect reproductions of documents, making Web sites perfectly scalable to user needs. LizardTech develops specific solutions that address the needs of the following markets: Internet and consumer users, e-commerce, business-to-business, health care, geospatial, business communications and publishing.

In February 1997 the Library of Congress became LizardTech's first MrSID customer. Since then, LizardTech has established relationships with a network of high-profile strategic partners and customers including Autodesk, Adobe Systems, Getty Images, Boeing, U.S. Navy, Photo Science Inc. and hundreds of other organizations. LizardTech was also recently voted the Washington Software Alliance's most promising new company. Investors and shareholders include Oak Investment Partners, AT&T, Mitsubishi Corporation, Hutchison Wampoa, Encompass Ventures, SeaPoint Ventures, Kirlan Ventures, Summit Ventures, Shurtleff Group, Staenberg Private Capital and others.

LizardTech leads the market in establishing new performance benchmarks for the efficient delivery of digital images and documents under constrained bandwidth or with limited storage conditions, and optimizing bandwidth for the dynamic display of content regardless of the viewing environment or device. LizardTech's team of talented, visionary professionals constantly upgrades and improves the company's software to bring the most advanced products to the public. Whether reducing a photograph to a microscopic image or enlarging it to the size of a billboard, LizardTech's groundbreaking imaging technologies lead the way, with perfect clarity, into the 21st century.

John Grizz Deal, president and CEO, brings his vision for the future of digital imaging to LizardTech where he directs both the future growth of the company and its strategic development.

LizardTech develops imaging software and solutions that simplify and enhance the distribution, management and control of digital images and documents.

NINTENDO OF AMERICA INC.

In 1889 Fusajiro Yamauchi began manufacturing "Hanafuda" playing cards in Kyoto, Japan. After decades of innovation, Nintendo has evolved from its humble beginnings to become the worldwide leader in interactive entertainment, so successful that over 40 percent of American households own a Nintendo game system. From Hanafuda to video game icons such as Mario®, Zelda®, Donkey Kong® and Pokémon®, Nintendo creates the world's most popular games.

Minoru Arakawa, president of Nintendo of America Inc.

Nintendo of America Inc. was formed in 1980 when Hiroshi Yamauchi, the great-grandson of Nintendo's founder, made the decision to expand Nintendo's video game operations to the United States to take advantage of the booming video game market. It didn't take long for Nintendo to make a name for itself. In 1981, led by President Minoru Arakawa, Nintendo of America Inc. released the Donkey Kong arcade game, which quickly became the hottest coin-operated video game on the market. The success continued with the launch of the Nintendo Entertainment System in 1985 and the introduction of the portable Game Boy in 1989. Their successors, the Super Nintendo Entertainment System, Nintendo 64, and the portable Game Boy Color have revolutionized the gaming industry. Over the years Nintendo has sold over 110 million Game Boy systems and is currently enjoying the multibillion dollar, worldwide success of the Pokémon phenomenon.

Nintendo's Mario

Nintendo Co. Ltd. remains headquartered in Kyoto, Japan, while the North American operations are managed by Nintendo of America Inc. in Redmond, Washington. Nintendo, responsible for bringing Pokémon to the West, is committed to

remaining the No. 1 video game developer in the world. DigiPen Institute of Technology, an accredited institute of higher learning located within the Nintendo of America complex, offers two- and four-year degrees in video game development. By teaching game creation in their own

backyard, Nintendo is sure of meeting its need for the fresh ideas and technological know-how necessary to create the most innovative forms of video entertainment. The first students graduated in 1998 with degrees in real time interactive simulation.

Since the end of the 19th century, Nintendo has been devoted to entertaining the world. That commitment extends beyond video games, however; Nintendo is a longtime partner with the Starlight Children's Foundation and the Make-A-Wish Foundation. In conjunction with the Starlight Children's Foundation, Nintendo has created mobile Fun Centers that provide a welcome diversion for sick children in hospitals across the nation.

With the introduction of the new Nintendo GameCube and Game Boy Advance in 2001, Nintendo will continue the success of the past by providing the best interactive entertainment to game players of all ages.

PWI TECHNOLOGIES

When it comes to implementing or improving complex computer systems, businesses in the tech-savvy Puget Sound region have depended on the expertise of PWI Technologies for more than 11 years.

Bellevue-based PWI's enterprise services team focuses on defining, designing and implementing B-to-B and B-to-C solutions for companies ranging from start-ups to Fortune 500 corporations. The company develops fully integrated server system architectures and network infrastructure solutions. Throughout its years in business, PWI has developed strategic planning methods and integrated service products to meet a wide variety of client needs. PWI's Enterprise Services include UNIX systems development, custom engineering, and integration of best-of-breed technologies from industry leaders such as Sun Microsystems™, Oracle® and Veritas®.

While PWI's comprehensive suite of products and services gives it a competitive advantage, the key to the company's success, according to President Barry Andersen, is a result of the company's founding principles.

"Our success is attributed to our employees, our perseverance in this industry and our focus on providing extraordinary service, not just products," says Andersen, who is also one of the company's founders.

In 1990 Barry Andersen and co-founder Gary Henderson saw the opportunity to help companies build leading-edge enterprise

solutions. Starting with just four employees, the company earned $1 million in revenue during its first year. Clients included Physio Control, Nintendo and Sharp Electronics.

A decade later, PWI's mission has evolved with the changing technology. The company now has 50 employees with sales exceeding $40 million. PWI credits ambitious clients — The Seattle Times and REI — for their willingness to test Internet business models that were still emerging. These companies helped position PWI to work with more recent Internet arrivals such as Go2Net and HomeGrocer.com. Current clients, including Nordstrom, SAFECO, Puget Sound Energy and Washington Mutual, suggest the future lies with traditional brick-and-mortar companies as they revamp their information technology systems and develop new ways of meeting customer needs.

PWI is convinced that one way to sustain excellent services in an ever-changing market is to reward its employees, particularly to confirm that success is a group effort. One way the company encourages its employees to rise to their fullest potential was best demonstrated by the trip the entire staff, including spouses, took to Hawaii after the company reached its 1999 sales goal. The entire company returned once again in 2001 when they achieved their sales goals for 2000.

PWI's commitment to returning dividends to its employees also extends to its belief in giving back to the community. The company contributes to and encourages its employees to volunteer and make donations to nonprofit organizations such as Northwest Harvest, Childhaven, Children's Orthopedic Hospital and Big Brothers/Big Sisters.

PWI's future may look rosy considering its years of experience, reputable history and wealth of regional clients, but the company doesn't plan to just sit back and reap the rewards of its carefully laid foundation. Instead, as Henderson is fond of saying, "luck is the intersection of opportunity and preparedness." That philosophy has led and will continue to lead PWI into yet another decade of success.

President Barry Andersen and Vice President Gary Henderson inspect the PWI SAN Lab.

Chief Technology Officer Matthew Reese diagrams white-board architectures in PWI's conference room.

2WAY CORPORATION

In an age in which technology is perceived as taking the humanity out of communication, 2WAY Corporation is giving it back. 2WAY's collaborative software helps businesses gather, compile and share feedback from customers, staff and colleagues in real time. The technology allows the concerns and opinions of the individuals who matter most to a company's bottom line reach the decision makers in an effective, timely way.

"Knowing your customer is ground zero," says Bruce Alper, CIO of American Management Association, a 2WAY client. "The simplicity of 2WAY is that you can use it in almost any situation where communication is part of your business."

2WAY products have indeed become standard communication tools among a variety of industries and applications. One company deployed a 2WAY to gather and respond to critical employee feedback during a billion-dollar merger. A major automobile manufacturer used a 2WAY solution to gather real-time information from its customers about design enhancements for its updated sports car line, helping it successfully launch it to the multibillion-dollar auto market.

The immediate feedback gathered using 2WAY software answers the current market demand for rapid decision making and instant collaboration, sometimes in innovative ways. For instance, in order to gauge audience responses, trade show presenters traditionally require participants to manually fill out paper questionnaires. But, they usually do not receive useful analysis until long after the shows have ended. One company eliminated that barrier to its audience by deploying 2WAY during a major industry trade show. Participants had the opportunity to provide immediate feedback using 2WAYs, and the speakers tailored their presentations to the audience's interests in real time. This real-time collaboration capability of 2WAY has led to its application in computer-based training, distance learning and distributed project management.

> 2WAY'S COLLABORATIVE SOFTWARE HELPS BUSINESSES GATHER, COMPILE AND SHARE FEEDBACK FROM CUSTOMERS, STAFF AND COLLEAGUES IN REAL TIME.

The company has applied its own software internally to a variety of interactive communication purposes, such an as internal help desk, development team collaboration, anonymous satisfaction surveys, interactive company newsletter and employee polls to determine company participation in community events. The increased employee involvement has already helped 2WAY sponsor a "Fun Run" with proceeds going to Fred Hutchinson Research and a scavenger hunt benefiting Childhaven.

2WAY's headquarters are located along Seattle's Elliott Bay, with an East Coast regional office in Boston, Massachusetts. The privately held company presently employs over 70 employees, doubling its staff of just a year ago. It is no wonder that 2WAY is getting plenty of write-ups in trade magazines as a major innovator in its field. 2WAY also has been recognized by *Upside's* Hot 100 Private Companies, the Smithsonian Institution's Permanent Research Collection of Information Technology, and the Washington Software Alliance's Best New Product Award in 1998.

There seems to be no end to the ways 2WAY can improve interactive business communications. This vision was precisely the reason that William Adams, Michael Libes and David Bluhm founded the company in 1997 — and it still resides at 2WAY's core. "Vision is not some nebulous direction," says Adams. "It is at the heart of what we do every day."

Pictured are some of 2WAY Corporation's dedicated team of 80 professionals whose mission is delivering innovative software solutions for corporate collaboration and communications. Their products have been used by numerous Global 2000 companies in a wide variety of industries since 1997.

Bibliography

Bagley, Clarence B. History of Seattle. Chicago: S.J. Clark, 1929.

Bass, Sophie Frye. Pigtail Days in Old Seattle. Portland: Metropolitan Press, 1937.

Denny, Arthur A. Pioneer Days on Puget Sound. Seattle: Alice Harriman, 1908.

Denny, Emily Inez. Blazing the Way. Seattle: Rainier Press, 1909.

Gates, Charles O. The First Century of the University of Washington. Seattle: U. of Wash. Press, 1961.

Hanford, C.H. Seattle and Environs. Chicago: Pioneer Historical Co., 1924.

Hines, Neal O. Denny's Knoll. Seattle: University of Washington Press, 1980.

Jones, Nard. Seattle. Doubleday, 1972.

Mumford, Esther Hall. Seattle's Black Victorians, 1852-1901. Seattle: Ananse Press, 1980.

Newell, Gordon. The H.W. McCurdy Marine History of the Pacific Northwest. Seattle: Superior, 1966.

_____. Westward to Alki. Seattle: Superior, 1977.

Sale, Roger. Seattle Past and Present. Seattle: University of Washington Press, 1976.

Selby, Kenneth E. Histories of the Seattle Public Schools. Seattle Public Schools, 1951.

Warren, James R. King County and its Queen City Seattle. Woodland Hills, CA: Windsor, 1981.

_____. The War Years. Seattle: History Ink and University of Washington Press, 2000.

Washington: A Guide to the Evergreen State. Writers Program of the Work Projects Administration, 1941.

Watt, Roberta Frye. Four Wagons West. Portland: Binfords and Mort, 1931.

Newspapers

The Seattle Times

The Seattle Post-Intelligencer

The Eastside Journal

Index

5th Avenue Theater 127

Adjusted Compensation Act..........................135

Alaska Gold Rush...107

Alaska-Pacific World's Fair 120

Alaska-Yukon-Pacific Exposition 129, 168

Alki Point 16,67

Allen, Eddie 151

Allen, Harry E. 133

Allen, Paul..196, 199

Allen, Raymond 166

Allen, William 165

American Airlines 166

Anderson, Eliza..93

Anti-Tuberculosis League 130

Arctic Brotherhood 129

Arlington National Cemetery 134

Arthur, President Chester A. 100

Back, John E. 105

Bagley, Clarence 73, 117

Bagley, Reverend Daniel 81

Baillargeon, Cebert 133

Bainbridge Island 153

Baker, Charles H...................................125

Balch, Captain Lafayette......................14

Ballinger, Richard A............................129

Baring Brothers 106

Beacon Hill..............................14, 92

Beatty, R.H. 83

Bell, William N.....................16, 68, 79

Bellingham 84, 125

Benaroya Hall....................................155

Benjamin, Captain Amos O. 111

Bering Sea 84

Bettman Brothers general store 80

Black River.......................................72

Blackford, John 132

Blaine, Catherine 74

Blaine, Reverend David 74

Boeing B-17 "Flying Fortress" 150

Boeing B-29 "Super Fortress"..........150

Boeing B-29 156

Boeing Company, The 121, 146, 165, 188

Boeing, William E...........120, 121, 146

Boren, Carson 14, 70, 76

Boren, Sarah Latimer......................14

Boyer, Mary Ann 73

Bremerton Navy Yard 149

British Columbia 112, 129

British-American War of 1812 12

Broadway High School....................132

Bronson, Deming 134

Buchanan, James 13

Burke, Thomas.................................93

Burnt River......................................15

Bush, George 14, 196

California Gold Rush...................69, 129

Camp Lewis..................................121

Camp Robinson 109

Capitol Hill 96, 117, 172

Carlson, Edward...........................168

Carnegie, Andrew..........................111

Carr, Edmund 80

Carr, Ossian J. 83

Carter, Jimmy................................178

Cascade Mountains 71, 94, 130

Casey, Colonel Silas 84

Chief Kanim....................................79

Chief Seattle 15, 70, 76

Churchill, Prime Minister Winston 150

Civil War 71, 83

Civilian Conservation Corps 144

Clairmont, Victor 100

Clark, E.A. 80

Cleveland, President Grover 97

Clinton, Mayor Gordon 166

Clinton, President Bill 196

Clise, Anna.....................................132

Clise, James W. 123

Close, Reverend Benjamin................74

Coe, Earl 184

Cold War 165

Coliseum Theater 118, 127

Collins, Josiah 100

Collins, L.M. 74

Collins, Luther................................14, 89

Colman, James M. 92

Columbia Rediviva 13

Columbia River 12, 94, 120

Commencement Bay 94

Condit, Phil 196

Conklin House................................73

Considine, John 127

Cornish, Nellie................................129

Cowlitz Prairie 81

Crosby, Bing...................................181

Crystal Vaudeville Theater 127

Cunningham, Ross............................168

Curtis, Edward S.............................75

Daughters of the American Revolution 130

Davis, John....................................70

DeLin House 85

DeLin, A.P......................................83

Demers, Bishop Modeste...................74

Denny Hill 100, 116, 143

Denny Party 14, 67

Denny Way...............................70, 117

Denny, Arthur 14, 69, 80, 81, 73, 94, 123

Denny, David T. 14, 68, 77, 93, 106

Denny, Emily Inez 76

Denny, John 14

Denny, Louisa Boren 14, 68, 77, 79

Denny, Mary Boren 14, 15, 68

Denny, Rolland H. 15

Dexter Horton Bank.........................73

Discovery Park 110

Dodd, Westley Allan..........................192

Doheny, Edward L. 138

Duwamish Head 16, 104

Duwamish River.......................14, 70, 94

Duwamish Valley 73, 92

Eagle Harbor 153

Eagleson, James B............................133

Ehrlichman, John 179

Eisenhower, Dwight 135

Ellensburg 120

Elliott Bay 13, 16, 92, 115, 149, 182

Ellis, James R. 166, 167

Environmental Protection Agency 193

Evans, Governor Dan 178

Evergreen Point Bridge....................................172

Evergreen State College....................................178

Fall, Albert B. 138

Fay, Captain Robert C. 15, 16

Federal Trade Commission 196

Felker House 73

Felker, Captain Leonard M............................73

Ferdinand, Archduke Franz............................133

Ferry, Governor Elisha P. 95, 99, 100

Fillmore, President Millard 89

Finch, Captain D.B. 93

First Hill..100

Fisher, Edmond 195

Folger, Captain Isaac.....................................16

Follett, Don 168

Fort Astoria 12

Fort Decatur 79

Fort Lawton 110, 154, 165

Fort Lewis 146, 195

Fort Nisqually 16, 75

Fort Steilacoom 84

Fort Sumter 83

Fort Vancouver 13, 84, 97

Fred Hutchinson Cancer

    Research Center............................195

Frederick and Nelson 158, 163, 196

Frink, James M. 123

Frye Art Museum............................199

Frye Opera House 104

Frye Packing Plant 151

Frye, George...81

Fuller, Dr. Richard 145

Gandy, Joseph P...168

Gates, Bill 188

Gerberding, William..199

GI Bill 135, 156, 162

Givens, Denny 168

Goodwill Games..195

Graham, Walter 80

Grant, Frederick James 16, 72

Grant, General Ulysses S. 84, 87

Gray, Captain Robert 13

Gray's Harbor..84

Great Depression.....................118, 139, 142, 157

Great Seattle Fire.....................................103, 125

Green Lake 109, 117

Greene, Judge Roger S. 98

Gross, Bill 97

Gustin, Paul 17

Haldeman, H.R. 179

Hamilton, Charles K. 120, 121

Hanford, Abbie Jane Holgate 77

Hanford, Judge Cornelius 80, 91, 112, 130

Hanford, Thaddeus 93

Hanover College..116

Harbor Island..134, 151

Harding, President Warren G. 136, 138

Harlin, Robert H. 142

Harris, Phil..181

Harrison, President Benjamin 100

Hartley, Governor Roland 143

Hendricks, Joseph L. 165

Hendrix, Jimi 177

Henry, H.C. 123

Higgins, David 93

Hill, James Jerome 94, 130

Hill, Sam 120

Hilton Hotel 179

Hine, S.B. 84

Hoeck, Jerry 168

Holgate, John 14, 89

Holgate, Milton 77

Holgate, Olivia 80

Holladay, Ben 87

Hoover, President Herbert 134, 135, 141

Hopkins, Ralph 119

Horton, Dexter 72, 80, 104, 123

Howard, Captain Daniel S. 69

Howard, William 97

Hudson's Bay Company 13

Hughes, Glenn 129

Husky Stadium 193

Igorrote, Filipino 129

Independent Asphalt Company 118

Jackson, Senator Henry 146, 178

James, Burton 129

Johanson, Dr. Nils 131

Johnson, Philip 165

Johnson, President Lyndon 87, 177

Jones, Mrs. Harvey 76

Kanim, Pat 79

Kaye, Danny 182

Kellogg Brothers Drugstore 84

Kendrick, William 199

Kennedy, President John F. 168

Kerry, A.S. 129

Kilbourne, Dr. E.C. 125

King County Airport (Boeing Field) 120, 146

Kingdome 182, 195

Kittitas Valley 14

Klickitat County 127

Klondike Creek 107

Klondike Gold Rush 107

Korean War 165

Krebs, Edwin 195

Kreielsheimer Theater 199

La Petite 127

Lake Keechelus 106

Lake Sammamish 191

Lake Union Shipyard 151

Lake Union 72, 95, 117

Lake View Park 109

Lake Washington ..94, 96, 116, 150, 167, 182, 191

Lander, Judge Edward 81

Langlie, Arthur 168

Latimer, W.G. 74

Lawton, Major General Henry Ware 110

Leary, John 93

Lenora, Margaret 14

Leschi Park 110

Leslie's Weekly 106

Lewis and Clark Expedition 13, 129

Lincoln, President Abraham 85

Lindbergh, Colonel Charles 121, 122

Littler, Bob 181

Locke, Gary 199

Low, John.........................14, 15, 16, 68, 69

Lowman, Bill 182

"Lucky Lindy"...................................139

MacArthur, General Douglas 135, 165

Magnolia Bluff 110, 154

Magnuson, Senator Warren G. ....

................................146, 168, 178, 184

Maple, Jane 81

Martin, Governor Clarence 143

Mason, Dr. Tate 132

Matthews, Dr. Mark A................................132

Maynard, Dr. David S.........................69, 70, 71

McCarthy, Senator Joseph 166

McCarty, Clara 83

McCaw Cellular Communications 196

McCaw, Craig 196

McChord Air Force Base 195

McConaha, George V. 70, 80

McConaha, Ursula 80

McCormack, James M. 76

McCulloch, Sheriff Tim 184

McCurdy, H.W.......................................163

McGraw, John H................96, 97, 98, 129

McKinney, Reverend Dr. Samuel B. ....

....109, 174

McLean, John 120

McNeil Island 138

Meadowdale Beach............................138

Meany, Edmund.........................76, 130

Meeker, Ezra 112, 121

Mercer Island Floating Bridge 195

Mercer Island..............................150, 194

Mercer, Asa S. 83, 87, 89

Mercer, Mary Jane 80

Mercer, Thomas 73, 131

Metropolitan Theater 127

Microsoft 188, 196

Montlake Bridge...............................163

Moran, Robert 93, 105

Mount Everest 177

Mount Rainier 92, 125, 130, 144, 188

Mount St. Helens 187, 188

Murrow, Edward R. 150

Nethercutt, George 199

Nextel Communications 196

Nixon, President Richard..................177, 179

Northern Pacific Railroad 93, 118

Odegaard, Charles 175, 177

Olmstead Brothers 130

Olmstead, Elise 138

Olmstead, Roy 138

Ord, General E.O.C. 84

Ordway, Lizzie 85

Oregon Trail 15

Oregon-Washington Railroad and

  Navigation Co. 118

Orpheum Theater 181

Osgood, Frank 117

Pacific Car and Foundry......................151

Pacific Science Center..............168, 179, 189

Pantages, Alexander 127

Park Place Office Building...................179

Parrington Hall....................................130, 132

Parsons, Henry G. 80

Pay Streak..129

Payne, Charles 97

Pearl Harbor..153

Penthouse Theater 129

Pershing, General John J. 133

Phelps, Lieutenant Thomas S. 78

Phillips, David 73

Pickett, General George...........................84

Pierce, President Franklin 71

Pike Place Market 173

Pike, Harvey..96

Pike, John...83

Pioneer Square.....................72, 158, 179, 197

Places Rating Almanac 199

Plummer, Charles 89

Polk, President James Knox 13

Port of Seattle 156, 165

Port Townsend 14, 85

Profanity Hill 112

Prohibition 138

Prosch, Charles 84

Puget Sound Bridge 134, 151

Puget Sound Herald 84

Puget Sound Indians 69

Puget Sound 13, 92, 115, 146, 167, 193

Puyallup River 69

Queen Anne Hill 73, 106, 131, 182

Rainier Tower 179

Ramage Press 88

Ray, Dr. Dixie Lee 178

Red Cross 134, 135, 155

Renton, William 94

Ressam, Ahmad 199

Reynolds, George 96

Rice, Mayor Norm 199

Ridgeway, General Matthew 165

Ringling Brothers Circus 164

Rininger, Dr. E.M. 131

Rochester, Al 168

Roosevelt, President Franklin 135, 138, 156

Rose Bowl 188

Rosellini, Governor Albert 168

Ross, J.D. 125

Russell, Mary Jane 80, 81

SAFECO Field..197

Salmon Bay 96

San Juan Island 84

Sand Point Naval Air Station 146, 153, 175

Sanderson, C.M. 85

Schell, Mayor Paul 199

Schrontz, Frank 196

SeaFirst Bank..73

SeaFirst Building 179

Seattle Aquarium 167

Seattle Art Museum 145, 181

Seattle Automobile Club 120

Seattle Carnegie Library..........................111

Seattle Chamber of Commerce 95, 96, 131

Seattle City Council................................168

Seattle Electric Light Company..................123

Seattle First National Bank 73

Seattle Mariners..............................182, 195

Seattle Opera House 103, 145, 168, 181

Seattle Port of Embarkation 154

Seattle Post-Intelligencer 93, 139

Seattle Press Club 137

Seattle Press-Times 106

Seattle Public Schools 199

Seattle Repertory Theater 129, 181, 199

Seattle Supersonics 182

Seattle Symphony 181, 199

Seattle Times, The 129, 188

Seattle Yacht Club 131

Seattle-Tacoma International Airport.............157

Seward, General William H. 130

Sheridan, General Phil.....................................84

Sherman, General 84

Shilshole Bay...131

Shorey, O.C...83

Showboat Theater 129

Sick's Stadium...182

Sieg, Lee Paul..157

Simmons, Michael...14

Sinclair, Harry...138

Skid Road...72

Skinner and Eddy Shipyard....................134

Slaughter, Lieutenant W.A................76, 79

Smith Cove 70, 153

Smith, Dr. Henry A. 70, 75

Smith, L.C..123

Snake River 14, 89

Snohomish River 14, 112

Snoqualmie Falls..............................125

Space Needle..........................168, 179

Spanish flu 135

Spanish-American War......................................109

Spellman, Governor John..................................193

Spirit of St. Louis 122, 123

Spokane, Portland and Seattle Railroad 118

Squire, Governor Watson............................97, 98

Stanford, John 199

Stanton, Richard 89

Stephens, Annie E...89

Stevens, Isaac I. 71, 76, 84, 92

Stewart, Charles..98

Sullivan, James 97

Suzzalo Library...133

Sylvester, Edmund 14

Taft, President William Howard.......................130

Telenews Theater 150

Terry, Charles C. 68, 71

Terry, Lee 15, 68, 84

Thiry, Paul 168

Thomas, Dr. E. Donall 195

Thomson, Reginald H. 116, 125, 172

Treaty of Ghent 12

Truman, President Harry S. 165

U.S. Government Pavilion 129

Umatilla Landing 15

Unbedacht, Ivan...152

Union Bay Village.....................................157, 162

Union Trust Bank...100

University of Washington ....

....................81, 95, 129, 131, 132, 146, 162, 188

University Village 158

Van Asselt, Henry...81

Van Trump, P.B. 92

Vessels, N.B. 71

Vietnam War 175, 177

Volunteer Park 109, 130, 146, 181

Wah Mee Social Club 192

Walla Walla 94, 120

Walsh, Thomas J. 138

Washington Athletic Club 167

Washington High School 132

Washington Plaza Hotel 179

Washington State College 150

Watergate 179

Watson, James R. 89

Watt, Roberta Frye 15, 79

Wayside Mission Hospital 110, 111

Webster, John 81

Westervelt, Commander Conrad 121

Westlake Mall 173

Whidbey Island Naval Air Base 195

White River Valley 94

Wholly, Lieutenant John H. 110

Willamette Valley 14, 15, 70

Williamson, Joe 84

Wilson, President Woodrow 133

Wilson, Robert 77

Wood, James A. 129

Woodland Park Zoo 182

World War I 110, 133, 134, 135, 161

World War II 110, 125, 135, 146, 150, 162

WPPSS disaster 192

Wright, General George 84

Wright, Howard S. 168

Wyckoff, Sheriff L.V. 81, 84, 96

Yamasaki, Minoru 168

Yesler Way 14, 70, 96, 116, 159

Yesler, Henry L. 72, 92

Yesler, Sarah 96

Yesler's Mill 84, 106

YMCA 111

Yukon Mining School 109

Yukon Territory 129

Zioncheck, Marion 146

Partners & Web Site Index

Alaska Airlines 388
www.alaskaair.com

Argosy Cruises 260
www.argosycruises.com

Art Institute of Seattle, The 467
www.ais.edu

Ballard Blossom 368
www.ballardblossom.com

Bay Pavilion 369
www.fishermansrestaurant.com

Bayview Manor 456
www.bayviewmanor.org

Bensussen Deutsch 430
& Associates, Inc.
www.bdainc.com

Best Western Executive Inn 356
www.bwexec-inn.com

Boeing Company, The 484
www.boeing.com

BRE Properties, Inc. 296
www.breproperties.com

Budget Rent a Car. 358
www.budget.com

Business Network International 431
www.bninw.com

Canlis Restaurant 370
www.canlis.com

Catholic Community Services and the
Archdiocesan Housing Authority 458
www.ccsww.org

Center for Career Alternatives 418
www.centerforcareeralternatives.org

Childhaven 419
www.childhaven.org

Children's Home Society
of Washington 408
www.chs-wa.org

Children's Hospital &
Regional Medical Center 438
www.seattlechildrens.org

Cinerama Theatre 261
www.seattlecinerama.com

Clise Properties, Inc. 286

Conner Homes Co. 285
www.connerhomes.com

Corixa Corporation 457
www.corixa.com

Corporate Council for the Arts/
Arts Fund 262
www.cca-artsfund.org

Covenant Shores 460
www.covenantretirement.org

Cruise West. 254
www.cruisewest.com

Dain Rauscher. 332
www.dainrauscher.com

Division Five 350
www.divisionfive.com

Dunn Lumber Co. 371
www.dunnlum.com

Economic Development Council 440
www.edc-sea.org

Elephant Car Wash 360
www.elephantcarwash.com

Expeditors International
of Washington, Inc. 336
www.expd.com

Experience Music Project 258
www.emplive.com

Farmers New World
Life Insurance Company 314
www.farmers.com

5th Avenue Theatre, The 271
www.5thavenuetheatre.org

Fox Sports Net 474
www.foxsports.com

Fred Hutchinson Cancer
Research Center 486
www.fhcrc.org

Full House Sports
& Entertainment 476
www.fullhousesports.com

Gary Quinn's PhotoMagic 372
www.photomagic1.com

George White
Location Photography 374
www.aa.net/~gwlp/

Giant Pacific Companies 373
www.members.aol.com/paciron

Greater Seattle Chamber
of Commerce 442
www.seattlechamber.com

Guy Carpenter & Company. 324
www.guycarp.com

Happy Guests International, Inc. 362
www.happyguests.com

Highline Community Hospital
Health Care Network 444
www.hchnet.org

HomeStreet Bank 326
www.homestreetbank.com

Horton Lantz Marocco 461
www.hlm.com

Industrial Crating & Packing, Inc. . . . 349
www.indcrate.com

InfoSpace, Inc. 492
www.infospace.com

Isernio Sausage Company 346
www.isernio.com

KCTS 405
www.kcts.org

Kiewit Construction Company 298
www.kiewit.com

KING 5 390
www.king5.com

KOMO 4 Television 392
www.komotv.com

Lifelong AIDS Alliance 420
www.lifelongaidsalliance.org

LizardTech, Inc. 493
www.lizardtech.com

Lucks Company, The 352
www.lucks.com

March of Dimes 421
www.modimes-wa.org

Marine Resources
Company International 340
www.mrcsea.com

Marsh & McLennan Companies 426
www.mmc.com

Master Builders Association of King and
Snohomish Counties 300
www.mba-ks.com

McKinsey & Company 428
www.mckinsey.com

Metropolis 375

Microsoft 488
www.microsoft.com

Millionair Club Charity, The 412
www.millionairclub.org

Mount Zion Baptist Church 462
www.mountzion.net

Museum of History & Industry 264
www.seattlehistory.org

MWW/Savitt 432
www.mww.com

Nintendo of America Inc. 494
www.nintendo.com

Nitze-Stagen & Co., Inc. 302
www.nitze-stagen.com

Nordic Heritage Museum 265
www.nordicmuseum.com

Nordstrom, Inc. 364
www.nordstrom.com

Northwest Building LLC 310

Northwest Center 463
www.nwcenter.org

Nowogroski Rupp Insurance Group . . 328
www.nrgseattle.com

OfficeLease. 433
www.officelease.com

On the Boards. 263
www.ontheboards.org

Pacific Market International. 342
www.pmiseattle.com

Pacific Northwest Ballet 266
www.pnb.org

Pacific Science Center. 267
www.pacsci.org

Pike Place Bar and Grill. 366
www.pikeplacebarandgrill.com

Pike Place Fish 376
www.pikeplacefish.com

Pike Place Market. 366
www.pikeplacemarket.org

Pilchuck Glass School 464
www.pilchuck.com

Pink Door, The 377
www.pinkdoorrestaurant.com

Piroshky Piroshky 366
www.piroshkypiroshky.com

Planned Parenthood. 446
www.ppww.org

Plymouth Congregational Church . . . 465
www.plymouthchurchseattle.org

Porcelain Gallery 378
www.porcelaingalleryinc.com

Port of Seattle 343
www.portseattle.org

Preston Gates & Ellis LLP. 434
www.prestongates.com

PWI Technologies 495
www.pwi.com

R.D. Merrill Company. 274
www.merrillgardens.com

Ray's Boathouse. 379
www.rays.com

Rock Bottom Brewery 380
www.rockbottom.com

SAFECO Corporation 320
www.safeco.com

Seattle Academy 448
www.seattleacademy.org

Seattle Aquarium, The. 268
www.seattleaquarium.org

Seattle Children's Theatre 263
www.sct.org

Seattle City Light 394
www.ci.seattle.wa.us/light/

Seattle Community College District. . 450
www.sccd.ctc.edu

Seattle Foundation, The. 414
www.seattlefoundation.org

Seattle-King County Association
of REALTORS 304
www.nwrealtor.com

Seattle Mariners 480
www.mariners.org

Seattle Men's Chorus 269
www.seattlemenschorus.org

Seattle Opera 263
www.seattleopera.org

Seattle Public Utilities 396
www.ci.seattle.wa.us/util/

Seattle Repertory Theatre 270
www.seattlerep.org

Seattle Seahawks 478
www.seahawks.com

Seattle Sounders 481
www.seattlesounders.net

Seattle Symphony 263
www.seattlesymphony.com

Seattle's Union Gospel Mission 410
www.ugm.org

Seattle Times, The 400
www.seattletimes.com

Seattle University 466
www.seattleu.edu

Senior Services of
Seattle-King County 422
www.seniorservices.org

710 KIRO 404
www.710kiro.com

Shapiro and Associates, Inc. 435
www.shap.com

Sorrento Hotel 381
www.hotelsorrento.com

Sound Transit 398
www.soundtransit.org

South of Downtown Development . . . 306

Starbucks Coffee Company 382
www.starbucks.com

Starwood Hotels 383
www.starwoodhotels.com

St. James Cathedral 459
www.stjames-cathedral.org

Studio Solstone Ltd. 367
www.seattlewatercolors.com

Sur La Table 367
www.surlatable.com

Swedish Medical Center 452
www.swedish.org

Tarragon Development Company 294
www.tarragonllc.com

13 Coins 384
www.13coins.com

Three Girls Bakery 367

Trendwest Resorts, Inc. 454
www.trendwestresorts.com

Turner Construction Company 290
www.turnernw.com

2WAY Corporation 496
www.2way.com

UltraBac.com 490
www.ultrabac.com

Unico Properties, Inc. 308
www.unicoprop.com

United Airlines 402
www.ual.com

University of Washington 468
www.washington.edu

University of Washington Academic
Medical Center 469
www.washington.edu/medical/

Washington Athletic Club 470
www.wac.net

Washington Mutual 330
www.wamu.com

WorksiteMassage/Optimal
Performance, Inc. 385
www.worksitemassage.com

World Vision 416
www.worldvision.org

Wright Runstad & Company 280
www.wrightrunstad.com

Patron:
Seed Intellectual Property Law Group PLLC
www.seedlaw.com

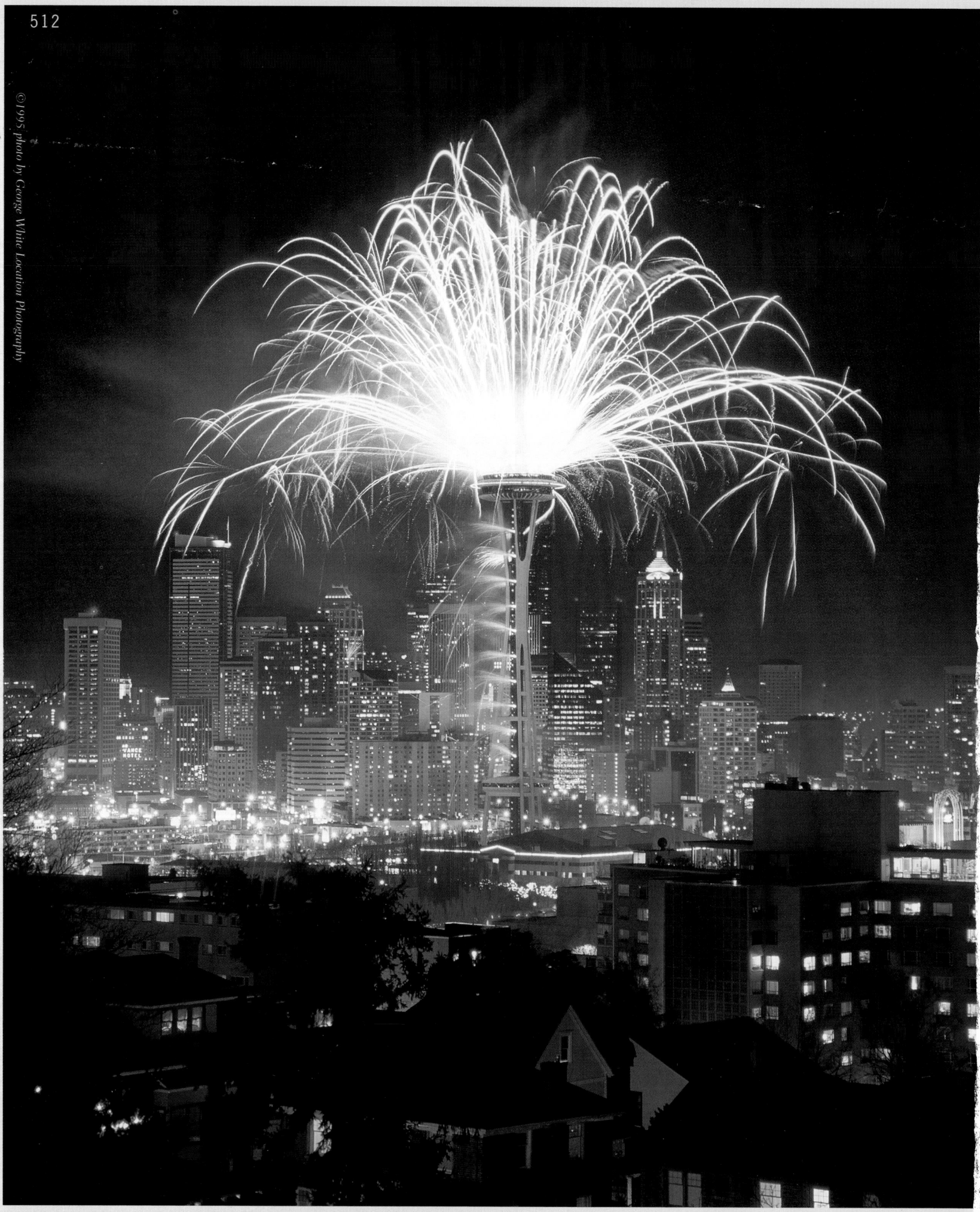
VANCE HOTEL